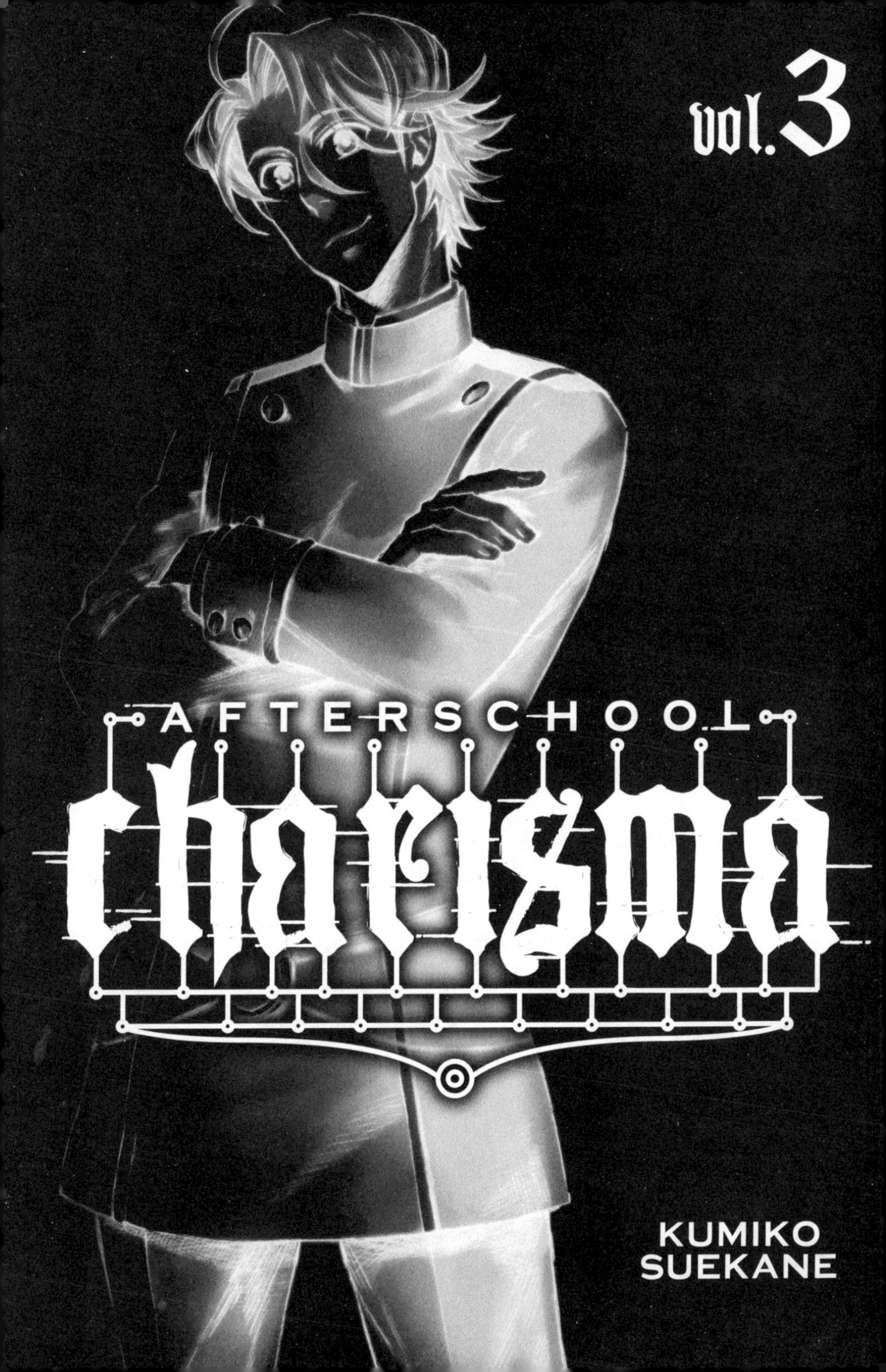
vol.3
AFTERSCHOOL
charisma
KUMIKO
SUEKANE

afterschool
charisma

c o n t e n t s

# Chapter thirteen

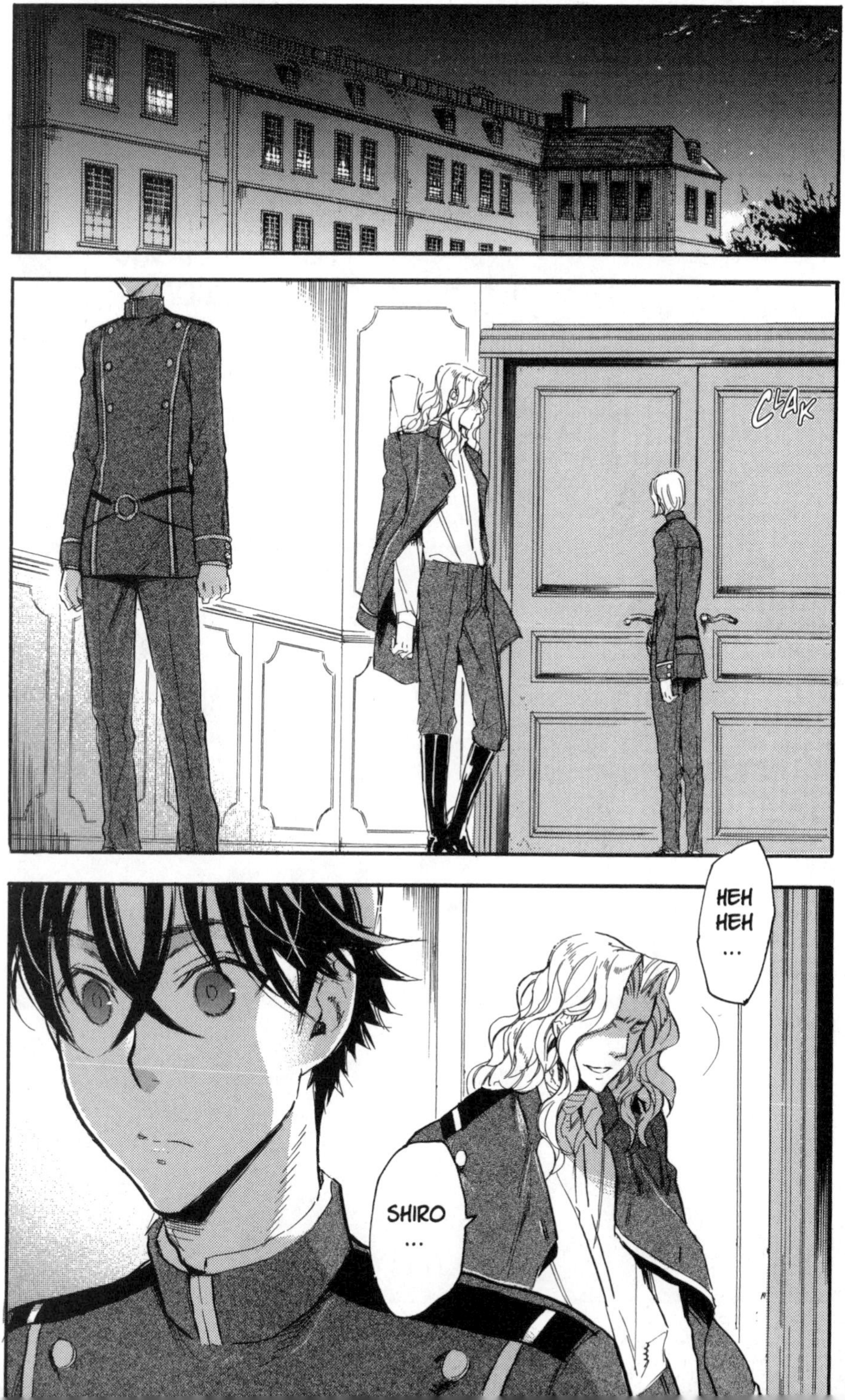
CLAK
HEH HEH ...
SHIRO ...

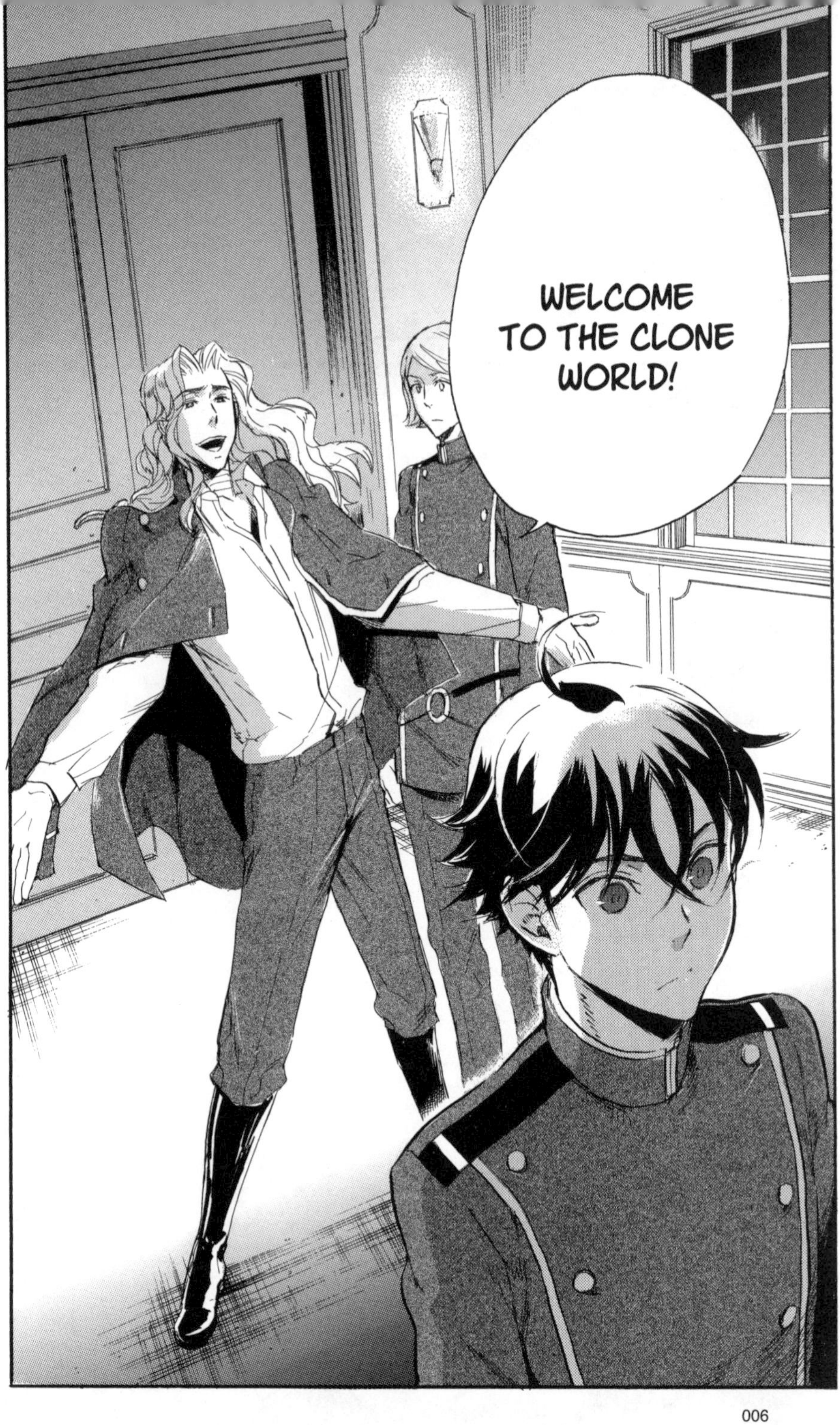
WELCOME TO THE CLONE WORLD!

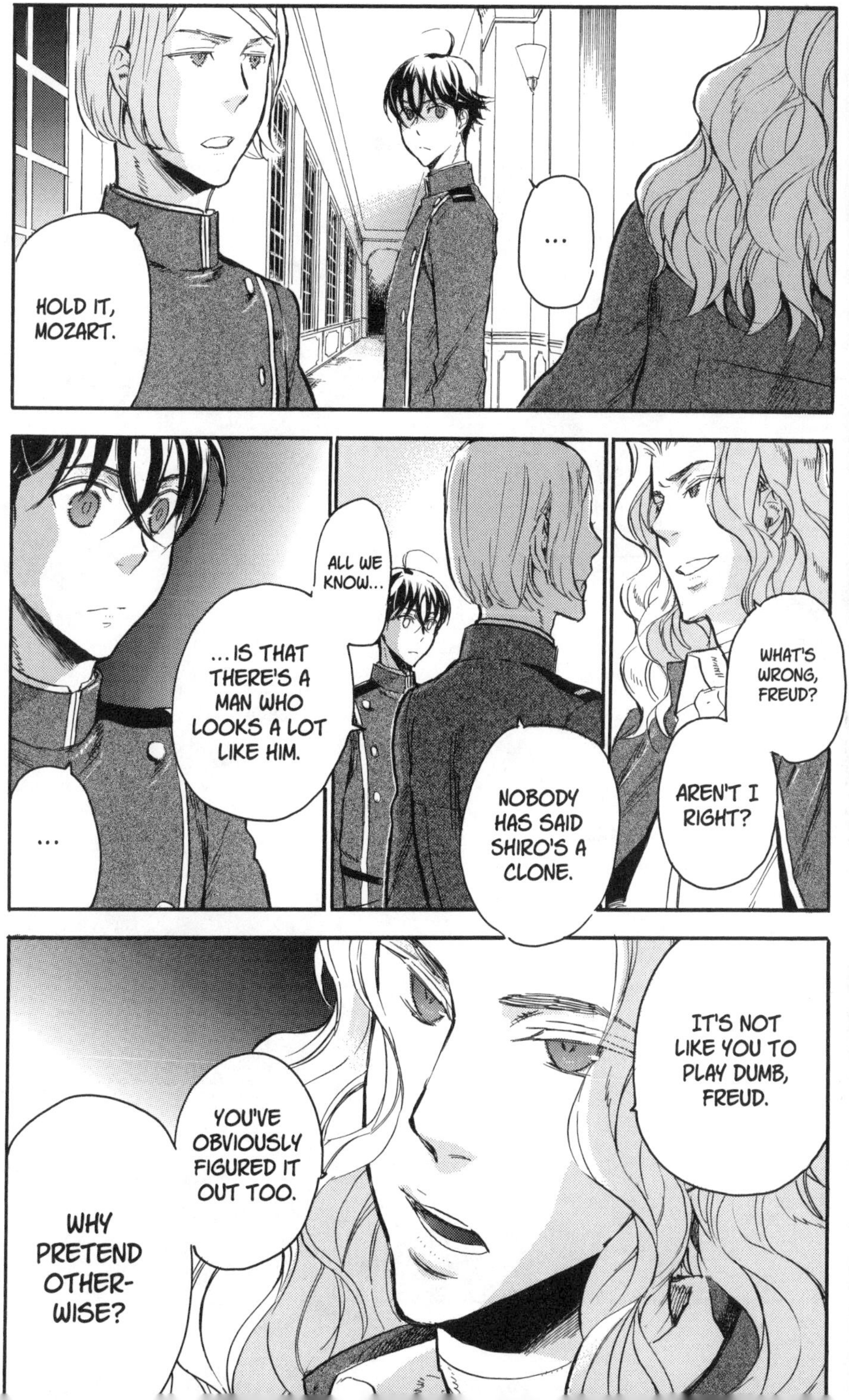
…
HOLD IT, MOZART.
WHAT'S WRONG, FREUD?
AREN'T I RIGHT?
NOBODY HAS SAID SHIRO'S A CLONE.
ALL WE KNOW…
…IS THAT THERE'S A MAN WHO LOOKS A LOT LIKE HIM.
…
IT'S NOT LIKE YOU TO PLAY DUMB, FREUD.
YOU'VE OBVIOUSLY FIGURED IT OUT TOO.
WHY PRETEND OTHER-WISE?

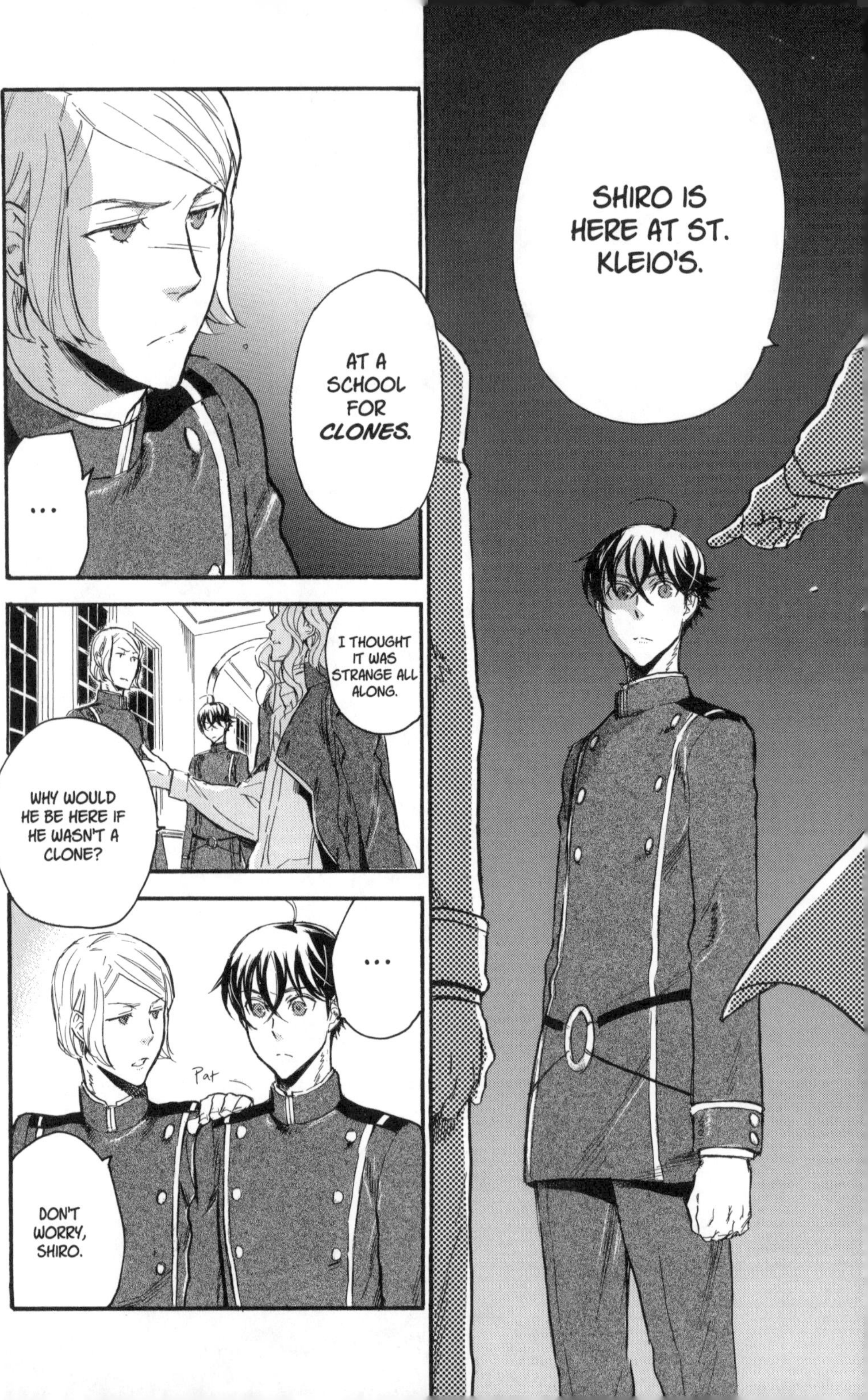
SHIRO IS HERE AT ST. KLEIO'S.
AT A SCHOOL FOR *CLONES*.
...
I THOUGHT IT WAS STRANGE ALL ALONG.
WHY WOULD HE BE HERE IF HE WASN'T A CLONE?
...
Pat
DON'T WORRY, SHIRO.

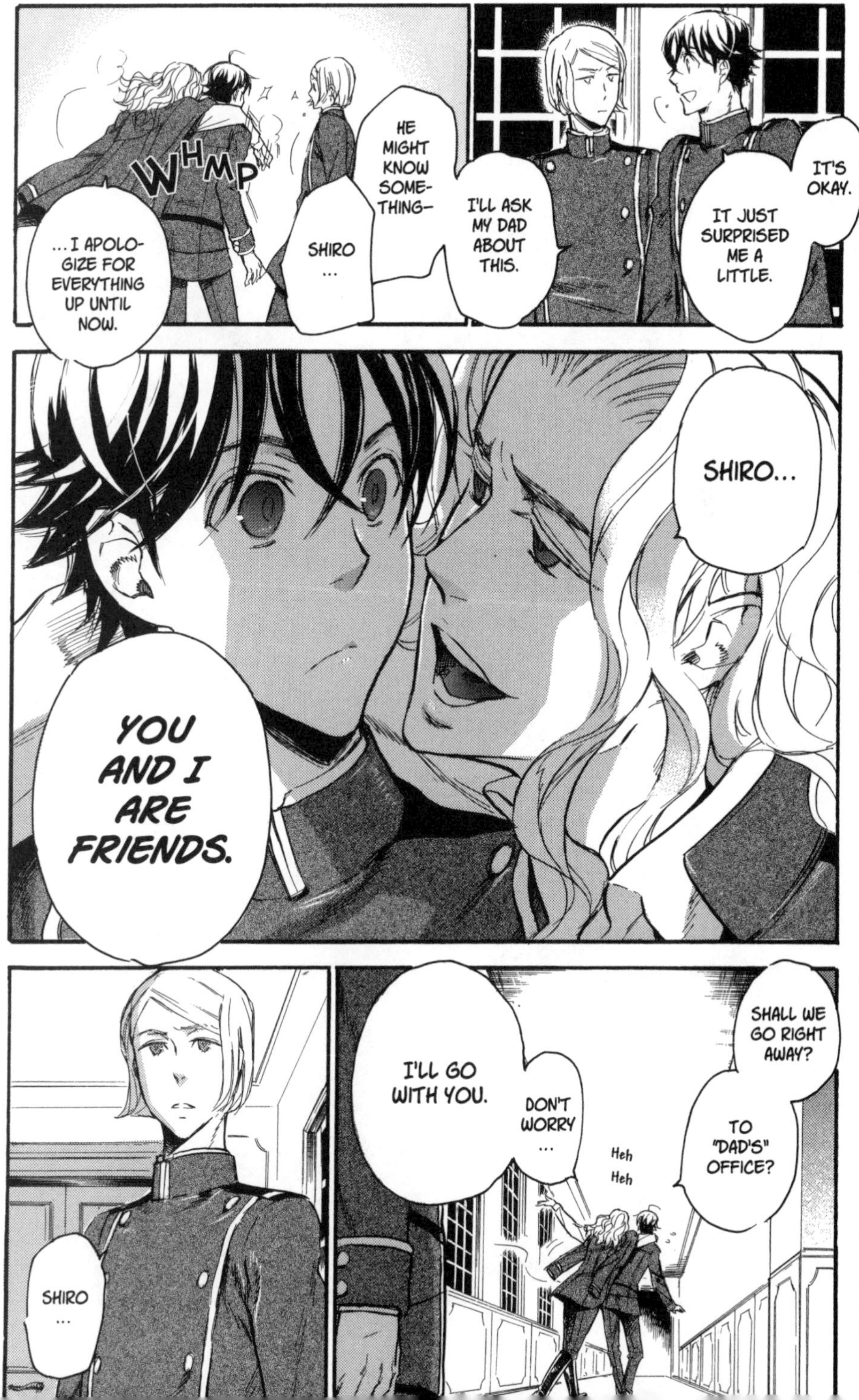
IT'S OKAY.
IT JUST SURPRISED ME A LITTLE.
I'LL ASK MY DAD ABOUT THIS.
HE MIGHT KNOW SOME-THING—
WHMP
SHIRO ...
...I APOLO-GIZE FOR EVERYTHING UP UNTIL NOW.
SHIRO...
YOU AND I ARE FRIENDS.
SHALL WE GO RIGHT AWAY?
TO "DAD'S" OFFICE?
Heh Heh
I'LL GO WITH YOU.
DON'T WORRY ...
SHIRO ...

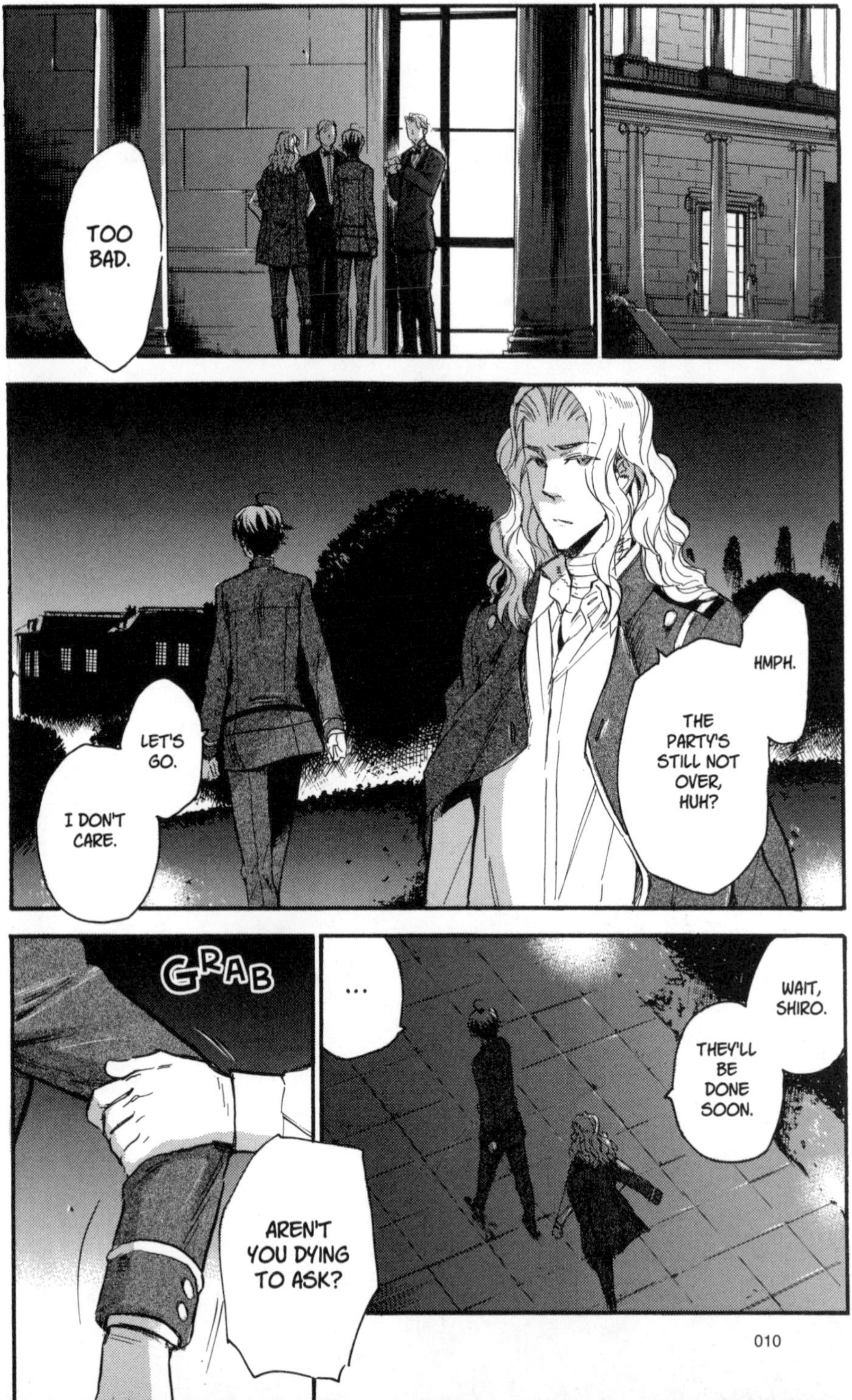
TOO BAD.
HMPH.
THE PARTY'S STILL NOT OVER, HUH?
LET'S GO.
I DON'T CARE.
WAIT, SHIRO.
THEY'LL BE DONE SOON.
...
GRAB
AREN'T YOU DYING TO ASK?

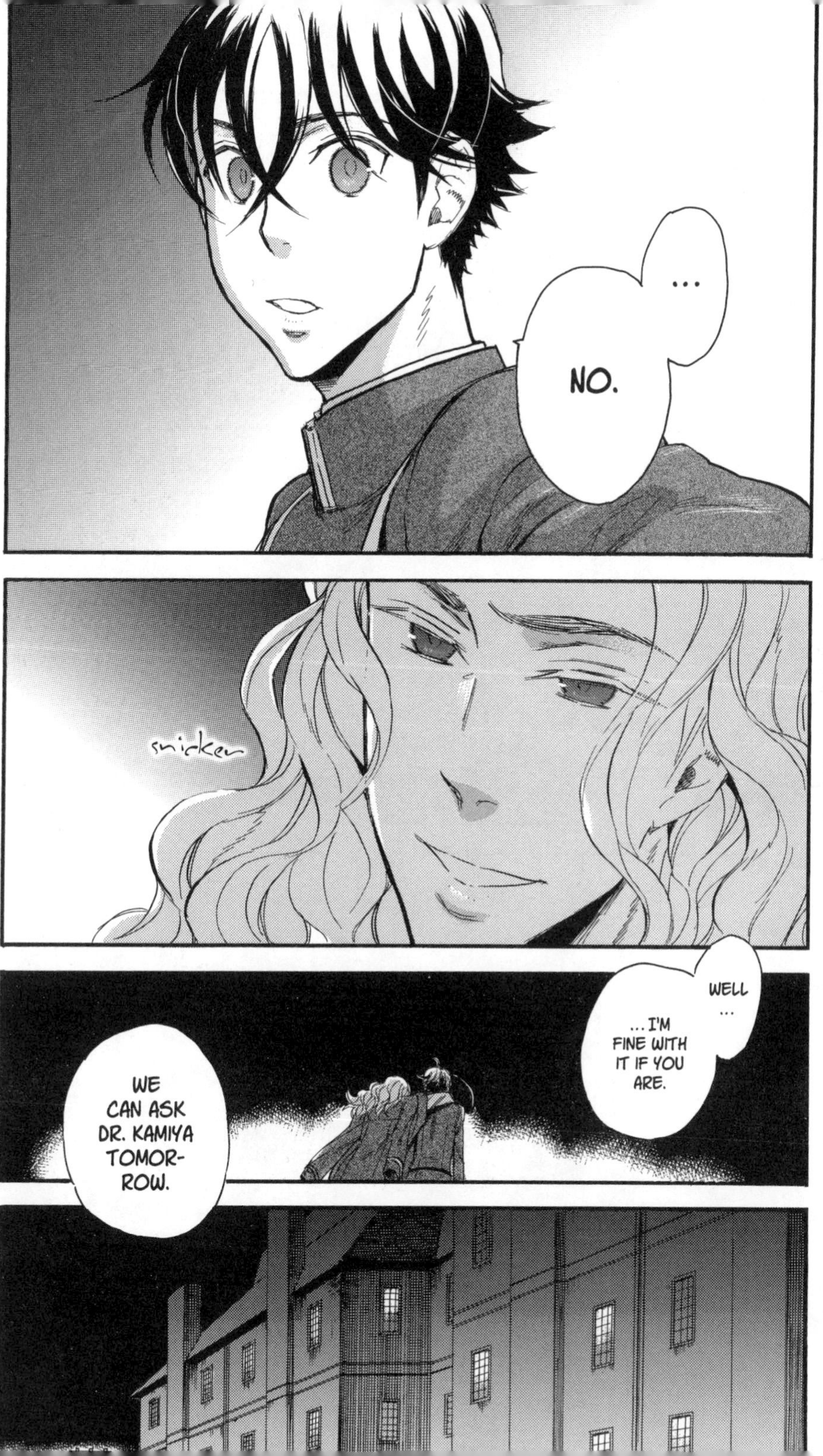
...
NO.
snicker
WELL ...
... I'M FINE WITH IT IF YOU ARE.
WE CAN ASK DR. KAMIYA TOMOR-ROW.

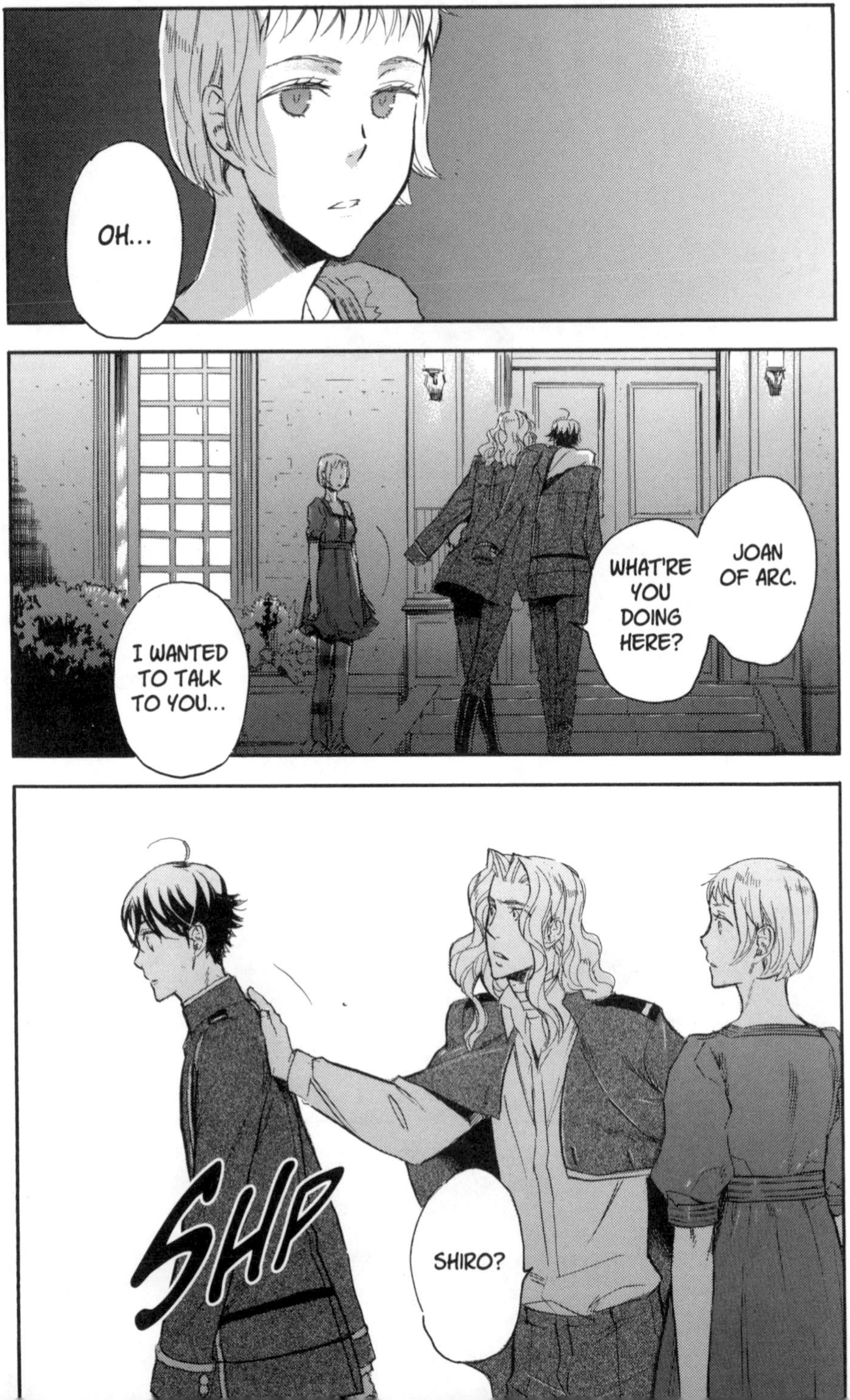
OH...
JOAN OF ARC.
WHAT'RE YOU DOING HERE?
I WANTED TO TALK TO YOU...
SHIP
SHIRO?

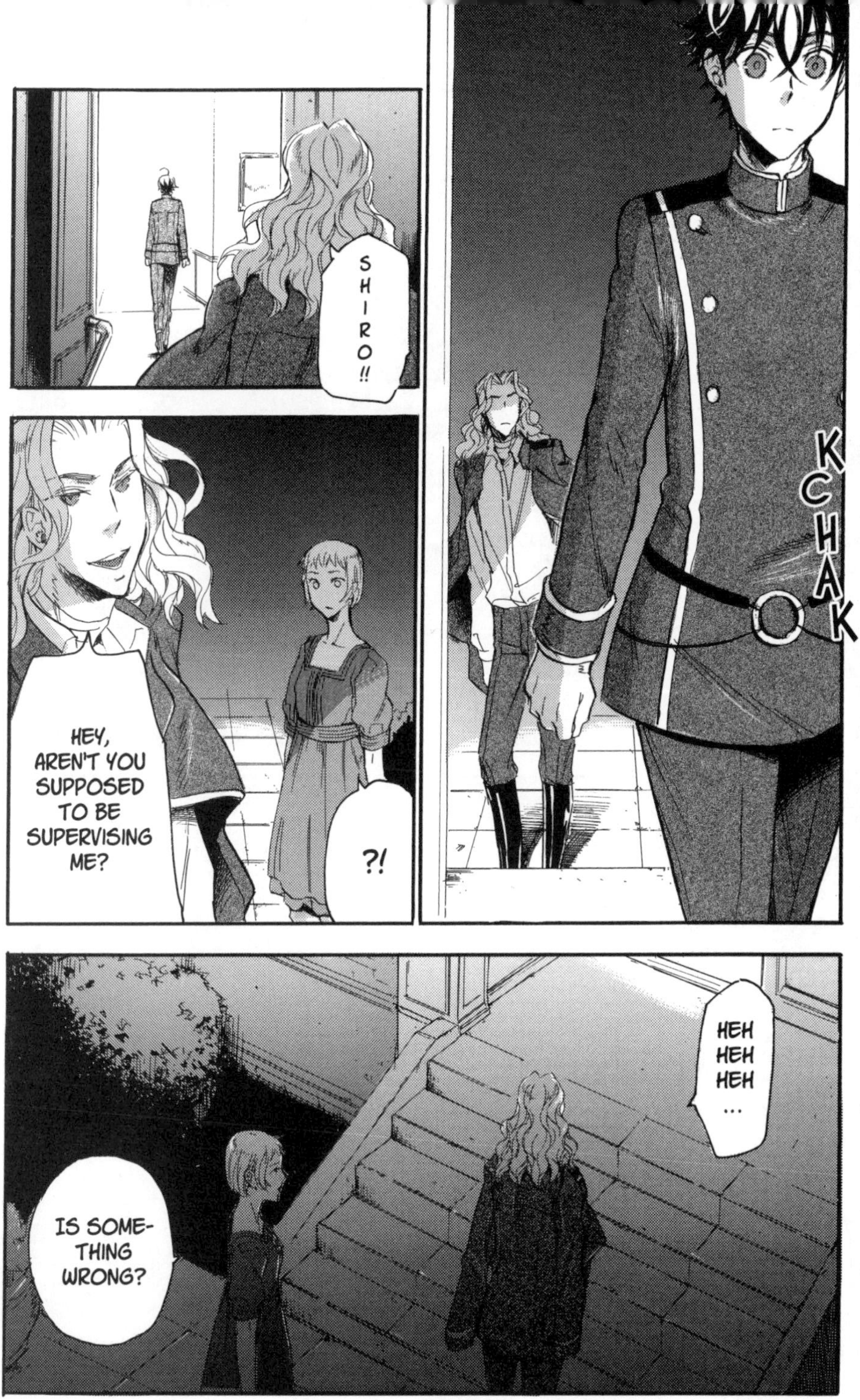
KCHAK
SHIRO!!
HEY, AREN'T YOU SUPPOSED TO BE SUPERVISING ME?
?!
HEH HEH HEH ...
IS SOME-THING WRONG?

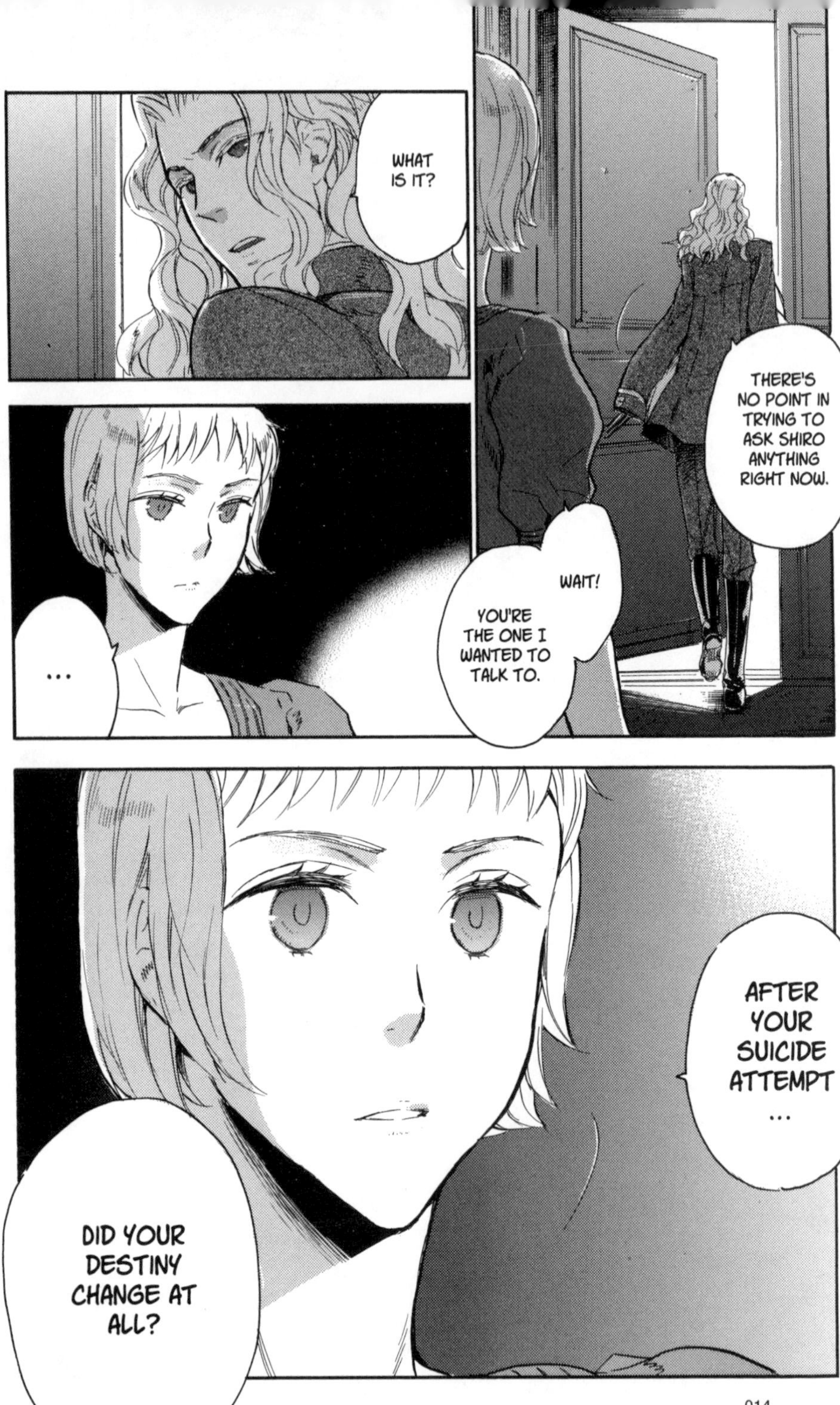
THERE'S NO POINT IN TRYING TO ASK SHIRO ANYTHING RIGHT NOW.
WAIT!
YOU'RE THE ONE I WANTED TO TALK TO.
WHAT IS IT?
...
AFTER YOUR SUICIDE ATTEMPT ...
DID YOUR DESTINY CHANGE AT ALL?

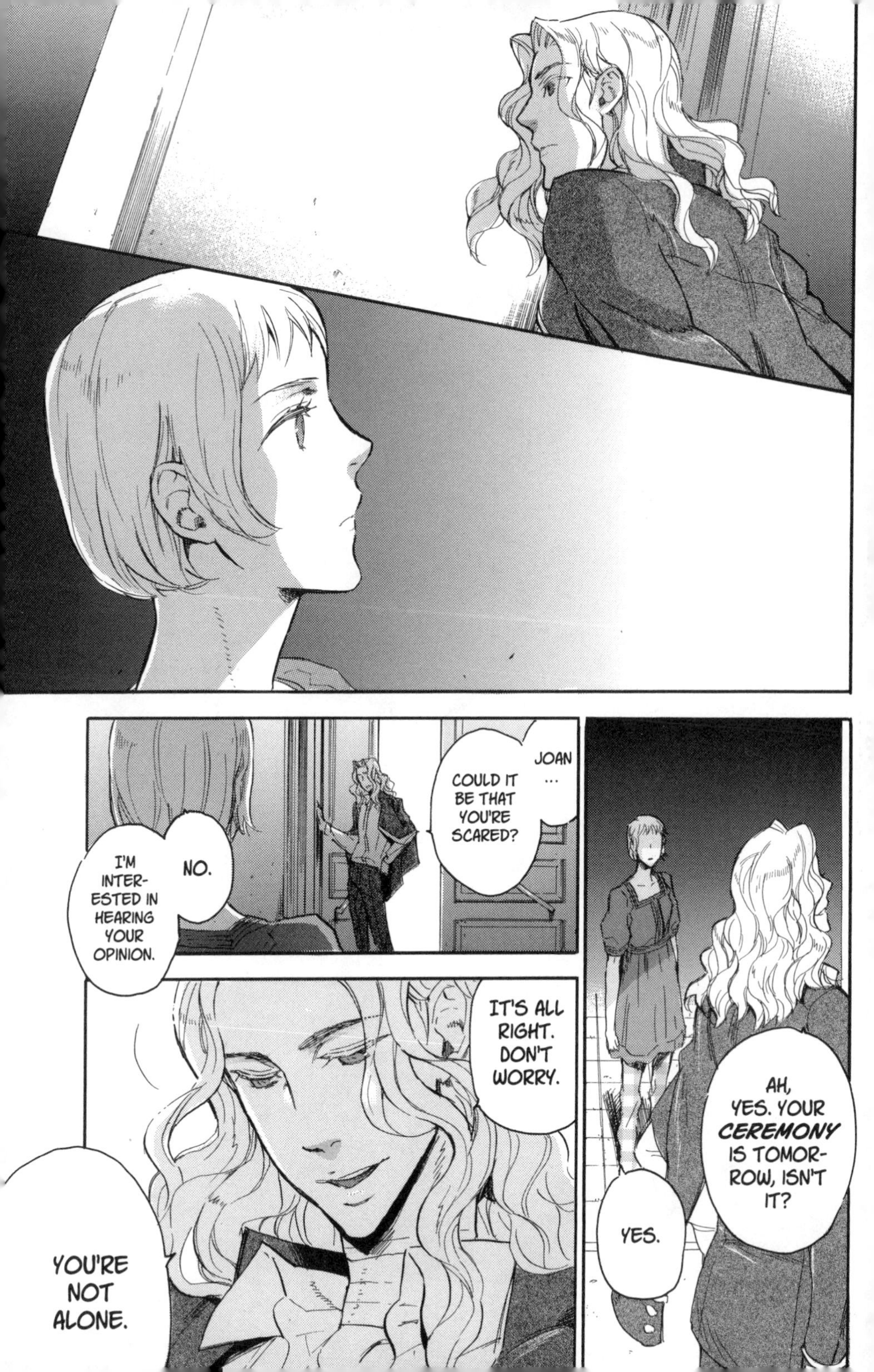
AH, YES. YOUR CEREMONY IS TOMORROW, ISN'T IT?
YES.
JOAN ...
COULD IT BE THAT YOU'RE SCARED?
NO.
I'M INTERESTED IN HEARING YOUR OPINION.
IT'S ALL RIGHT. DON'T WORRY.
YOU'RE NOT ALONE.

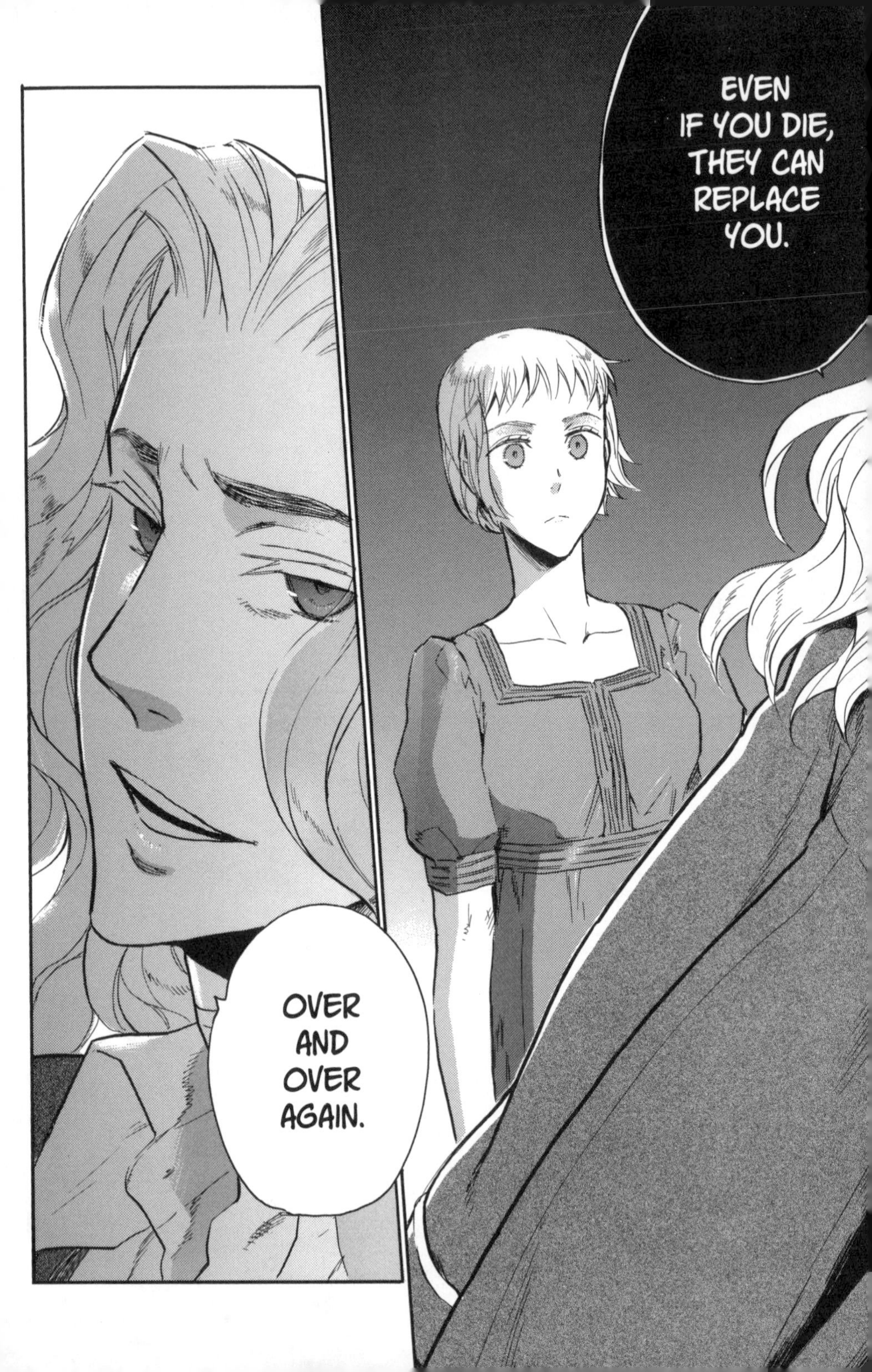
EVEN IF YOU DIE, THEY CAN REPLACE YOU.
OVER AND OVER AGAIN.

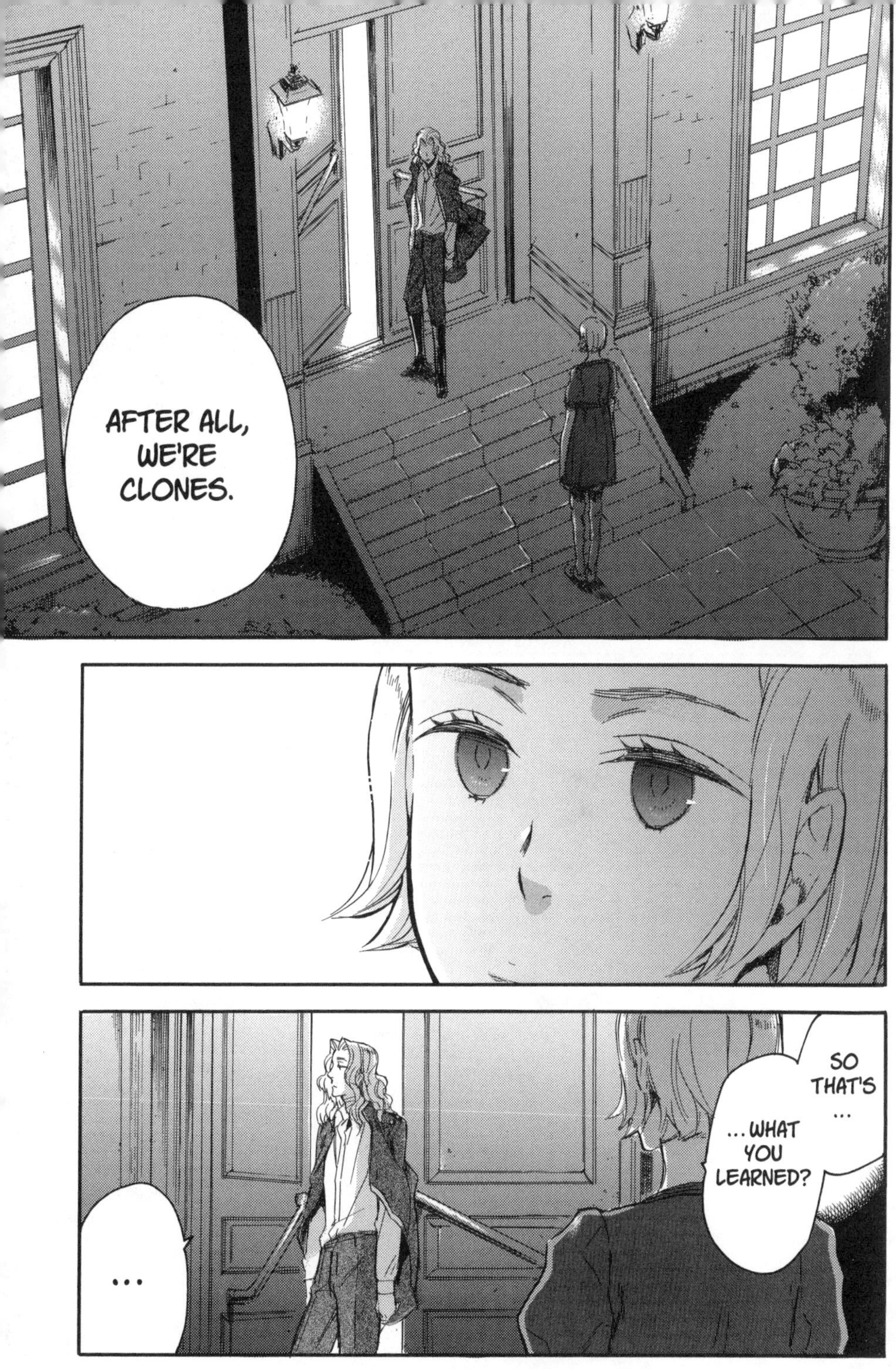
AFTER ALL, WE'RE CLONES.
SO THAT'S ...
... WHAT YOU LEARNED?
...

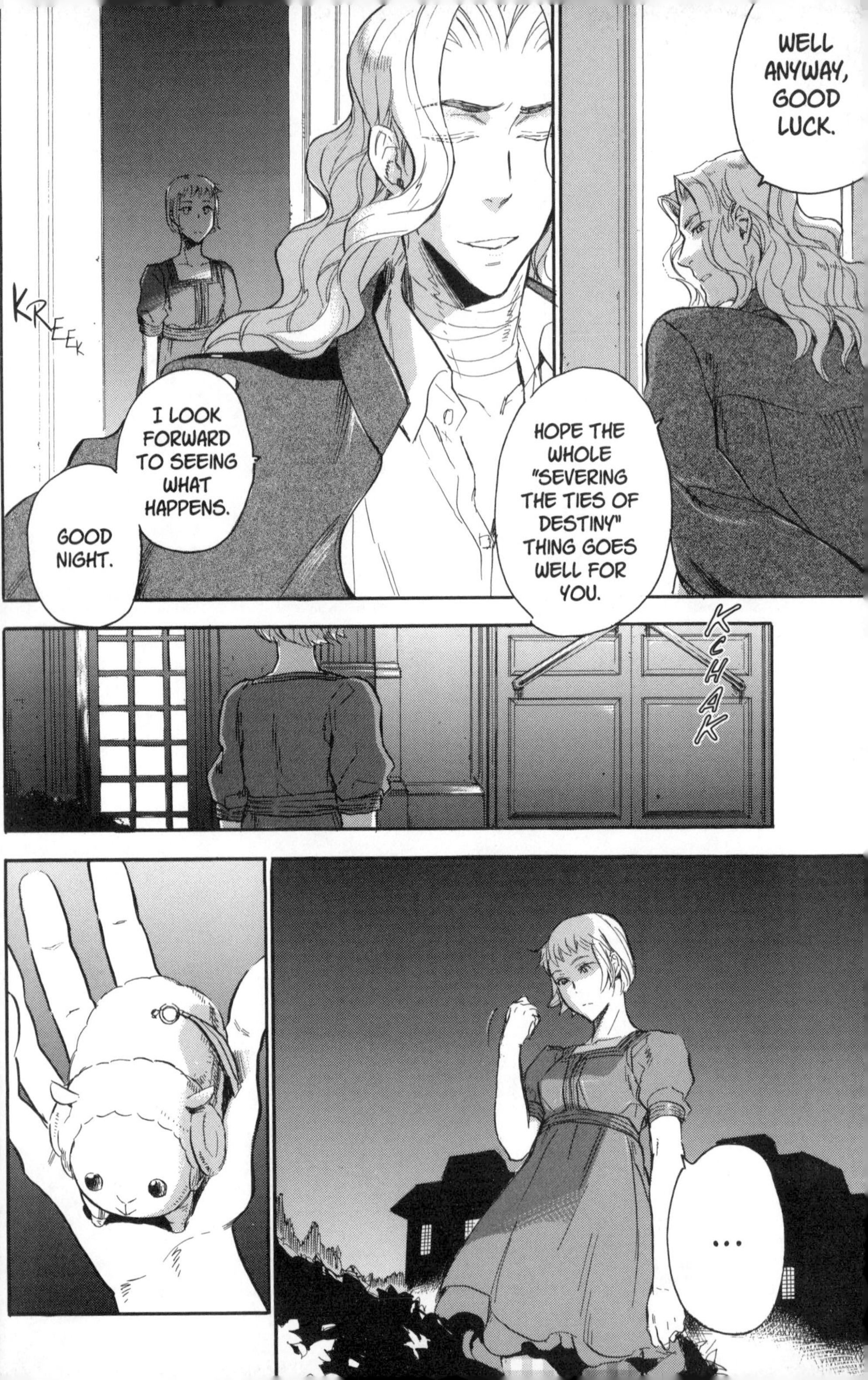
WELL ANYWAY, GOOD LUCK.
HOPE THE WHOLE "SEVERING THE TIES OF DESTINY" THING GOES WELL FOR YOU.
KREEEK
I LOOK FORWARD TO SEEING WHAT HAPPENS.
GOOD NIGHT.
KCHAK
...

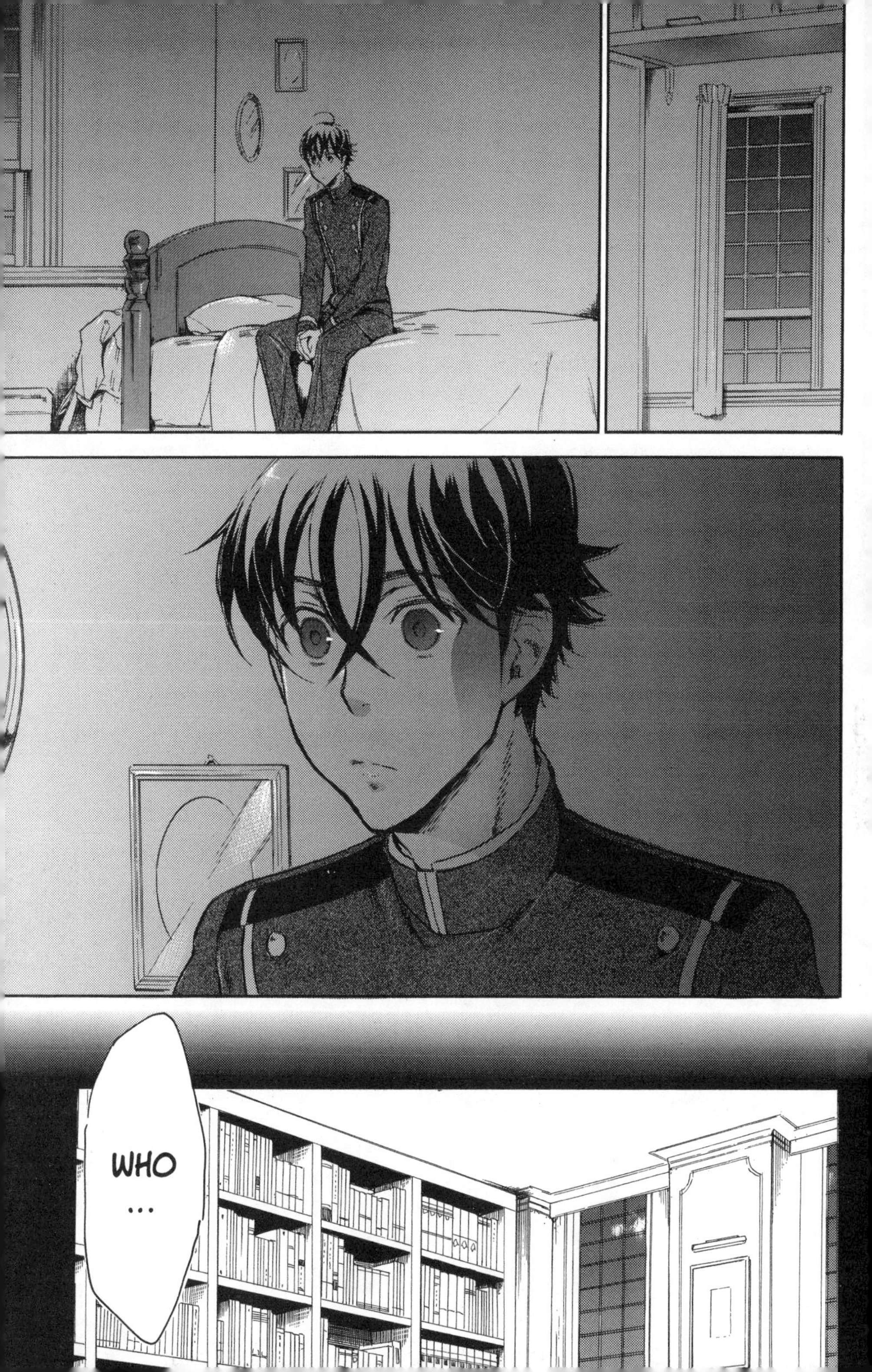
WHO
...

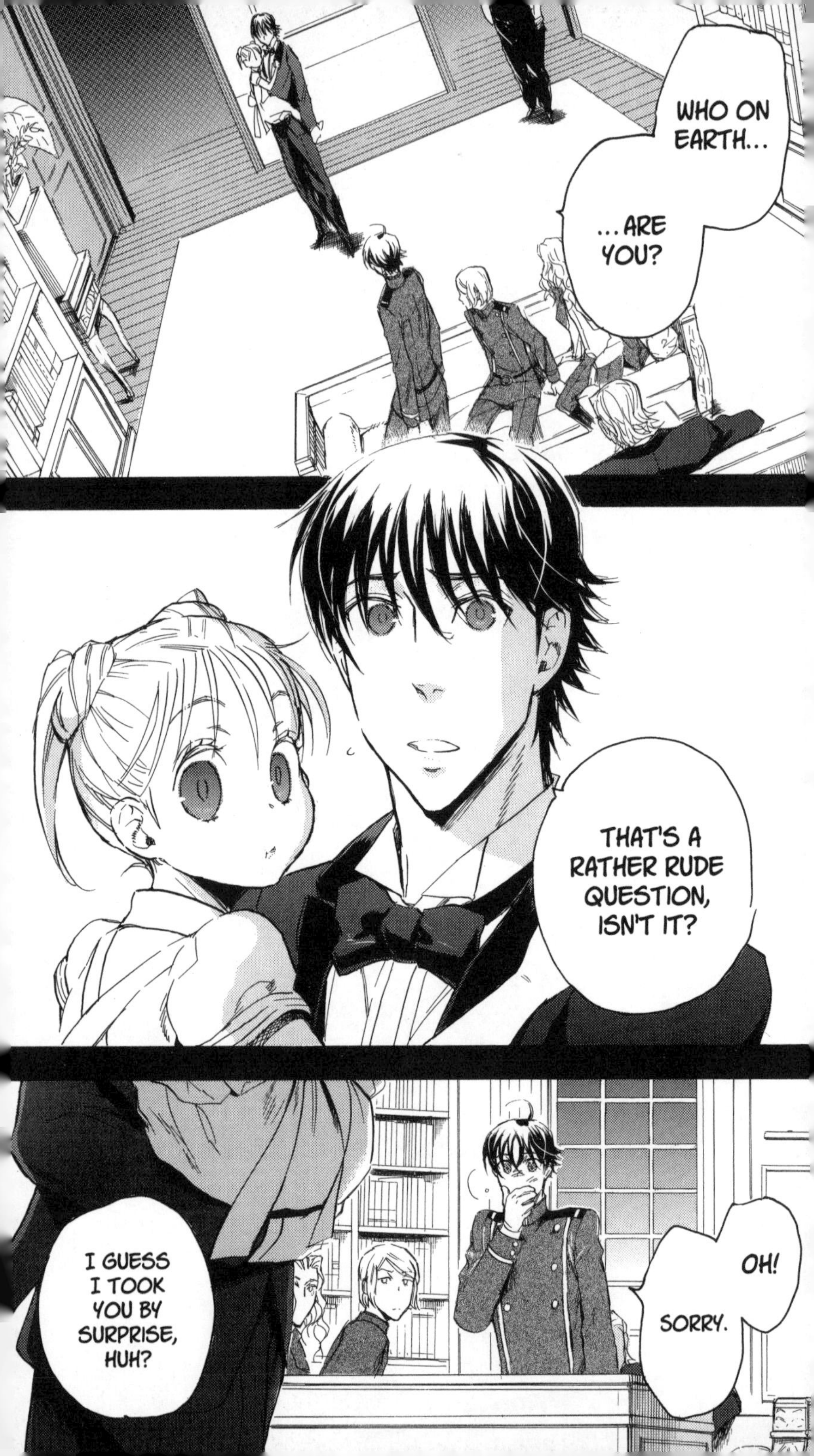
WHO ON EARTH...
...ARE YOU?
THAT'S A RATHER RUDE QUESTION, ISN'T IT?
OH!
SORRY.
I GUESS I TOOK YOU BY SURPRISE, HUH?

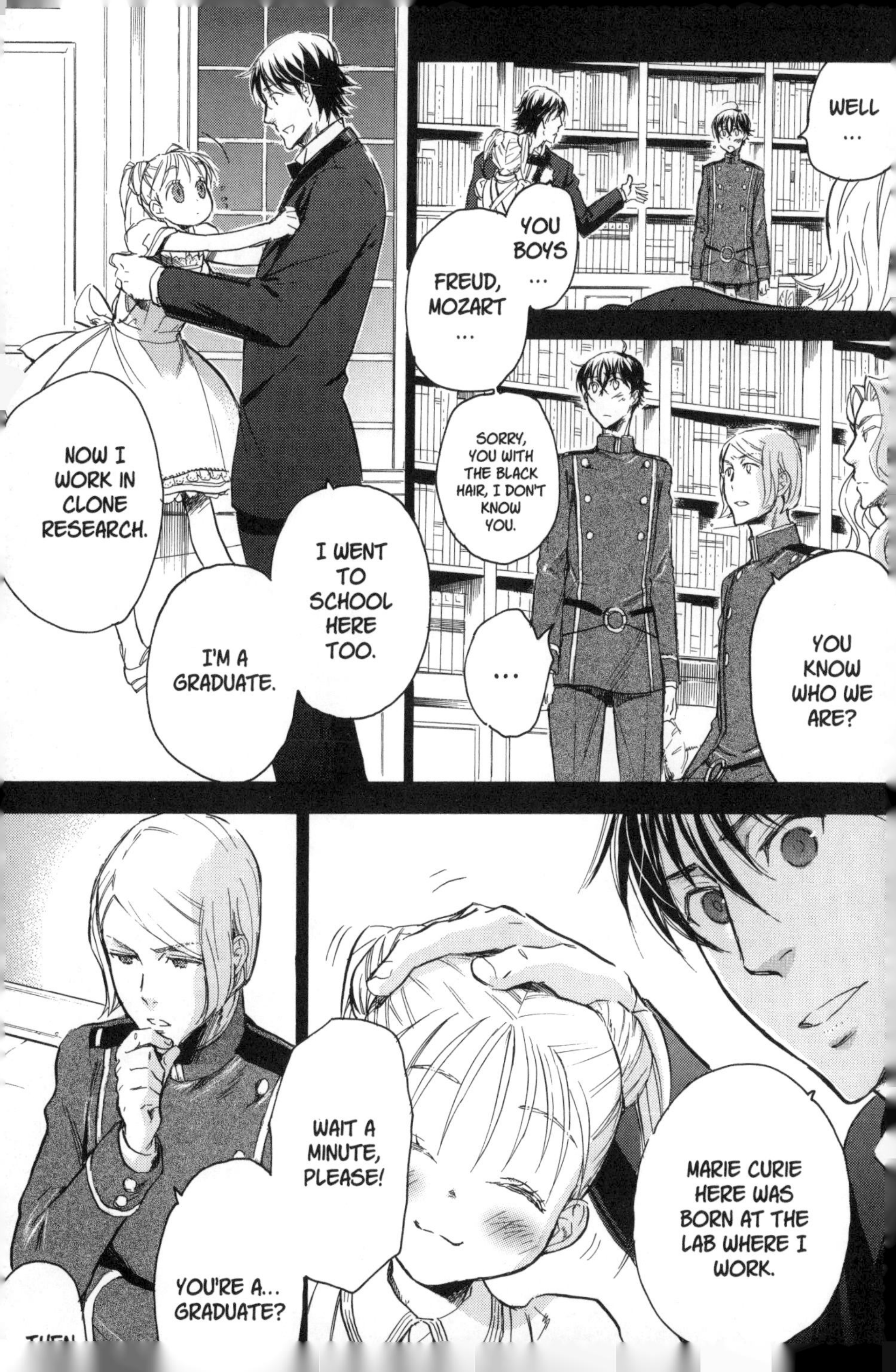
WELL …
YOU BOYS …
FREUD, MOZART …
SORRY, YOU WITH THE BLACK HAIR, I DON'T KNOW YOU.
YOU KNOW WHO WE ARE?
…
I WENT TO SCHOOL HERE TOO.
I'M A GRADUATE.
NOW I WORK IN CLONE RESEARCH.
MARIE CURIE HERE WAS BORN AT THE LAB WHERE I WORK.
WAIT A MINUTE, PLEASE!
YOU'RE A… GRADUATE?

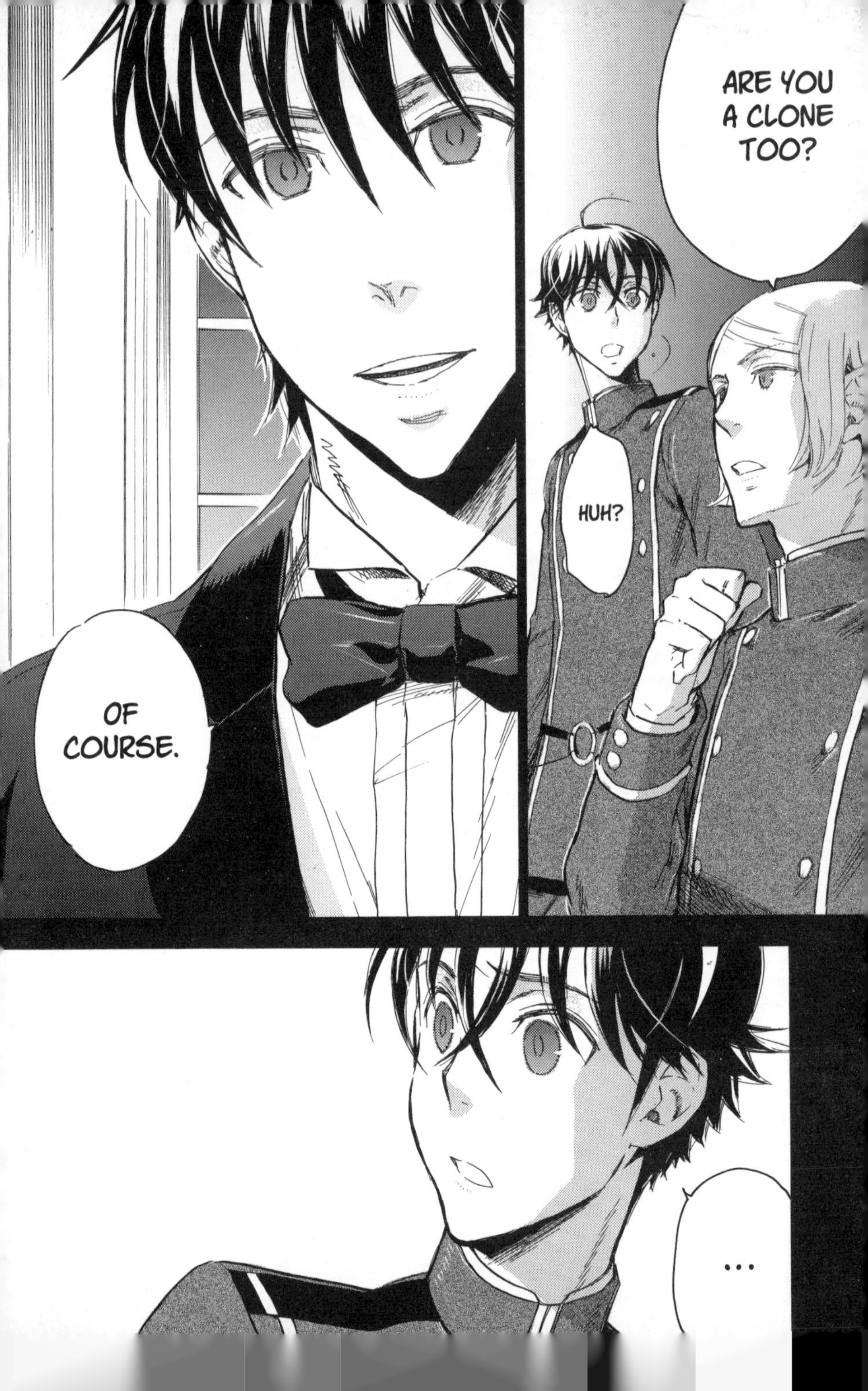
ARE YOU A CLONE TOO?
HUH?
OF COURSE.
...

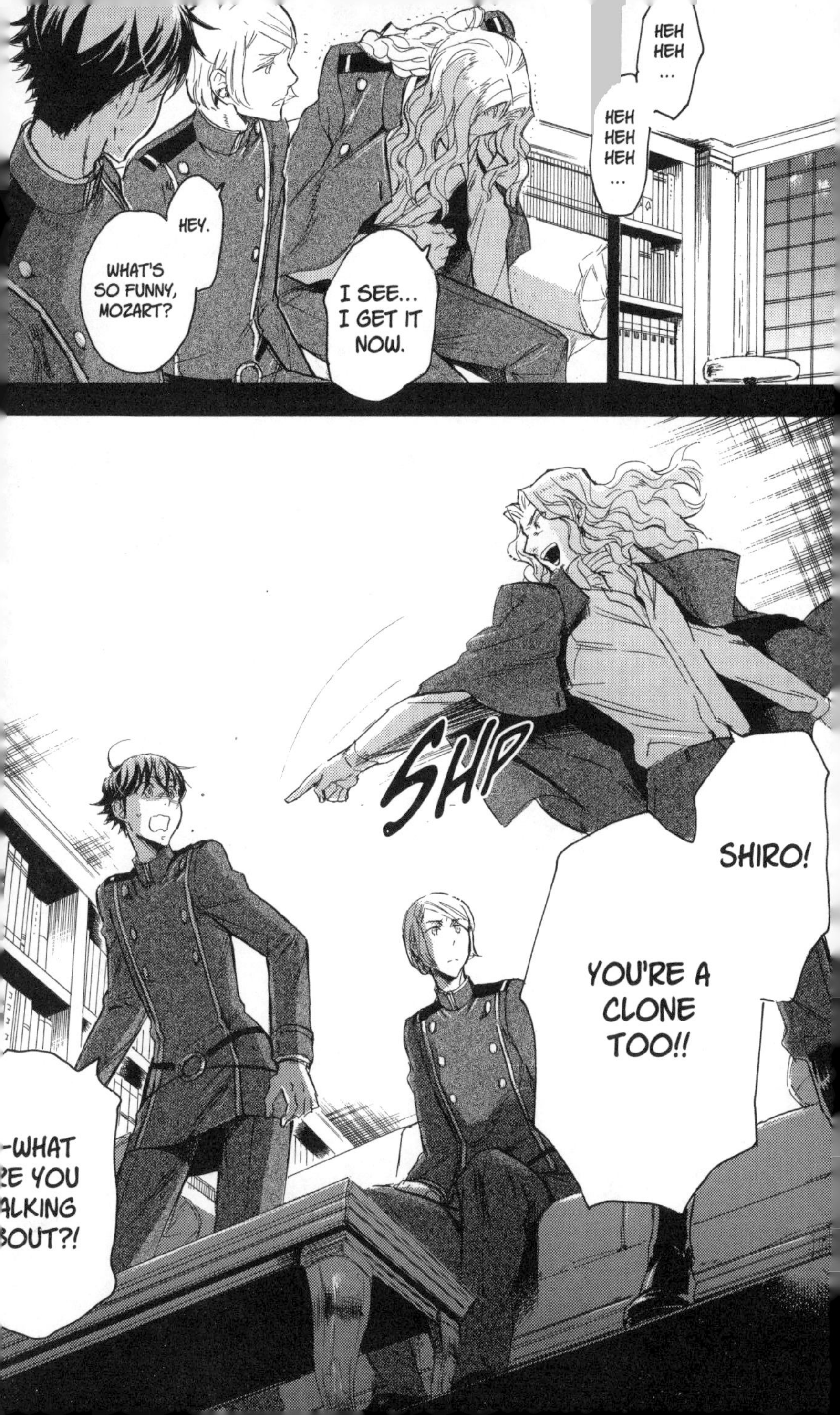
HEH HEH ...
HEH HEH HEH ...
I SEE... I GET IT NOW.
HEY.
WHAT'S SO FUNNY, MOZART?
SHIP
SHIRO!
YOU'RE A CLONE TOO!!
-WHAT RE YOU ALKING BOUT?!

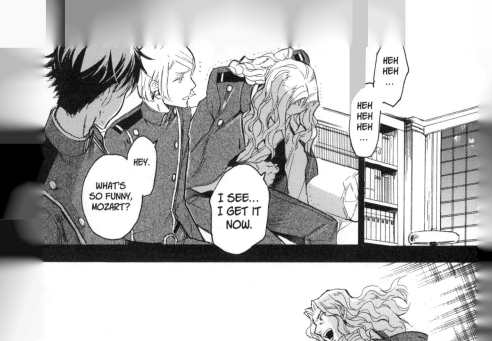

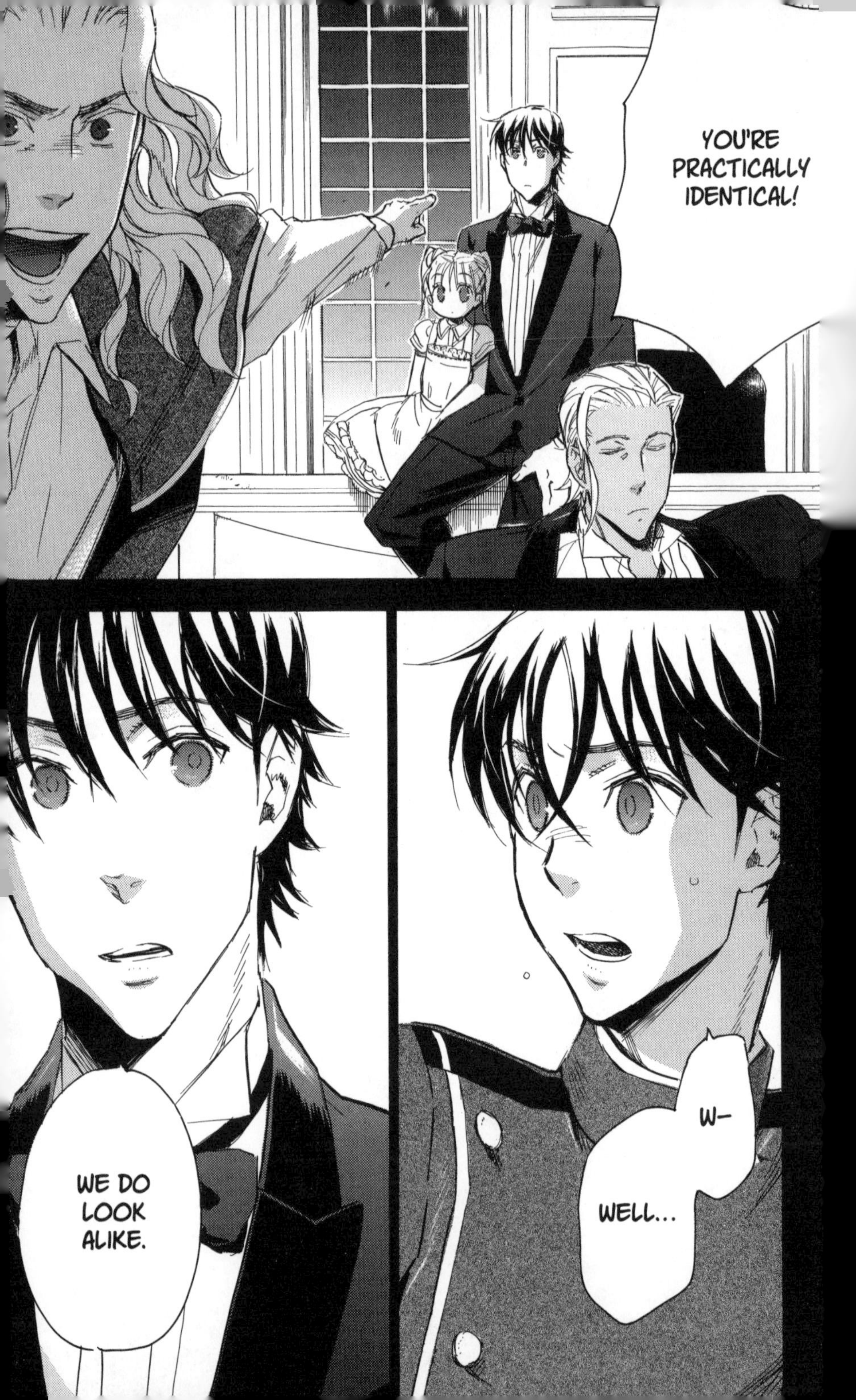

YOU'RE PRACTICALLY IDENTICAL!
W—
WELL...
WE DO LOOK ALIKE.

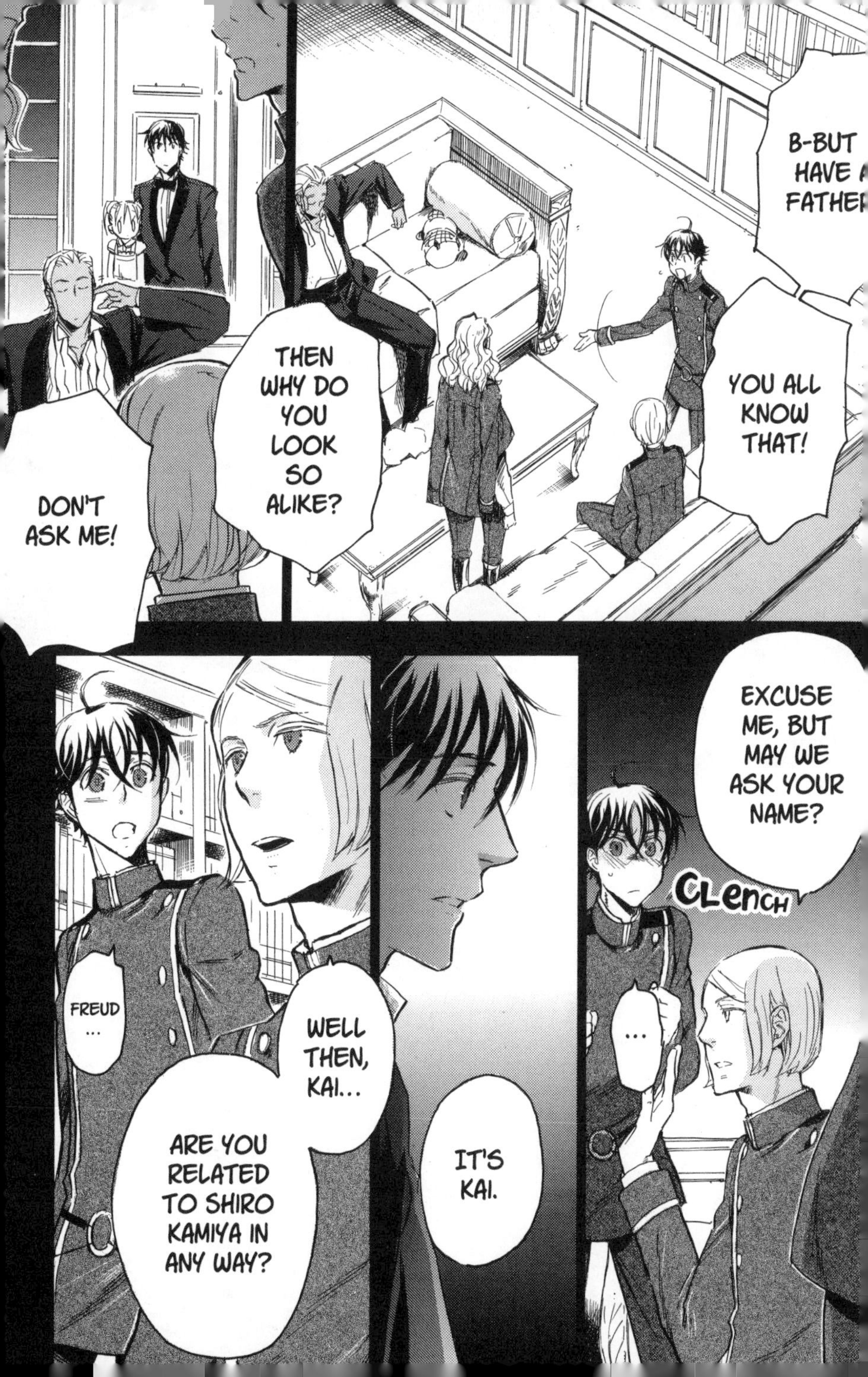
B-BUT HAVE A FATHER
YOU ALL KNOW THAT!
THEN WHY DO YOU LOOK SO ALIKE?
DON'T ASK ME!
EXCUSE ME, BUT MAY WE ASK YOUR NAME?
CLENCH
...
IT'S KAI.
WELL THEN, KAI...
FREUD...
ARE YOU RELATED TO SHIRO KAMIYA IN ANY WAY?

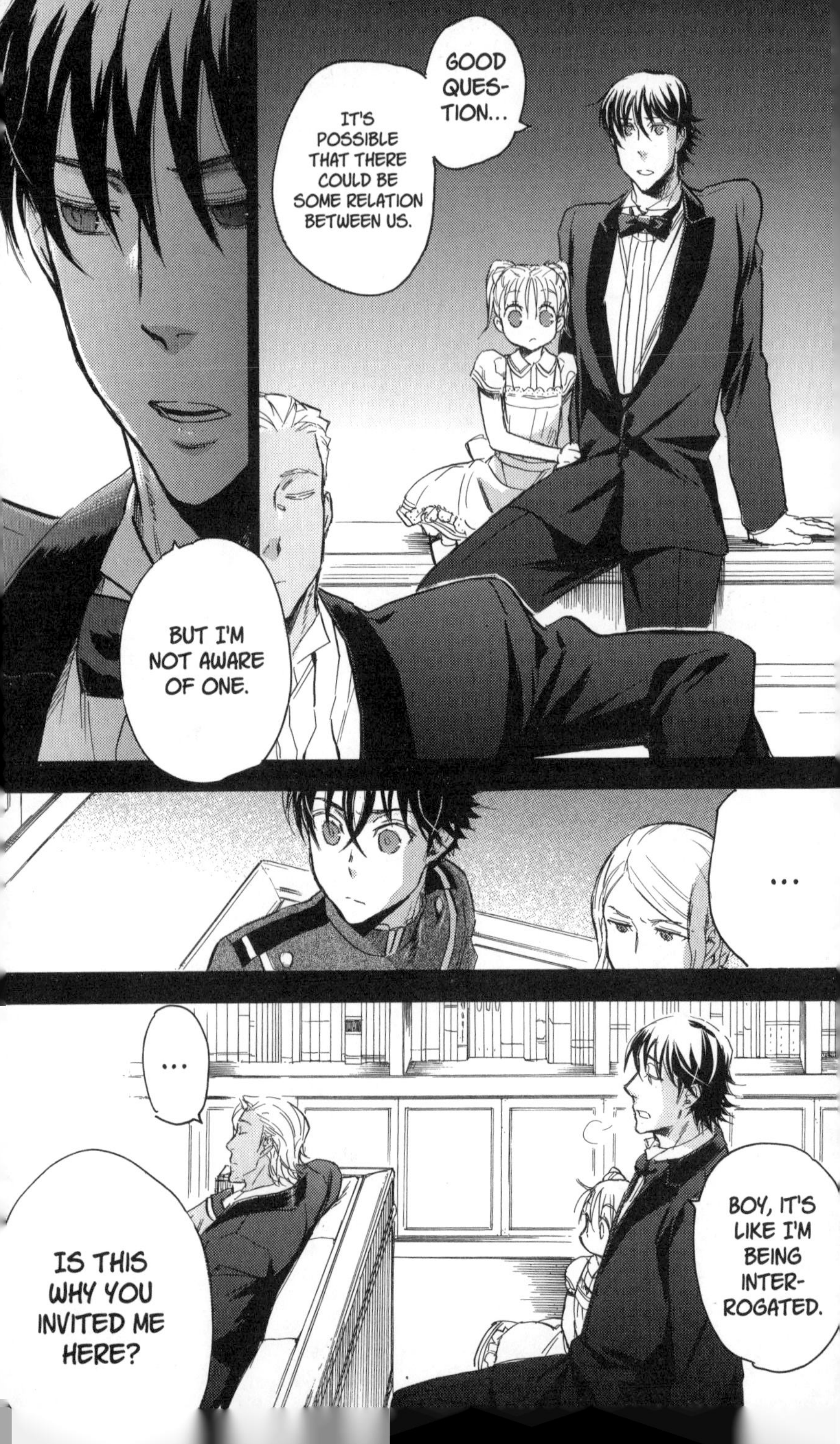
GOOD QUES-TION...
IT'S POSSIBLE THAT THERE COULD BE SOME RELATION BETWEEN US.
BUT I'M NOT AWARE OF ONE.
...
...
BOY, IT'S LIKE I'M BEING INTER-ROGATED.
IS THIS WHY YOU INVITED ME HERE?

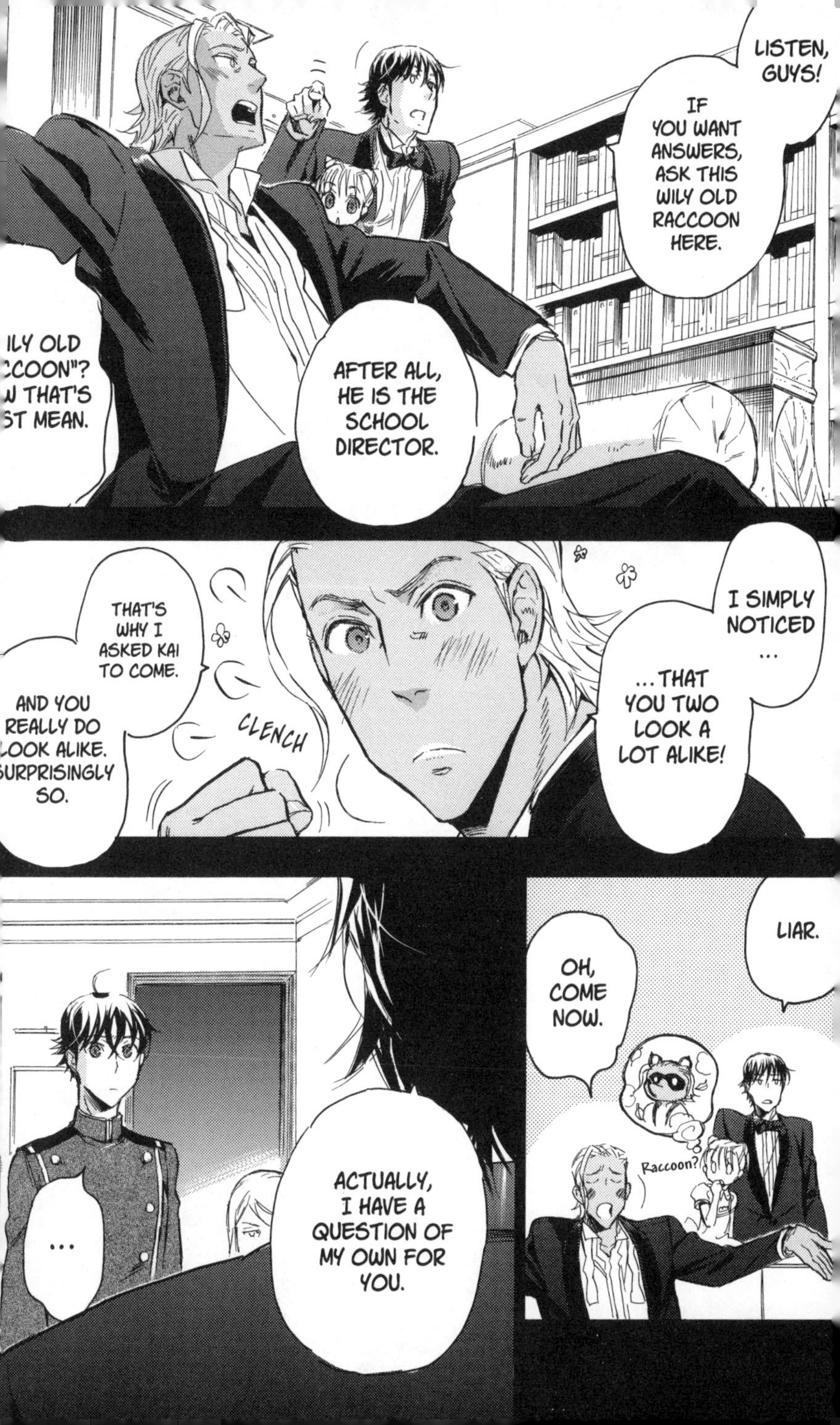
LISTEN, GUYS!
IF YOU WANT ANSWERS, ASK THIS WILY OLD RACCOON HERE.
AFTER ALL, HE IS THE SCHOOL DIRECTOR.
ILY OLD CCOON"? W THAT'S ST MEAN.
I SIMPLY NOTICED ...
...THAT YOU TWO LOOK A LOT ALIKE!
CLENCH
THAT'S WHY I ASKED KAI TO COME.
AND YOU REALLY DO OOK ALIKE. URPRISINGLY SO.
LIAR.
OH, COME NOW.
Raccoon?
ACTUALLY, I HAVE A QUESTION OF MY OWN FOR YOU.
...

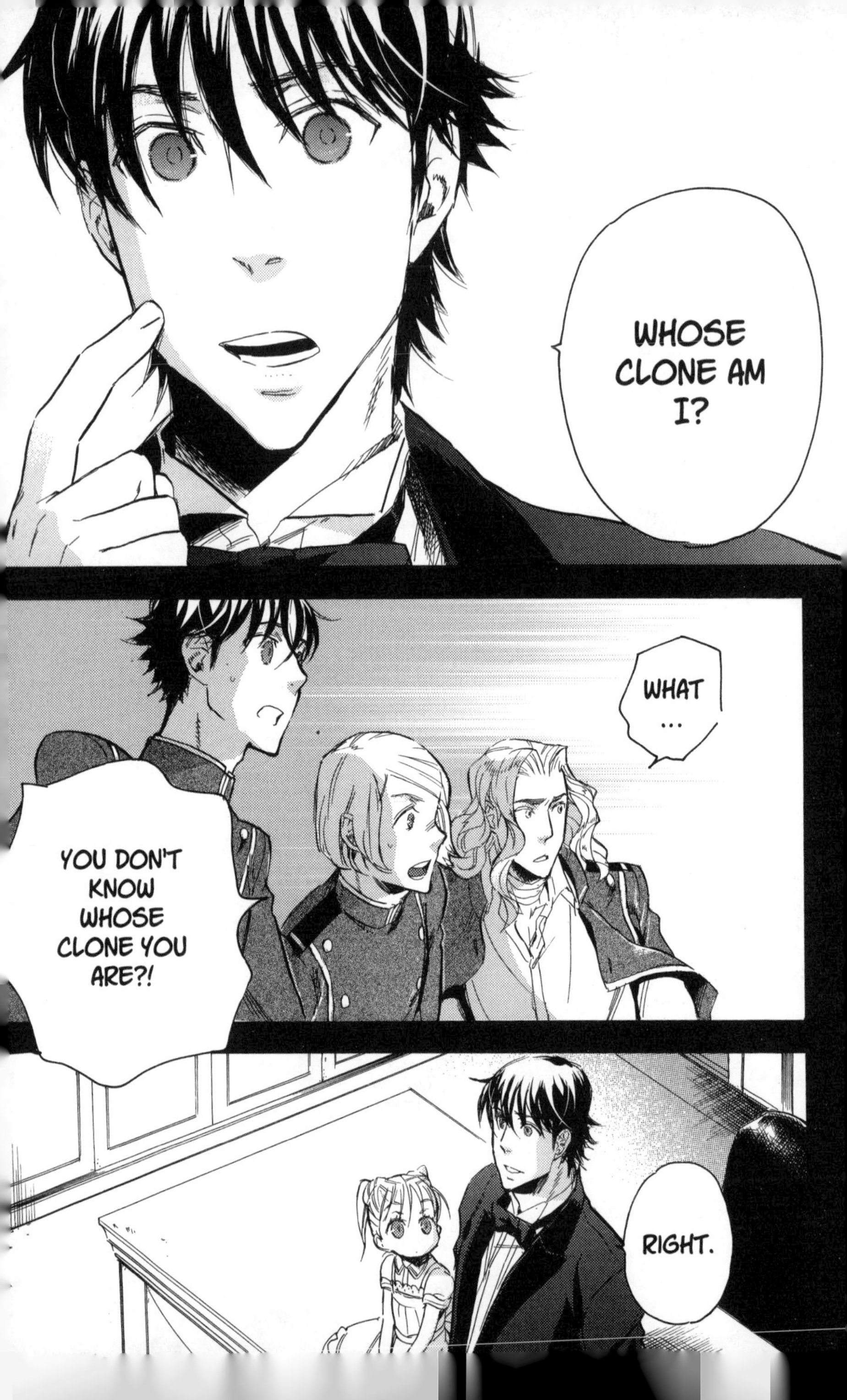
WHOSE CLONE AM I?
WHAT ...
YOU DON'T KNOW WHOSE CLONE YOU ARE?!
RIGHT.

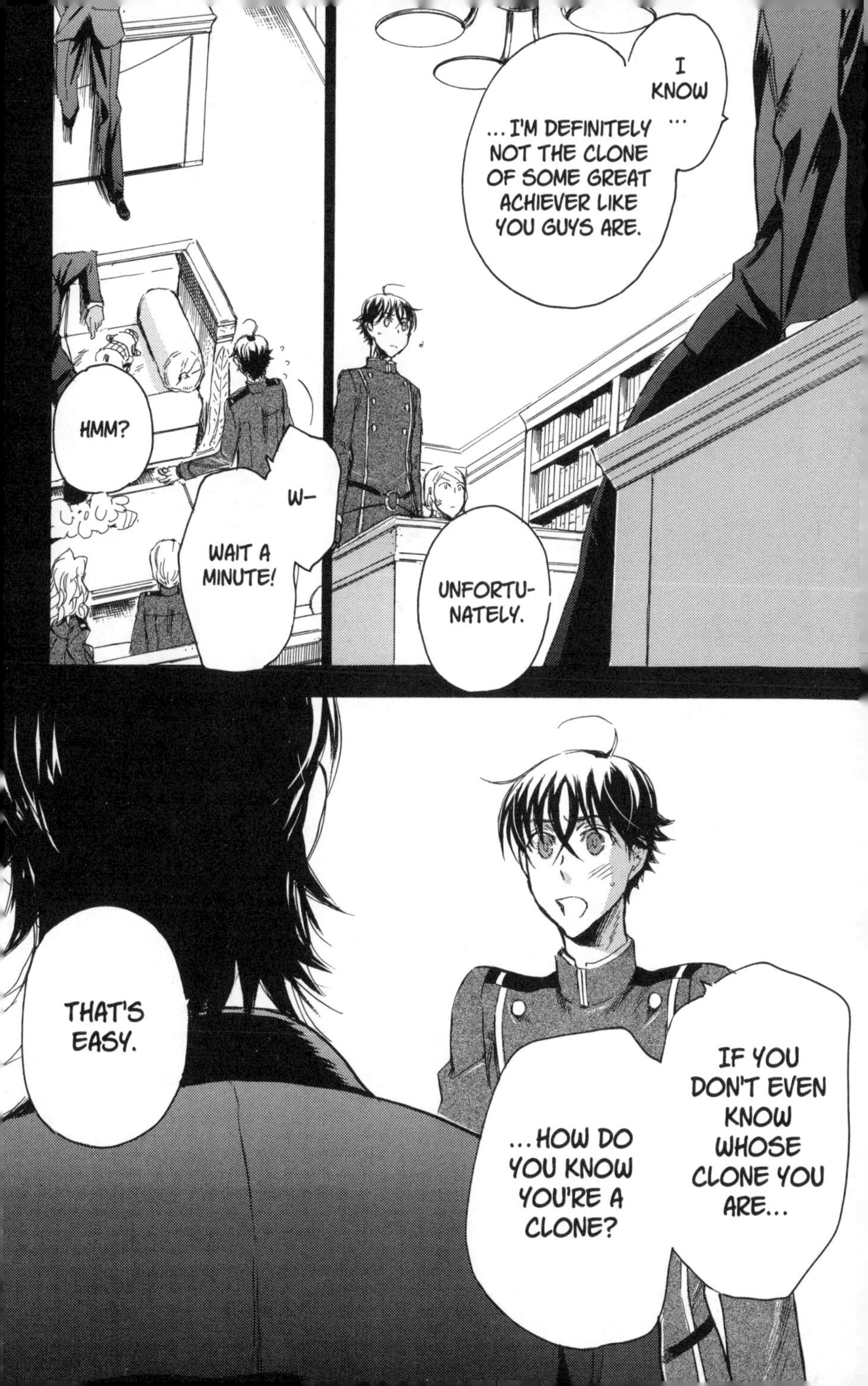
I KNOW ...
...I'M DEFINITELY NOT THE CLONE OF SOME GREAT ACHIEVER LIKE YOU GUYS ARE.
UNFORTUNATELY.
W— WAIT A MINUTE!
HMM?
IF YOU DON'T EVEN KNOW WHOSE CLONE YOU ARE...
...HOW DO YOU KNOW YOU'RE A CLONE?
THAT'S EASY.

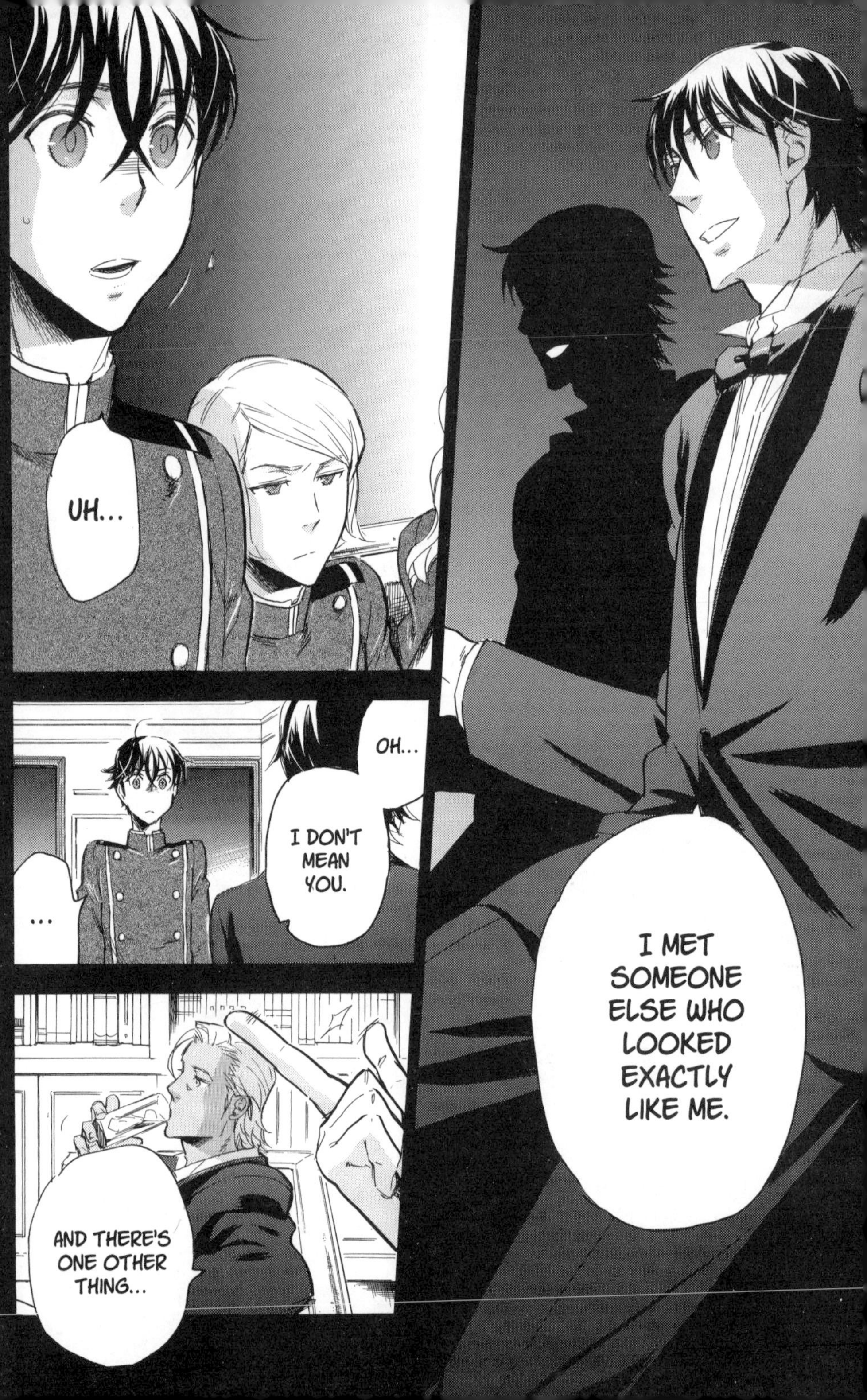
I MET SOMEONE ELSE WHO LOOKED EXACTLY LIKE ME.
UH...
OH...
I DON'T MEAN YOU.
...
AND THERE'S ONE OTHER THING...

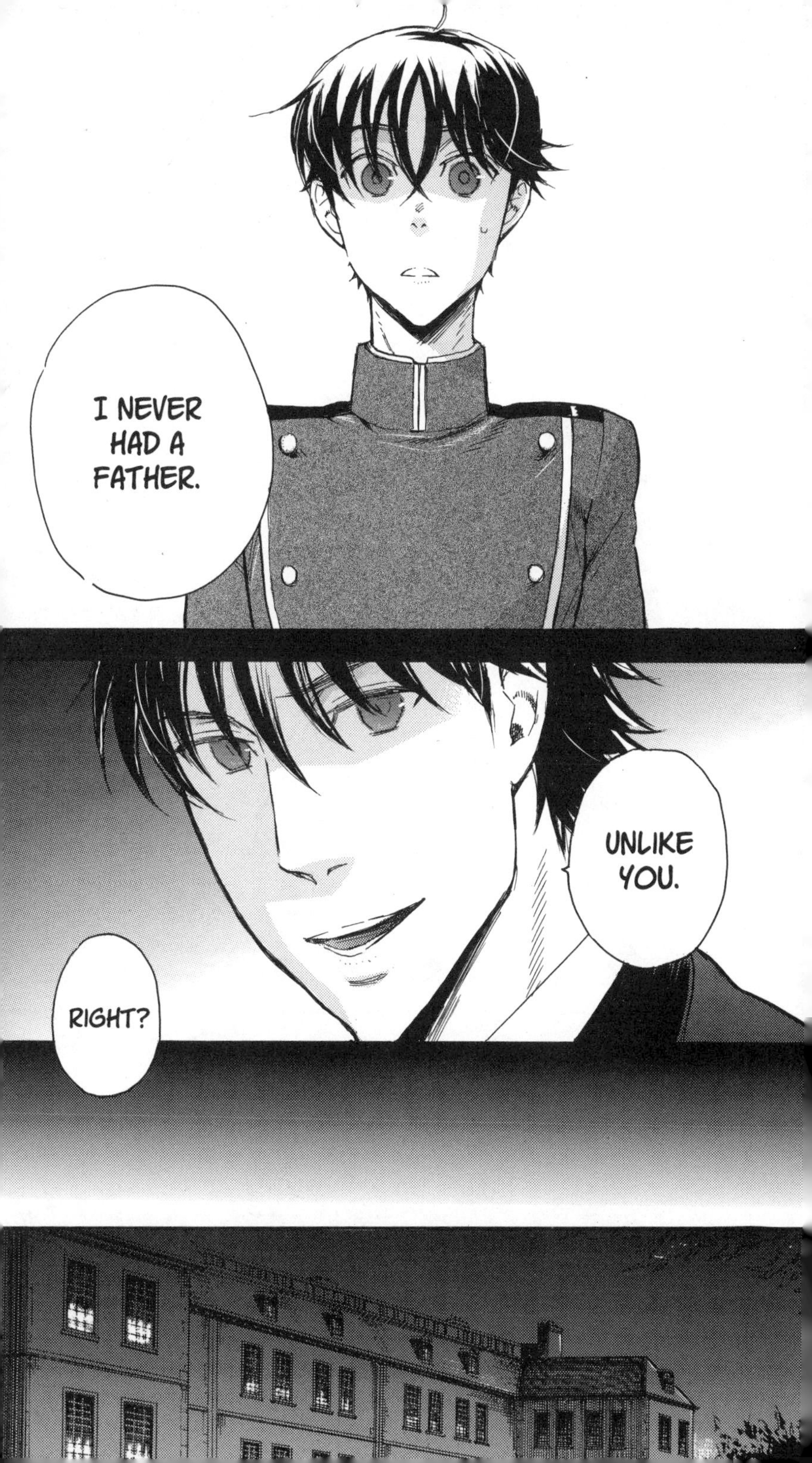
I NEVER HAD A FATHER.
UNLIKE YOU.
RIGHT?

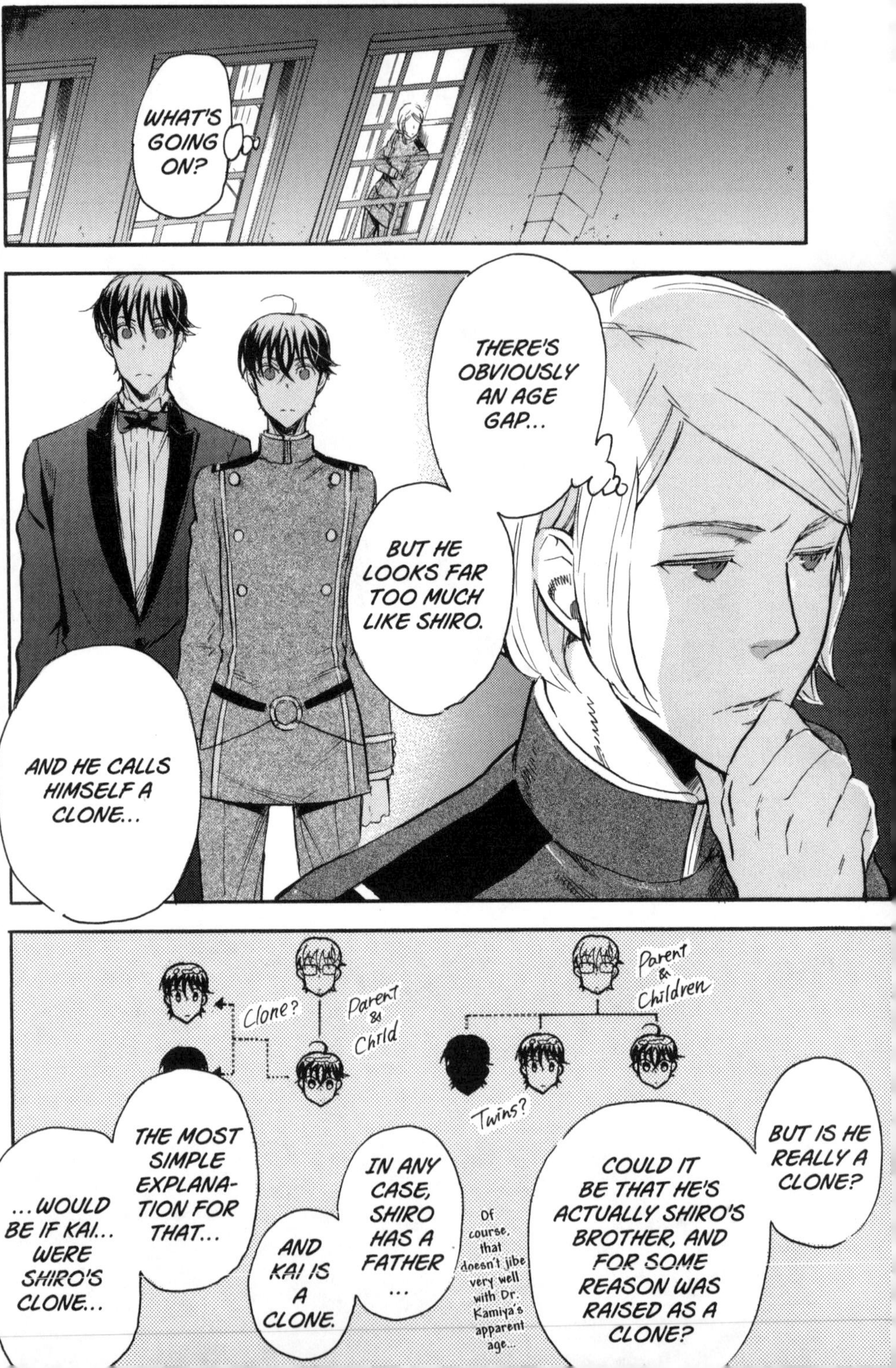
WHAT'S GOING ON?
THERE'S OBVIOUSLY AN AGE GAP...
BUT HE LOOKS FAR TOO MUCH LIKE SHIRO.
AND HE CALLS HIMSELF A CLONE...
Parent & Children
Twins?
Parent & Child
Clone?
BUT IS HE REALLY A CLONE?
COULD IT BE THAT HE'S ACTUALLY SHIRO'S BROTHER, AND FOR SOME REASON WAS RAISED AS A CLONE?
Of course, that doesn't jibe very well with Dr. Kamiya's apparent age...
IN ANY CASE, SHIRO HAS A FATHER...
AND KAI IS A CLONE.
THE MOST SIMPLE EXPLANATION FOR THAT...
...WOULD BE IF KAI... WERE SHIRO'S CLONE...

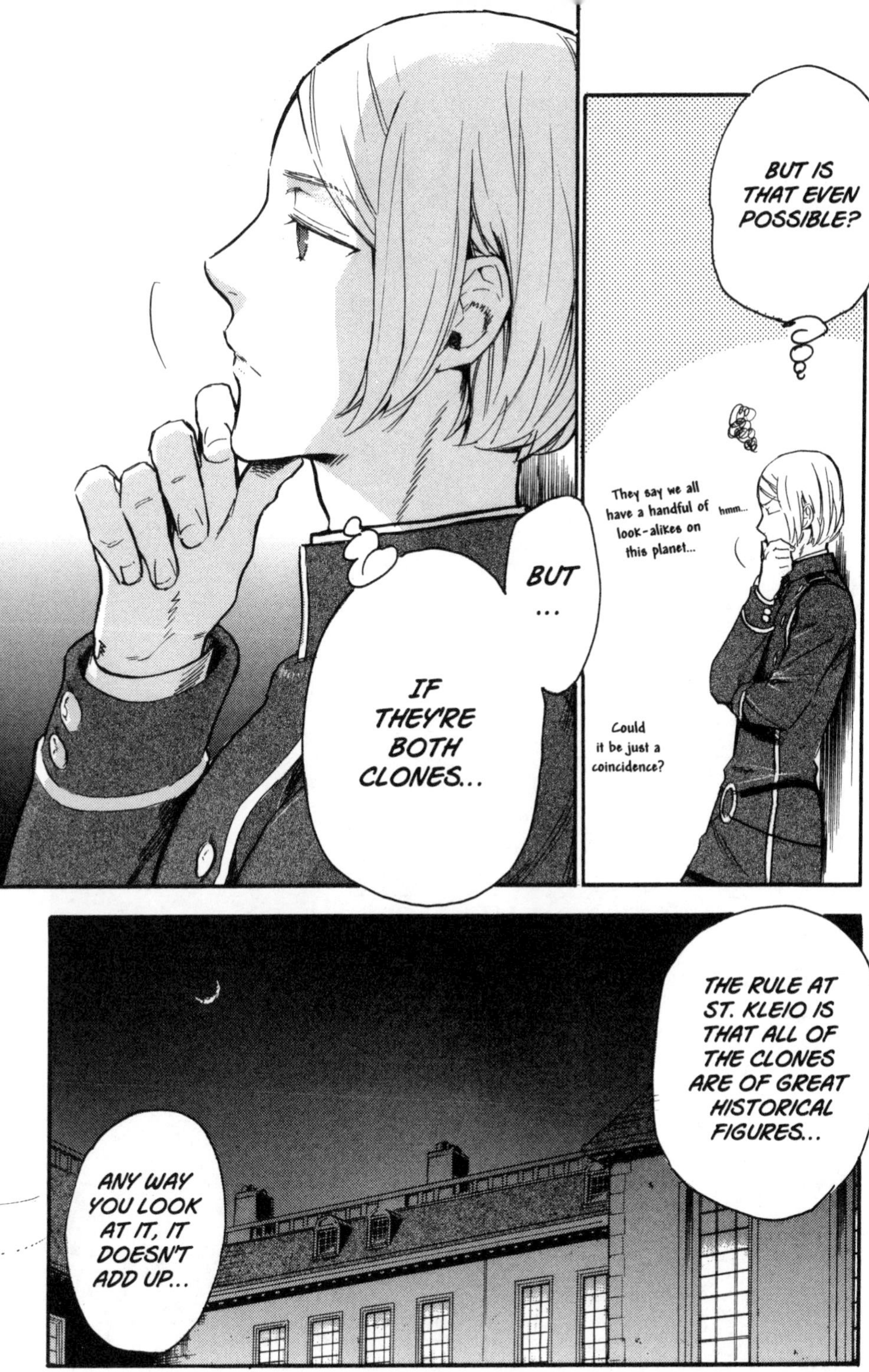
BUT IS THAT EVEN POSSIBLE?
They say we all have a handful of look-alikes on this planet...
hmm...
Could it be just a coincidence?
BUT... IF THEY'RE BOTH CLONES...
THE RULE AT ST. KLEIO IS THAT ALL OF THE CLONES ARE OF GREAT HISTORICAL FIGURES...
ANY WAY YOU LOOK AT IT, IT DOESN'T ADD UP...

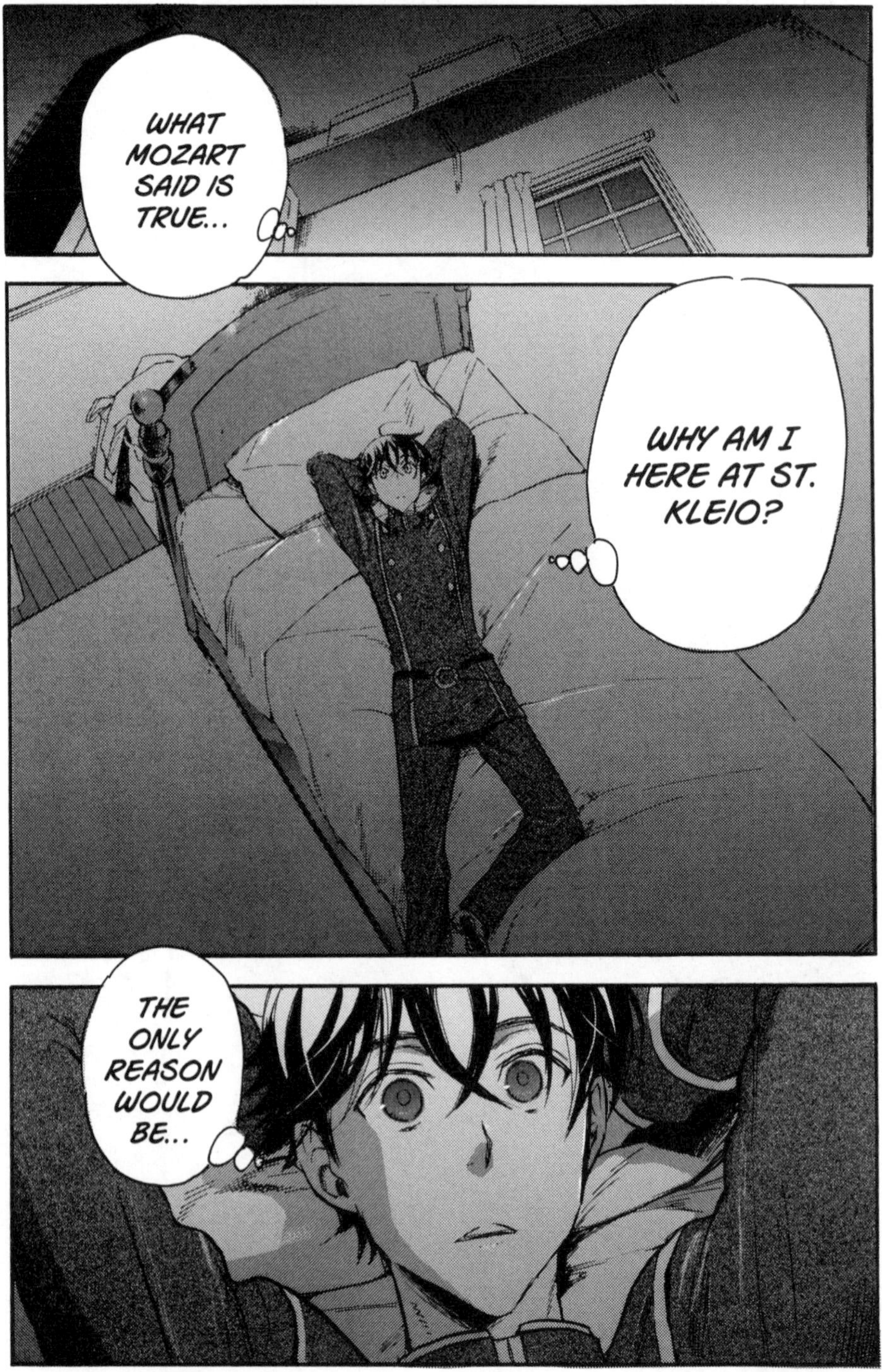
WHAT MOZART SAID IS TRUE...
WHY AM I HERE AT ST. KLEIO?
THE ONLY REASON WOULD BE...

IF I'M A CLONE, THAT WOULD EXPLAIN IT.

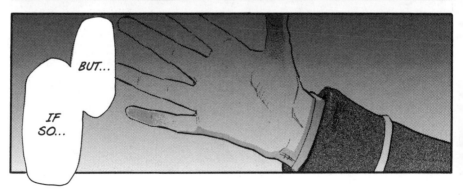

BUT...

IF SO...

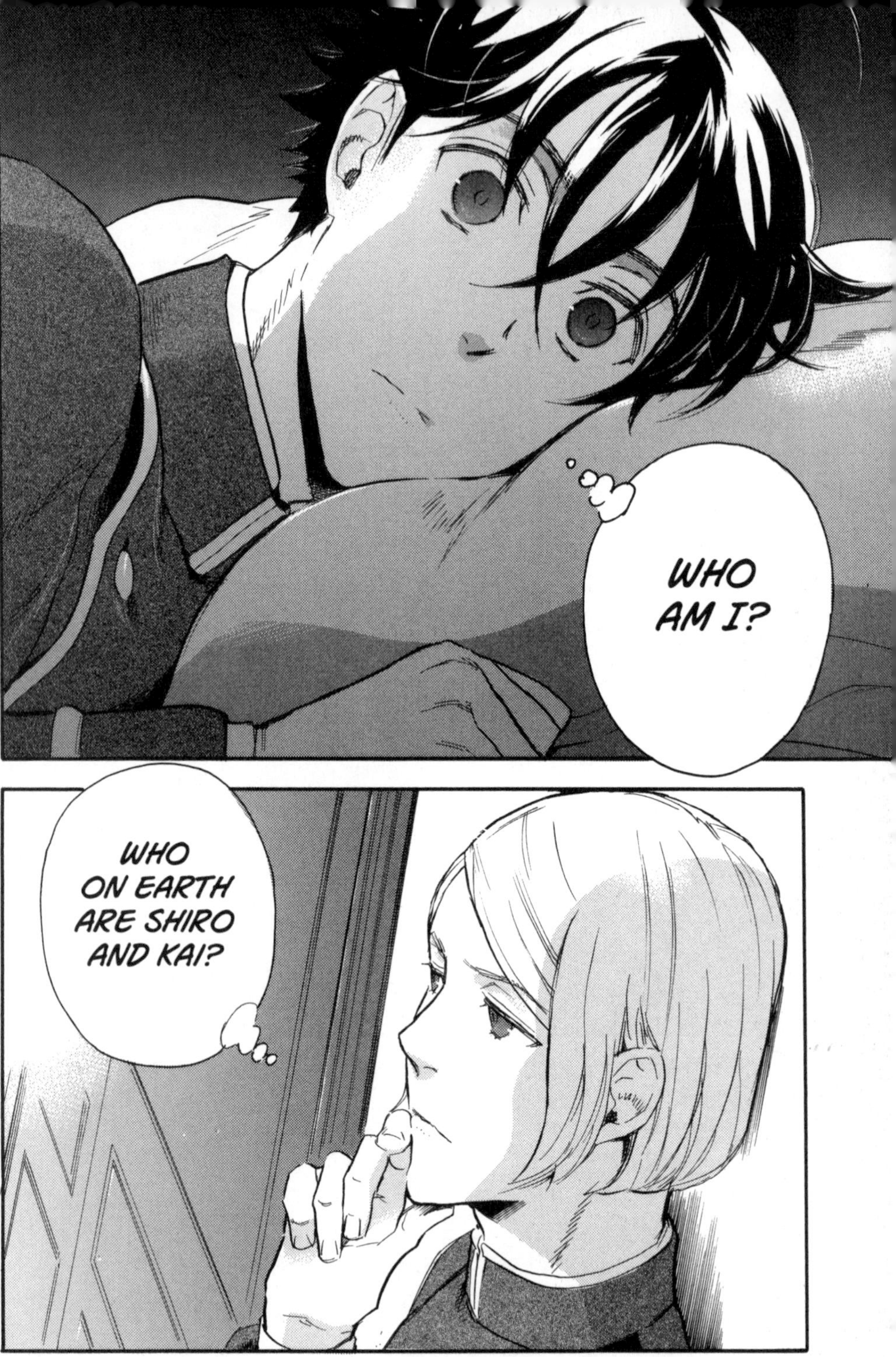
WHO AM I?
WHO ON EARTH ARE SHIRO AND KAI?

afterschool charisma

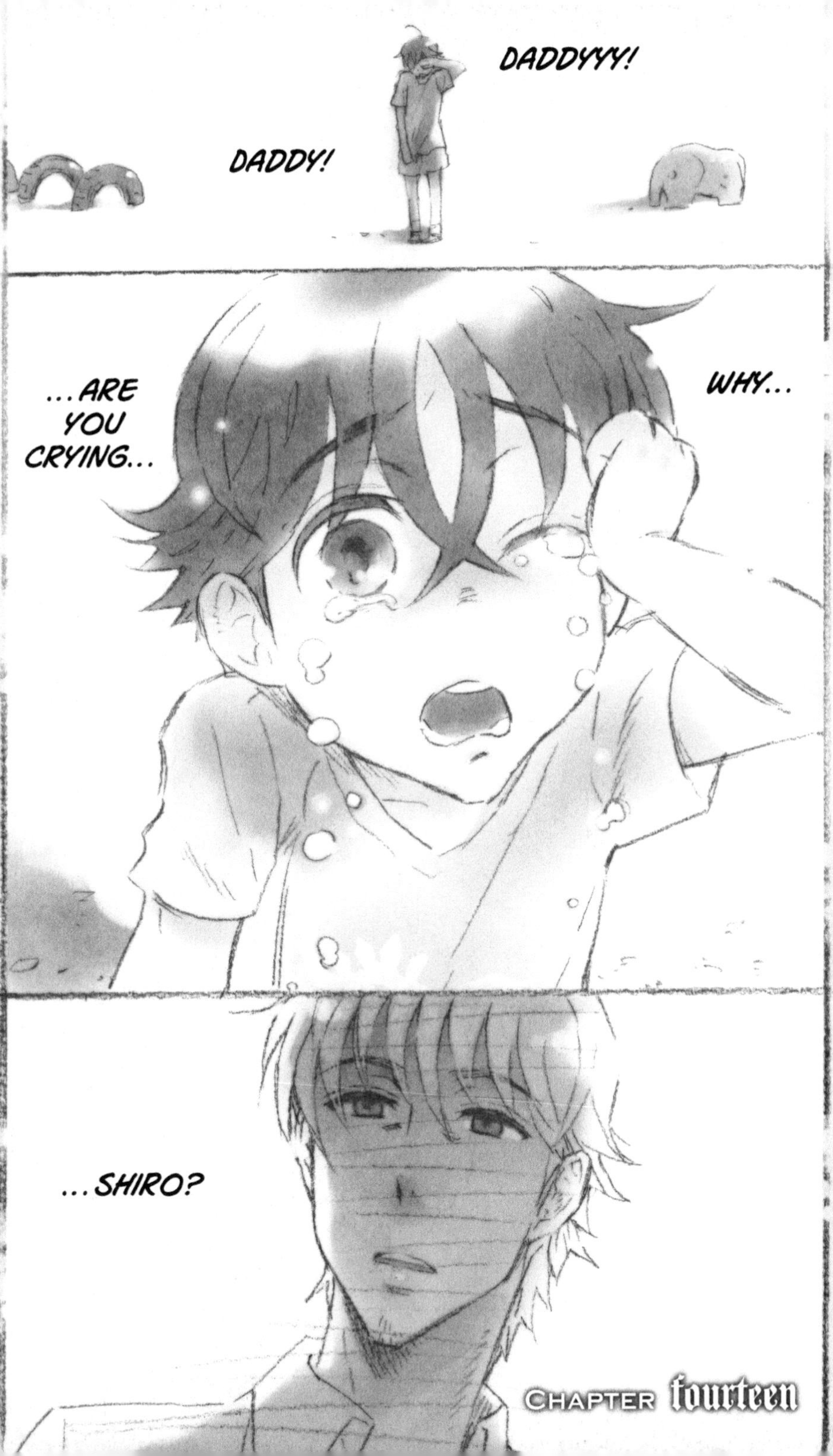
DADDYYY!
DADDY!
WHY...
...ARE YOU CRYING...
...SHIRO?
CHAPTER fourteen

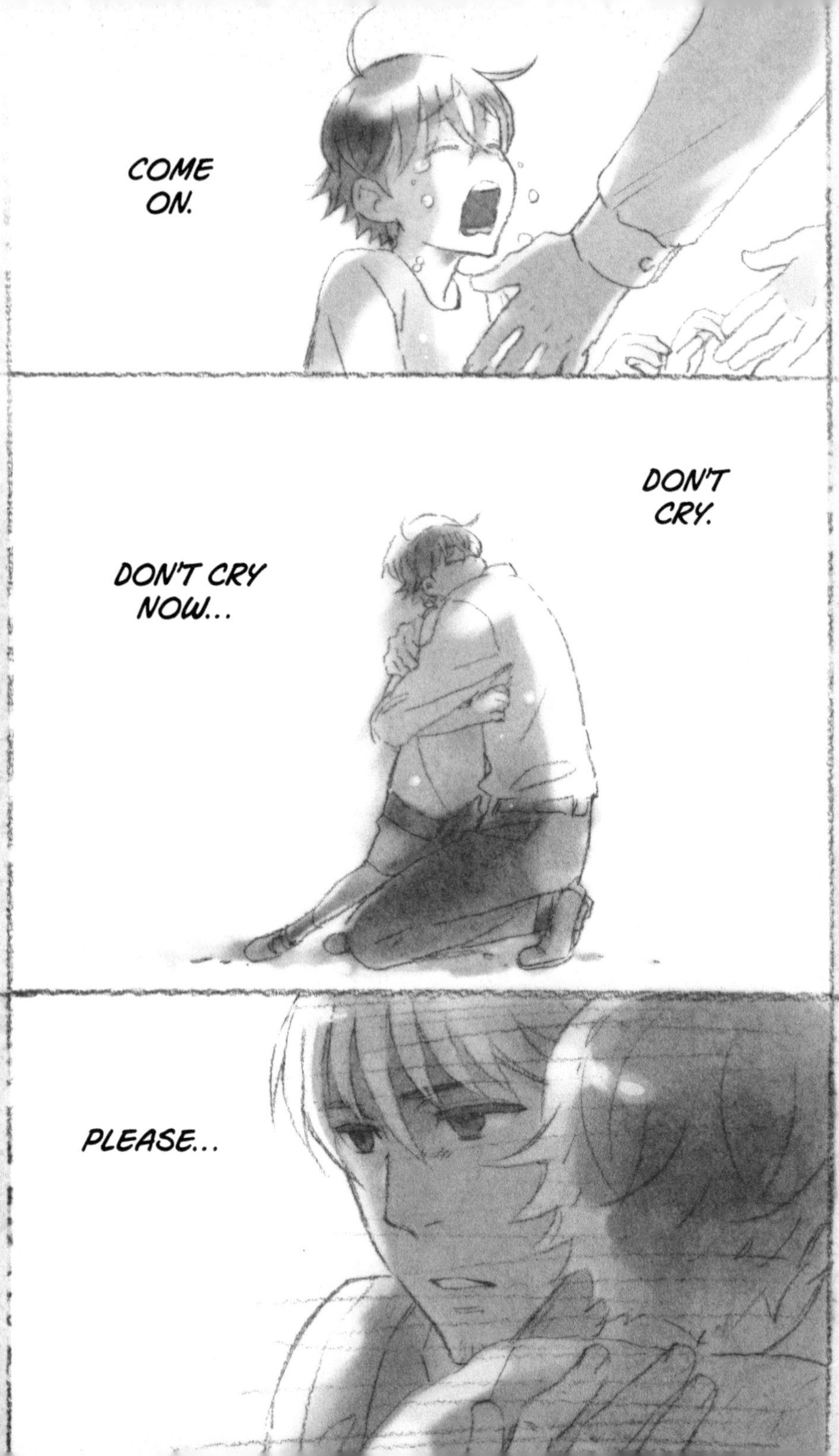
COME ON.
DON'T CRY.
DON'T CRY NOW...
PLEASE...

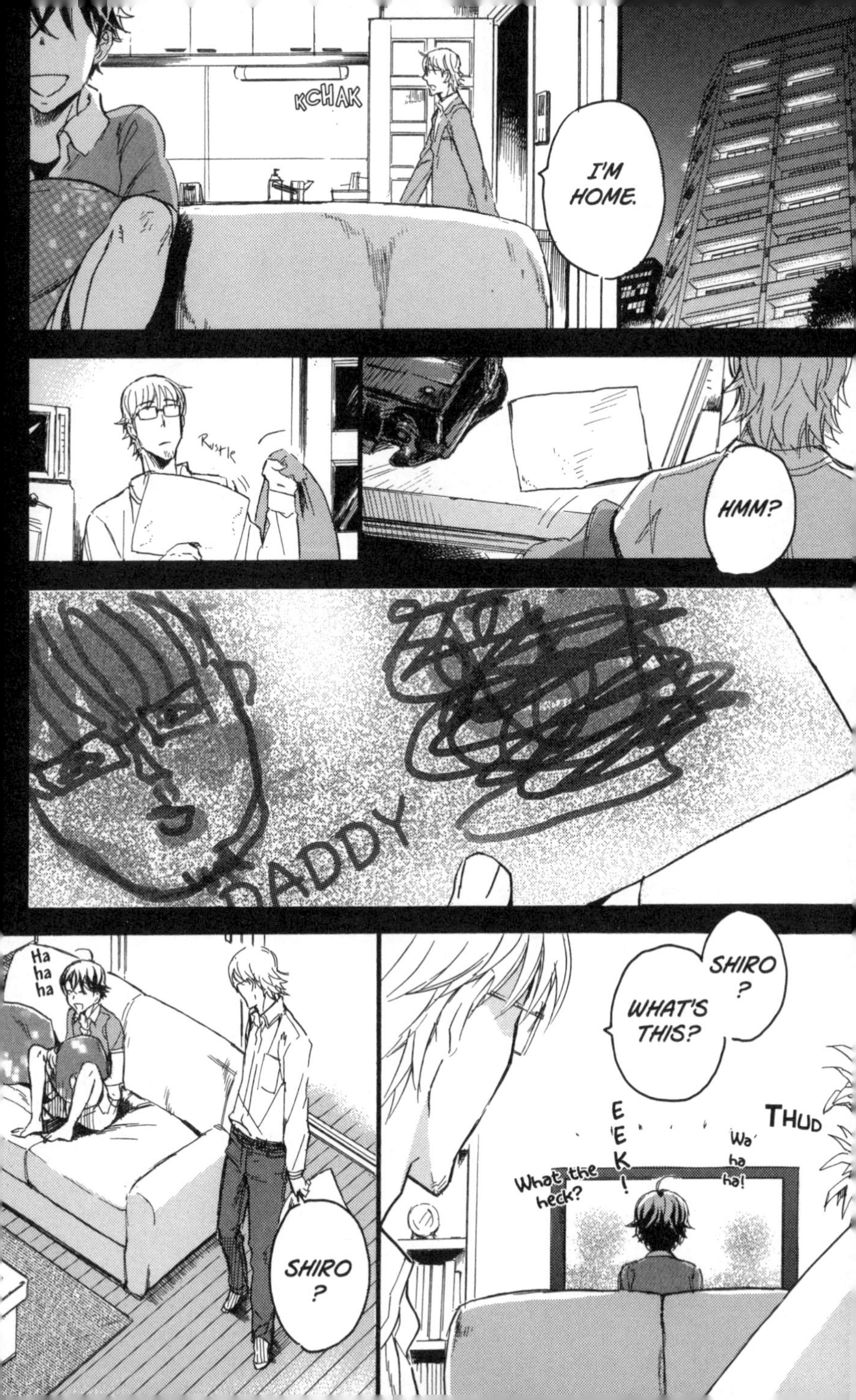
I'M HOME.
KCHAK
HMM?
Rustle
DADDY
SHIRO?
WHAT'S THIS?
THUD
Wa ha ha!
EEK!
What the heck?
SHIRO?
Ha ha ha

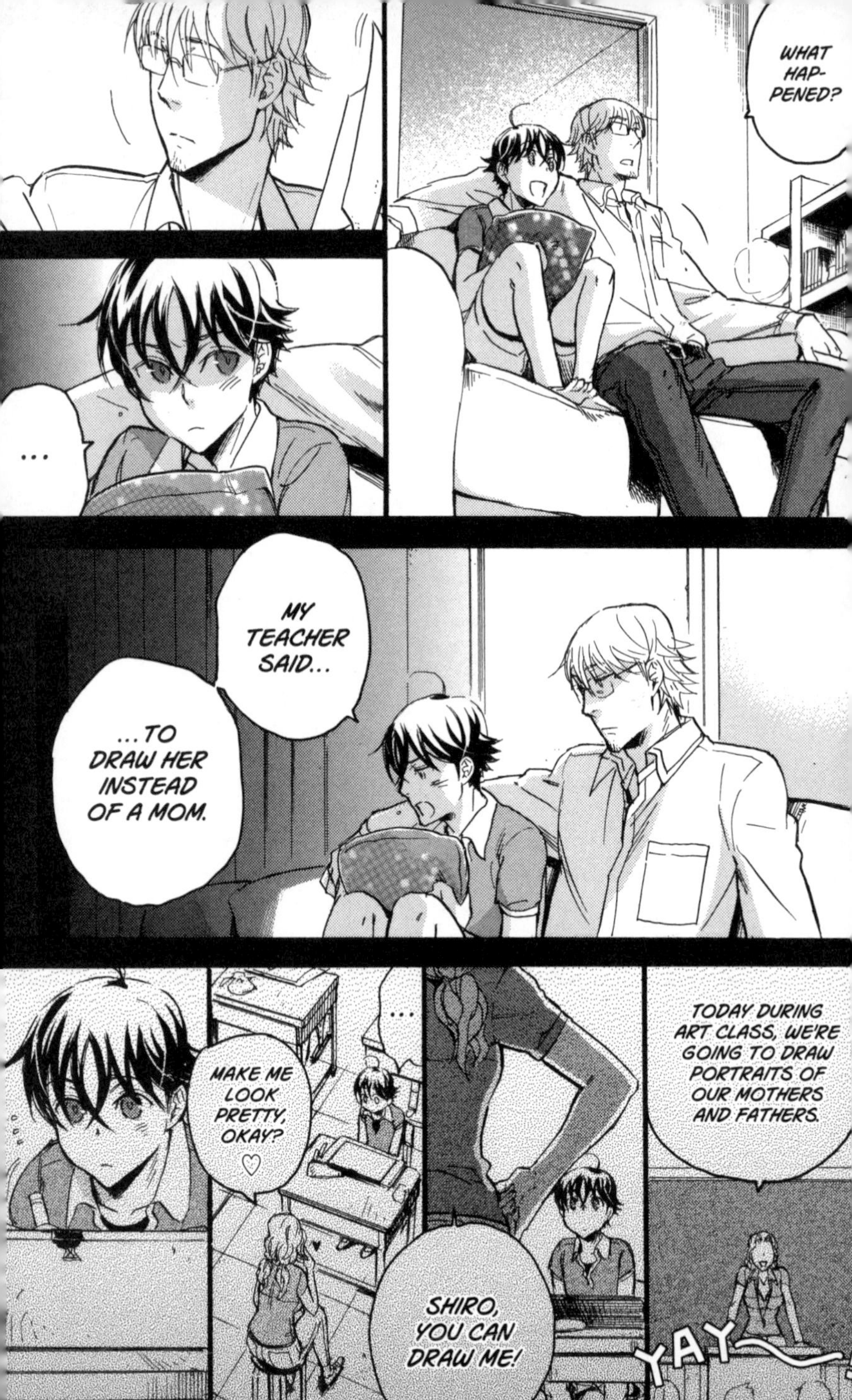
WHAT HAP-PENED?
...
MY TEACHER SAID...
...TO DRAW HER INSTEAD OF A MOM.
TODAY DURING ART CLASS, WE'RE GOING TO DRAW PORTRAITS OF OUR MOTHERS AND FATHERS.
YAY—
SHIRO, YOU CAN DRAW ME!
...
MAKE ME LOOK PRETTY, OKAY? ♡

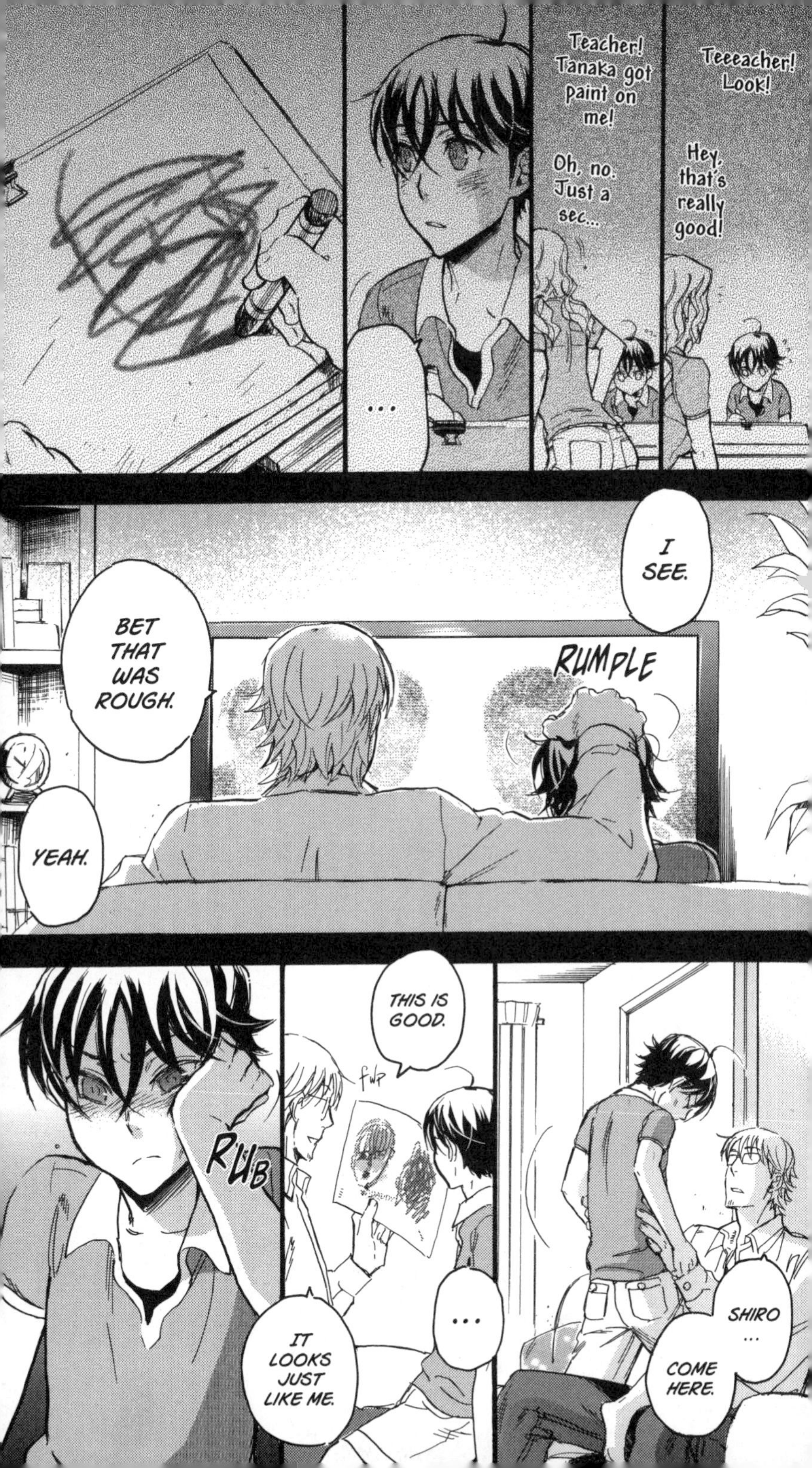
Teeeacher! Look!
Hey, that's really good!
Teacher! Tanaka got paint on me!
Oh, no. Just a sec...
...
I SEE.
RUMPLE
BET THAT WAS ROUGH.
YEAH.
SHIRO ... COME HERE.
THIS IS GOOD.
fwp
...
IT LOOKS JUST LIKE ME.
RUB

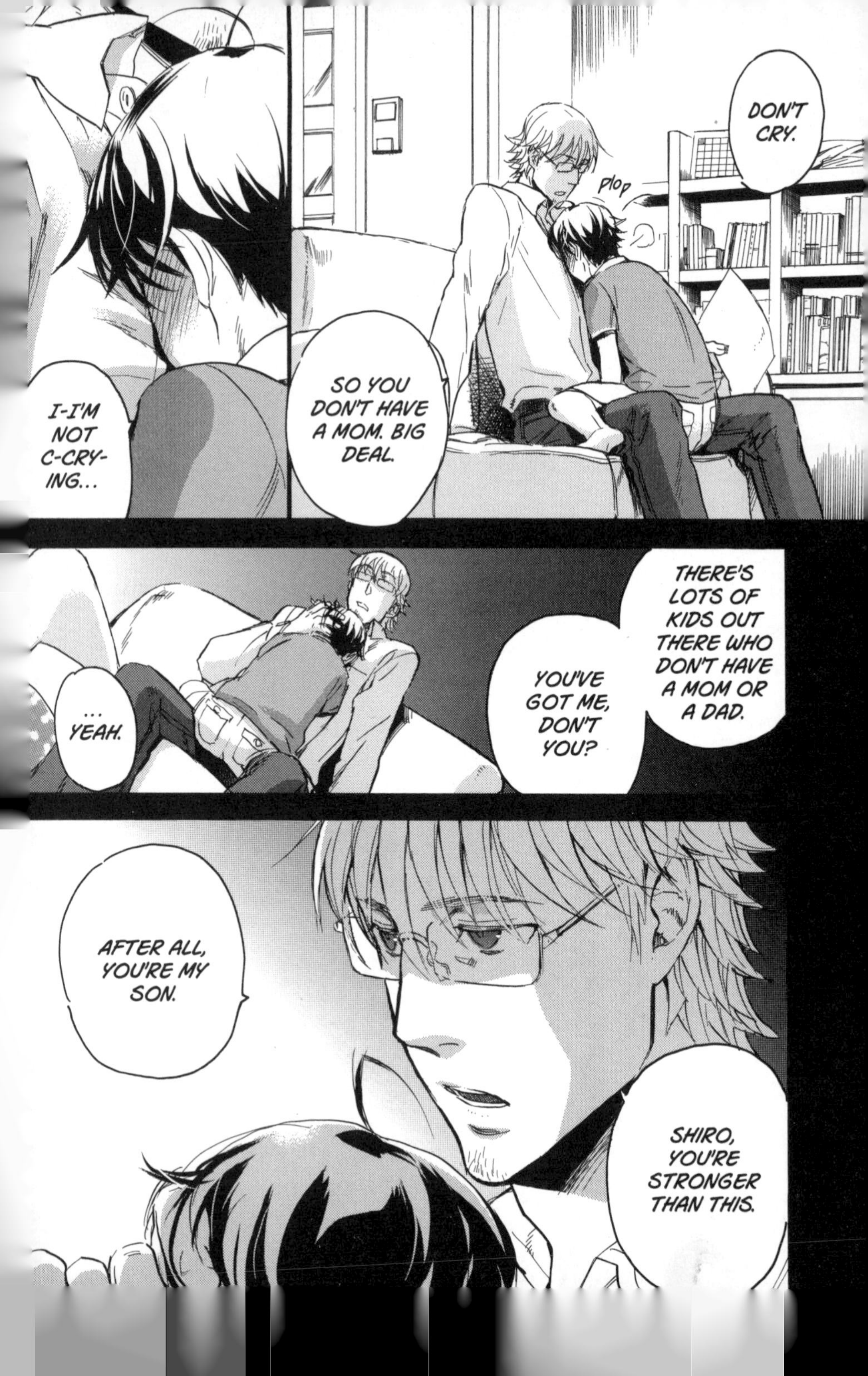
DON'T CRY.
plop
SO YOU DON'T HAVE A MOM. BIG DEAL.
I-I'M NOT C-CRY-ING...
THERE'S LOTS OF KIDS OUT THERE WHO DON'T HAVE A MOM OR A DAD.
YOU'VE GOT ME, DON'T YOU?
... YEAH.
SHIRO, YOU'RE STRONGER THAN THIS.
AFTER ALL, YOU'RE MY SON.

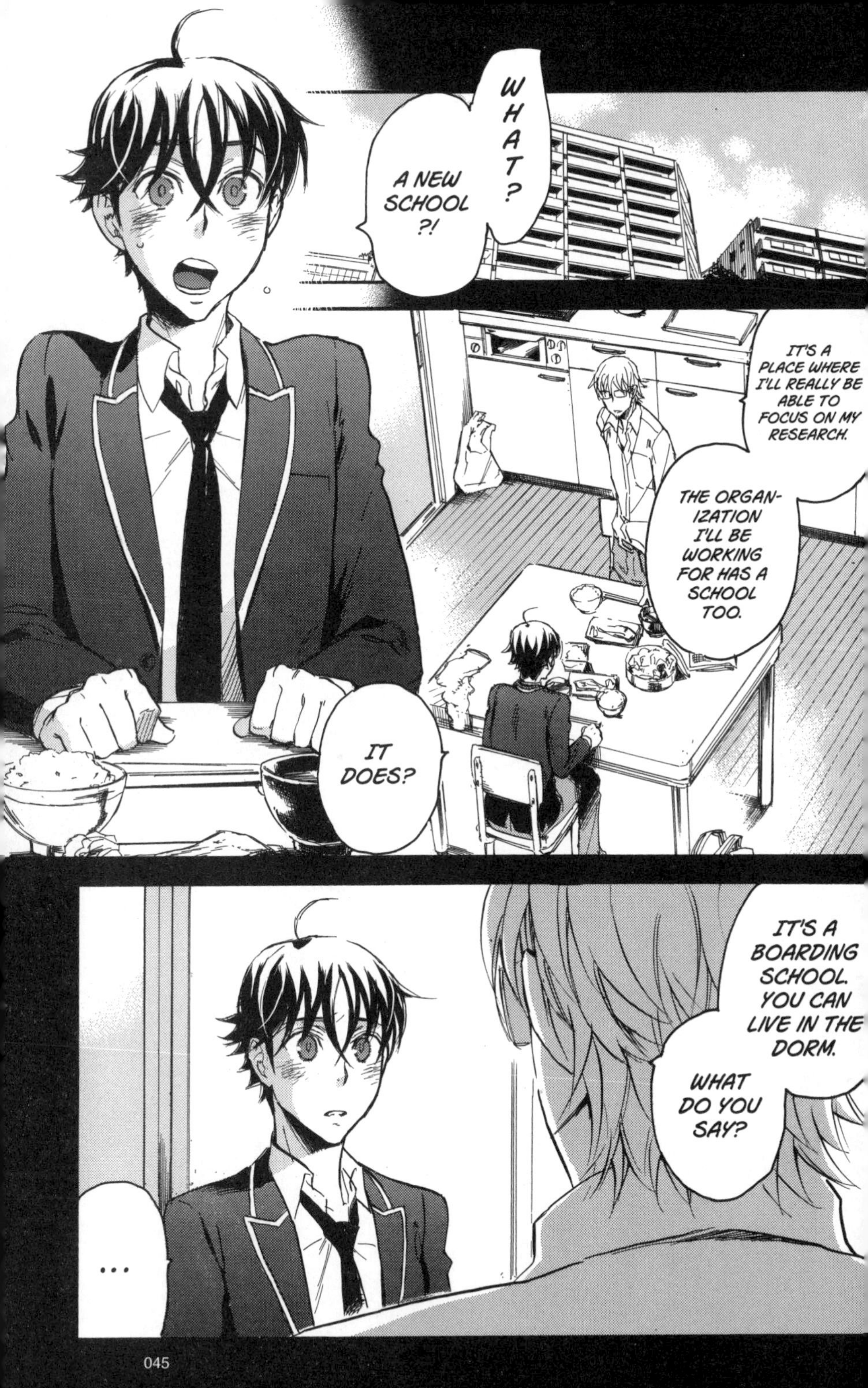
WHAT?
A NEW SCHOOL ?!
IT'S A PLACE WHERE I'LL REALLY BE ABLE TO FOCUS ON MY RESEARCH.
THE ORGAN-IZATION I'LL BE WORKING FOR HAS A SCHOOL TOO.
IT DOES?
IT'S A BOARDING SCHOOL. YOU CAN LIVE IN THE DORM.
WHAT DO YOU SAY?
...

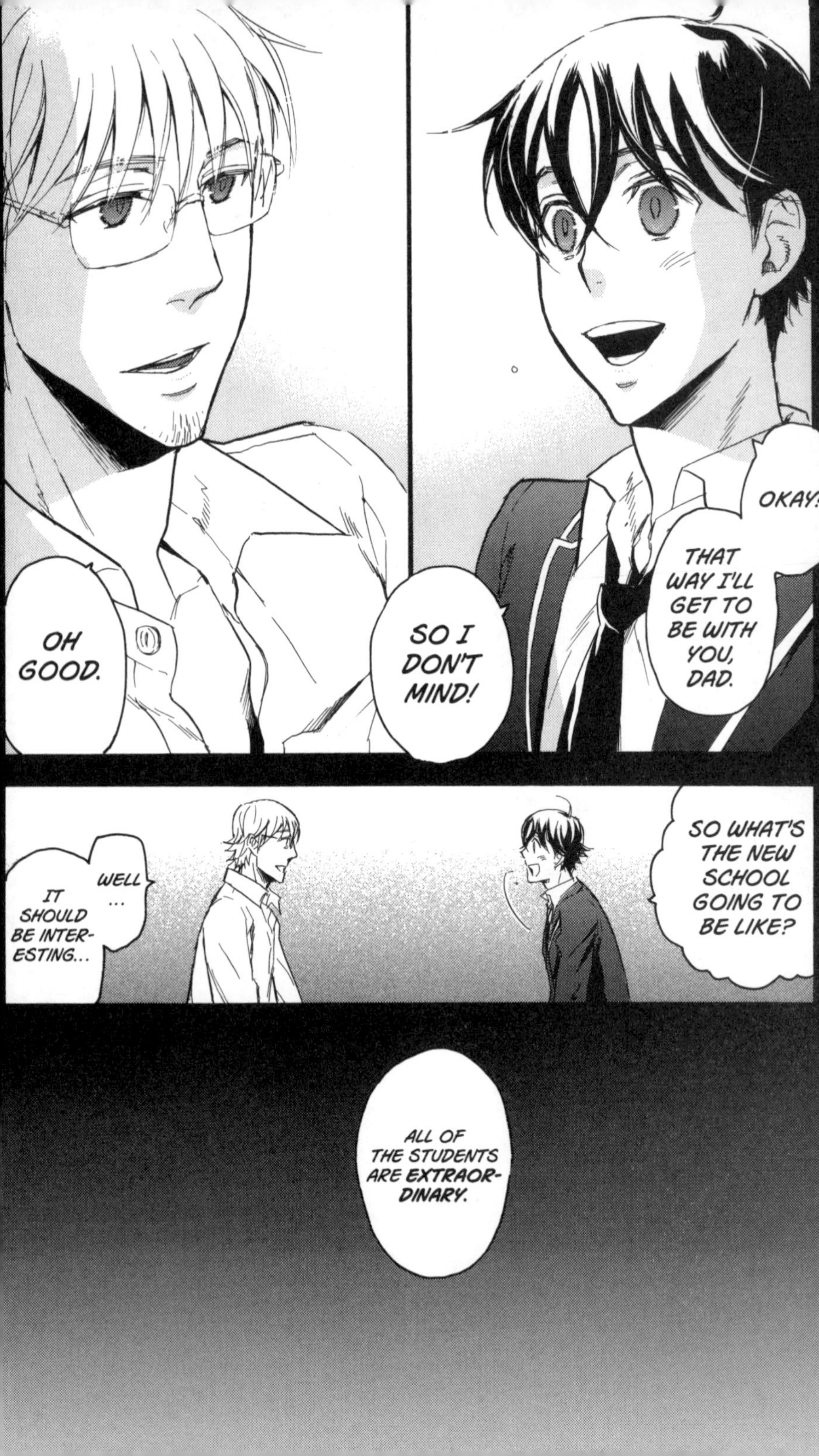
OKAY!
THAT WAY I'LL GET TO BE WITH YOU, DAD.
SO I DON'T MIND!
OH GOOD.
SO WHAT'S THE NEW SCHOOL GOING TO BE LIKE?
WELL...
IT SHOULD BE INTER-ESTING...
ALL OF THE STUDENTS ARE EXTRAOR-DINARY.

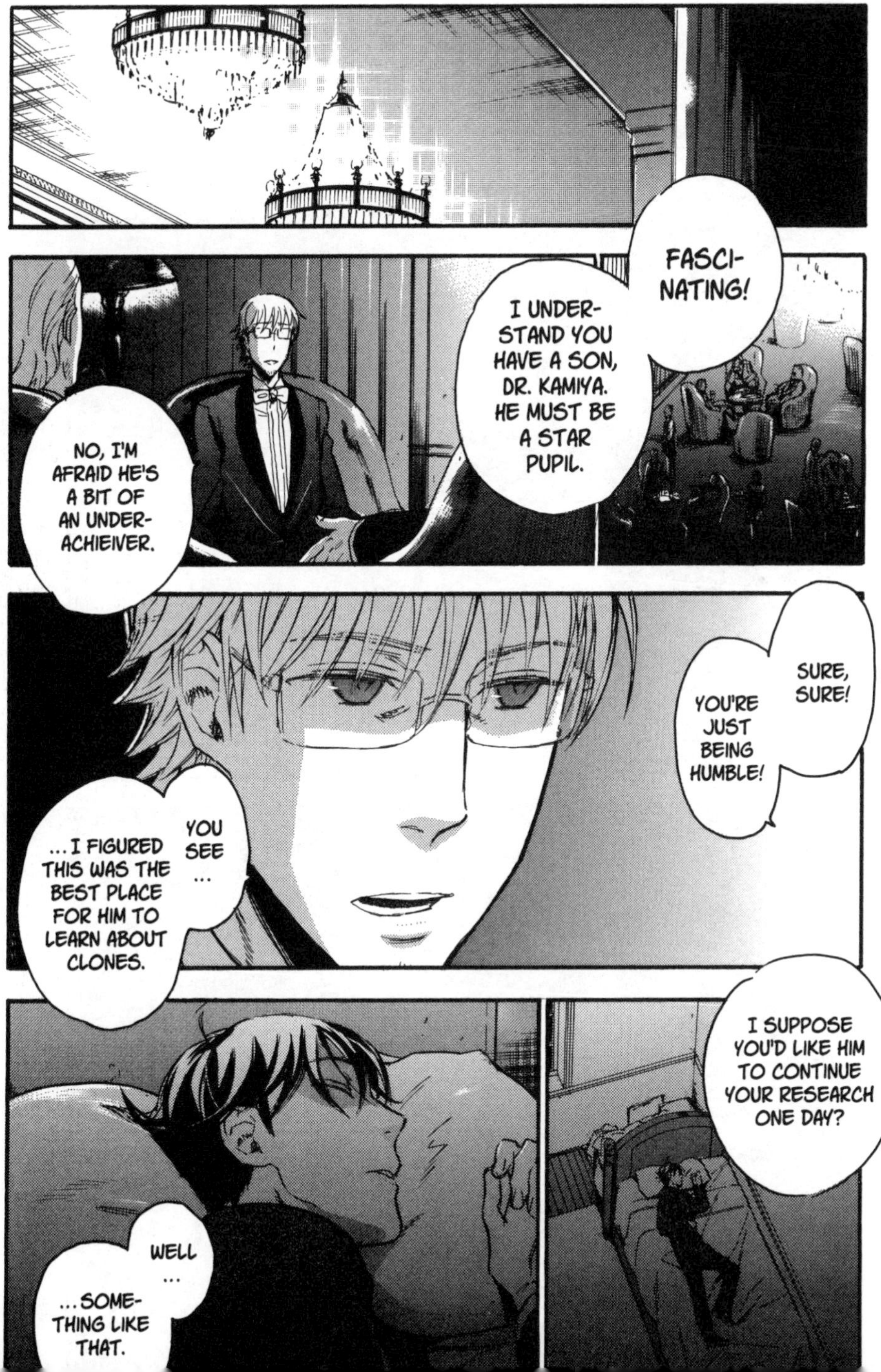
FASCI-NATING!
I UNDER-STAND YOU HAVE A SON, DR. KAMIYA. HE MUST BE A STAR PUPIL.
NO, I'M AFRAID HE'S A BIT OF AN UNDER-ACHIEIVER.
SURE, SURE!
YOU'RE JUST BEING HUMBLE!
YOU SEE ...
... I FIGURED THIS WAS THE BEST PLACE FOR HIM TO LEARN ABOUT CLONES.
I SUPPOSE YOU'D LIKE HIM TO CONTINUE YOUR RESEARCH ONE DAY?
WELL ...
... SOME-THING LIKE THAT.

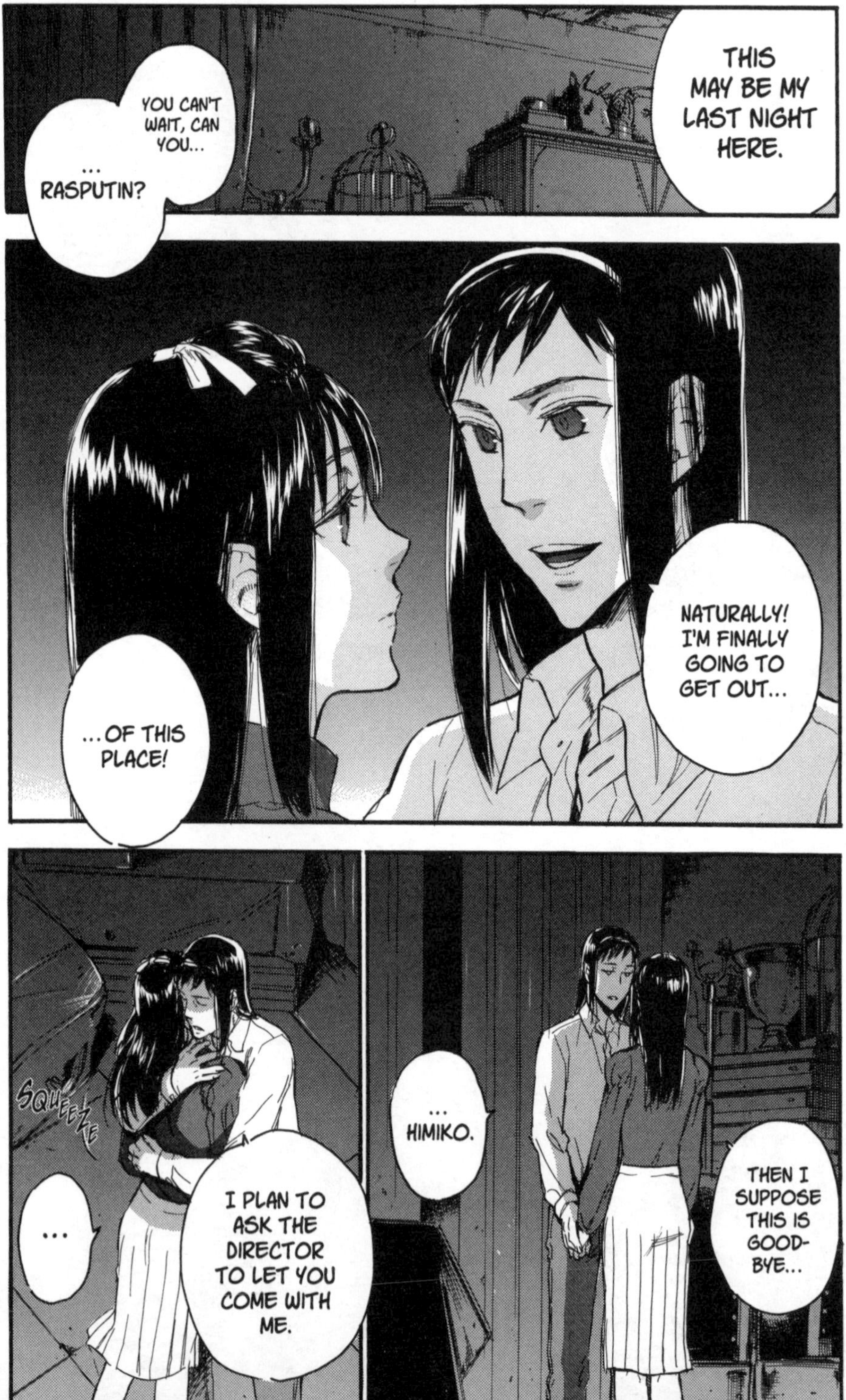
THIS MAY BE MY LAST NIGHT HERE.
YOU CAN'T WAIT, CAN YOU... ...RASPUTIN?
NATURALLY! I'M FINALLY GOING TO GET OUT...
...OF THIS PLACE!
THEN I SUPPOSE THIS IS GOOD-BYE...
...HIMIKO.
I PLAN TO ASK THE DIRECTOR TO LET YOU COME WITH ME.
SQUEEZE
...

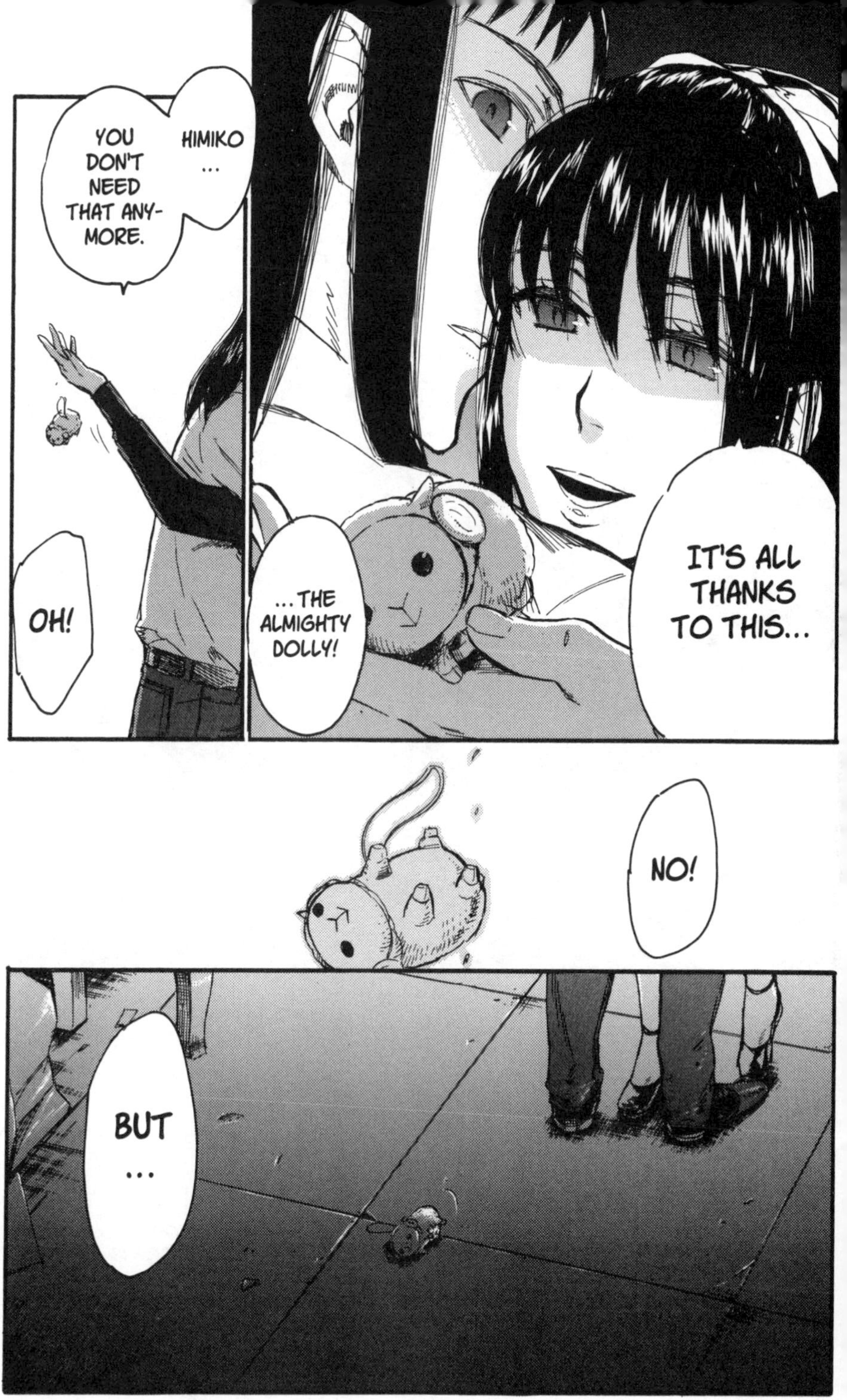
IT'S ALL THANKS TO THIS...
...THE ALMIGHTY DOLLY!
HIMIKO...
YOU DON'T NEED THAT ANY-MORE.
OH!
NO!
BUT...

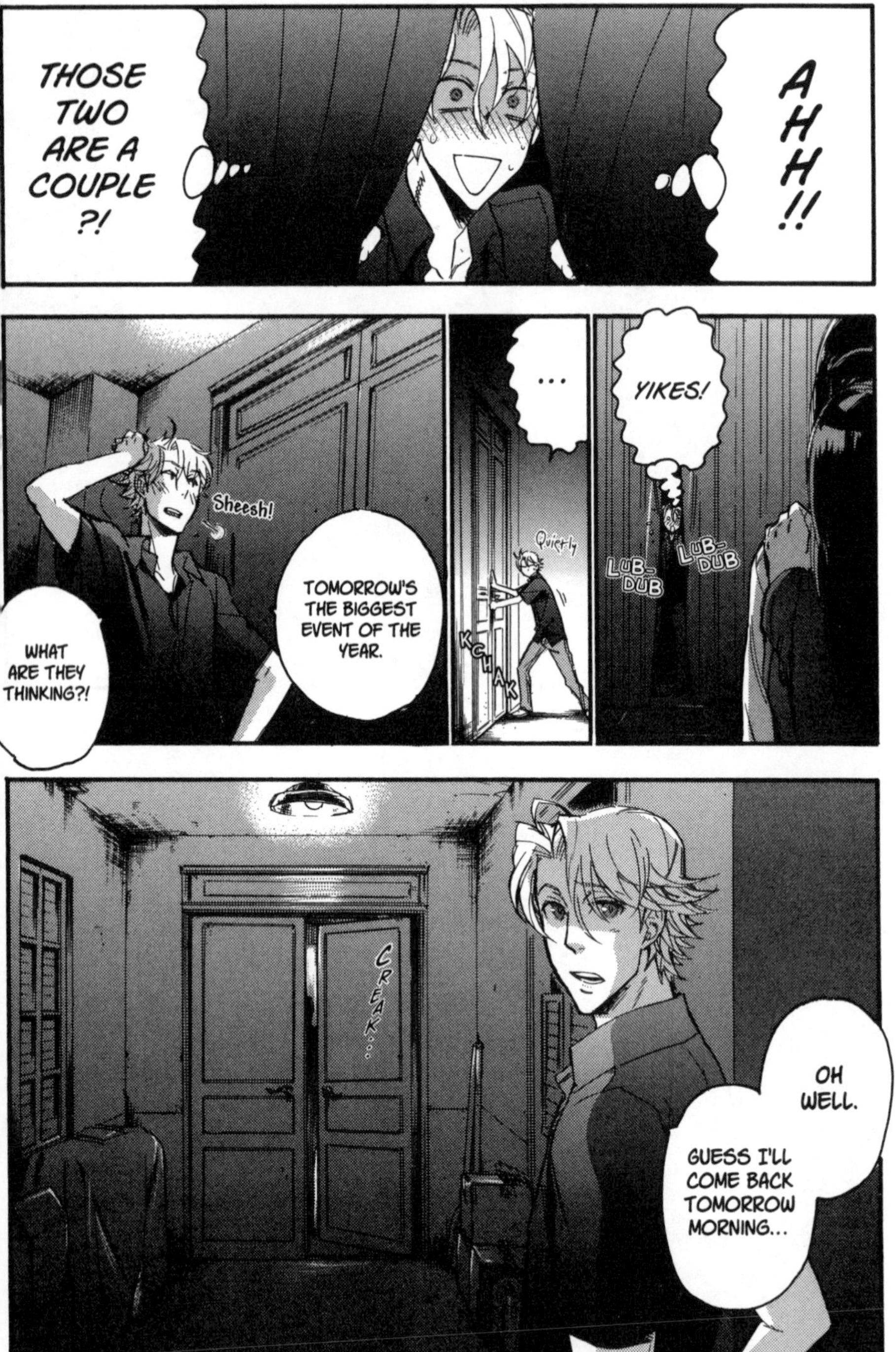
AHH!!
THOSE TWO ARE A COUPLE?!
YIKES!
LUB-DUB
LUB-DUB
...
Quietly
KCHAK
Sheesh!
TOMORROW'S THE BIGGEST EVENT OF THE YEAR.
WHAT ARE THEY THINKING?!
OH WELL.
GUESS I'LL COME BACK TOMORROW MORNING...
CREAK...

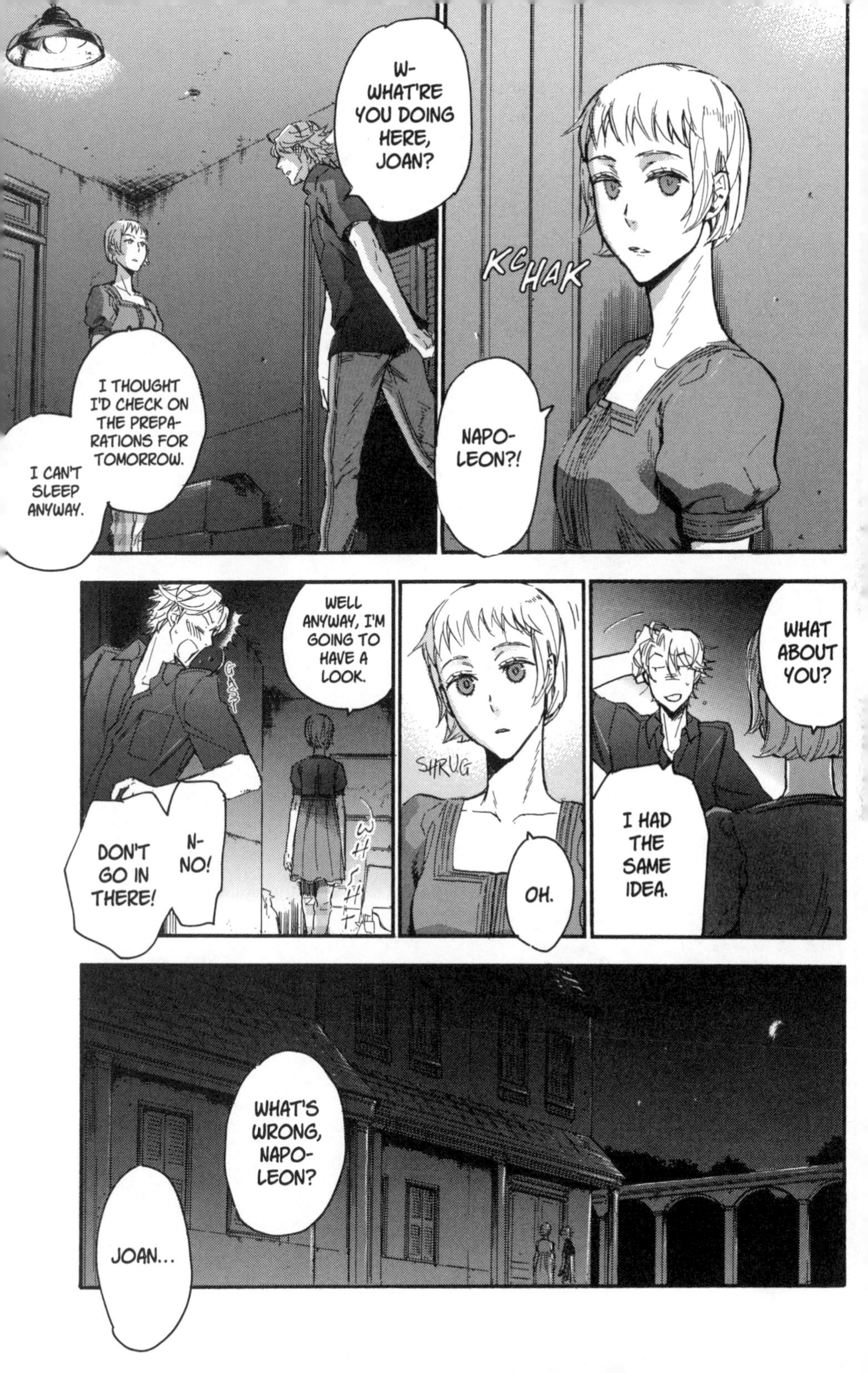

KCHAK
NAPO-LEON?!
W-WHAT'RE YOU DOING HERE, JOAN?
I THOUGHT I'D CHECK ON THE PREPA-RATIONS FOR TOMORROW.
I CAN'T SLEEP ANYWAY.
WHAT ABOUT YOU?
I HAD THE SAME IDEA.
SHRUG
OH.
WELL ANYWAY, I'M GOING TO HAVE A LOOK.
GASP
N-NO!
DON'T GO IN THERE!
WHAT'S WRONG, NAPO-LEON?
JOAN...

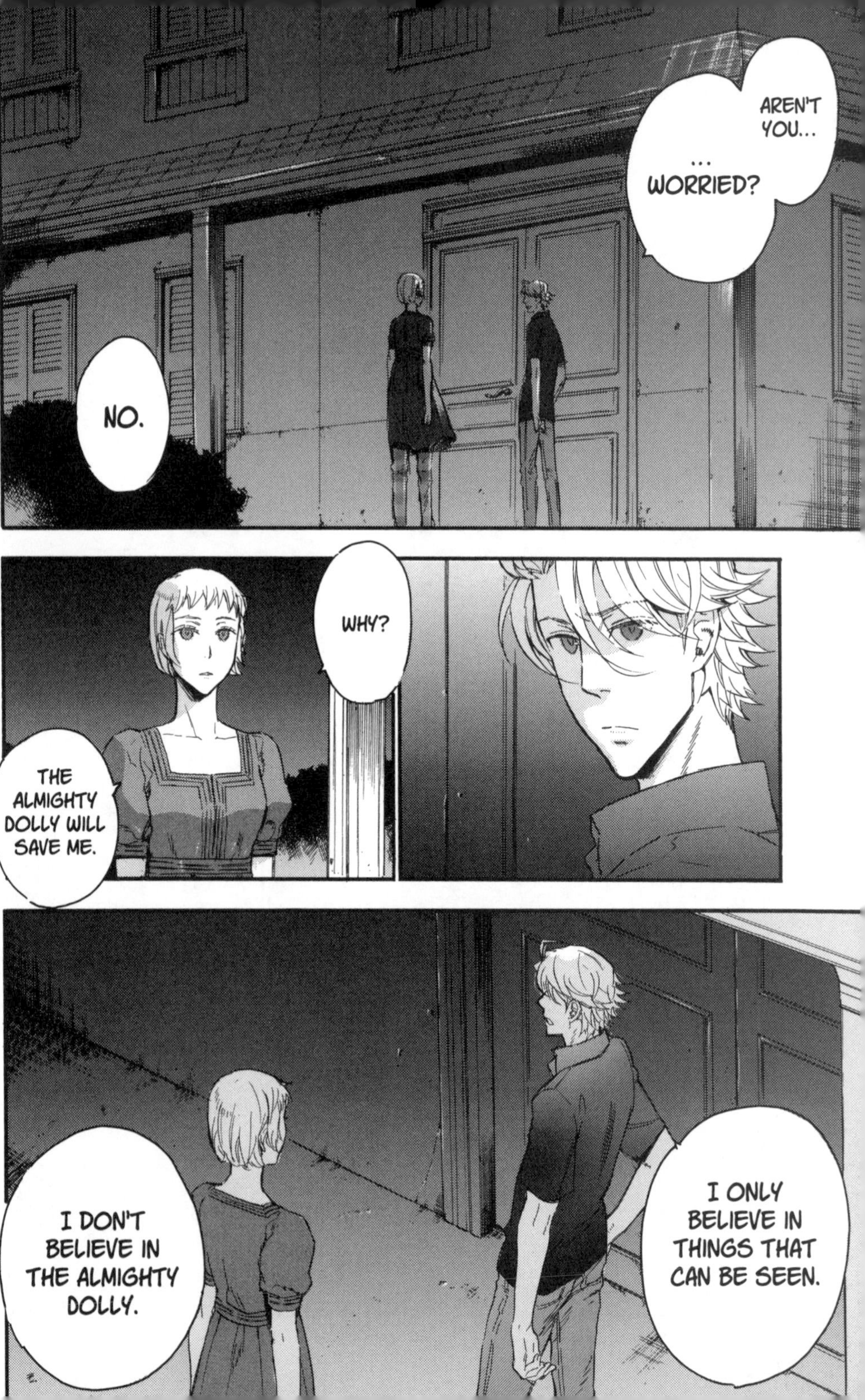
AREN'T YOU...
...WORRIED?
NO.
WHY?
THE ALMIGHTY DOLLY WILL SAVE ME.
I ONLY BELIEVE IN THINGS THAT CAN BE SEEN.
I DON'T BELIEVE IN THE ALMIGHTY DOLLY.

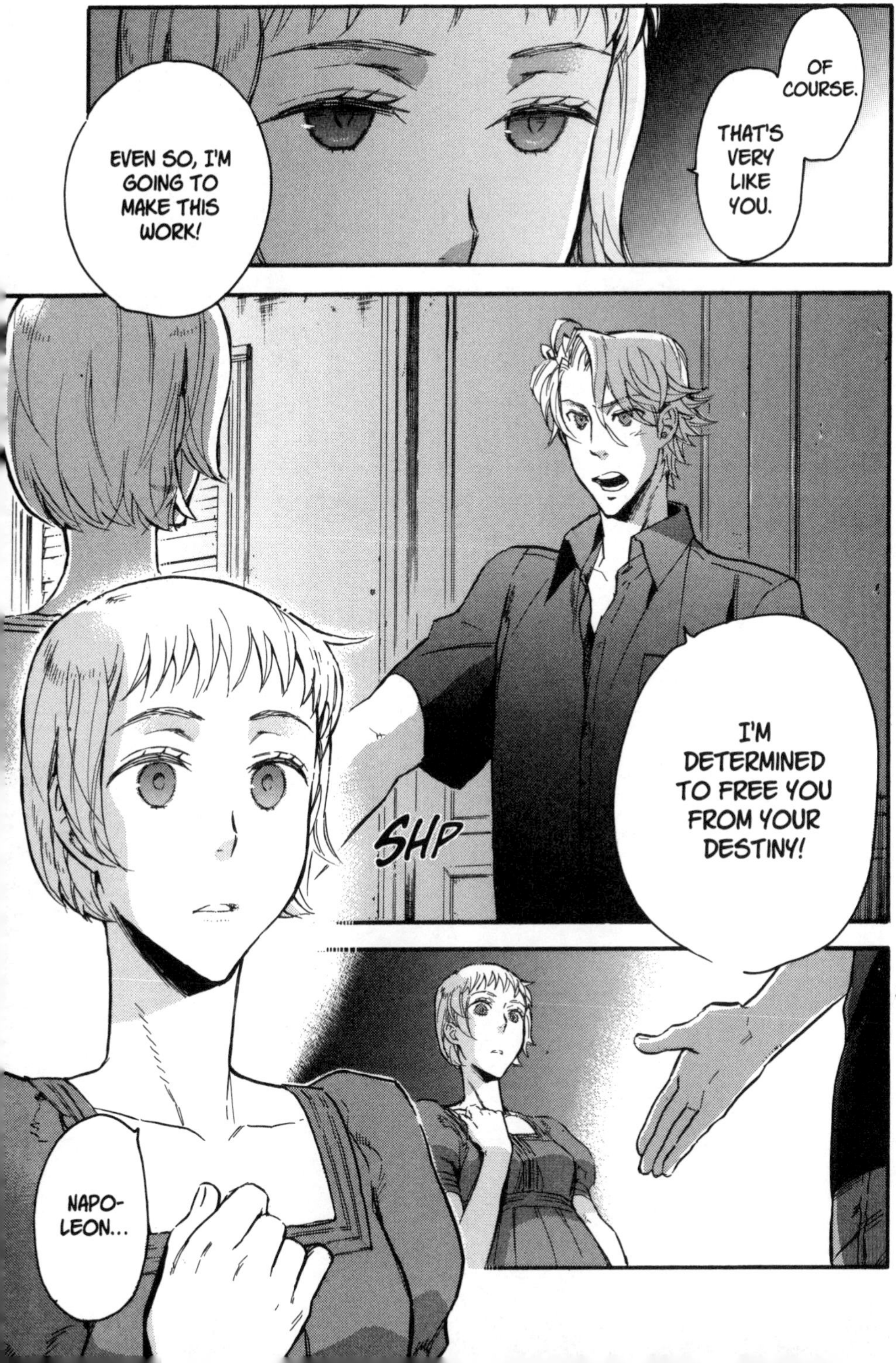
OF COURSE.
THAT'S VERY LIKE YOU.
EVEN SO, I'M GOING TO MAKE THIS WORK!
I'M DETERMINED TO FREE YOU FROM YOUR DESTINY!
SHP
NAPO-LEON...

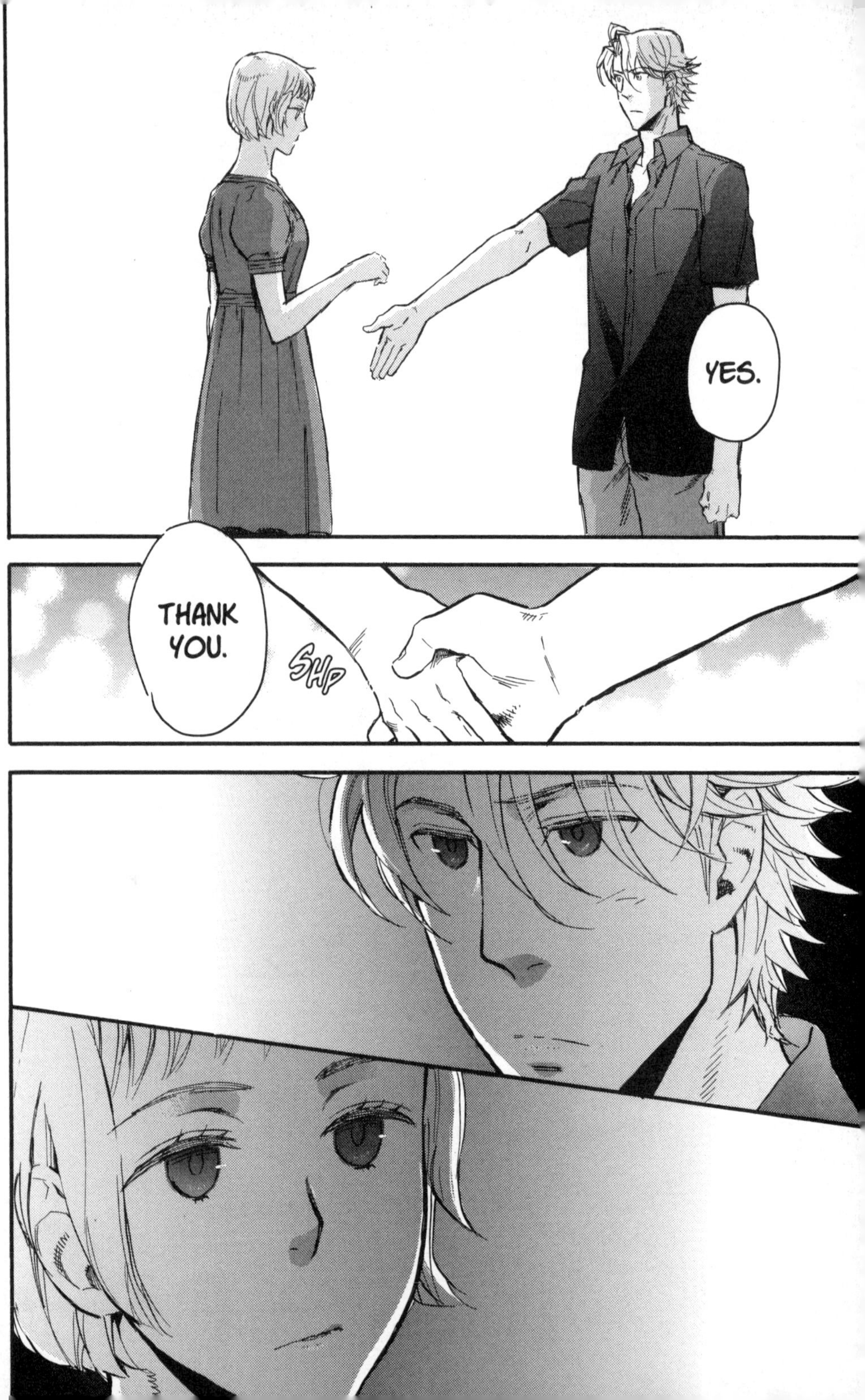
YES.
THANK YOU.
SHP

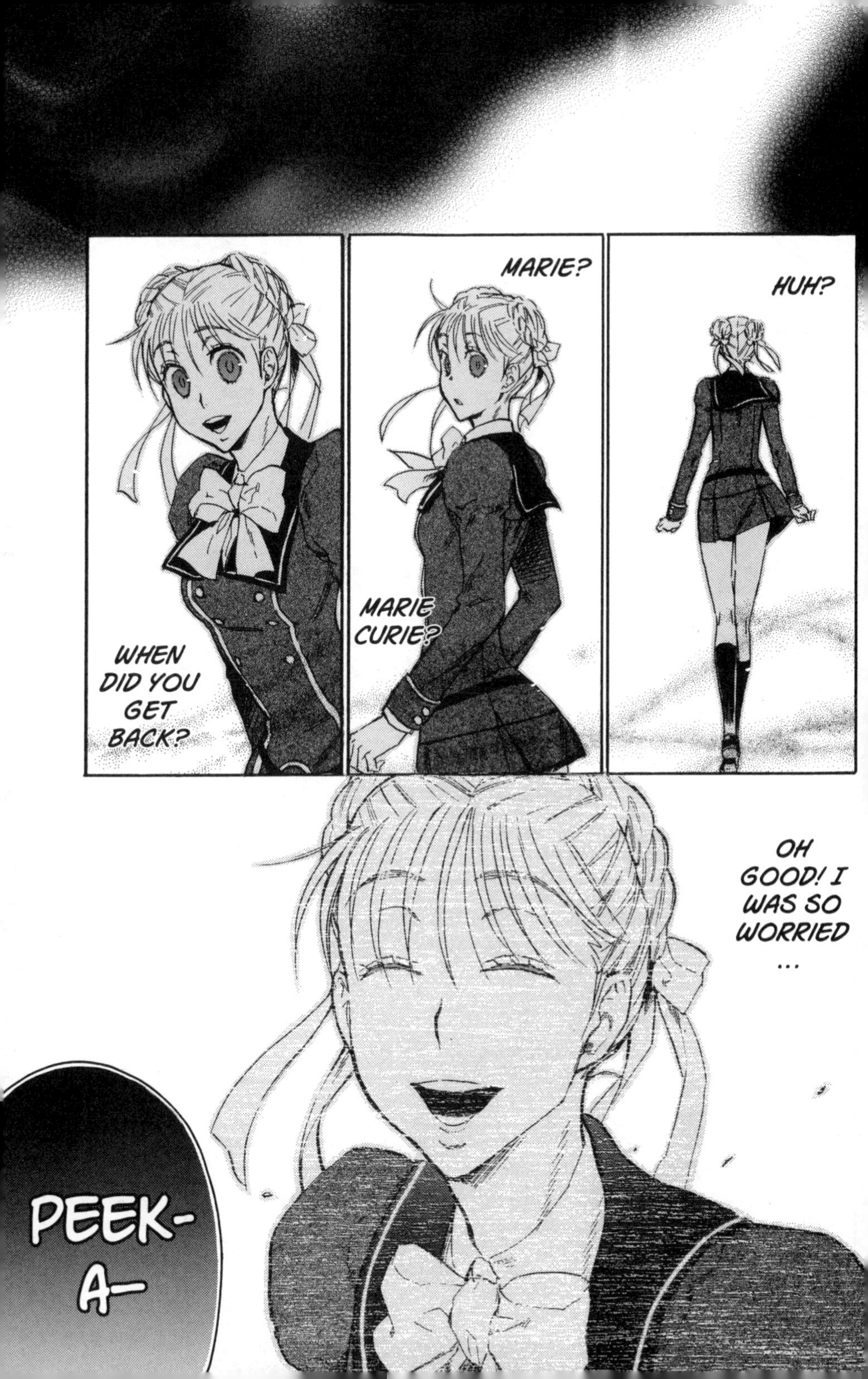
HUH?
MARIE?
MARIE CURIE?
WHEN DID YOU GET BACK?
OH GOOD! I WAS SO WORRIED ...
PEEK-A-

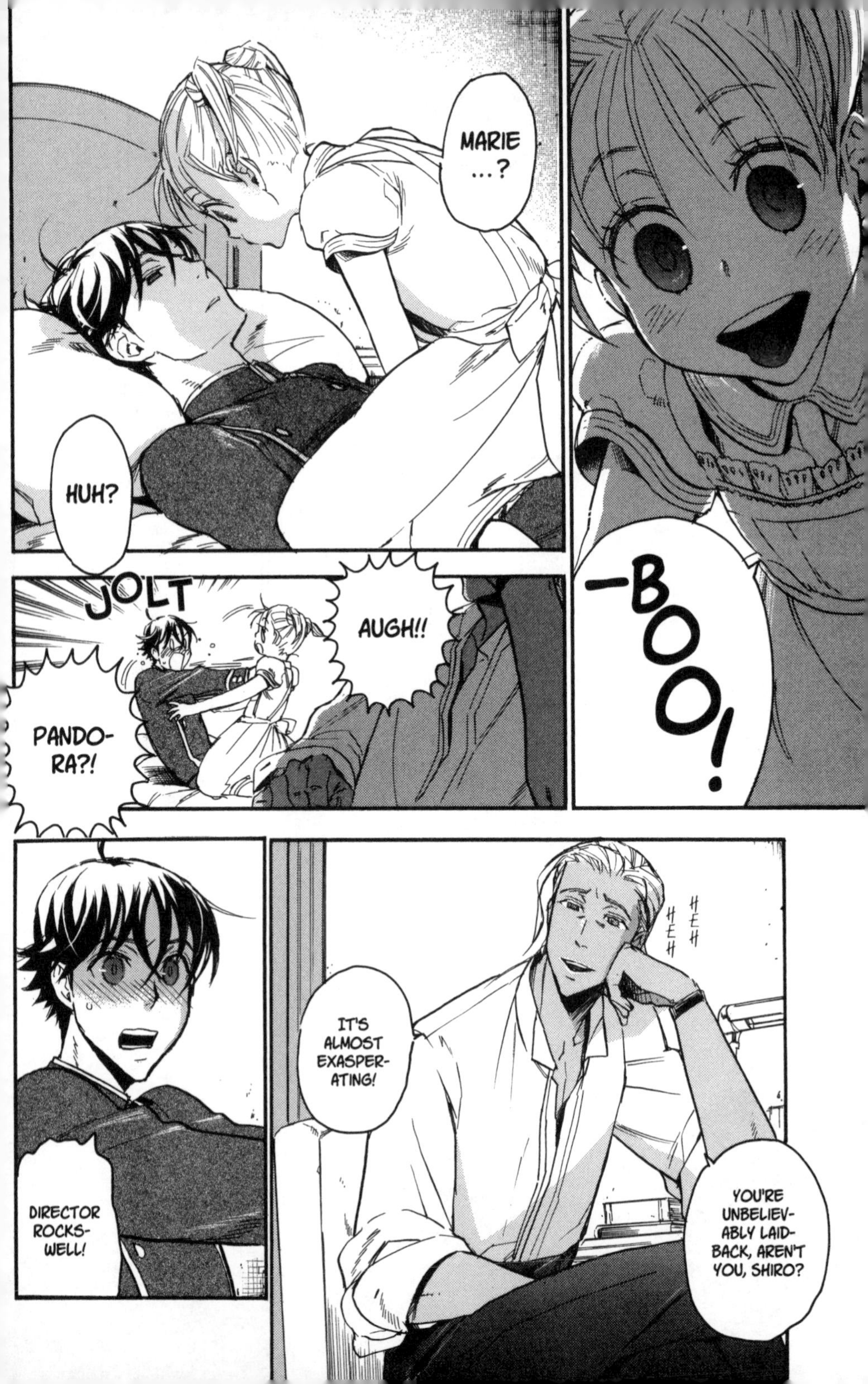
-BOO!
MARIE ...?
HUH?
AUGH!!
JOLT
PANDORA?!
HEH HEH
YOU'RE UNBELIEV-ABLY LAID-BACK, AREN'T YOU, SHIRO?
IT'S ALMOST EXASPER-ATING!
DIRECTOR ROCKS-WELL!

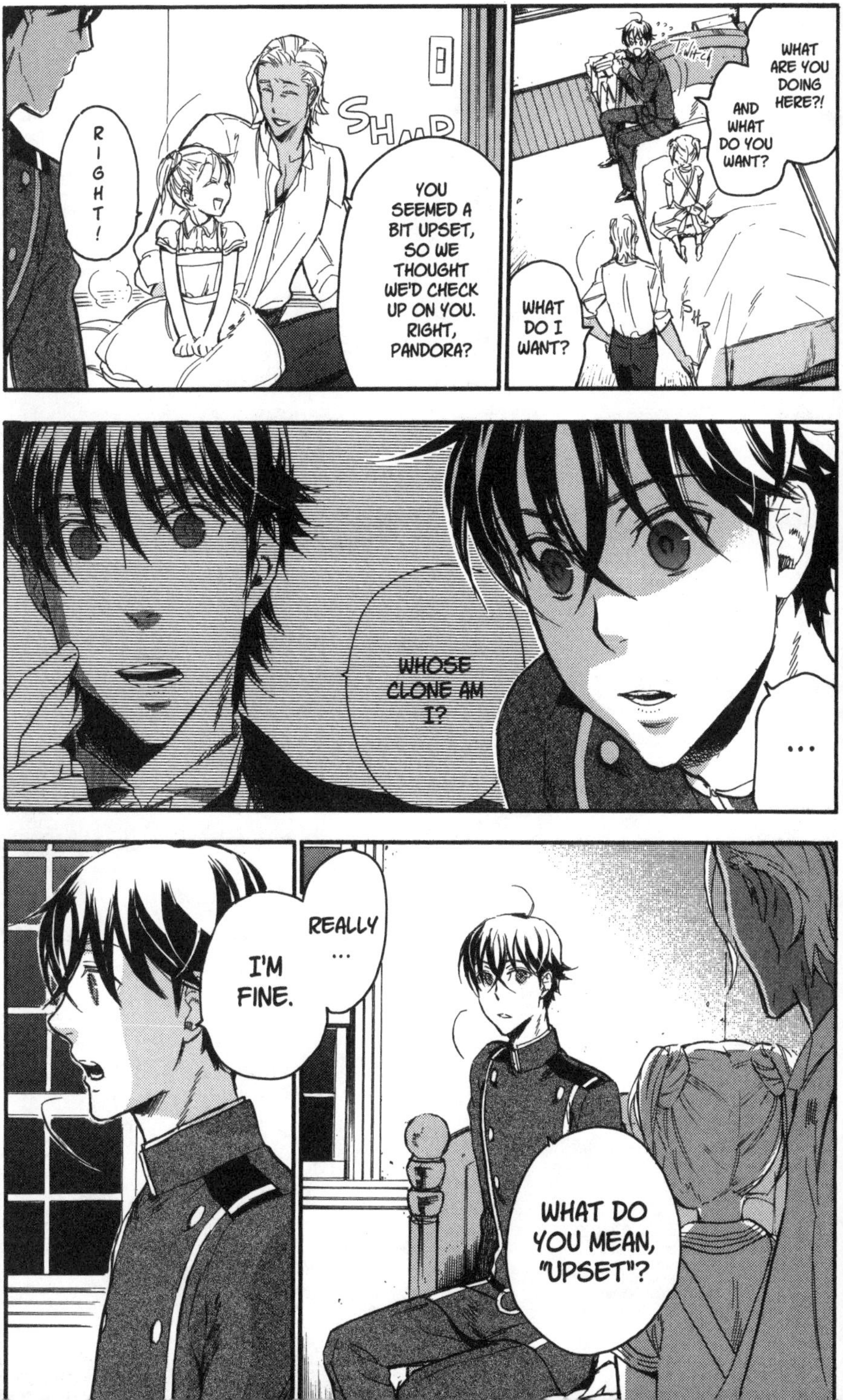
WHAT ARE YOU DOING HERE?!
AND WHAT DO YOU WANT?
WHAT DO I WANT?
YOU SEEMED A BIT UPSET, SO WE THOUGHT WE'D CHECK UP ON YOU. RIGHT, PANDORA?
RIGHT!
...
WHOSE CLONE AM I?
WHAT DO YOU MEAN, "UPSET"?
REALLY... I'M FINE.

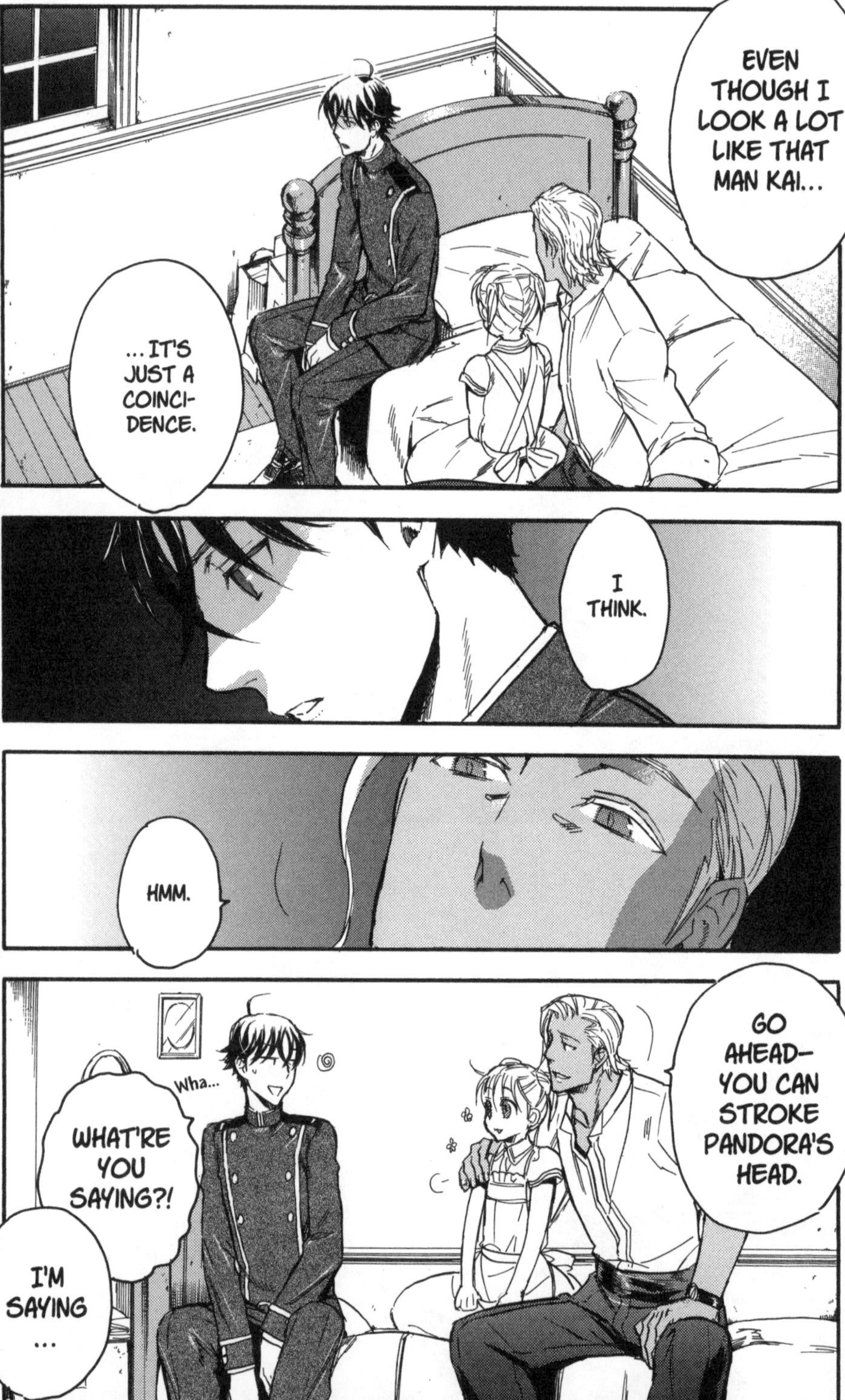
EVEN THOUGH I LOOK A LOT LIKE THAT MAN KAI...
...IT'S JUST A COINCI-DENCE.
I THINK.
HMM.
GO AHEAD- YOU CAN STROKE PANDORA'S HEAD.
Wha...
WHAT'RE YOU SAYING?!
I'M SAYING ...

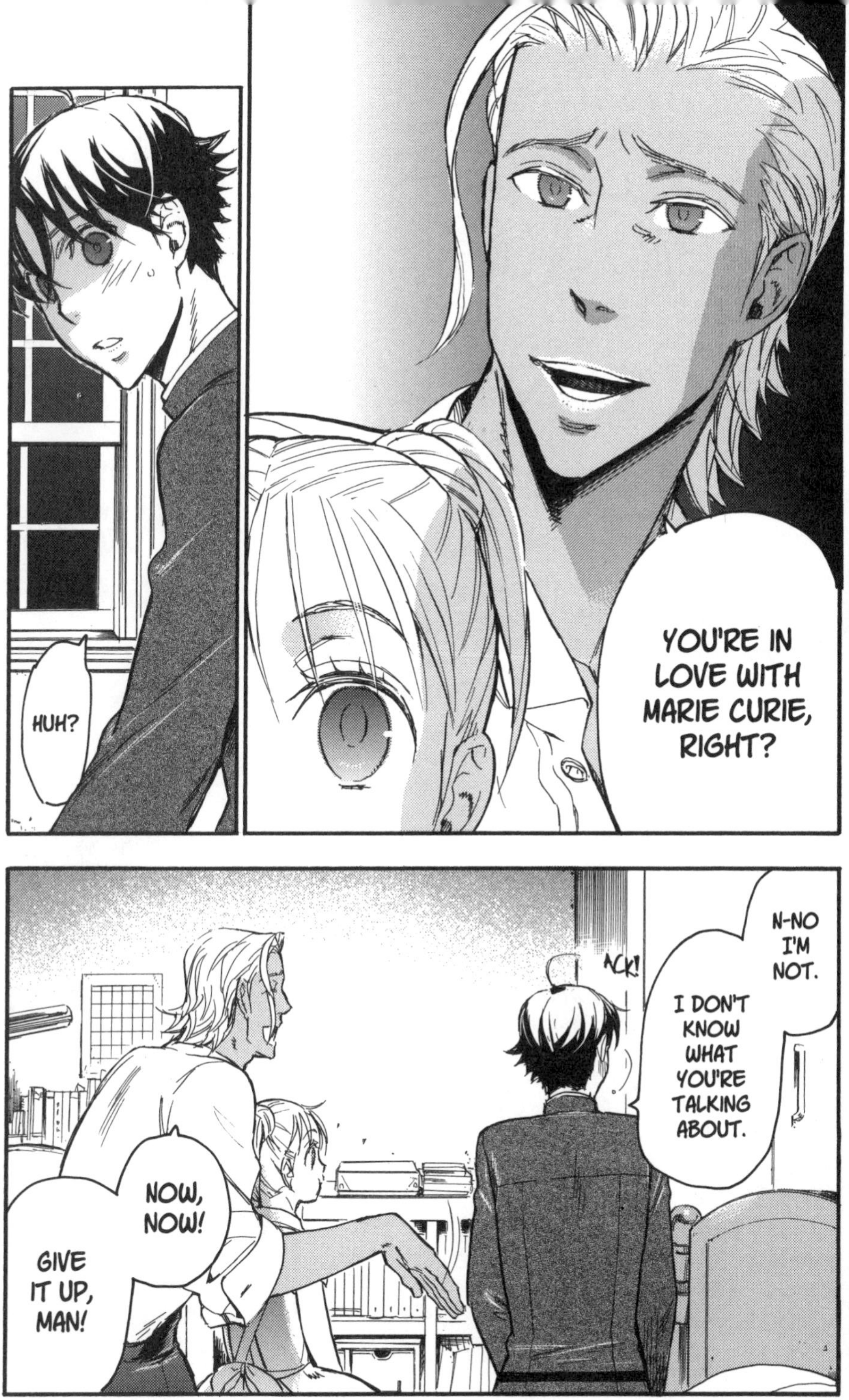
YOU'RE IN LOVE WITH MARIE CURIE, RIGHT?
HUH?
N-NO I'M NOT.
ACK!
I DON'T KNOW WHAT YOU'RE TALKING ABOUT.
NOW, NOW!
GIVE IT UP, MAN!

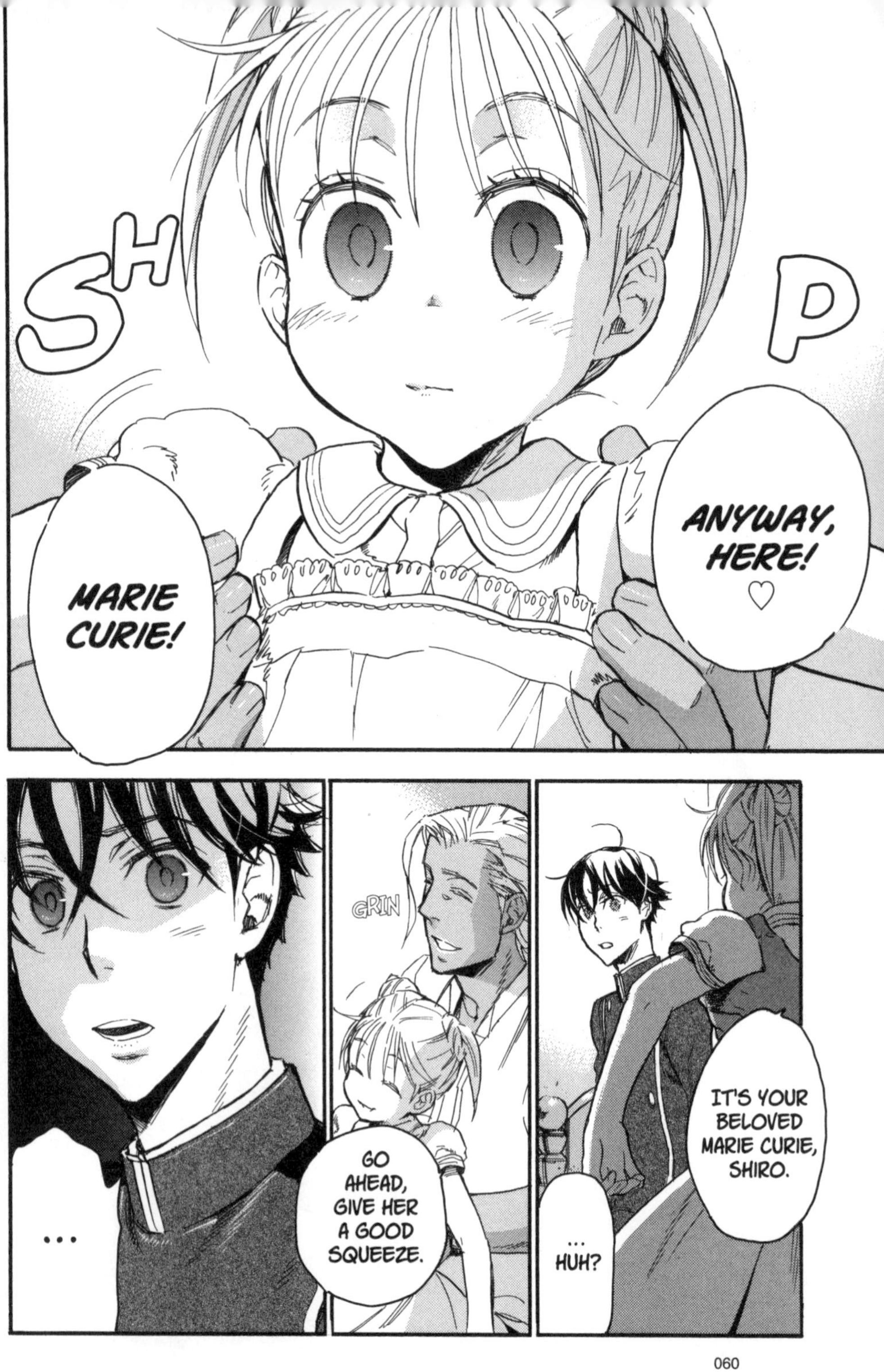
SHP
ANYWAY, HERE! ♡
MARIE CURIE!
IT'S YOUR BELOVED MARIE CURIE, SHIRO.
... HUH?
GRIN
GO AHEAD, GIVE HER A GOOD SQUEEZE.
...

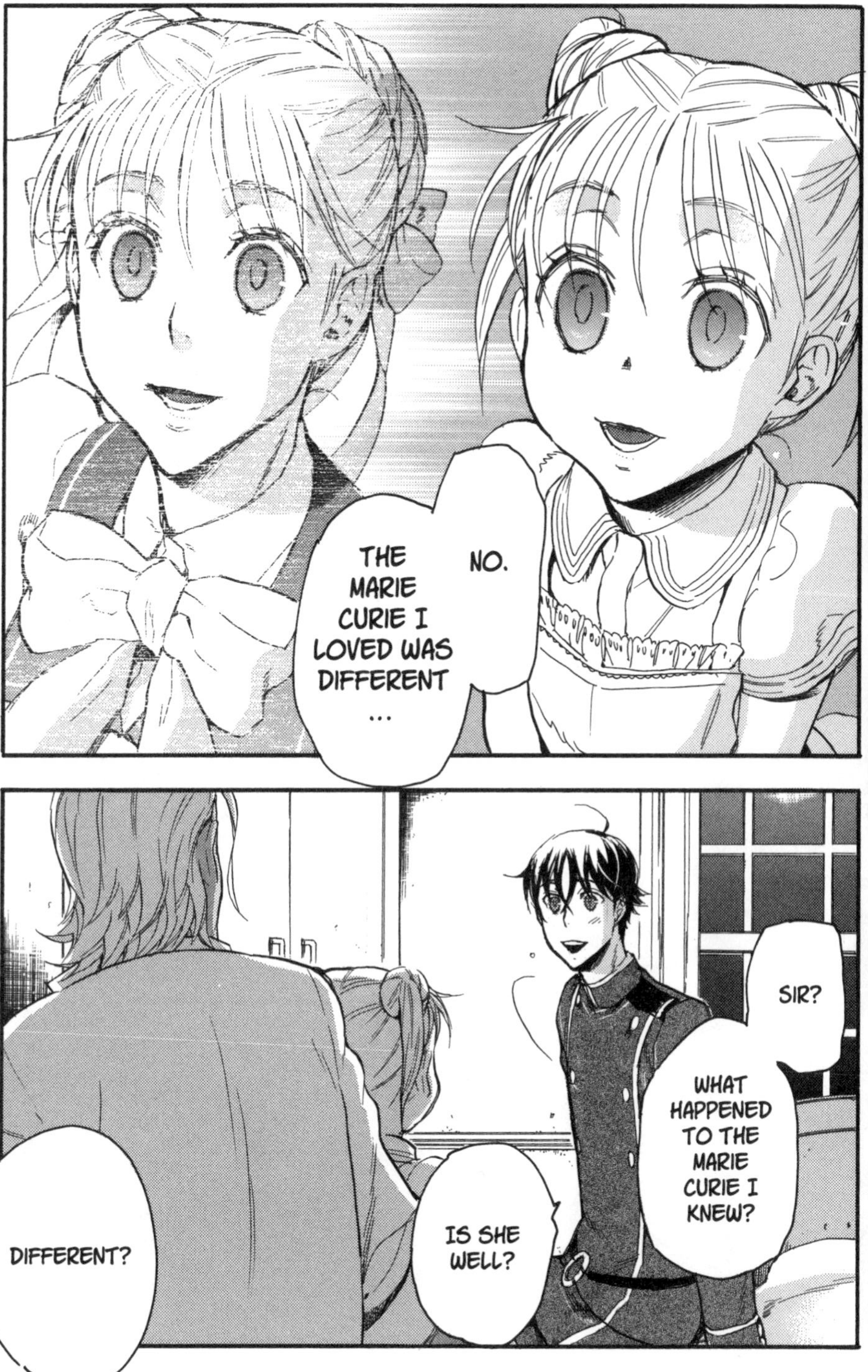
NO.
THE MARIE CURIE I LOVED WAS DIFFERENT...
SIR?
WHAT HAPPENED TO THE MARIE CURIE I KNEW?
IS SHE WELL?
DIFFERENT?

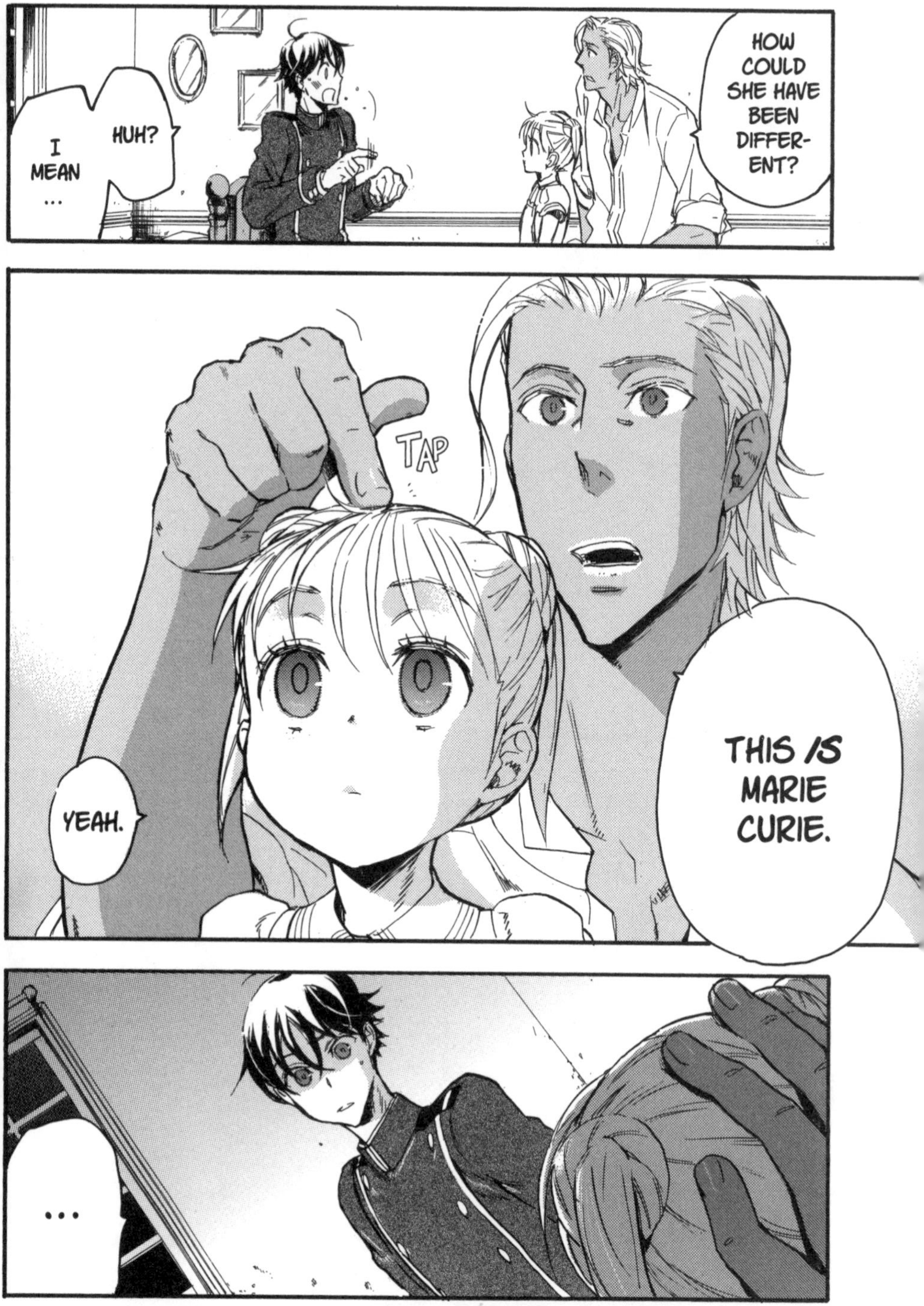
HOW COULD SHE HAVE BEEN DIFFERENT?
HUH?
I MEAN ...
TAP
THIS IS MARIE CURIE.
YEAH.
...

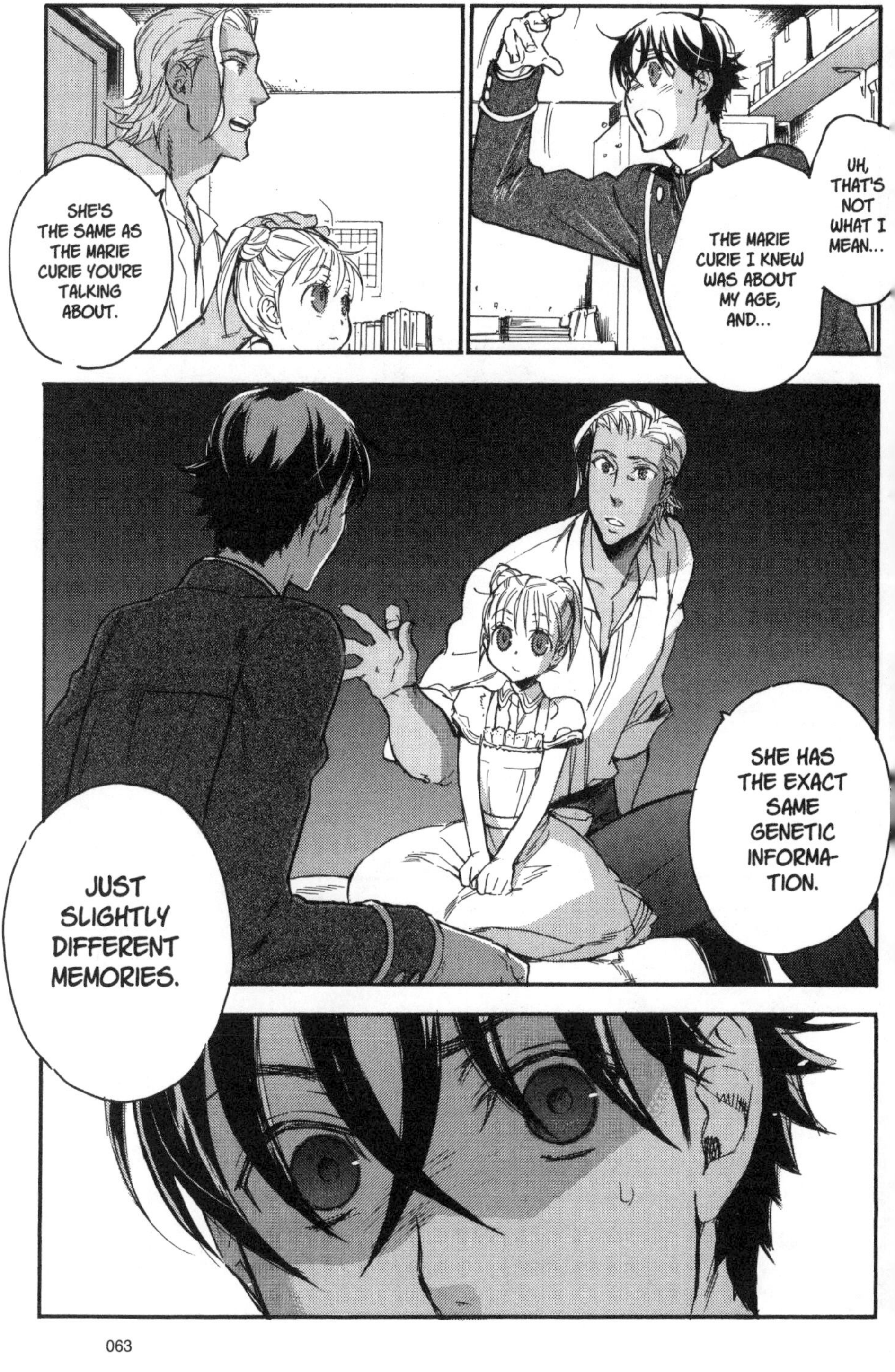
UH, THAT'S NOT WHAT I MEAN...
THE MARIE CURIE I KNEW WAS ABOUT MY AGE, AND...
SHE'S THE SAME AS THE MARIE CURIE YOU'RE TALKING ABOUT.
SHE HAS THE EXACT SAME GENETIC INFORMATION.
JUST SLIGHTLY DIFFERENT MEMORIES.

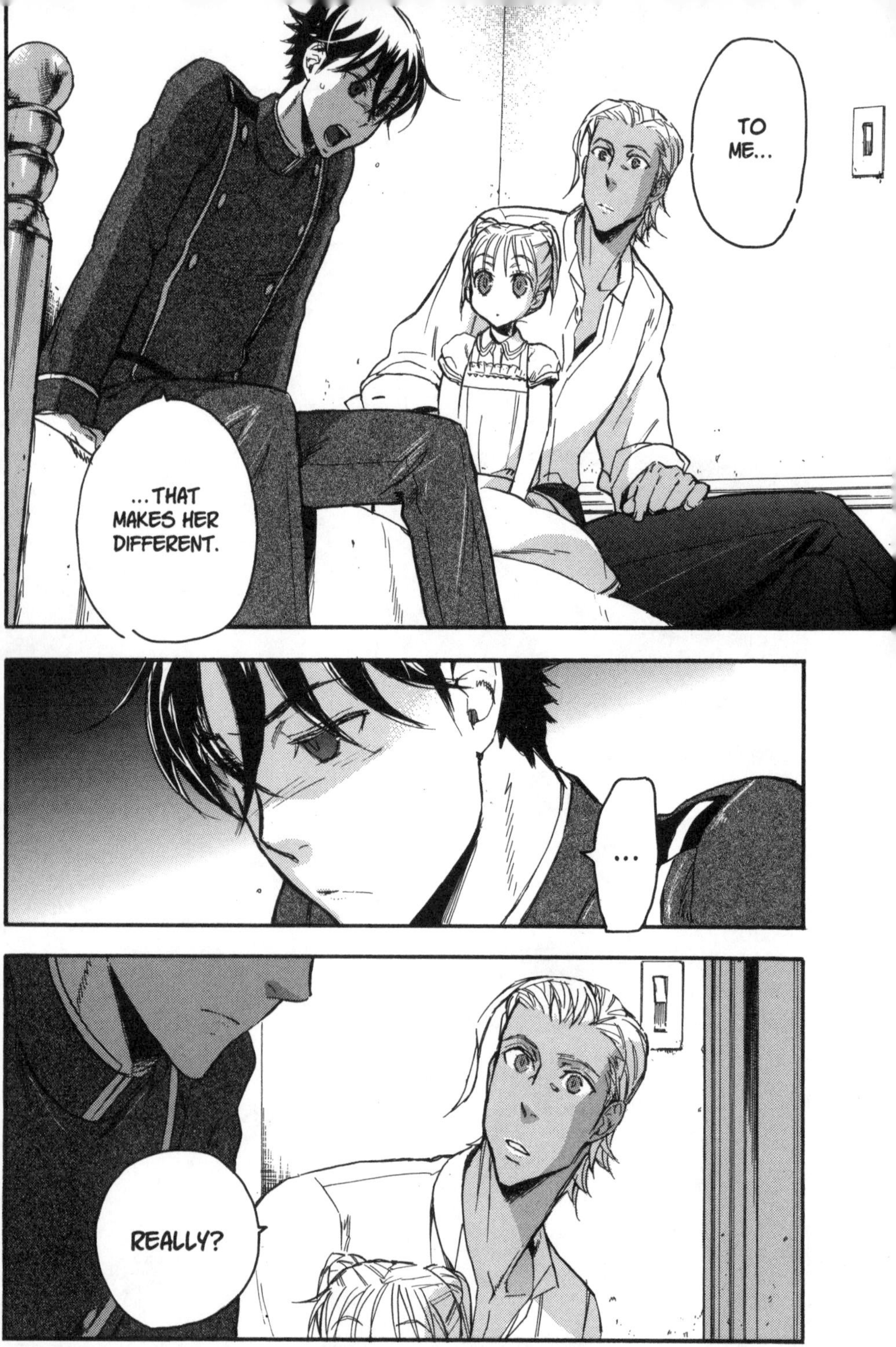
TO ME...
...THAT MAKES HER DIFFERENT.
...
REALLY?

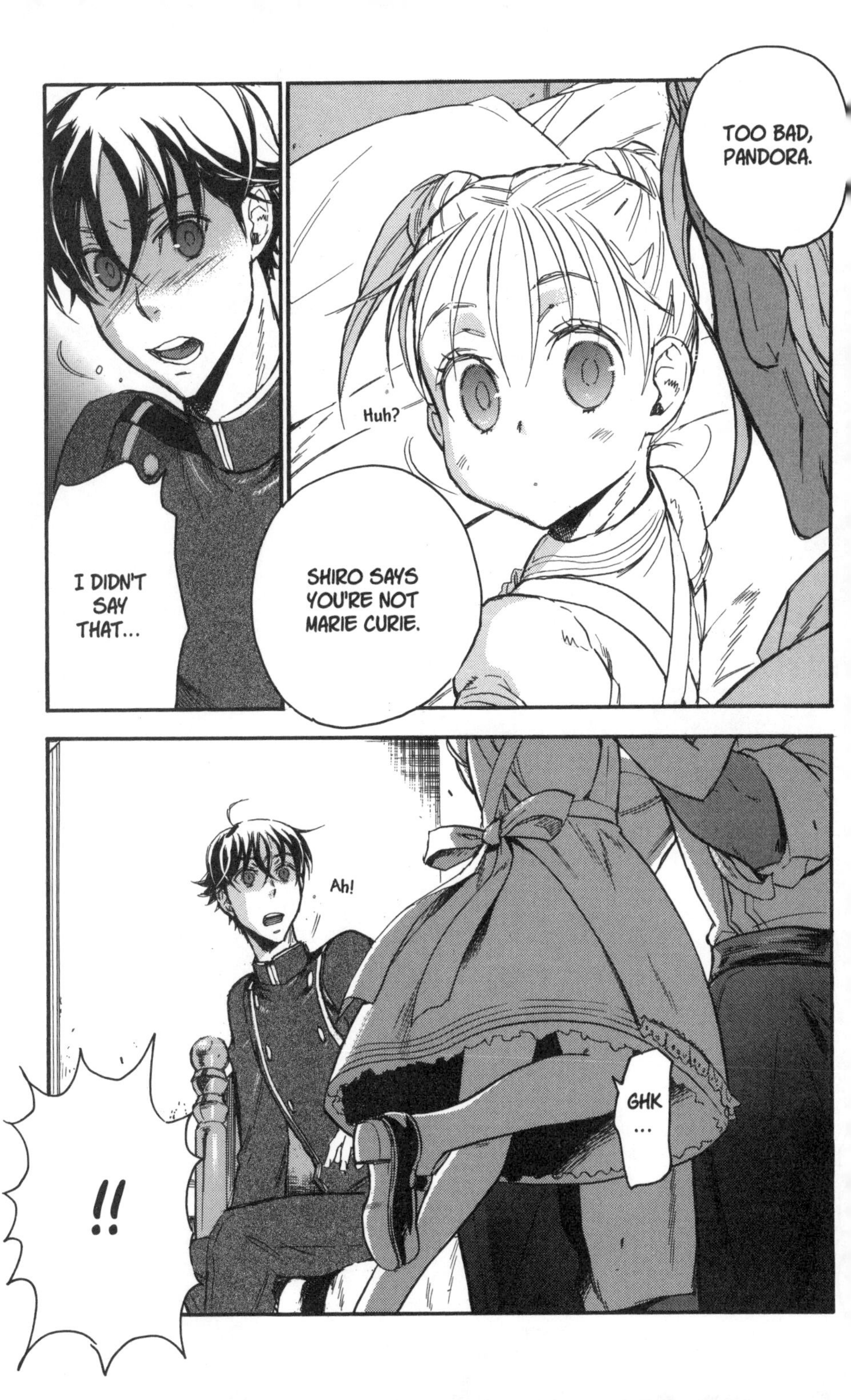
TOO BAD, PANDORA.
Huh?
SHIRO SAYS YOU'RE NOT MARIE CURIE.
I DIDN'T SAY THAT...
Ah!
GHK ...
!!

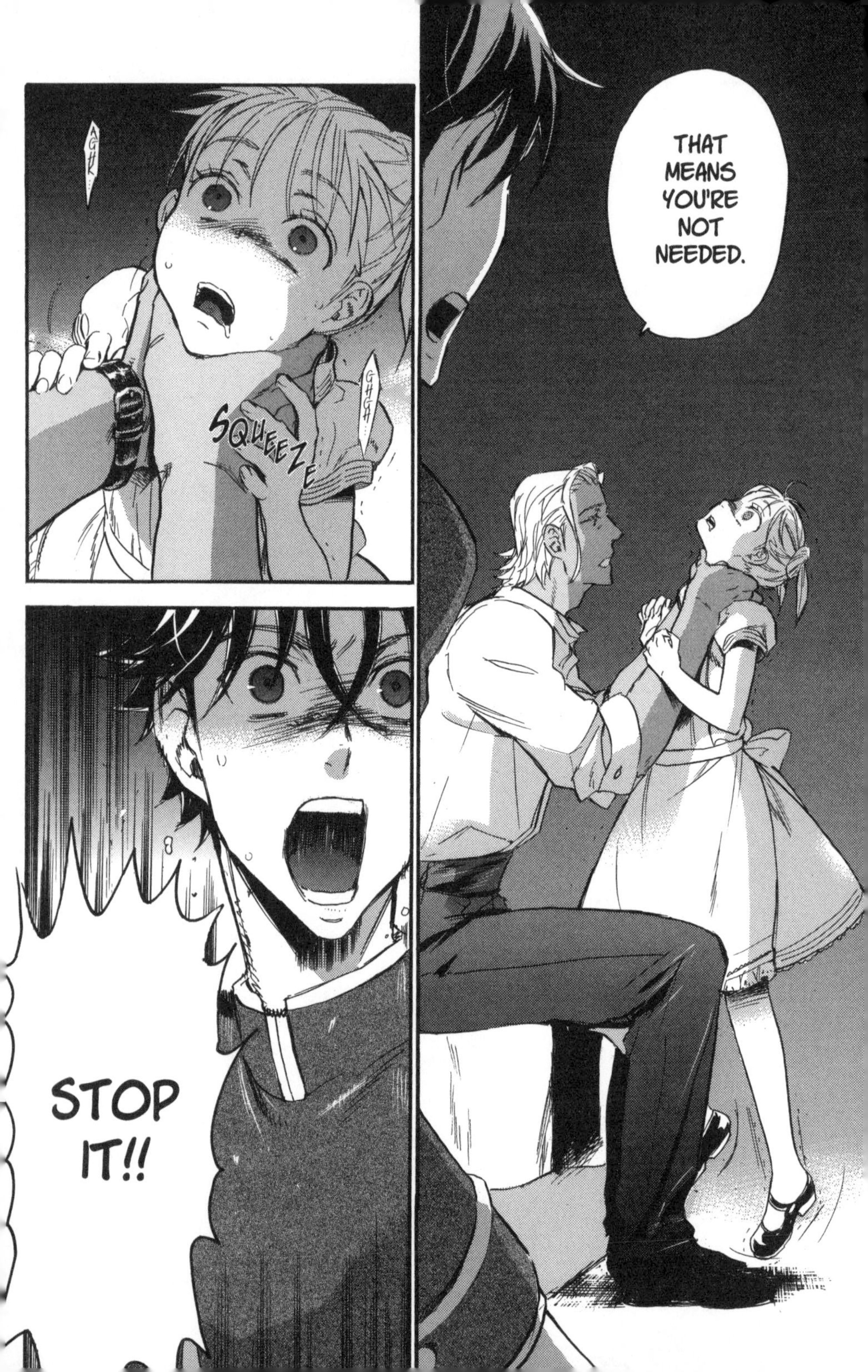
THAT MEANS YOU'RE NOT NEEDED.
AGHK...
GHGH...
SQUEEZE
STOP IT!!

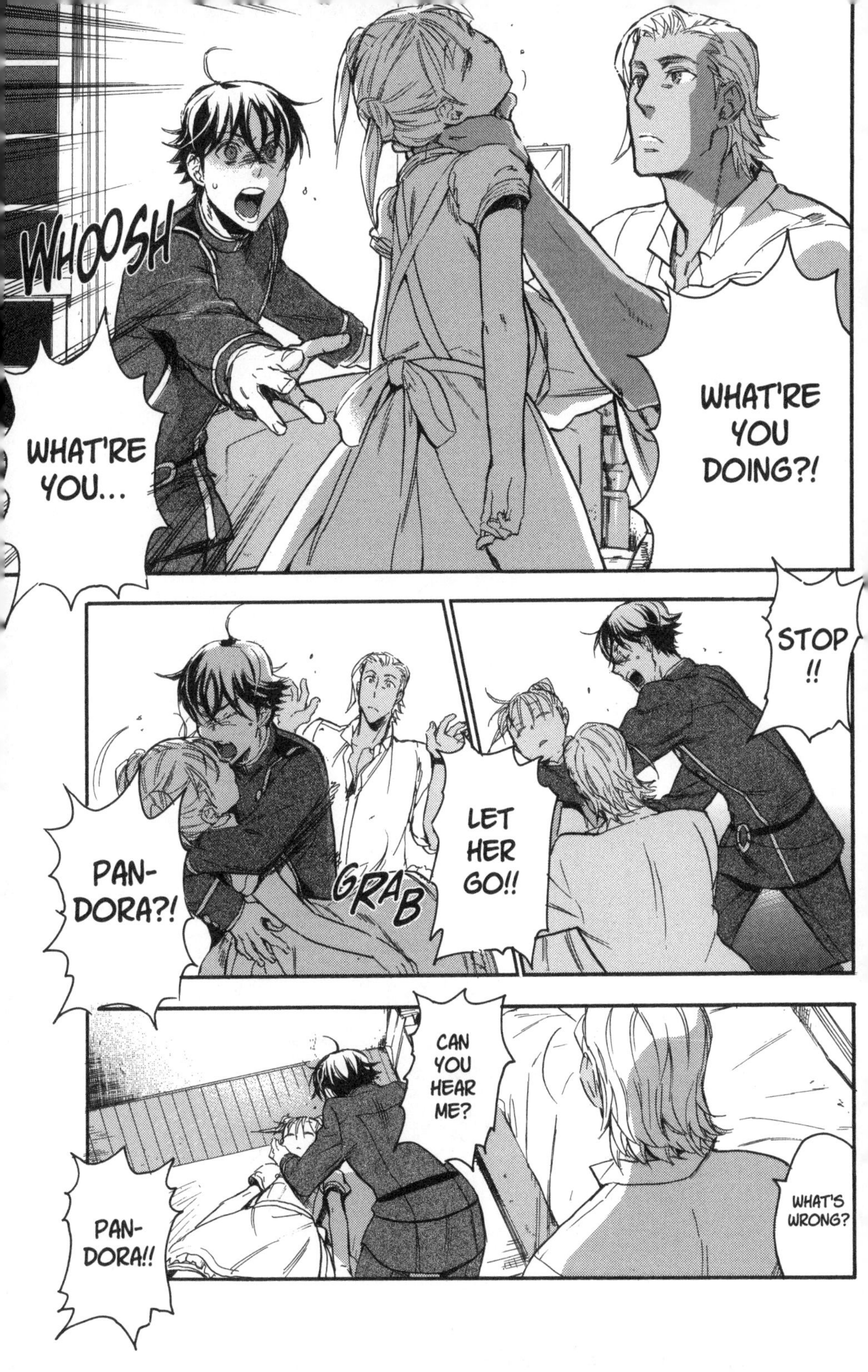
WHAT'RE YOU DOING?!
WHOOSH
WHAT'RE YOU...
STOP!!
LET HER GO!!
GRAB
PAN-DORA?!
WHAT'S WRONG?
CAN YOU HEAR ME?
PAN-DORA!!

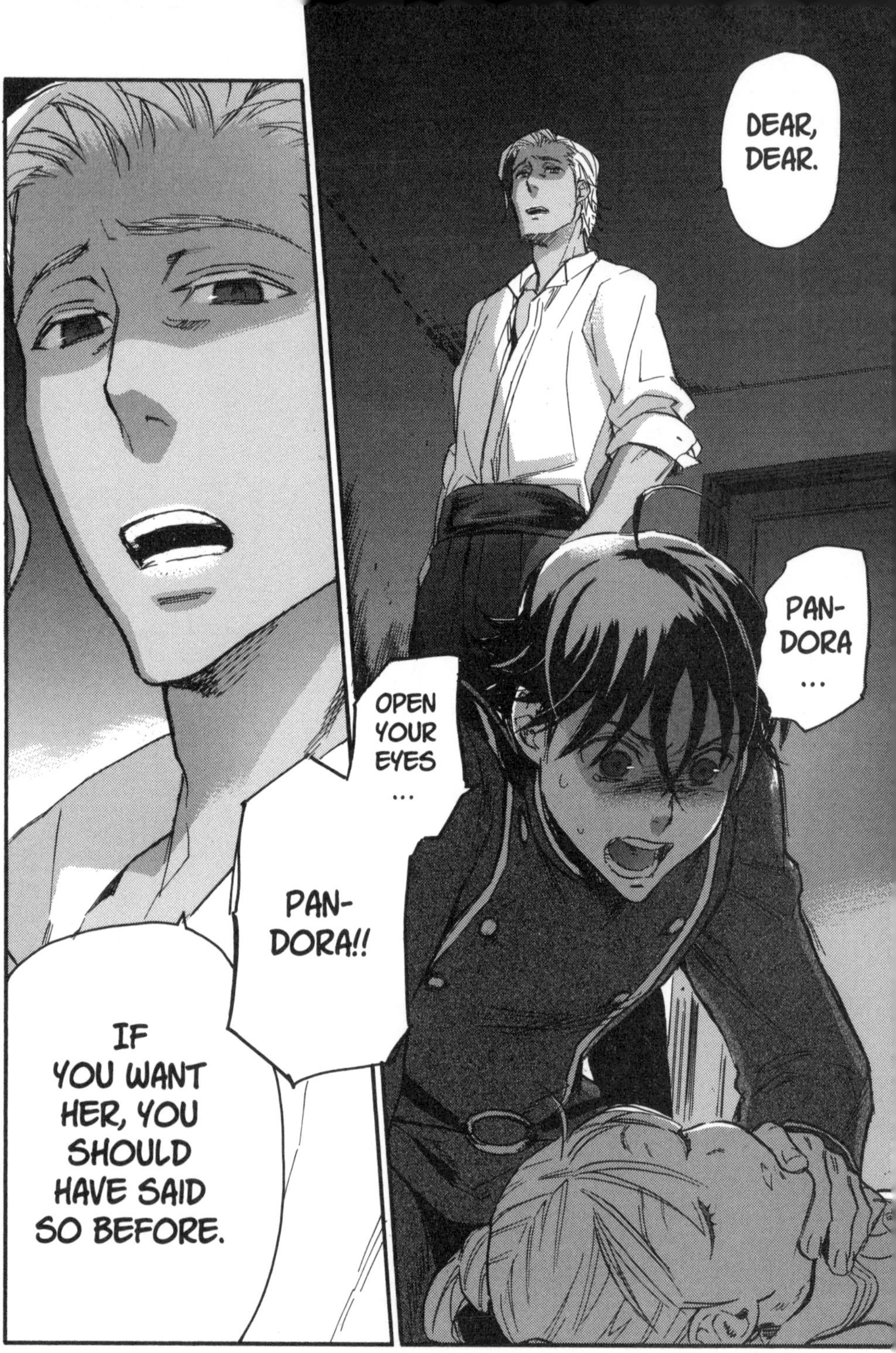
DEAR, DEAR.
PAN-DORA...
OPEN YOUR EYES...
PAN-DORA!!
IF YOU WANT HER, YOU SHOULD HAVE SAID SO BEFORE.

# CHAPTER fifteen

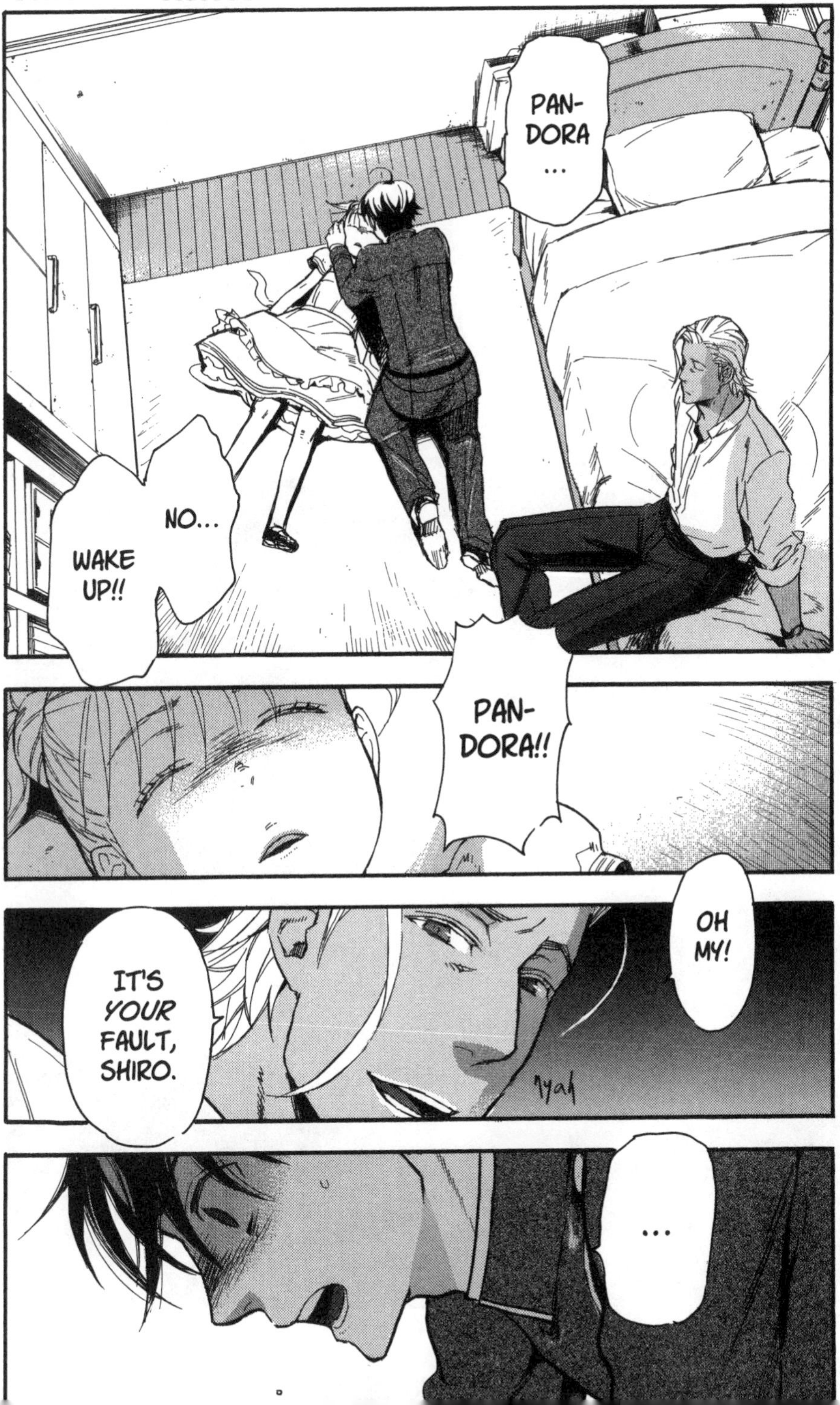

PAN-DORA ...
NO... WAKE UP!!
PAN-DORA!!
OH MY!
IT'S *YOUR* FAULT, SHIRO.
nyah
...

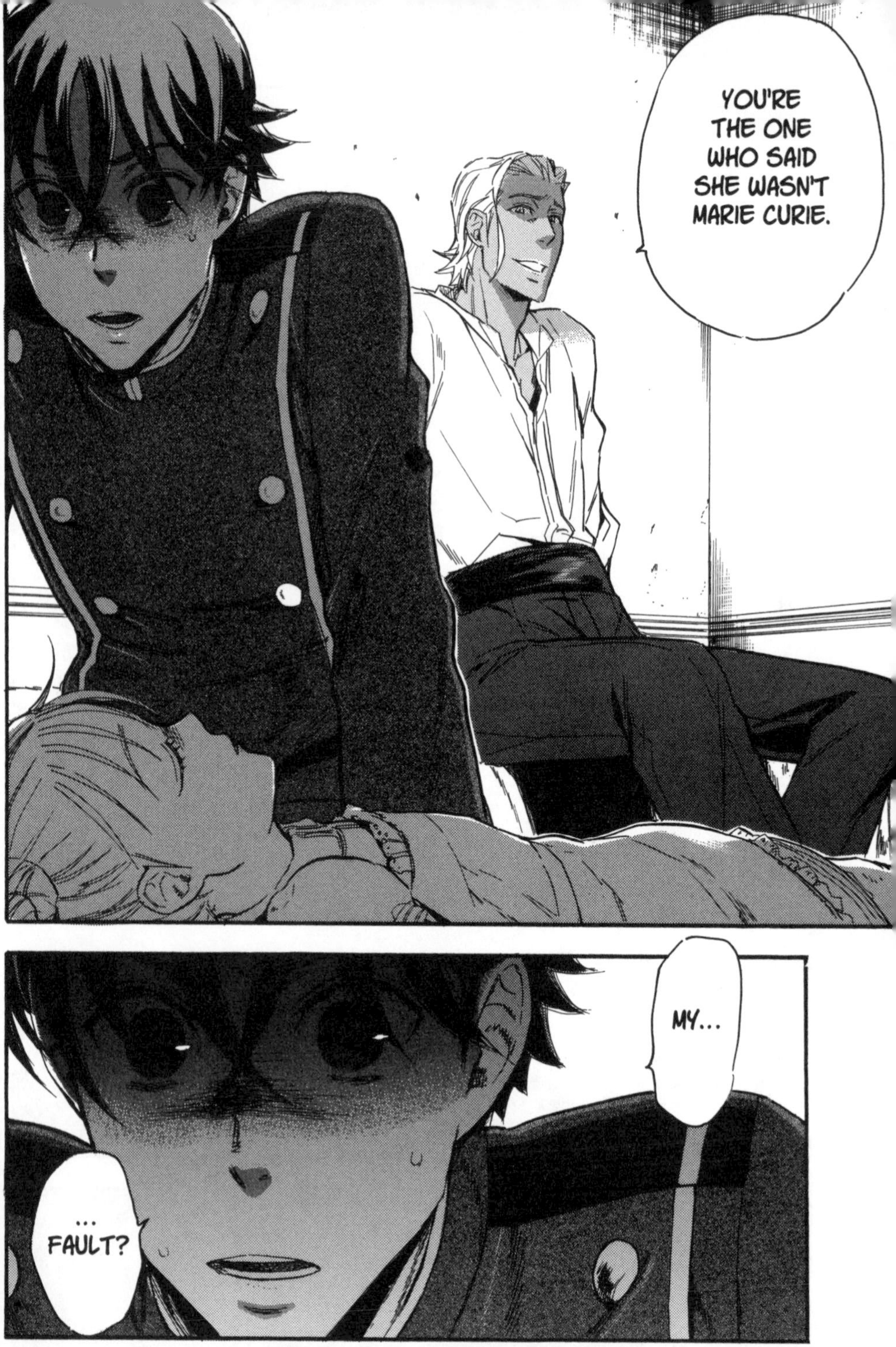
YOU'RE THE ONE WHO SAID SHE WASN'T MARIE CURIE.
MY...
... FAULT?

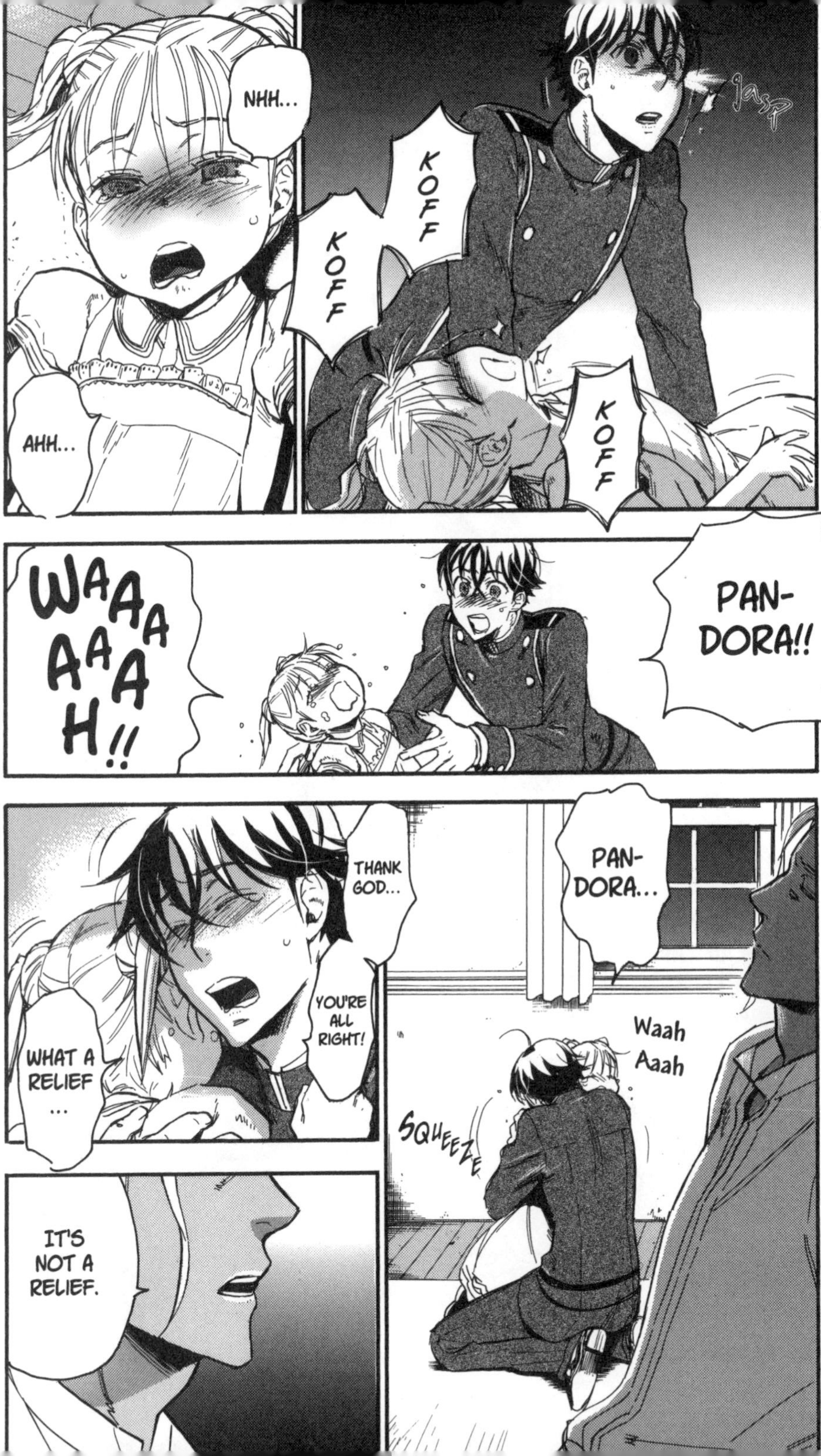
gasp
KOFF
KOFF
KOFF
NHH...
AHH...
PAN-DORA!!
WAAAAAAH!!
PAN-DORA...
Waah Aaah
SQUEEZE
THANK GOD...
YOU'RE ALL RIGHT!
WHAT A RELIEF...
IT'S NOT A RELIEF.

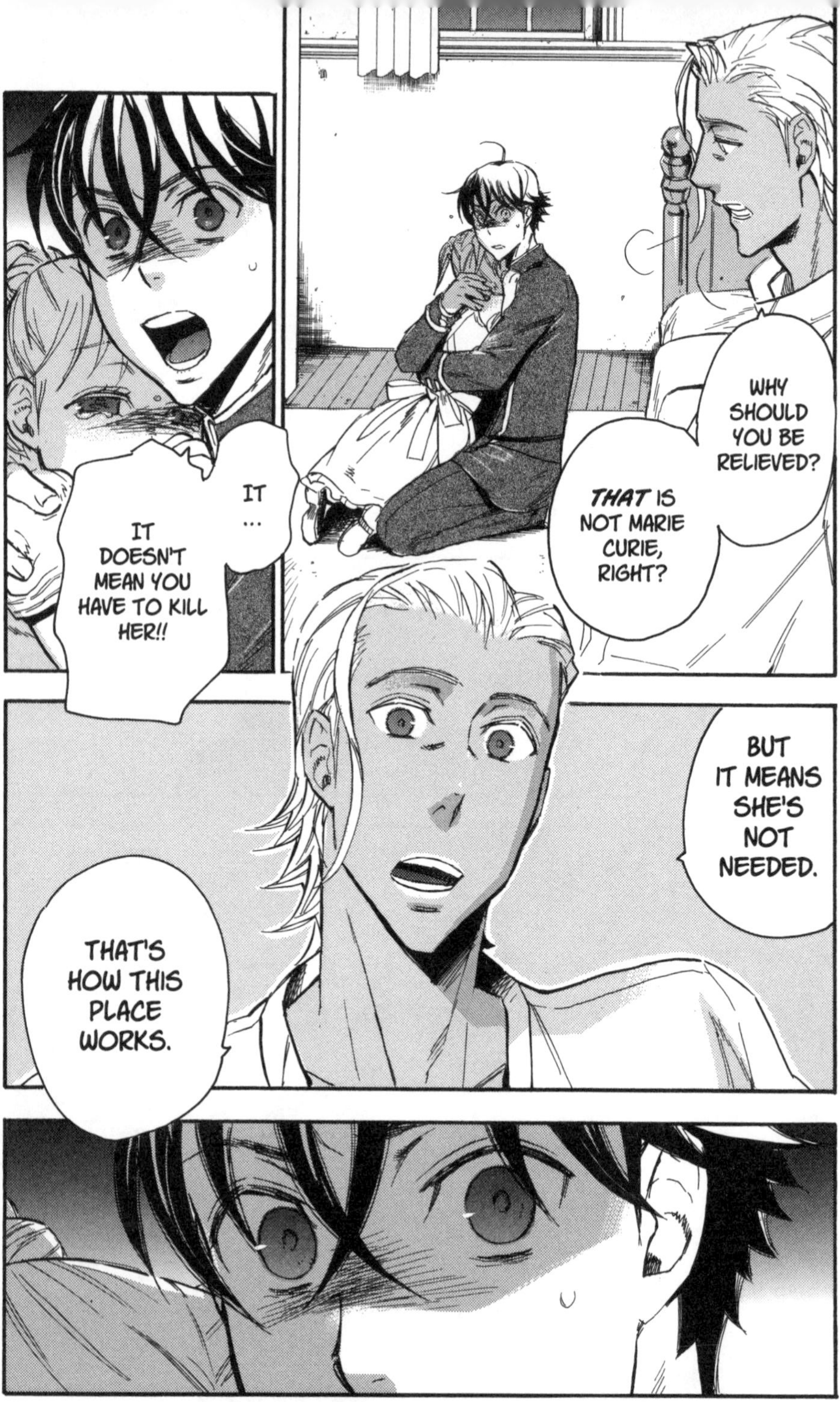
WHY SHOULD YOU BE RELIEVED?
*THAT* IS NOT MARIE CURIE, RIGHT?
IT ...
IT DOESN'T MEAN YOU HAVE TO KILL HER!!
BUT IT MEANS SHE'S NOT NEEDED.
THAT'S HOW THIS PLACE WORKS.

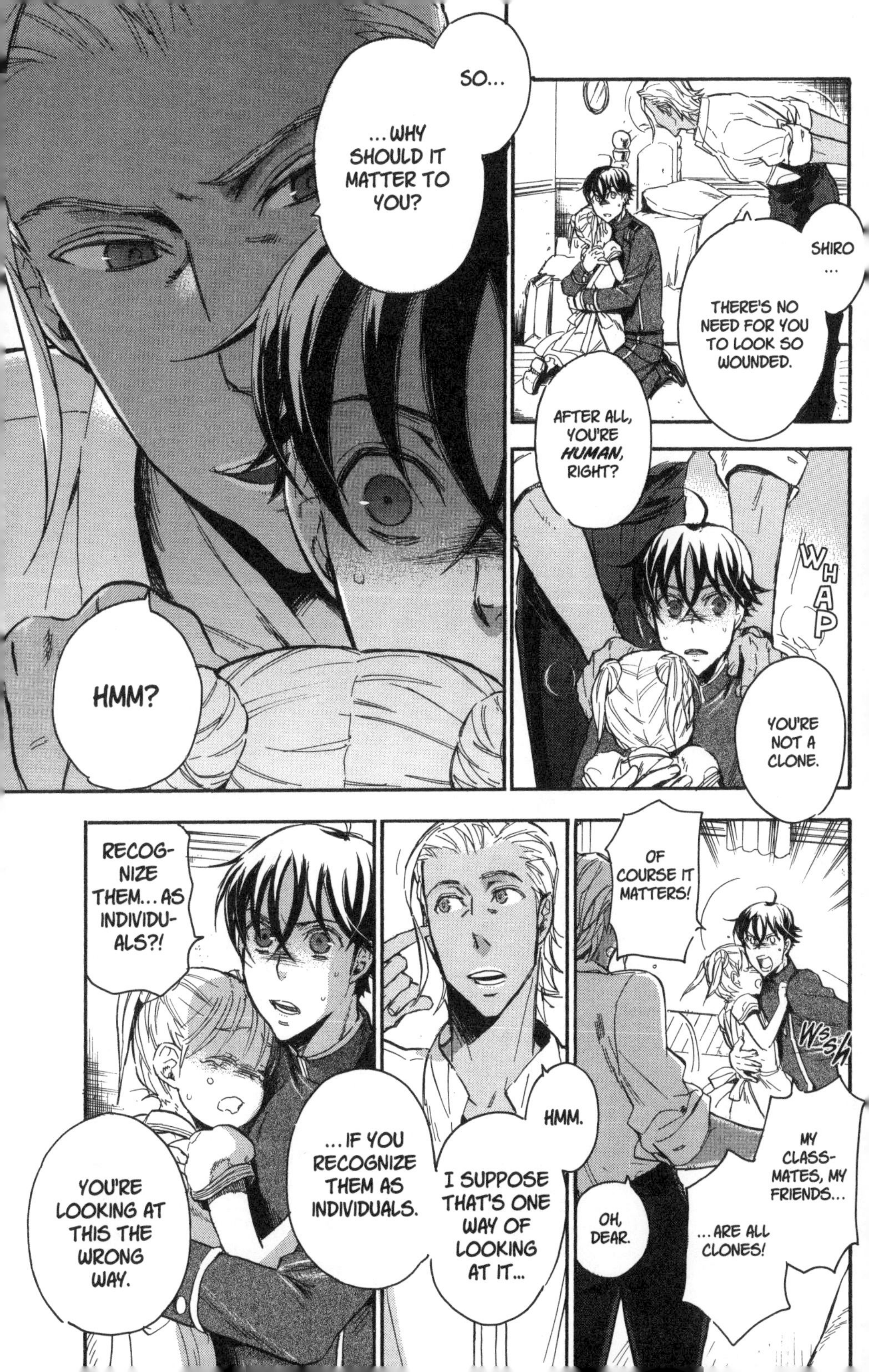
SHIRO ...
THERE'S NO NEED FOR YOU TO LOOK SO WOUNDED.
AFTER ALL, YOU'RE *HUMAN*, RIGHT?
WHAP
YOU'RE NOT A CLONE.
SO...
...WHY SHOULD IT MATTER TO YOU?
HMM?
OF COURSE IT MATTERS!
WSSH
MY CLASS-MATES, MY FRIENDS...
...ARE ALL CLONES!
OH, DEAR.
HMM.
I SUPPOSE THAT'S ONE WAY OF LOOKING AT IT...
...IF YOU RECOGNIZE THEM AS INDIVIDUALS.
RECOG-NIZE THEM...AS INDIVIDU-ALS?!
YOU'RE LOOKING AT THIS THE WRONG WAY.

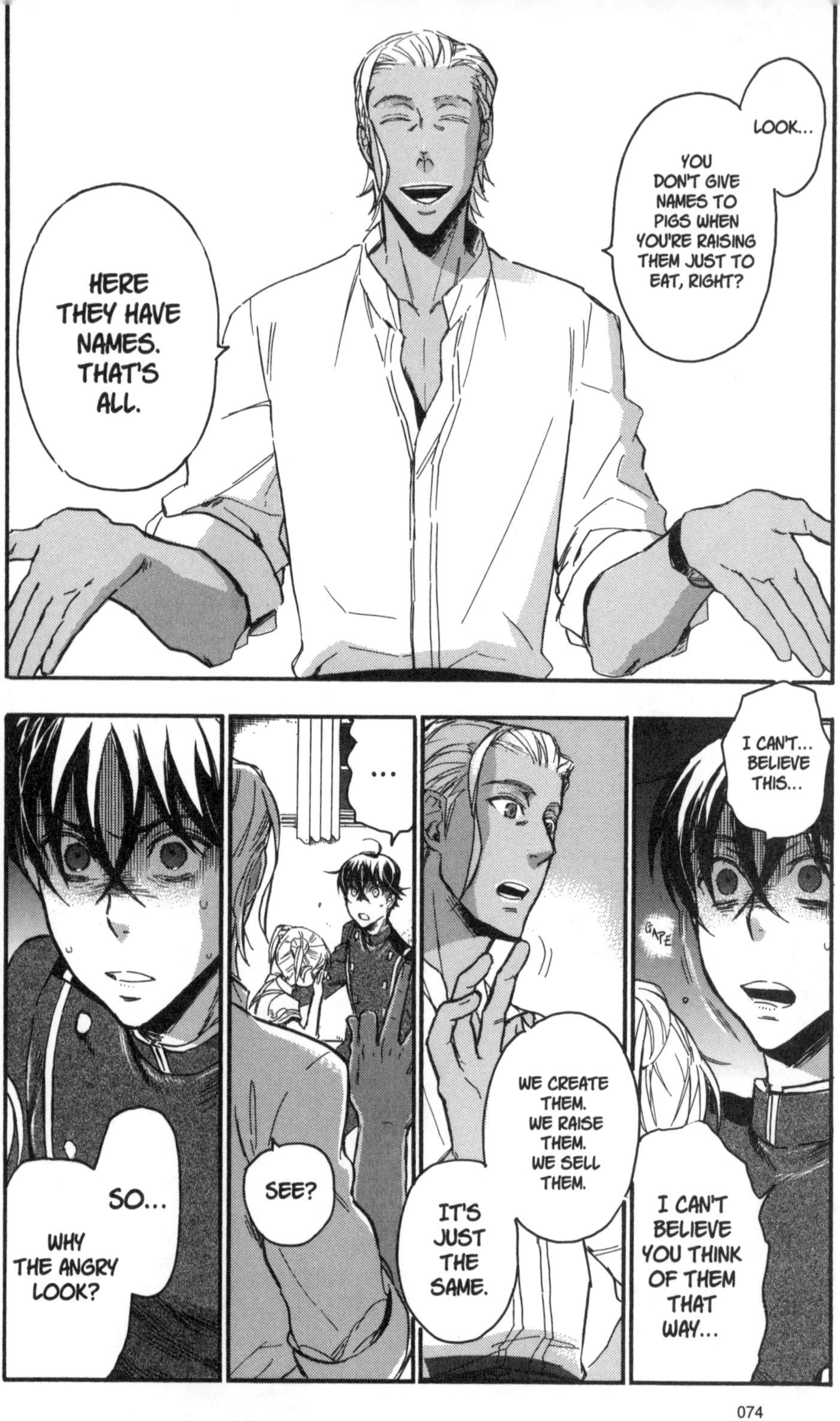
LOOK...
YOU DON'T GIVE NAMES TO PIGS WHEN YOU'RE RAISING THEM JUST TO EAT, RIGHT?
HERE THEY HAVE NAMES. THAT'S ALL.
I CAN'T... BELIEVE THIS...
GAPE
I CAN'T BELIEVE YOU THINK OF THEM THAT WAY...
WE CREATE THEM. WE RAISE THEM. WE SELL THEM.
IT'S JUST THE SAME.
...
SEE?
SO...
WHY THE ANGRY LOOK?

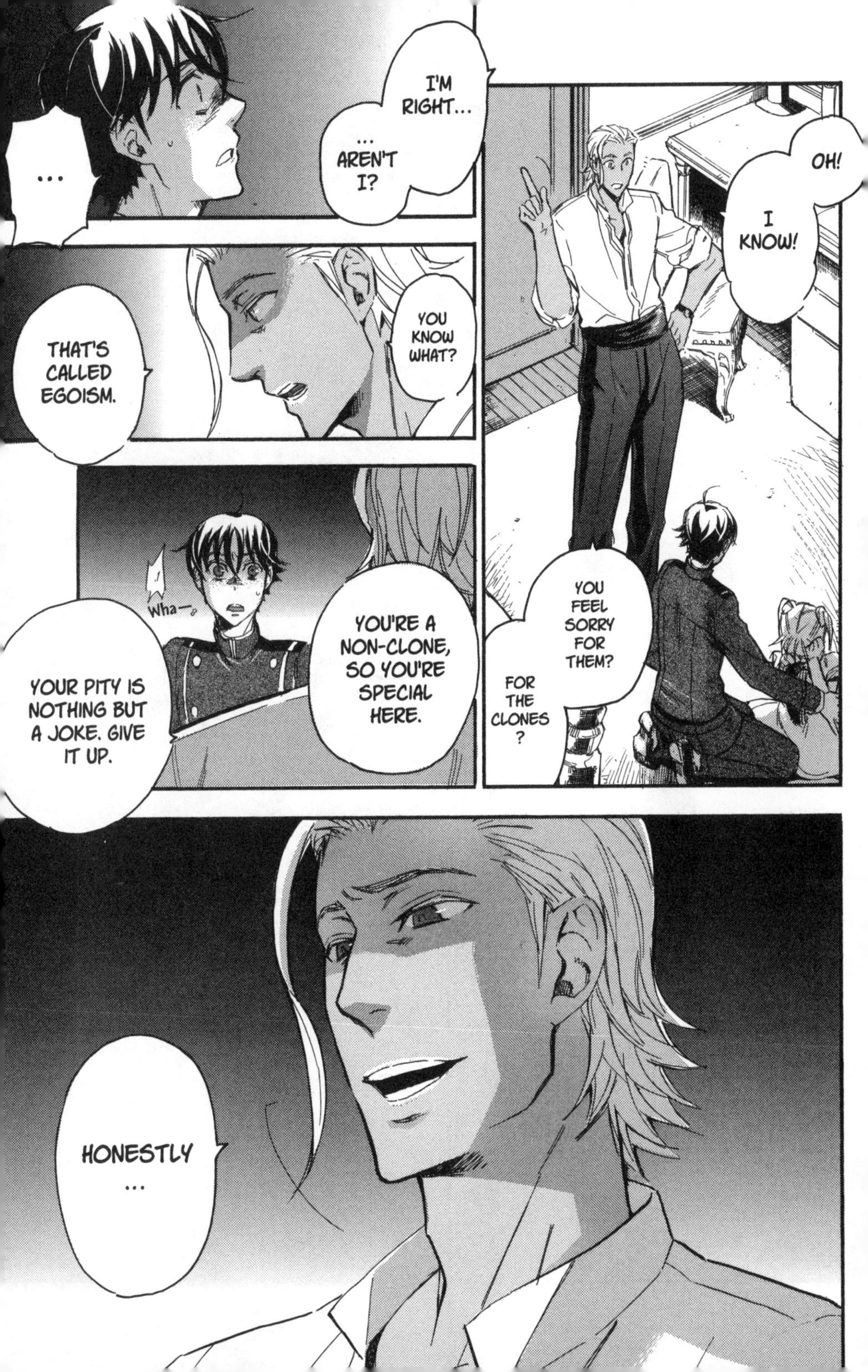
OH!
I KNOW!
YOU FEEL SORRY FOR THEM?
FOR THE CLONES?
I'M RIGHT...
... AREN'T I?
...
YOU KNOW WHAT?
THAT'S CALLED EGOISM.
YOU'RE A NON-CLONE, SO YOU'RE SPECIAL HERE.
Wha—
YOUR PITY IS NOTHING BUT A JOKE. GIVE IT UP.
HONESTLY ...

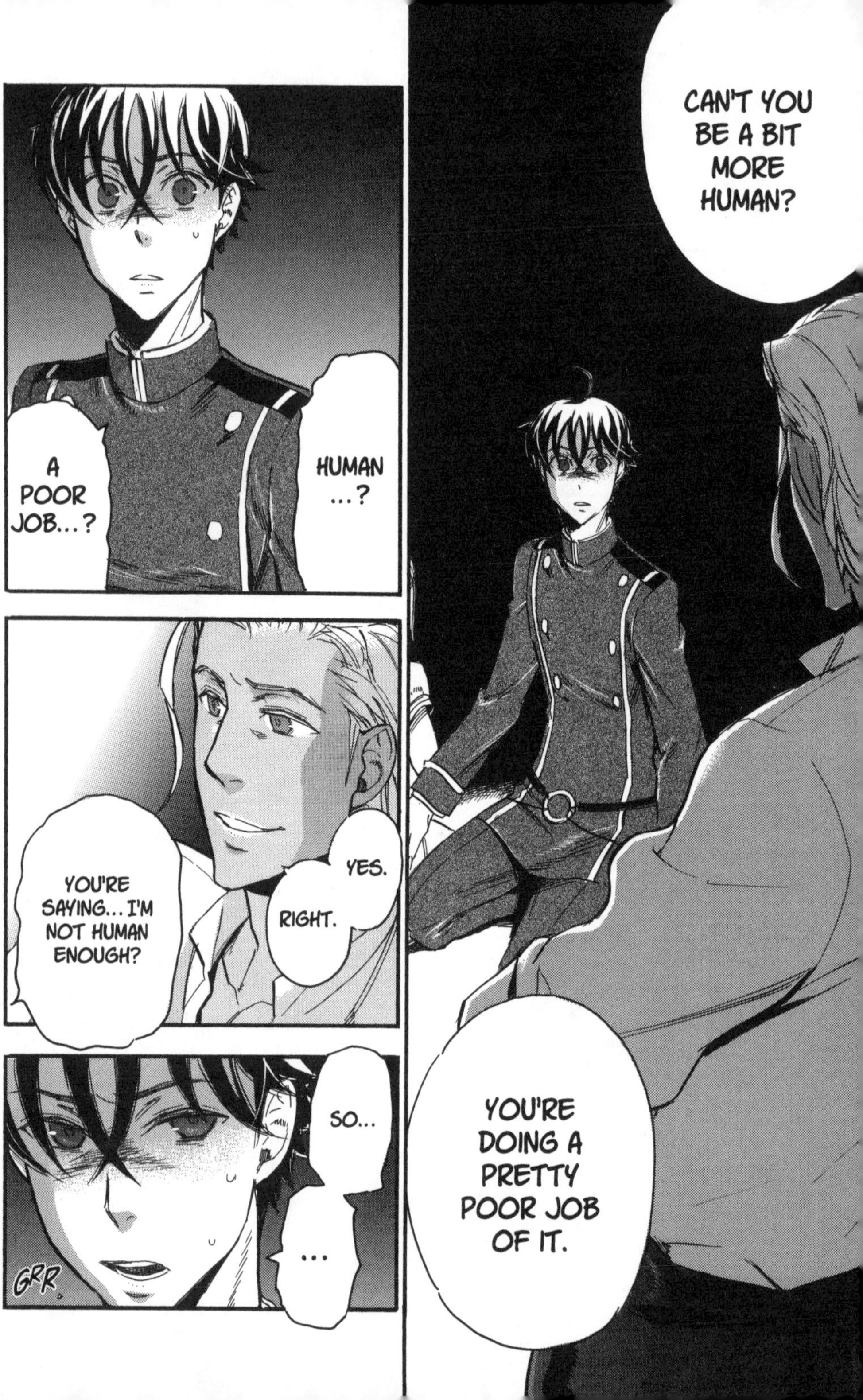
CAN'T YOU BE A BIT MORE HUMAN?
YOU'RE DOING A PRETTY POOR JOB OF IT.
HUMAN ...?
A POOR JOB...?
YES.
RIGHT.
YOU'RE SAYING... I'M NOT HUMAN ENOUGH?
SO...
...
GRR

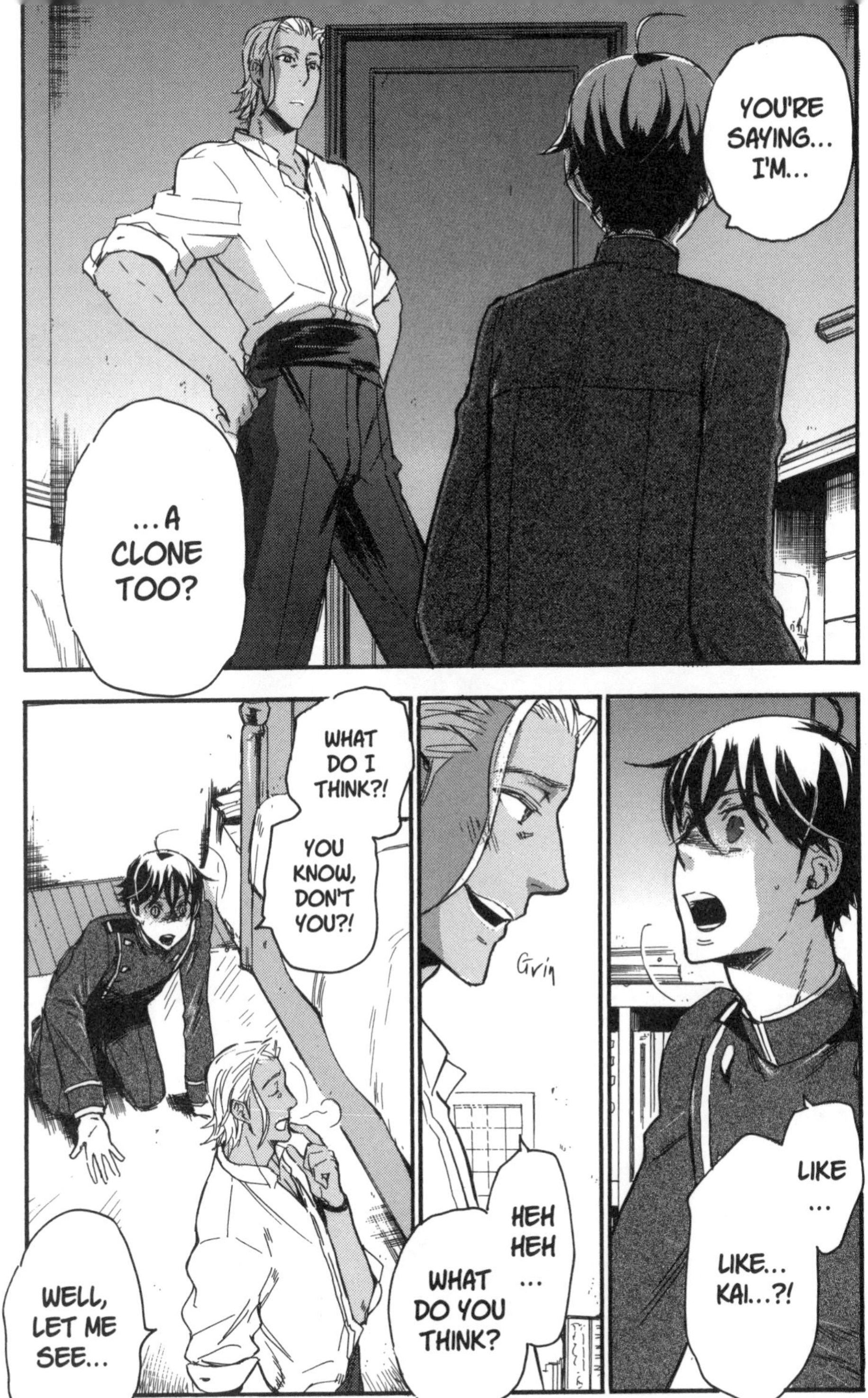
YOU'RE SAYING... I'M...
...A CLONE TOO?
LIKE ...
LIKE... KAI...?!
Grin
HEH HEH ...
WHAT DO YOU THINK?
WHAT DO I THINK?!
YOU KNOW, DON'T YOU?!
WELL, LET ME SEE...

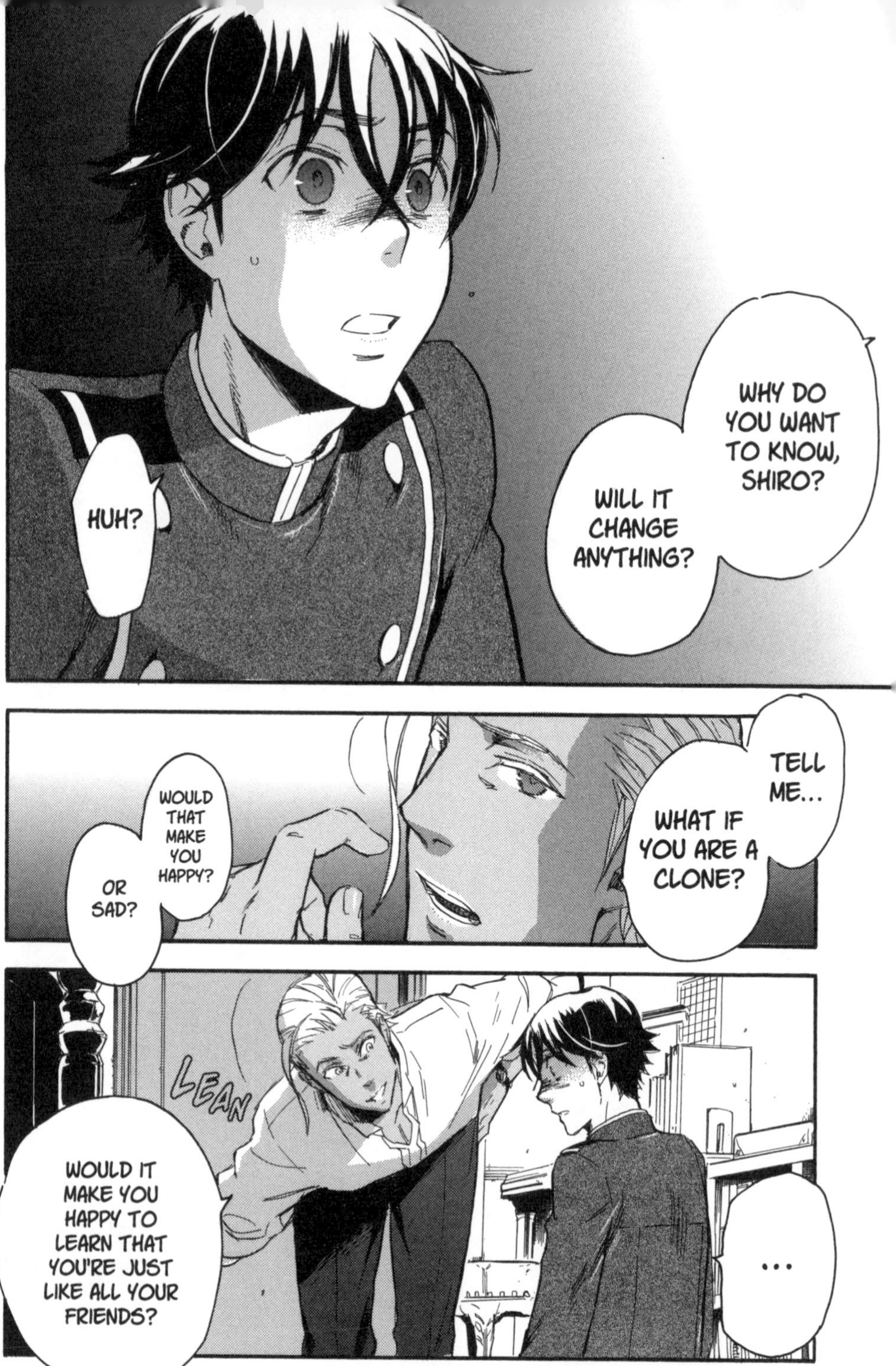
WHY DO YOU WANT TO KNOW, SHIRO?
WILL IT CHANGE ANYTHING?
HUH?
TELL ME...
WHAT IF YOU ARE A CLONE?
WOULD THAT MAKE YOU HAPPY?
OR SAD?
LEAN
WOULD IT MAKE YOU HAPPY TO LEARN THAT YOU'RE JUST LIKE ALL YOUR FRIENDS?
...

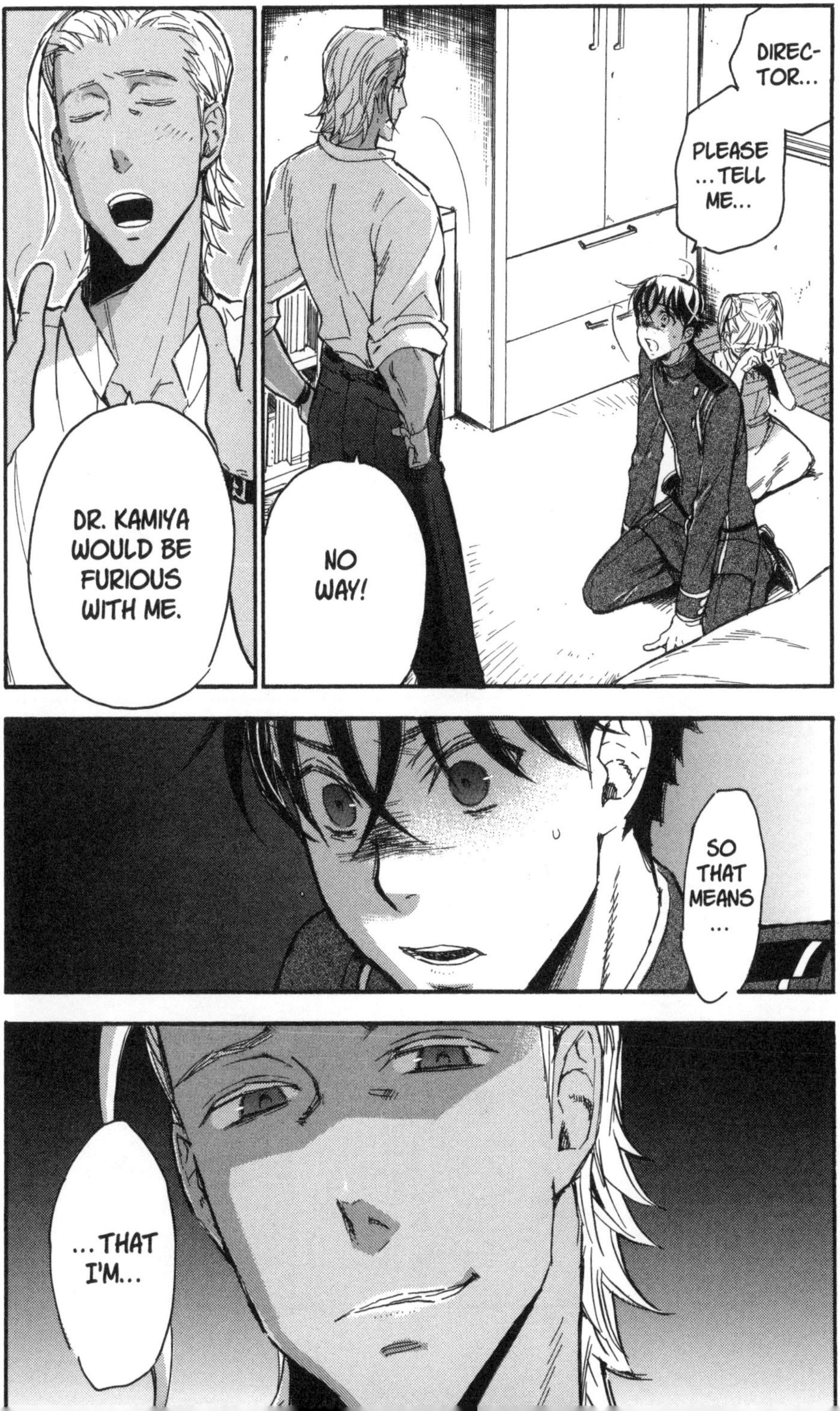
DIRECTOR...
PLEASE ...TELL ME...
NO WAY!
DR. KAMIYA WOULD BE FURIOUS WITH ME.
SO THAT MEANS ...
...THAT I'M...

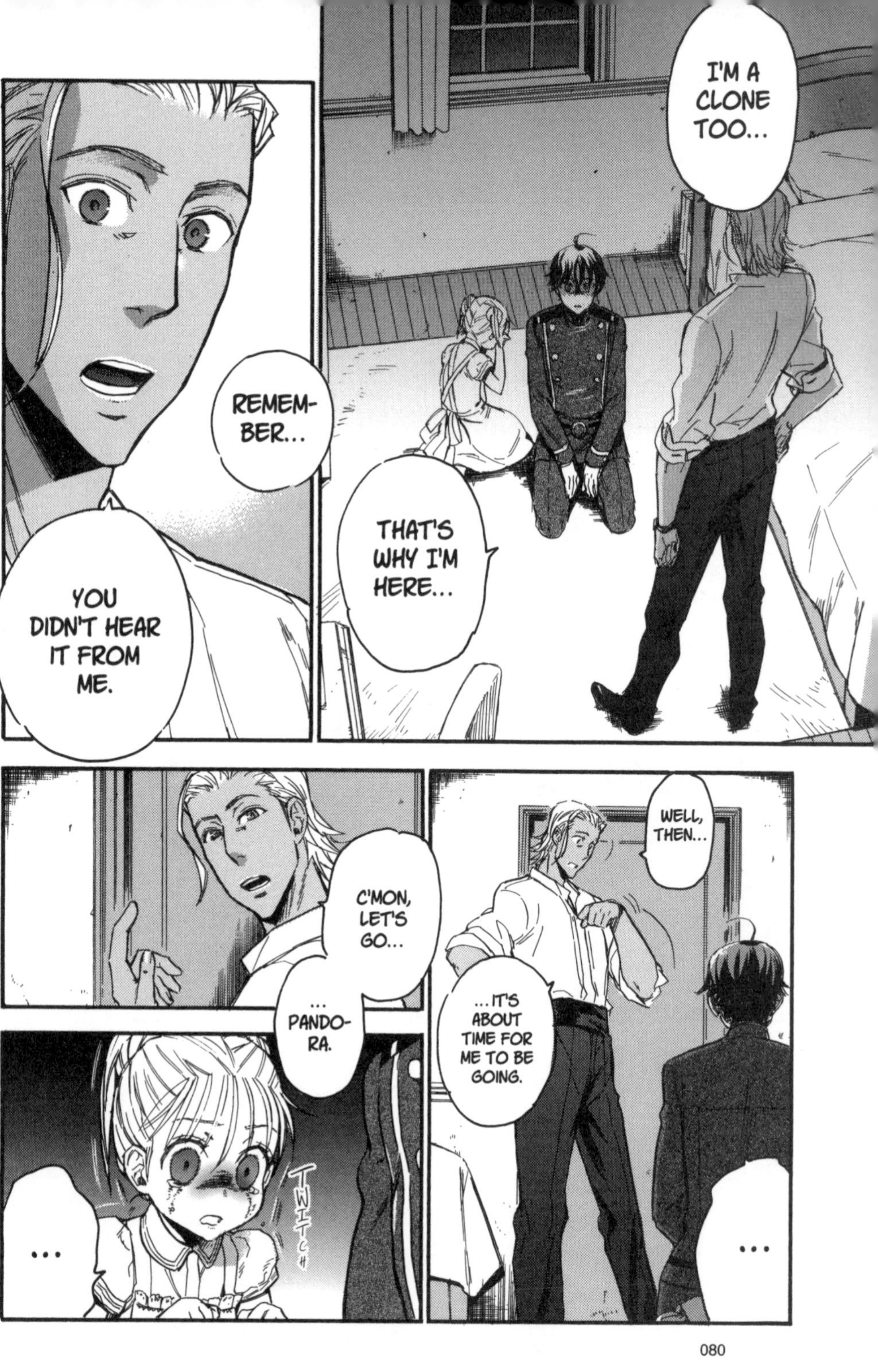
I'M A CLONE TOO...
THAT'S WHY I'M HERE...
REMEMBER...
YOU DIDN'T HEAR IT FROM ME.
WELL, THEN...
...IT'S ABOUT TIME FOR ME TO BE GOING.
...
C'MON, LET'S GO...
...PANDORA.
TWITCH
...

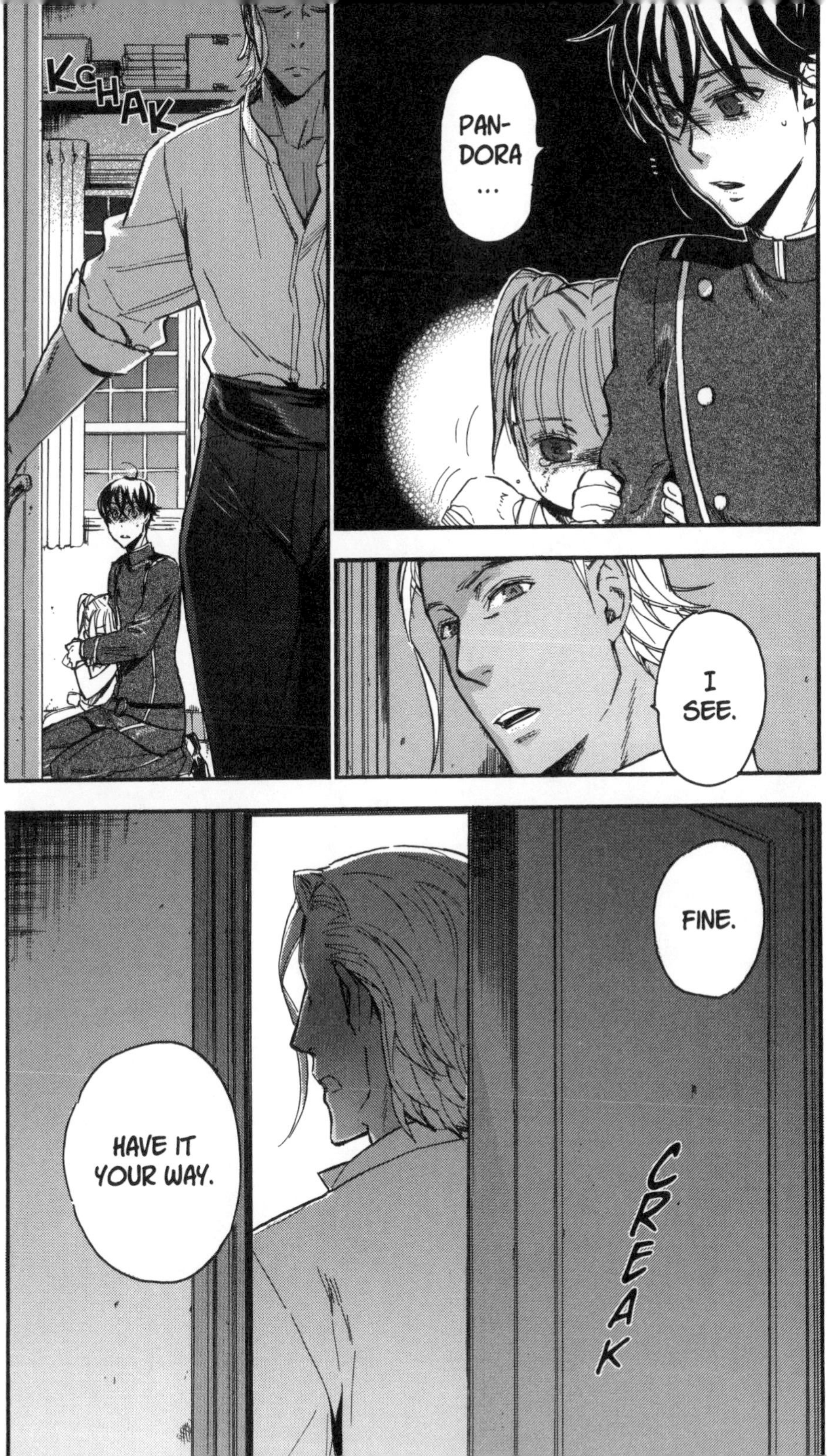
PAN-DORA...
I SEE.
KCHAK
FINE.
HAVE IT YOUR WAY.
CREAK

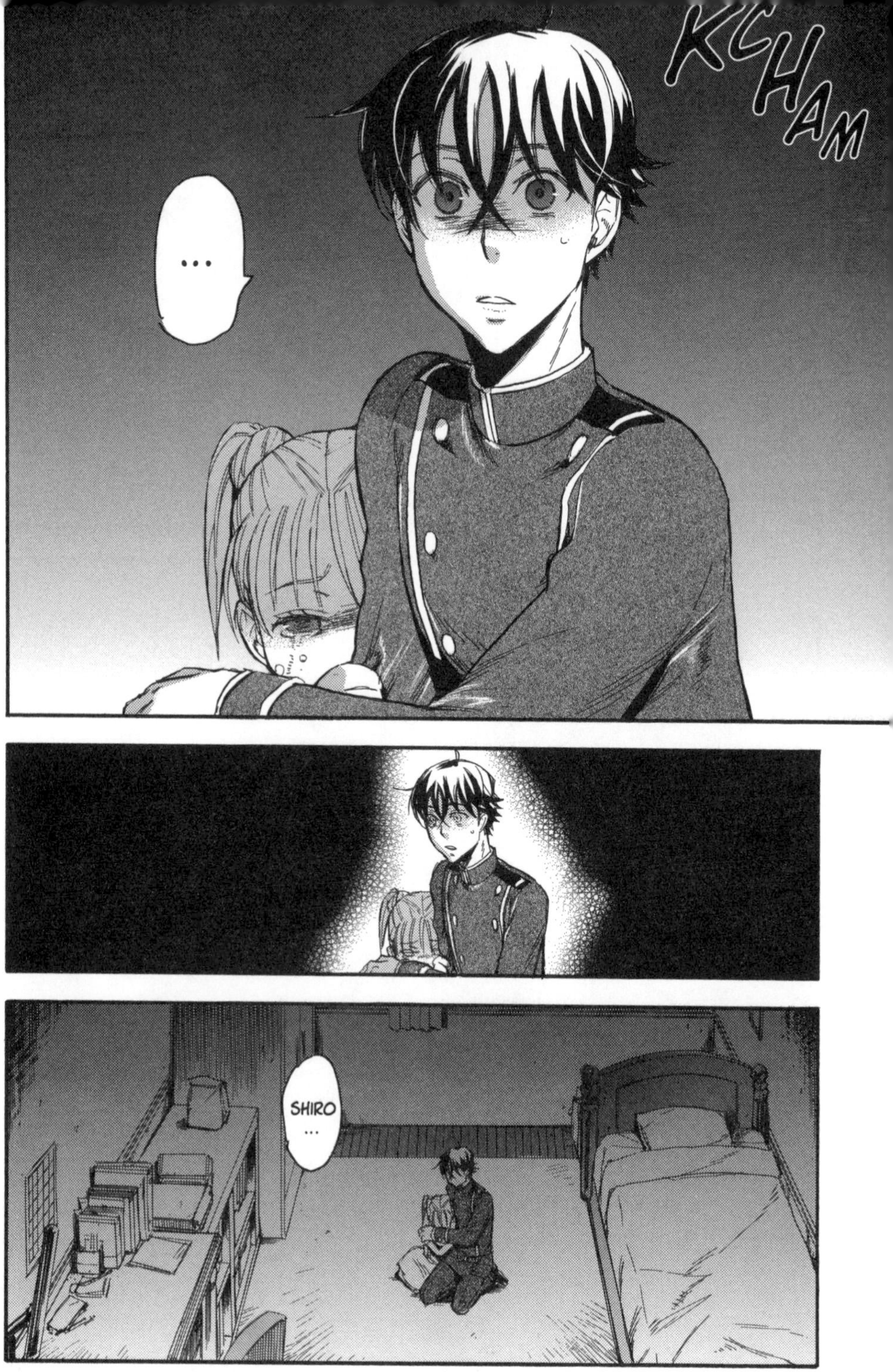
KCHAM
...
SHIRO ...

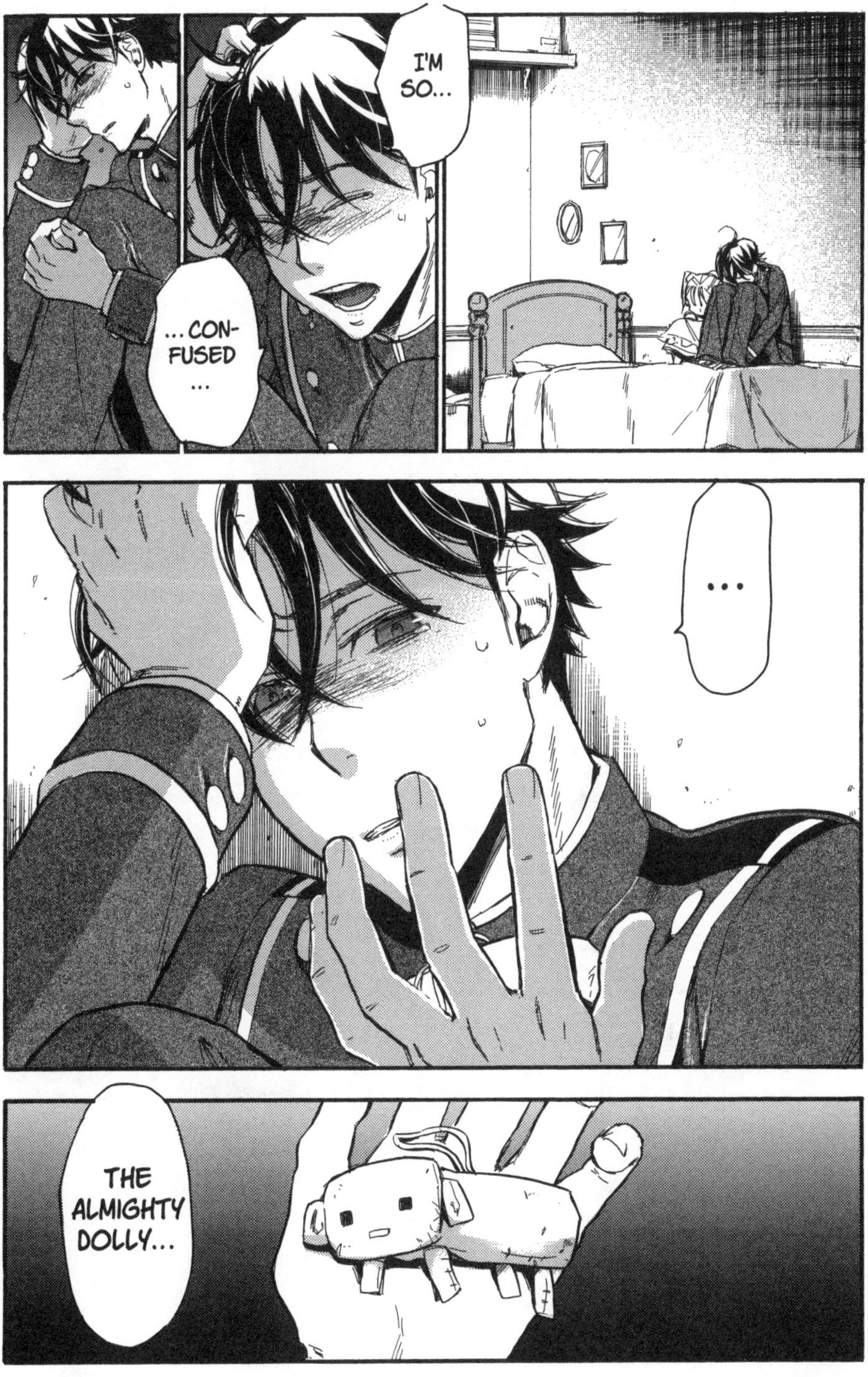
I'M SO...
...CON-FUSED ...
...
THE ALMIGHTY DOLLY...

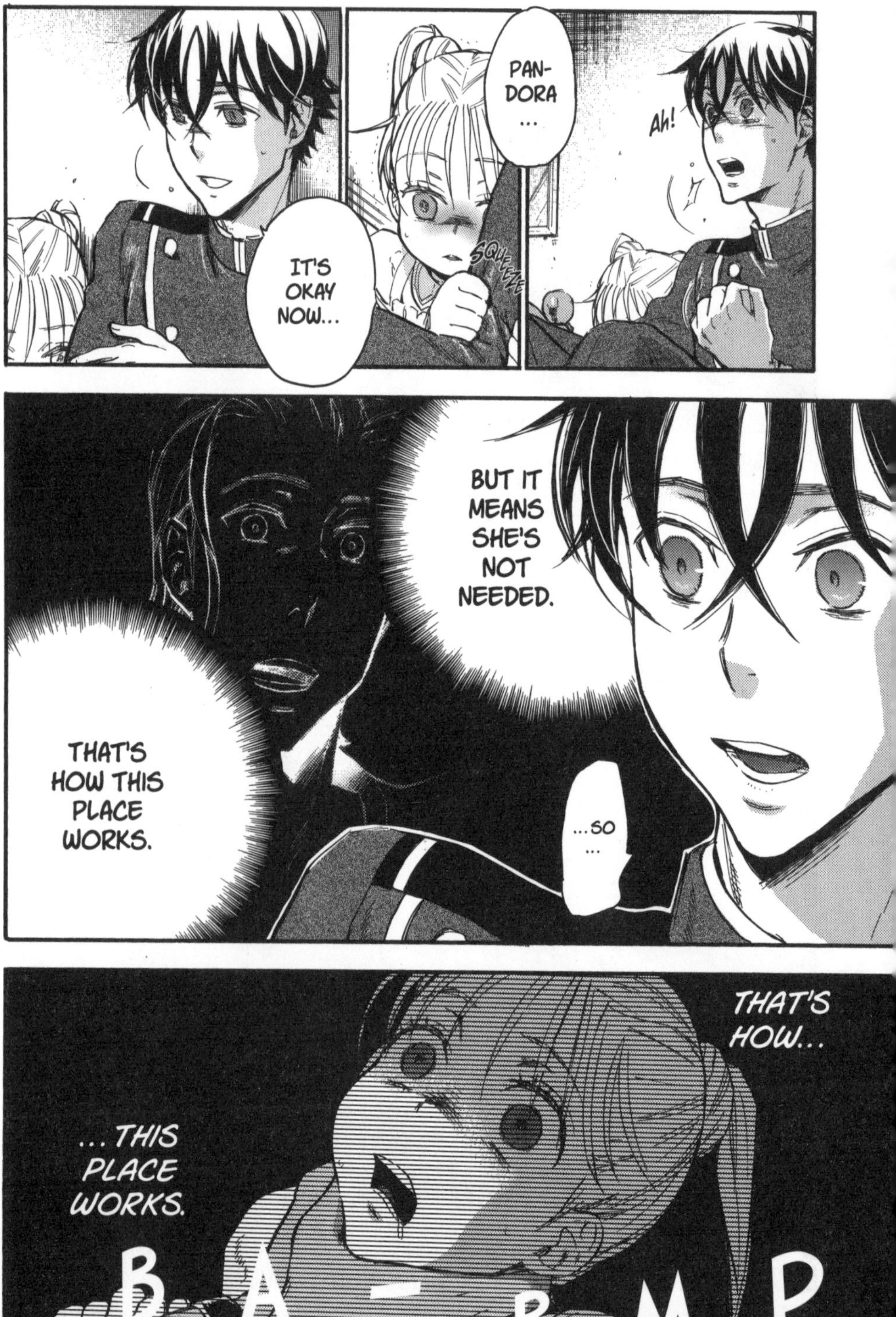
Ah!
PAN-DORA ...
SQUEEZE
IT'S OKAY NOW...
BUT IT MEANS SHE'S NOT NEEDED.
...SO ...
THAT'S HOW THIS PLACE WORKS.
THAT'S HOW...
...THIS PLACE WORKS.
BA-BMP

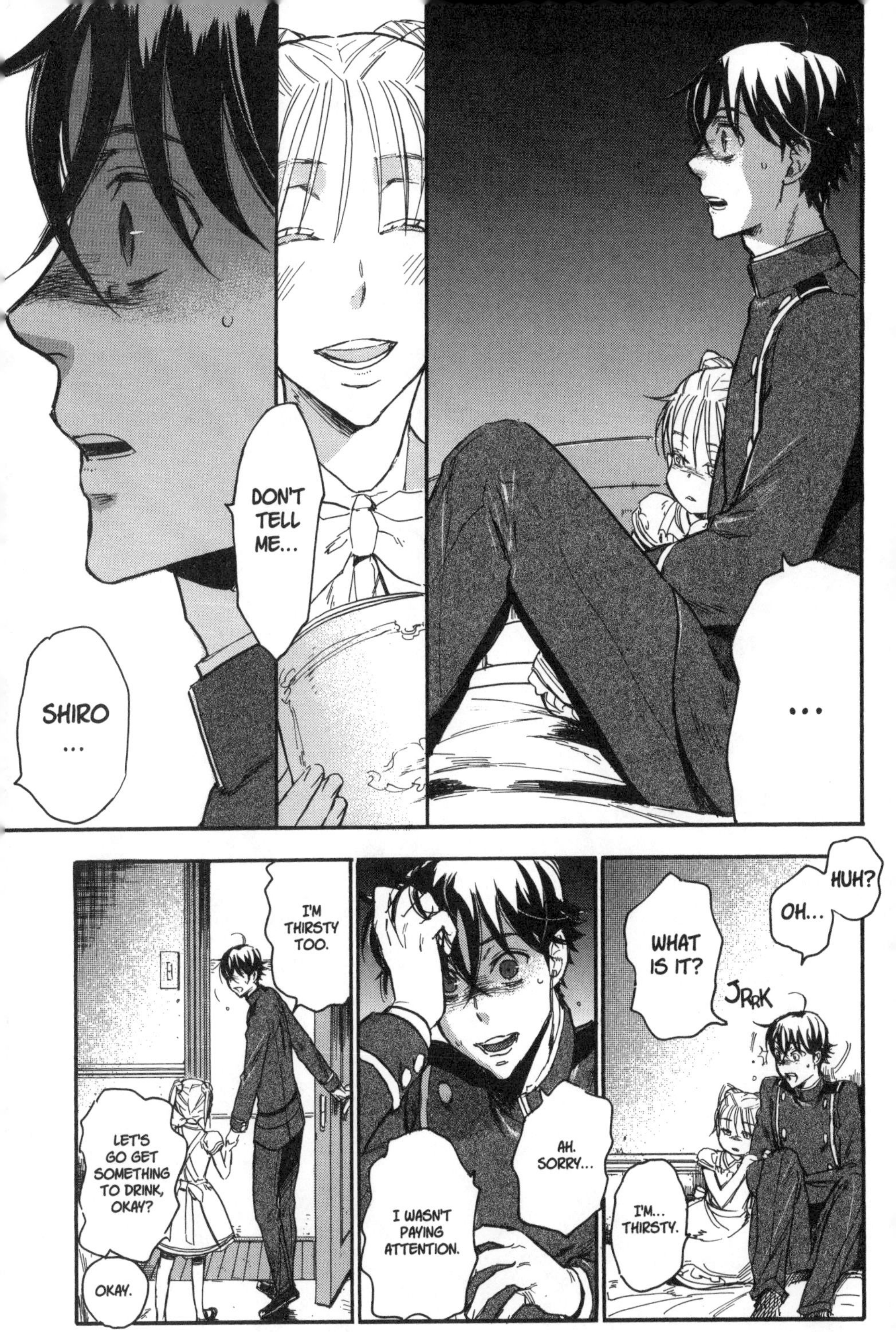
...
DON'T TELL ME...
SHIRO ...
HUH?
OH...
WHAT IS IT?
JRRK
I'M... THIRSTY.
AH. SORRY...
I WASN'T PAYING ATTENTION.
I'M THIRSTY TOO.
LET'S GO GET SOMETHING TO DRINK, OKAY?
OKAY.

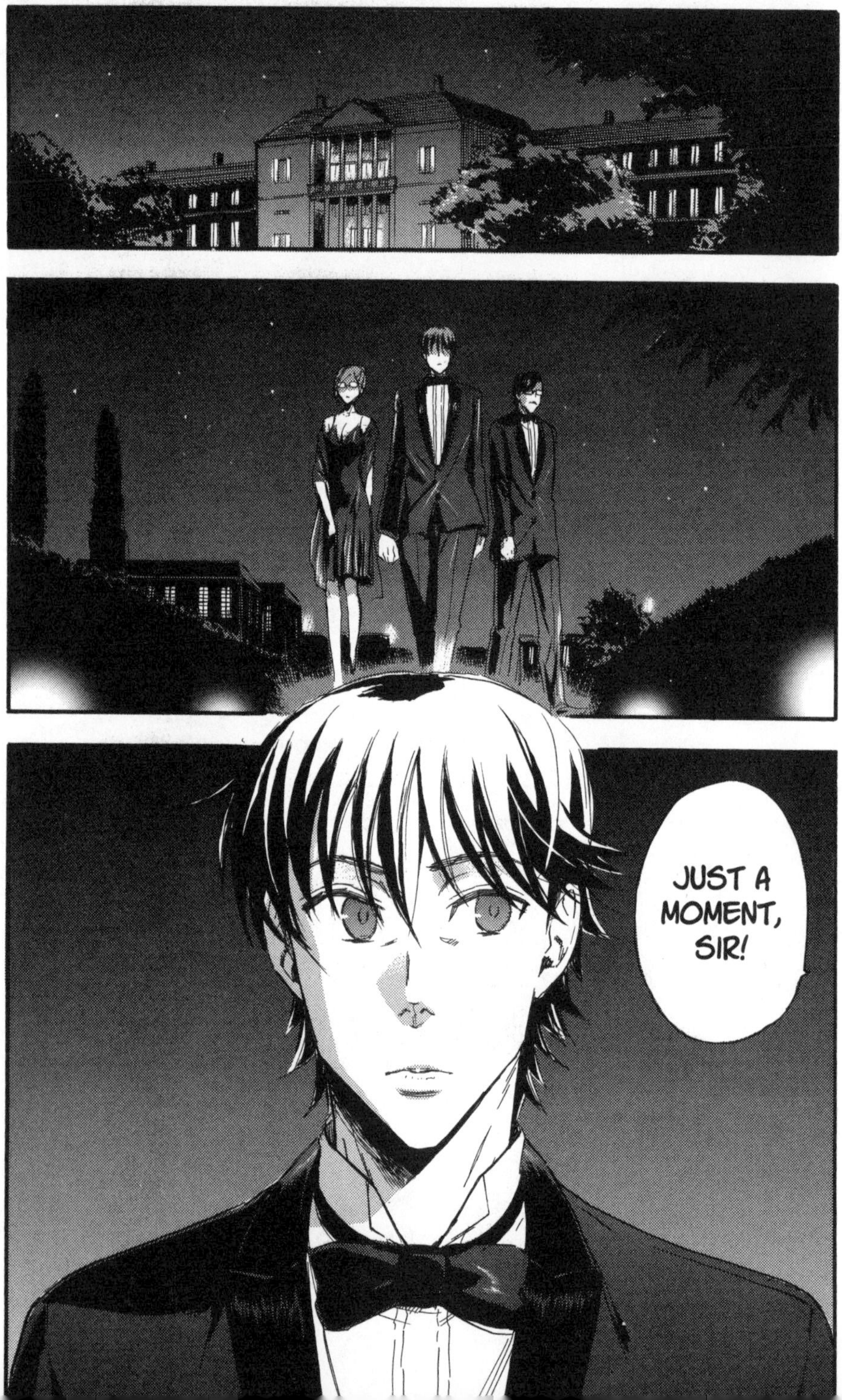
JUST A MOMENT, SIR!

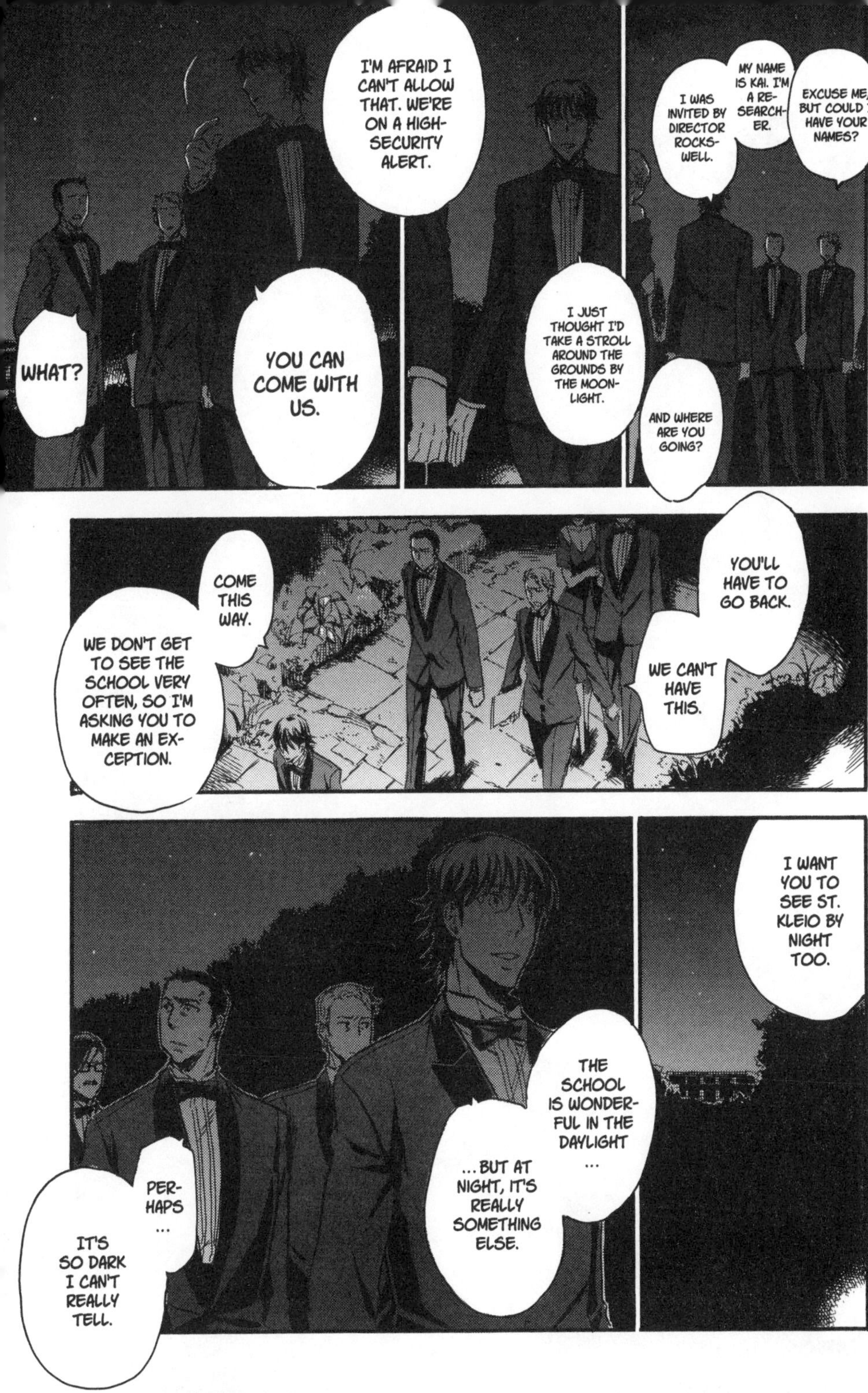
EXCUSE ME, BUT COULD I HAVE YOUR NAMES?
MY NAME IS KAI. I'M A RE-SEARCH-ER.
I WAS INVITED BY DIRECTOR ROCKS-WELL.
AND WHERE ARE YOU GOING?
I JUST THOUGHT I'D TAKE A STROLL AROUND THE GROUNDS BY THE MOON-LIGHT.
I'M AFRAID I CAN'T ALLOW THAT. WE'RE ON A HIGH-SECURITY ALERT.
YOU CAN COME WITH US.
WHAT?
YOU'LL HAVE TO GO BACK.
WE CAN'T HAVE THIS.
COME THIS WAY.
WE DON'T GET TO SEE THE SCHOOL VERY OFTEN, SO I'M ASKING YOU TO MAKE AN EX-CEPTION.
I WANT YOU TO SEE ST. KLEIO BY NIGHT TOO.
THE SCHOOL IS WONDER-FUL IN THE DAYLIGHT ...
... BUT AT NIGHT, IT'S REALLY SOMETHING ELSE.
PER-HAPS ...
IT'S SO DARK I CAN'T REALLY TELL.

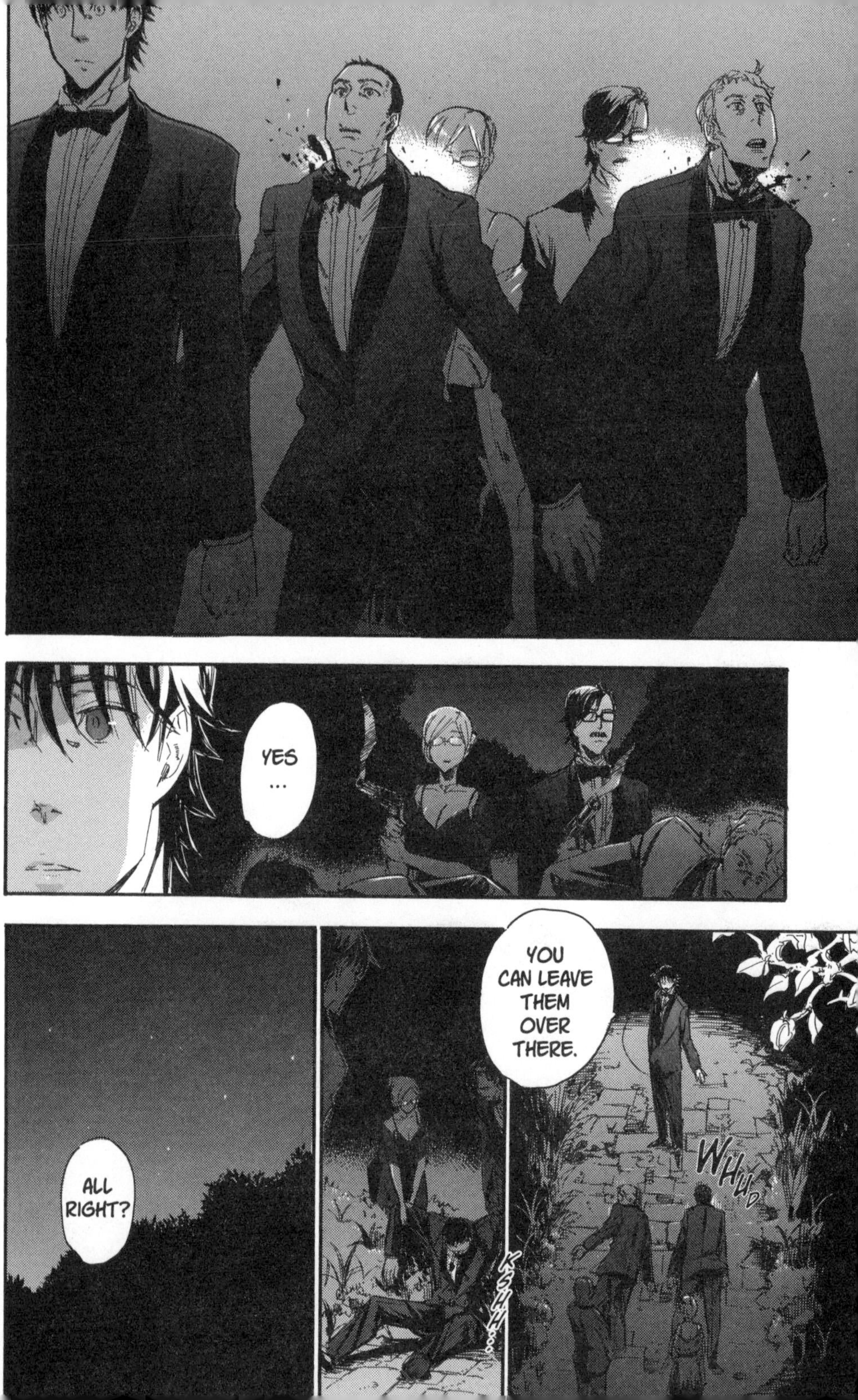
YES ...
YOU CAN LEAVE THEM OVER THERE.
WHUD
KSHH...
ALL RIGHT?

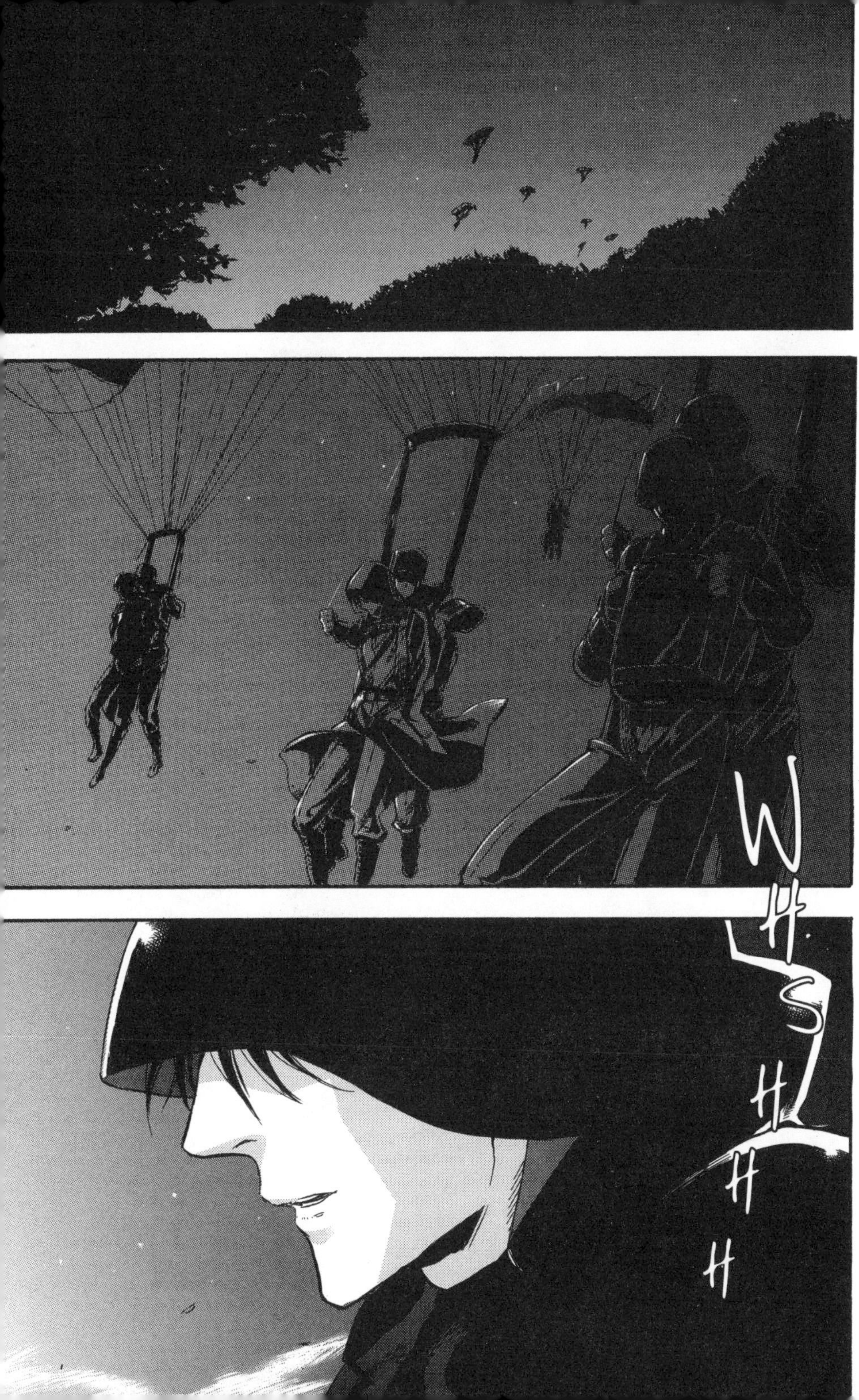
WHSHHH

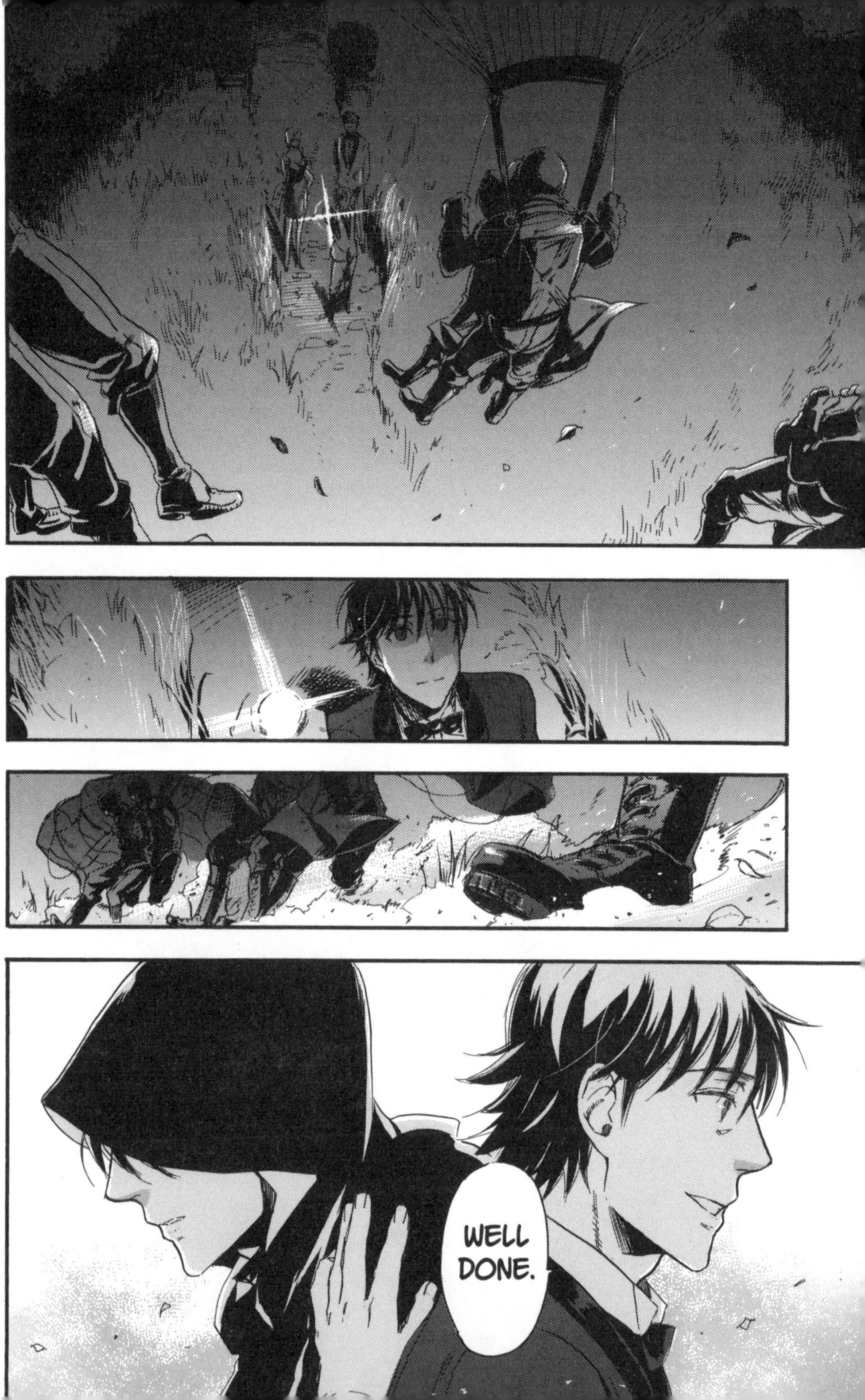
WELL DONE.

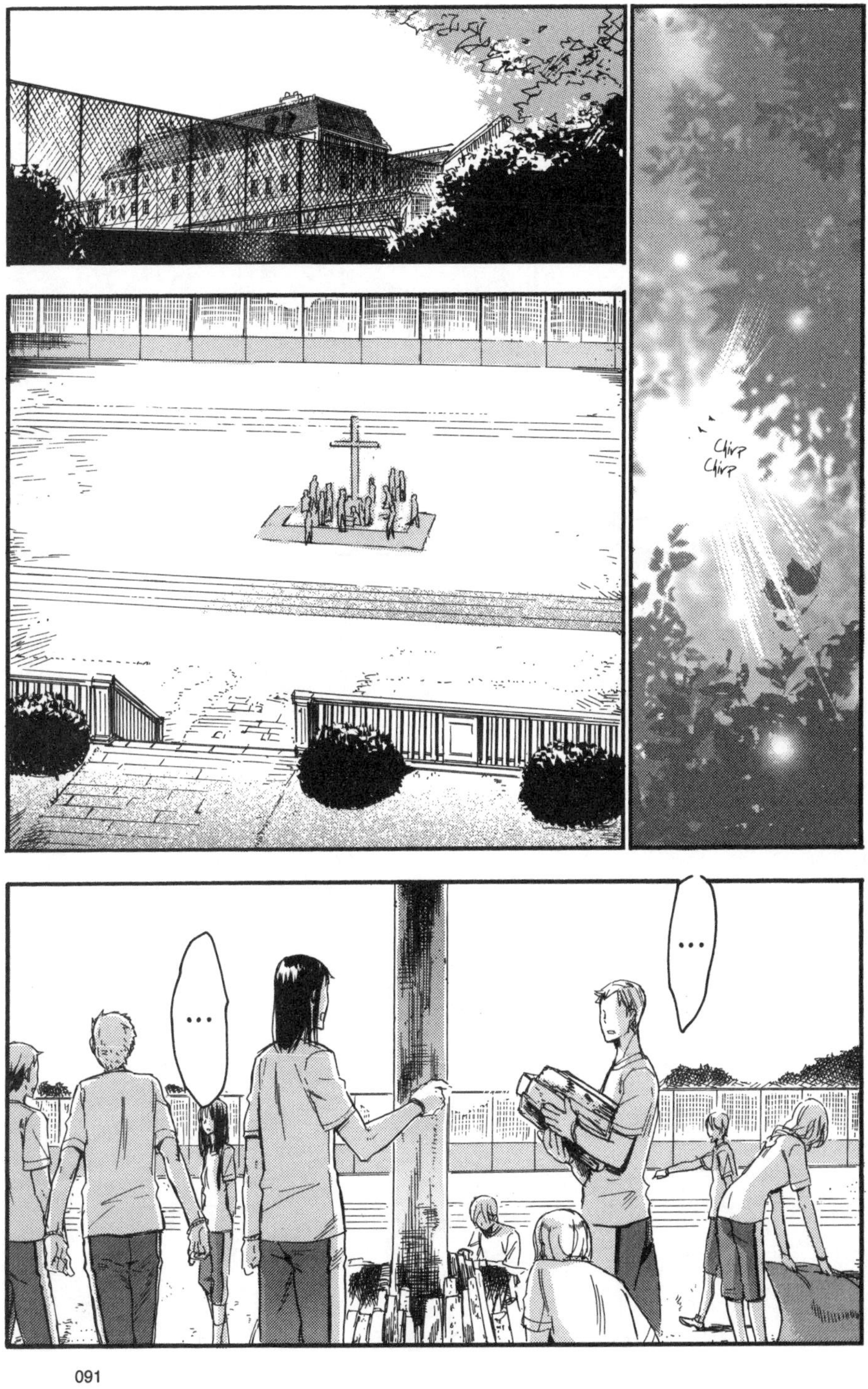
Chirp
Chirp
...
...

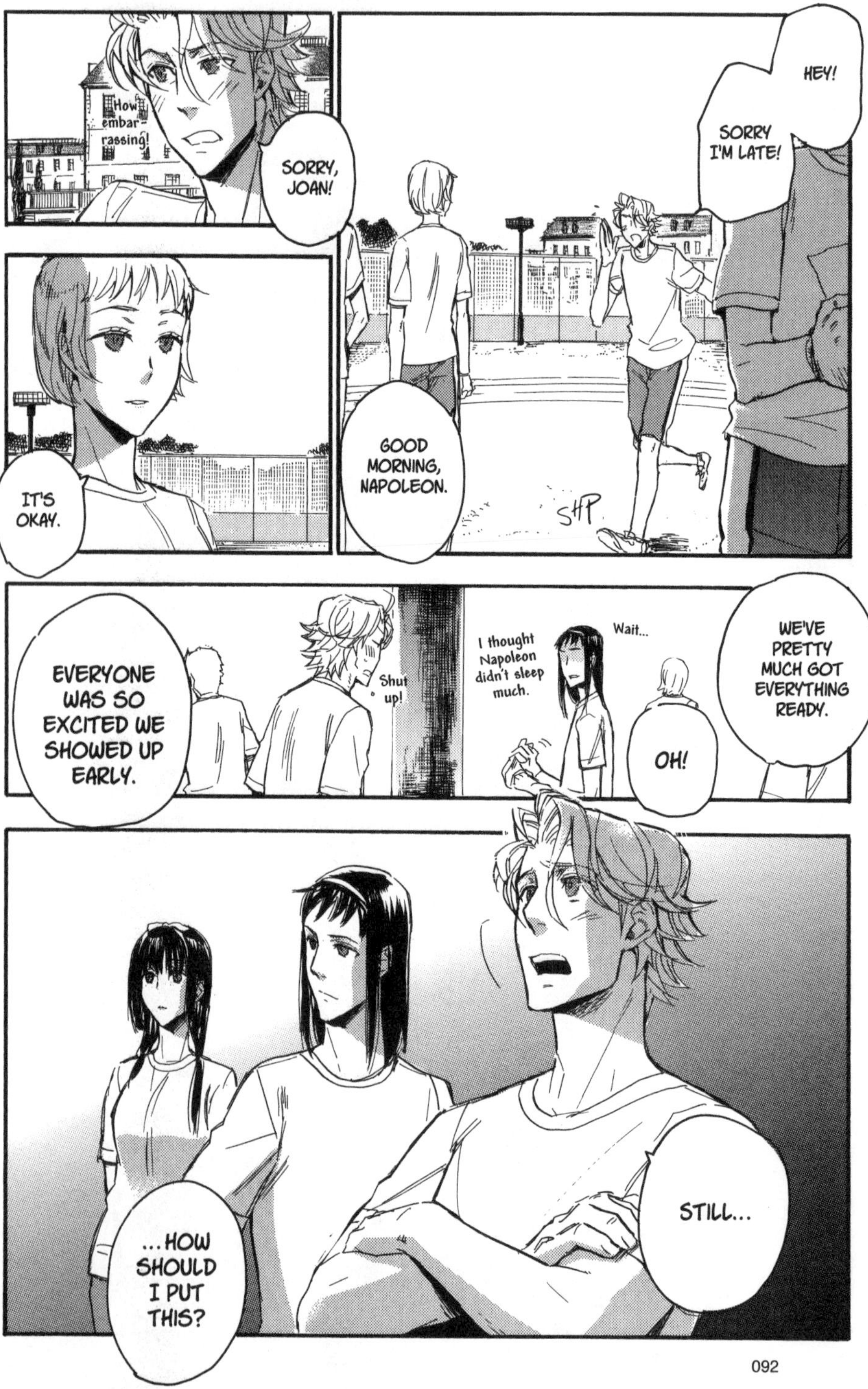
HEY!
SORRY I'M LATE!
GOOD MORNING, NAPOLEON.
SHP
How embarrassing!
SORRY, JOAN!
IT'S OKAY.
WE'VE PRETTY MUCH GOT EVERYTHING READY.
Wait...
I thought Napoleon didn't sleep much.
OH!
EVERYONE WAS SO EXCITED WE SHOWED UP EARLY.
Shut up!
STILL...
...HOW SHOULD I PUT THIS?

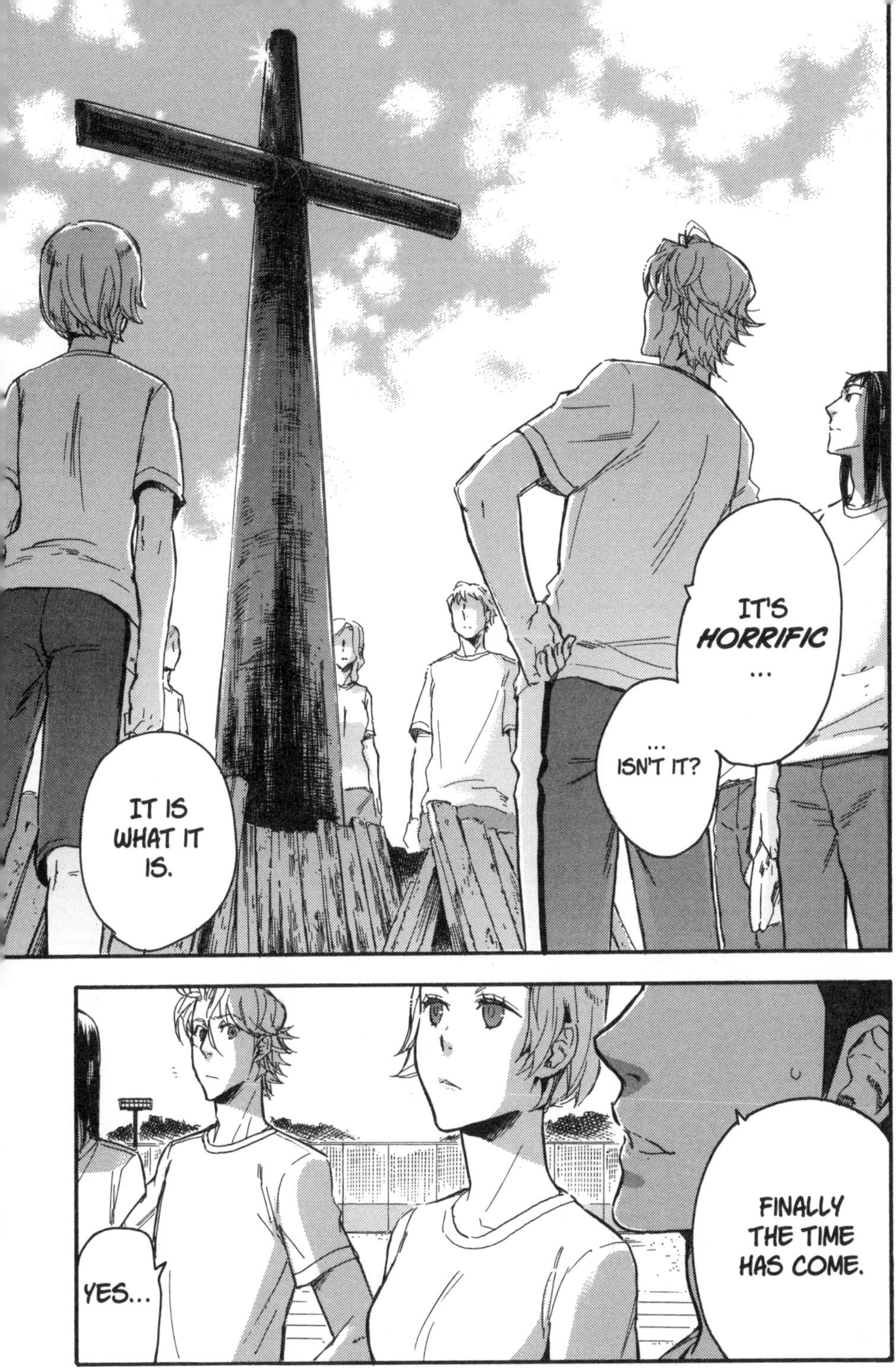
IT'S HORRIFIC ...
... ISN'T IT?
IT IS WHAT IT IS.
FINALLY THE TIME HAS COME.
YES...

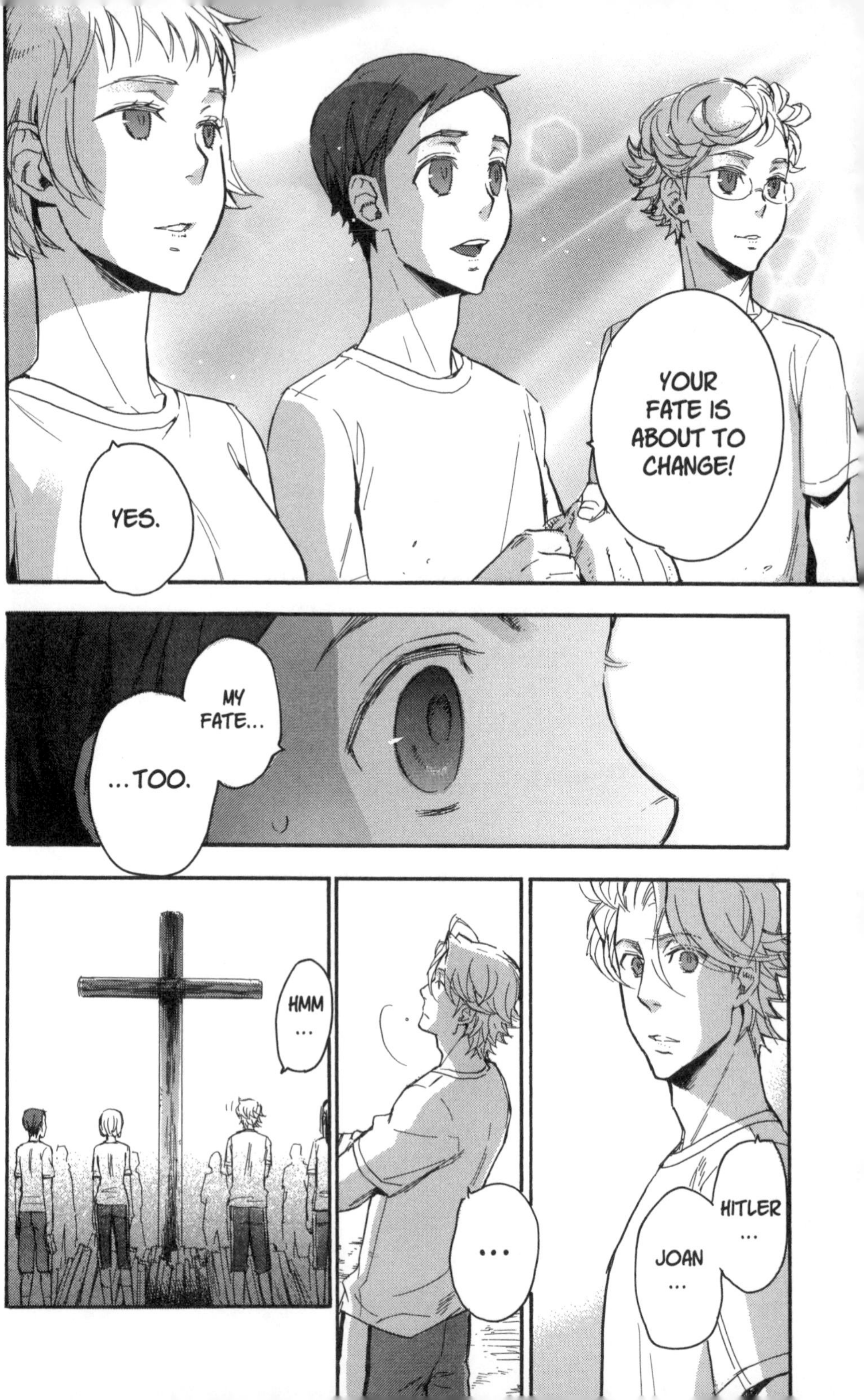
YOUR FATE IS ABOUT TO CHANGE!
YES.
MY FATE...
...TOO.
HITLER ...
JOAN ...
...
HMM ...

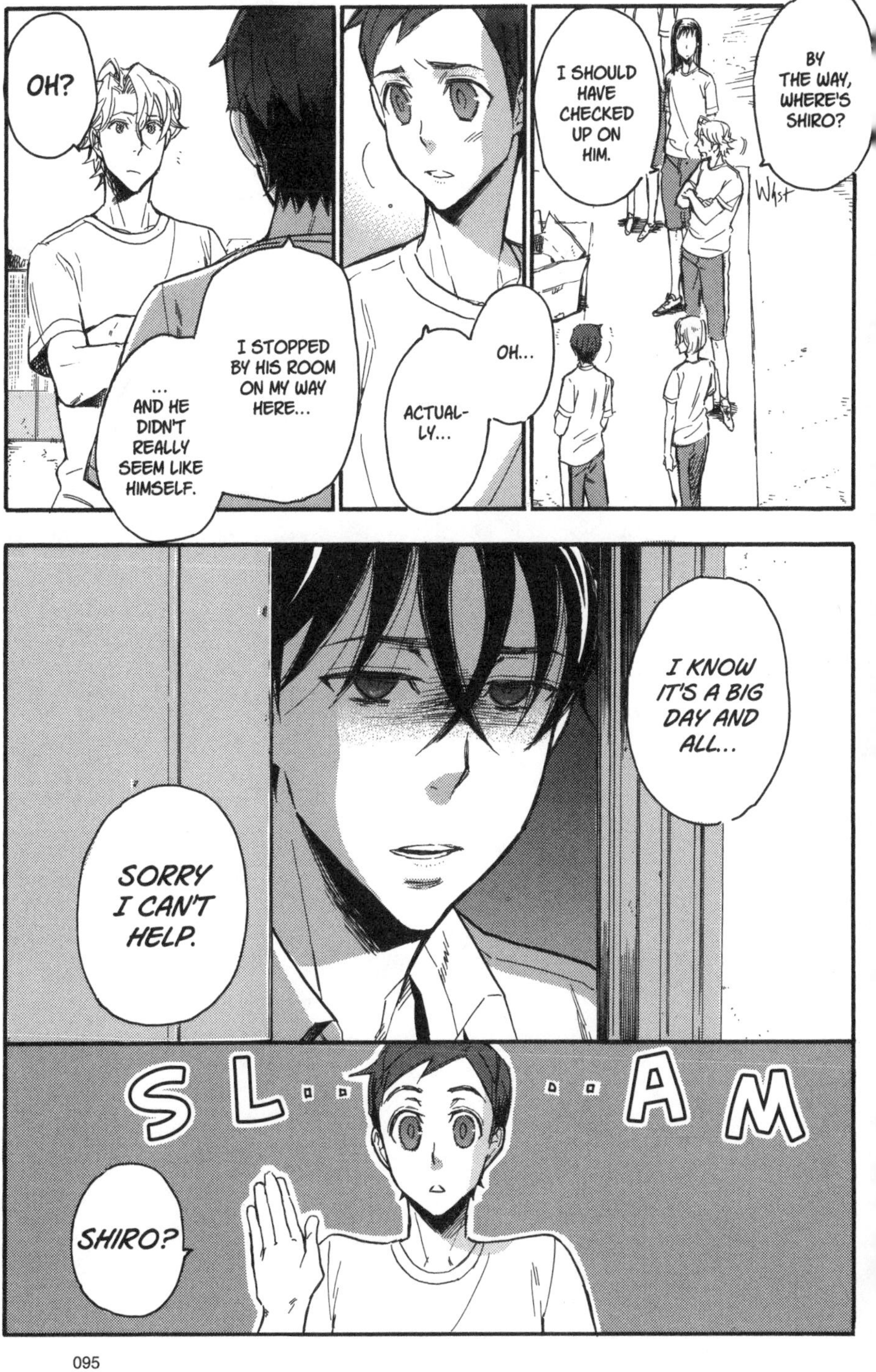
BY THE WAY, WHERE'S SHIRO?
I SHOULD HAVE CHECKED UP ON HIM.
OH... ACTUAL-LY...
OH?
I STOPPED BY HIS ROOM ON MY WAY HERE...
...AND HE DIDN'T REALLY SEEM LIKE HIMSELF.
I KNOW IT'S A BIG DAY AND ALL...
SORRY I CAN'T HELP.
SL...AM
SHIRO?

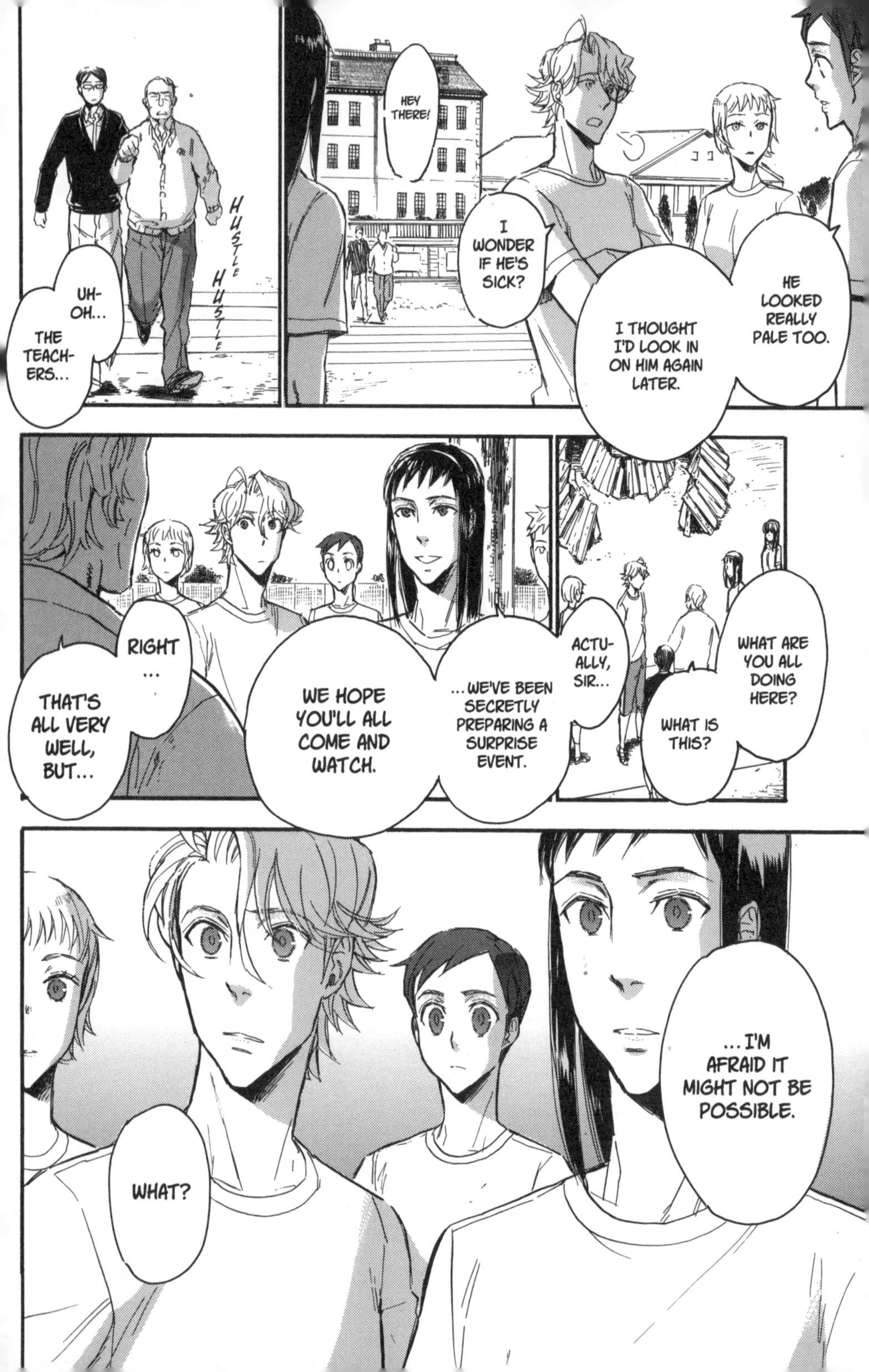
I WONDER IF HE'S SICK?
HE LOOKED REALLY PALE TOO.
I THOUGHT I'D LOOK IN ON HIM AGAIN LATER.
HEY THERE!
HUSTLE HUSTLE
UH-OH... THE TEACH-ERS...
WHAT ARE YOU ALL DOING HERE?
WHAT IS THIS?
ACTU-ALLY, SIR...
...WE'VE BEEN SECRETLY PREPARING A SURPRISE EVENT.
WE HOPE YOU'LL ALL COME AND WATCH.
RIGHT...
THAT'S ALL VERY WELL, BUT...
...I'M AFRAID IT MIGHT NOT BE POSSIBLE.
WHAT?

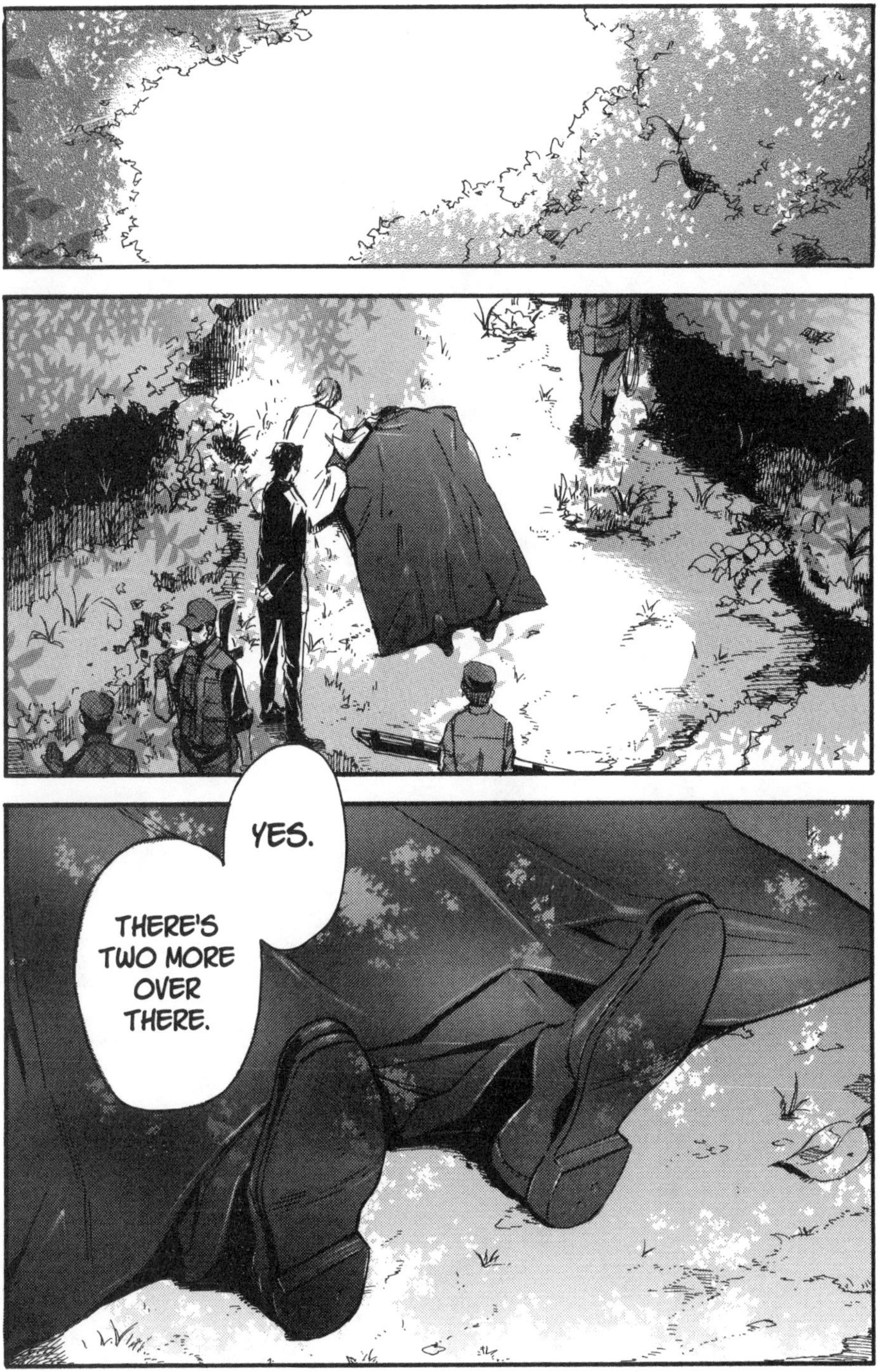
YES.
THERE'S TWO MORE OVER THERE.

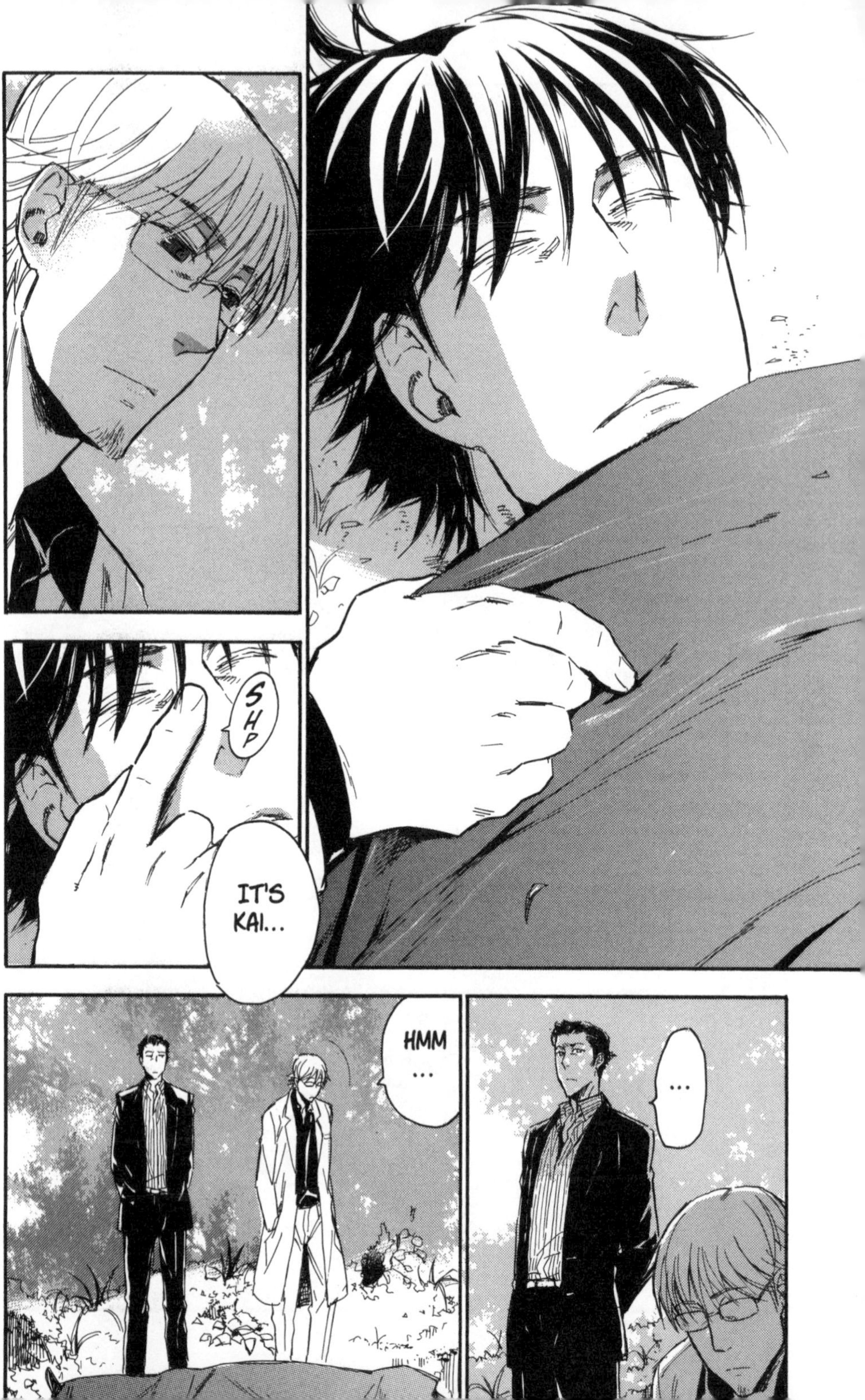
SHP
IT'S KAI...
...
HMM ...

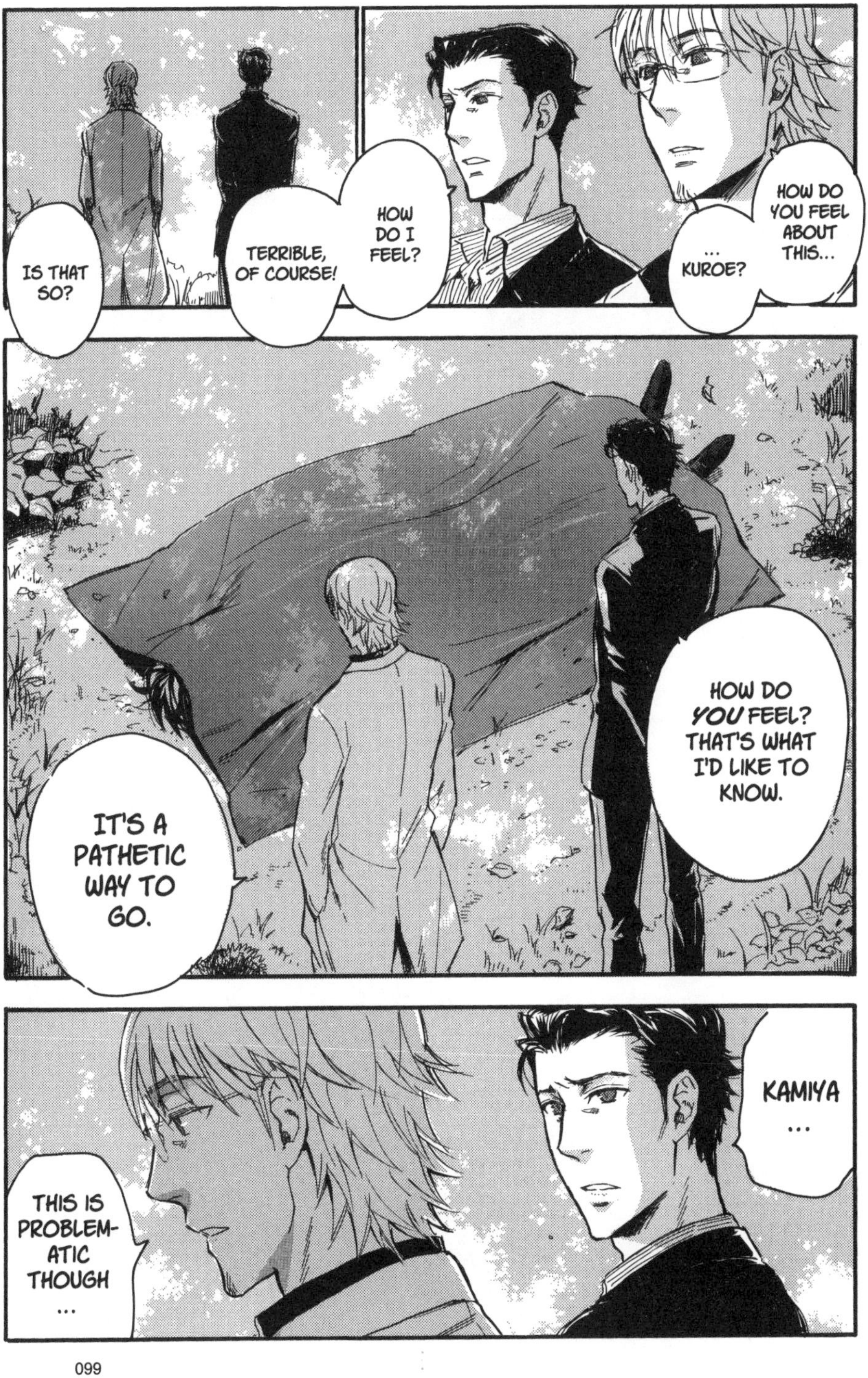
HOW DO YOU FEEL ABOUT THIS...
...KUROE?
HOW DO I FEEL?
TERRIBLE, OF COURSE!
IS THAT SO?
HOW DO *YOU* FEEL? THAT'S WHAT I'D LIKE TO KNOW.
IT'S A PATHETIC WAY TO GO.
KAMIYA...
THIS IS PROBLEM-ATIC THOUGH...

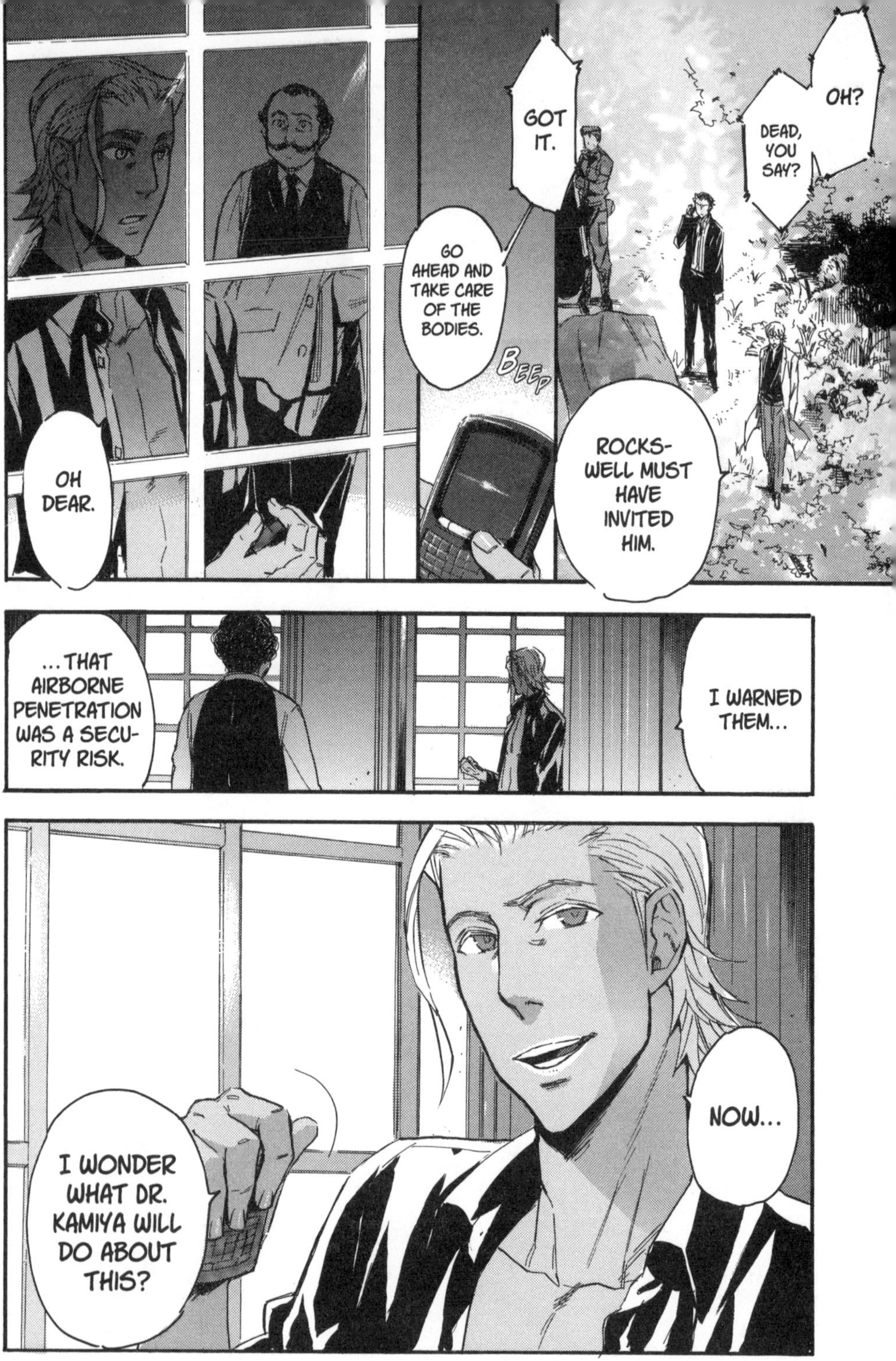
OH?
DEAD, YOU SAY?
GOT IT.
ROCKS-WELL MUST HAVE INVITED HIM.
GO AHEAD AND TAKE CARE OF THE BODIES.
BEEP
OH DEAR.
I WARNED THEM...
...THAT AIRBORNE PENETRATION WAS A SECU-RITY RISK.
NOW...
I WONDER WHAT DR. KAMIYA WILL DO ABOUT THIS?

# CHAPTER sixteen

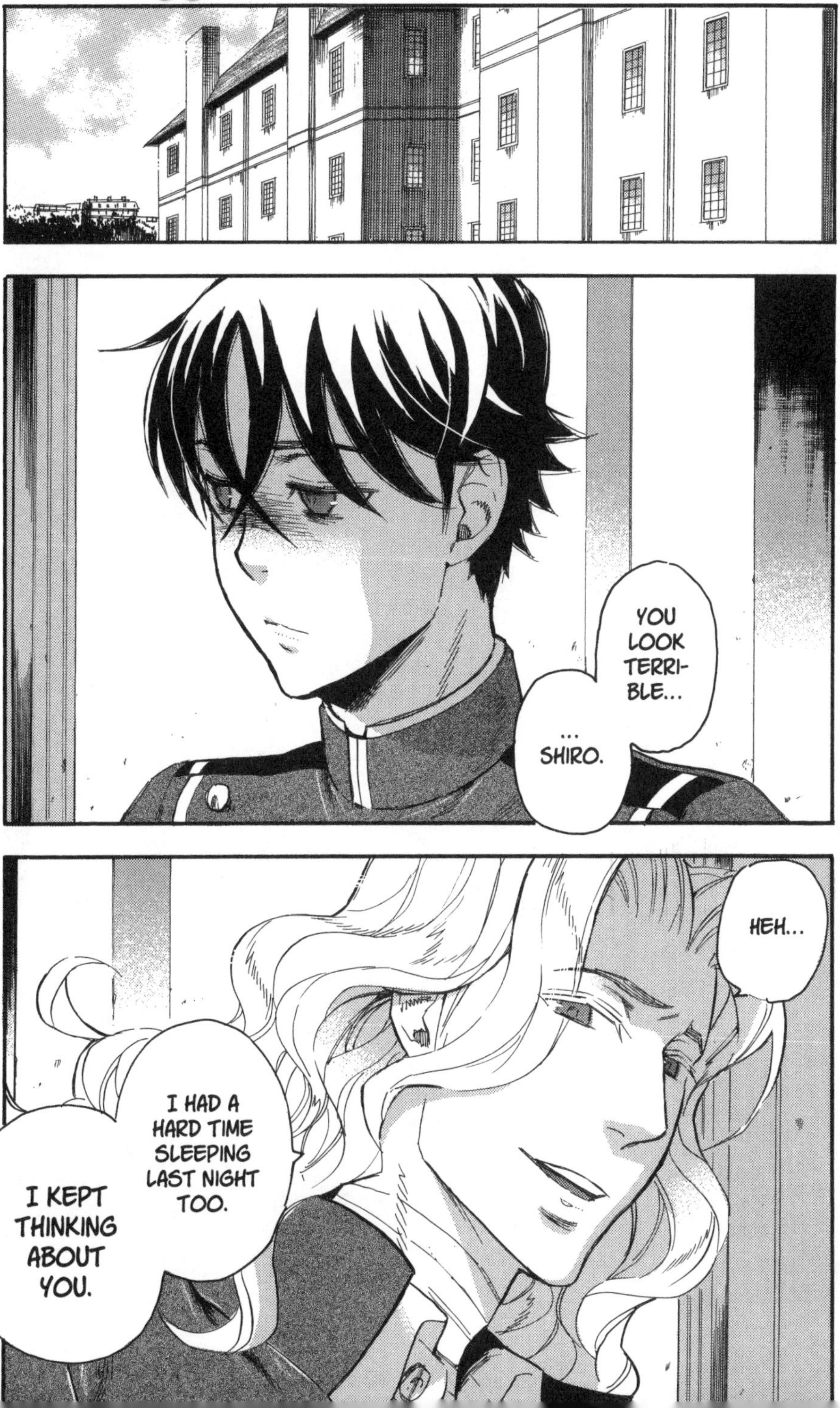
YOU LOOK TERRIBLE...
...SHIRO.
HEH...
I HAD A HARD TIME SLEEPING LAST NIGHT TOO.
I KEPT THINKING ABOUT YOU.

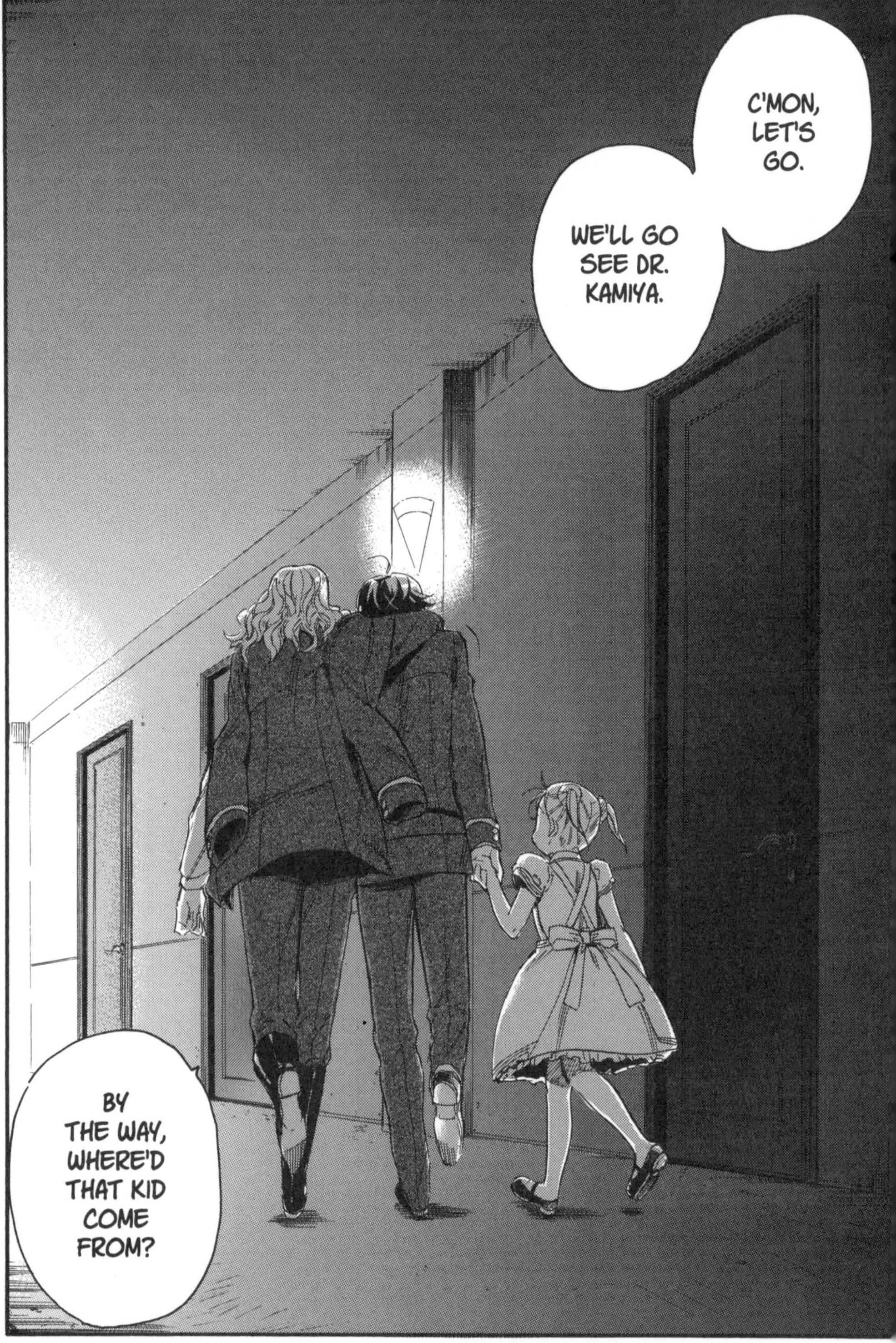
C'MON, LET'S GO.
WE'LL GO SEE DR. KAMIYA.
BY THE WAY, WHERE'D THAT KID COME FROM?

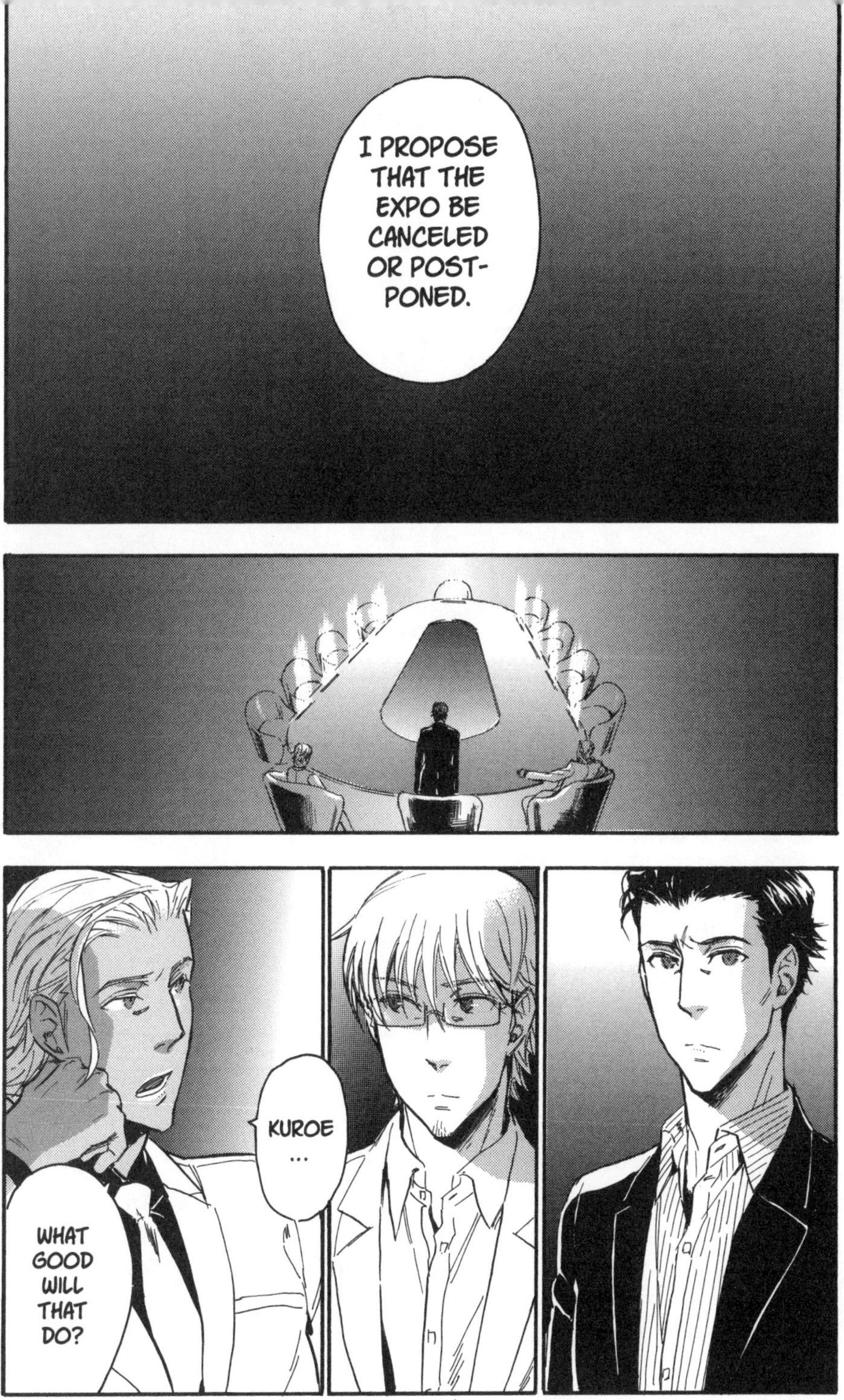
I PROPOSE THAT THE EXPO BE CANCELED OR POST-PONED.
KUROE ...
WHAT GOOD WILL THAT DO?

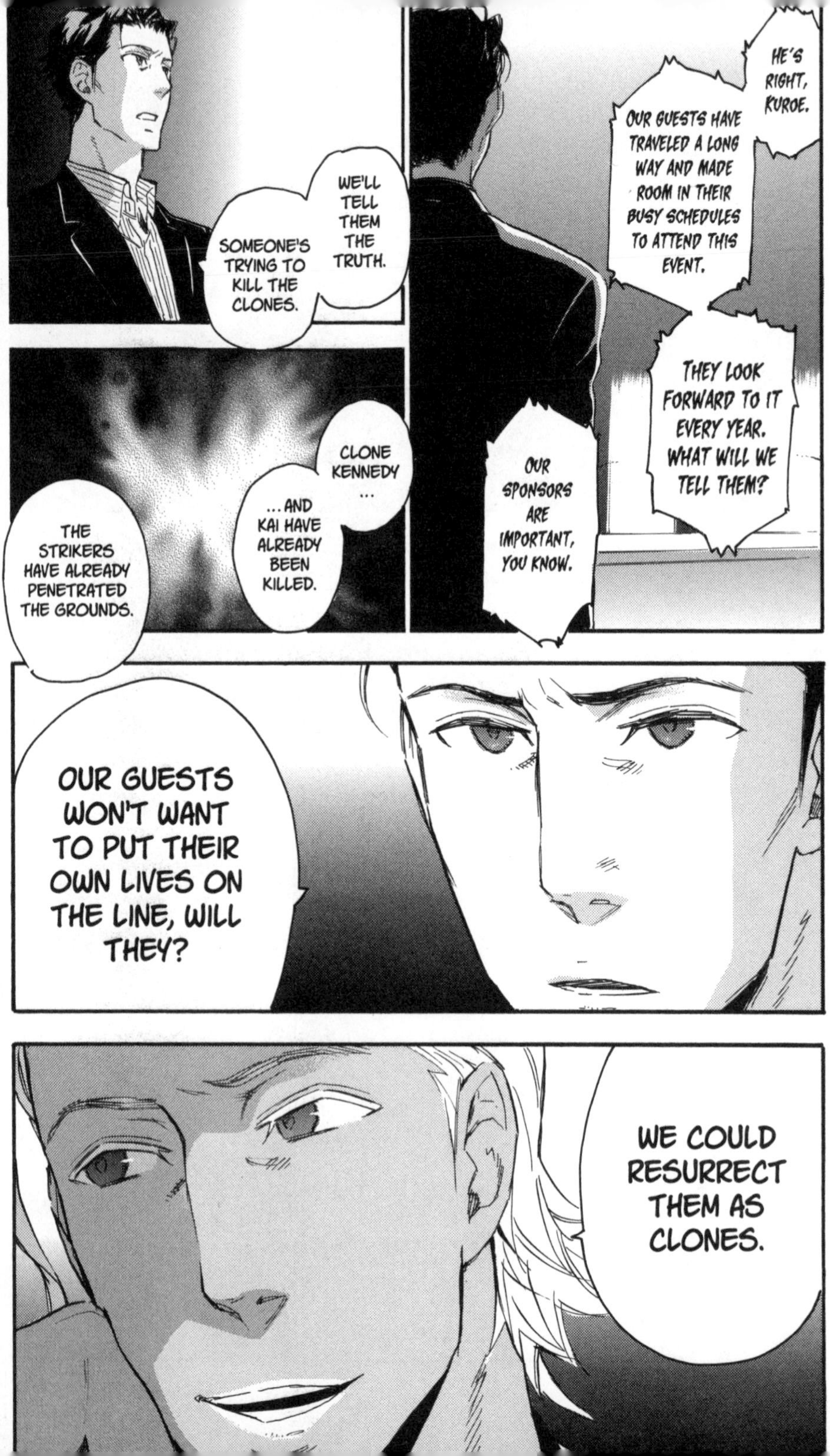
HE'S RIGHT, KUROE.
OUR GUESTS HAVE TRAVELED A LONG WAY AND MADE ROOM IN THEIR BUSY SCHEDULES TO ATTEND THIS EVENT.
THEY LOOK FORWARD TO IT EVERY YEAR. WHAT WILL WE TELL THEM?
OUR SPONSORS ARE IMPORTANT, YOU KNOW.
WE'LL TELL THEM THE TRUTH.
SOMEONE'S TRYING TO KILL THE CLONES.
CLONE KENNEDY ...
...AND KAI HAVE ALREADY BEEN KILLED.
THE STRIKERS HAVE ALREADY PENETRATED THE GROUNDS.
OUR GUESTS WON'T WANT TO PUT THEIR OWN LIVES ON THE LINE, WILL THEY?
WE COULD RESURRECT THEM AS CLONES.

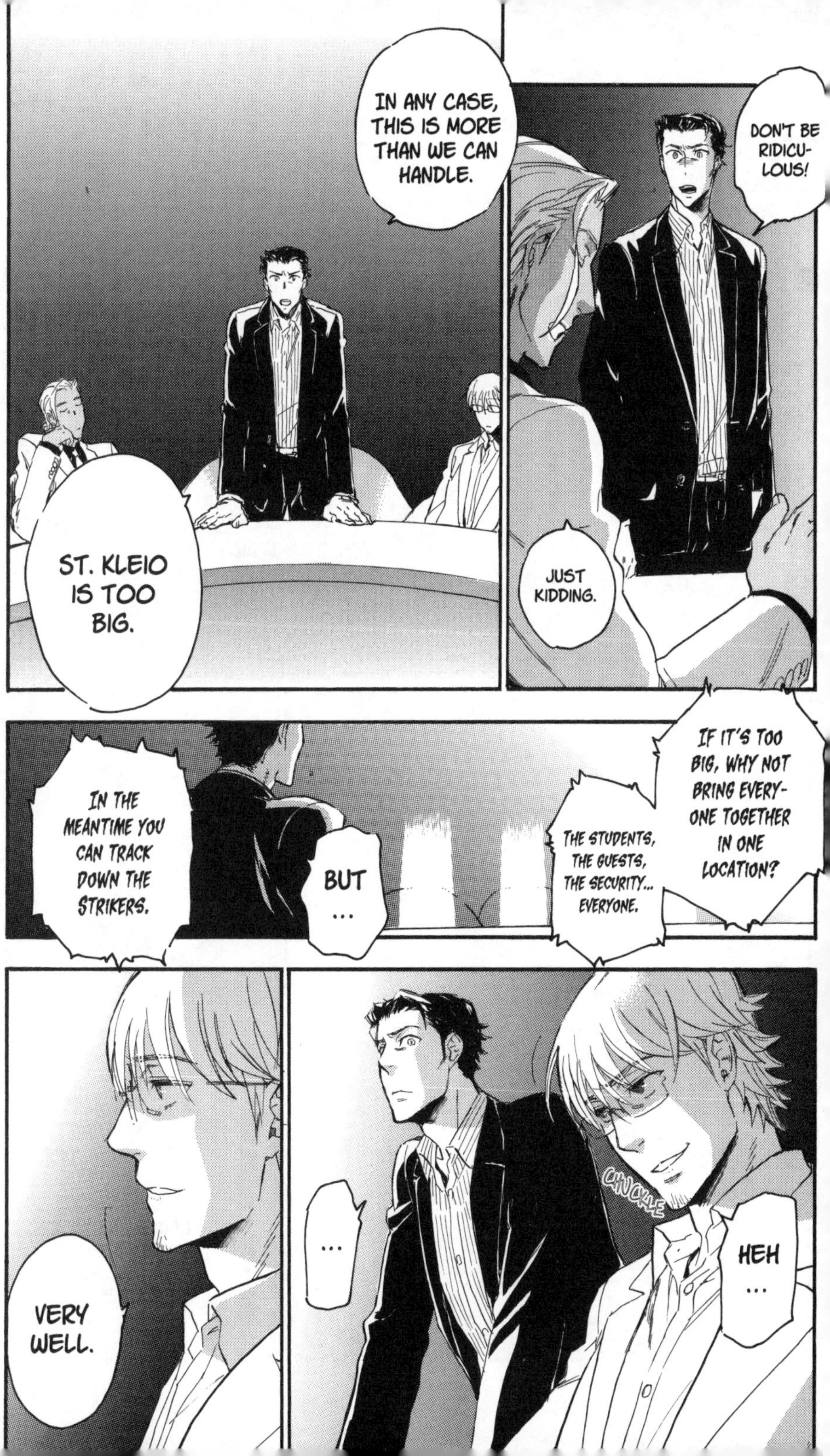
DON'T BE RIDICULOUS!
JUST KIDDING.
IN ANY CASE, THIS IS MORE THAN WE CAN HANDLE.
ST. KLEIO IS TOO BIG.
IF IT'S TOO BIG, WHY NOT BRING EVERYONE TOGETHER IN ONE LOCATION?
THE STUDENTS, THE GUESTS, THE SECURITY... EVERYONE.
BUT ...
IN THE MEANTIME YOU CAN TRACK DOWN THE STRIKERS.
HEH ...
CHUCKLE
...
VERY WELL.

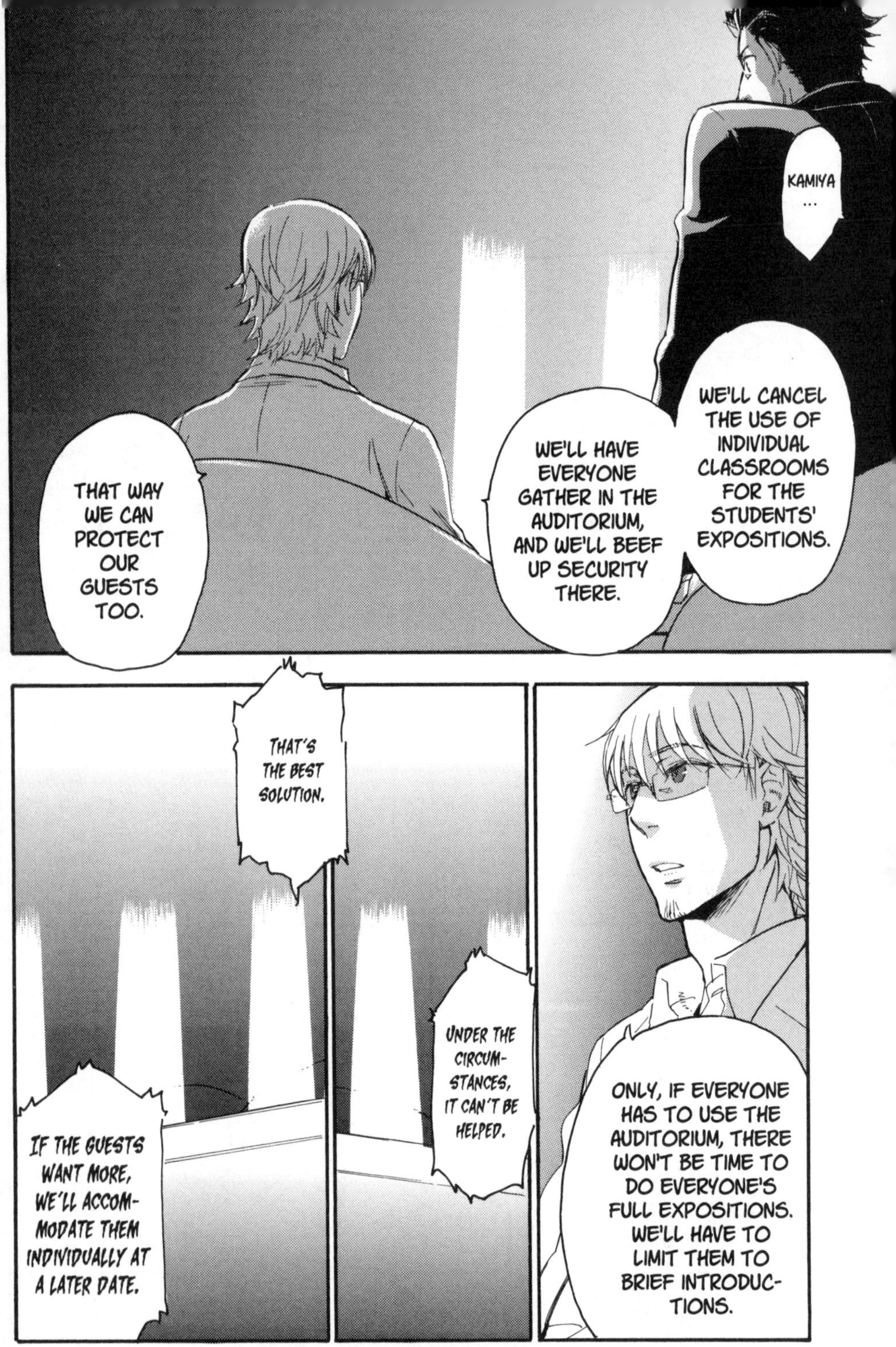
KAMIYA ...
WE'LL CANCEL THE USE OF INDIVIDUAL CLASSROOMS FOR THE STUDENTS' EXPOSITIONS.
WE'LL HAVE EVERYONE GATHER IN THE AUDITORIUM, AND WE'LL BEEF UP SECURITY THERE.
THAT WAY WE CAN PROTECT OUR GUESTS TOO.
ONLY, IF EVERYONE HAS TO USE THE AUDITORIUM, THERE WON'T BE TIME TO DO EVERYONE'S FULL EXPOSITIONS. WE'LL HAVE TO LIMIT THEM TO BRIEF INTRODUCTIONS.
THAT'S THE BEST SOLUTION.
UNDER THE CIRCUMSTANCES, IT CAN'T BE HELPED.
IF THE GUESTS WANT MORE, WE'LL ACCOMMODATE THEM INDIVIDUALLY AT A LATER DATE.

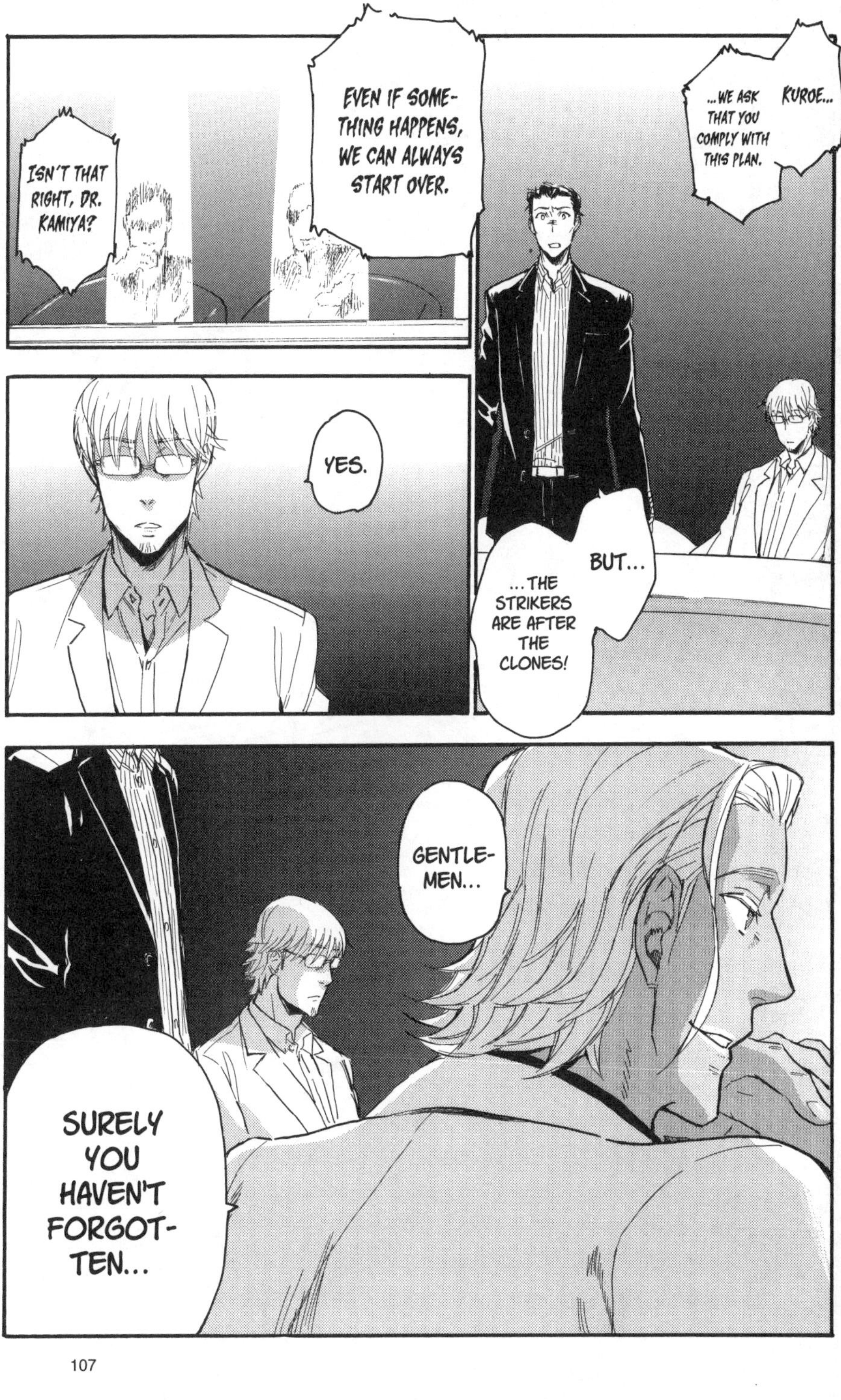
KUROE...
...WE ASK THAT YOU COMPLY WITH THIS PLAN.
BUT...
...THE STRIKERS ARE AFTER THE CLONES!
EVEN IF SOME-THING HAPPENS, WE CAN ALWAYS START OVER.
ISN'T THAT RIGHT, DR. KAMIYA?
YES.
GENTLE-MEN...
SURELY YOU HAVEN'T FORGOT-TEN...

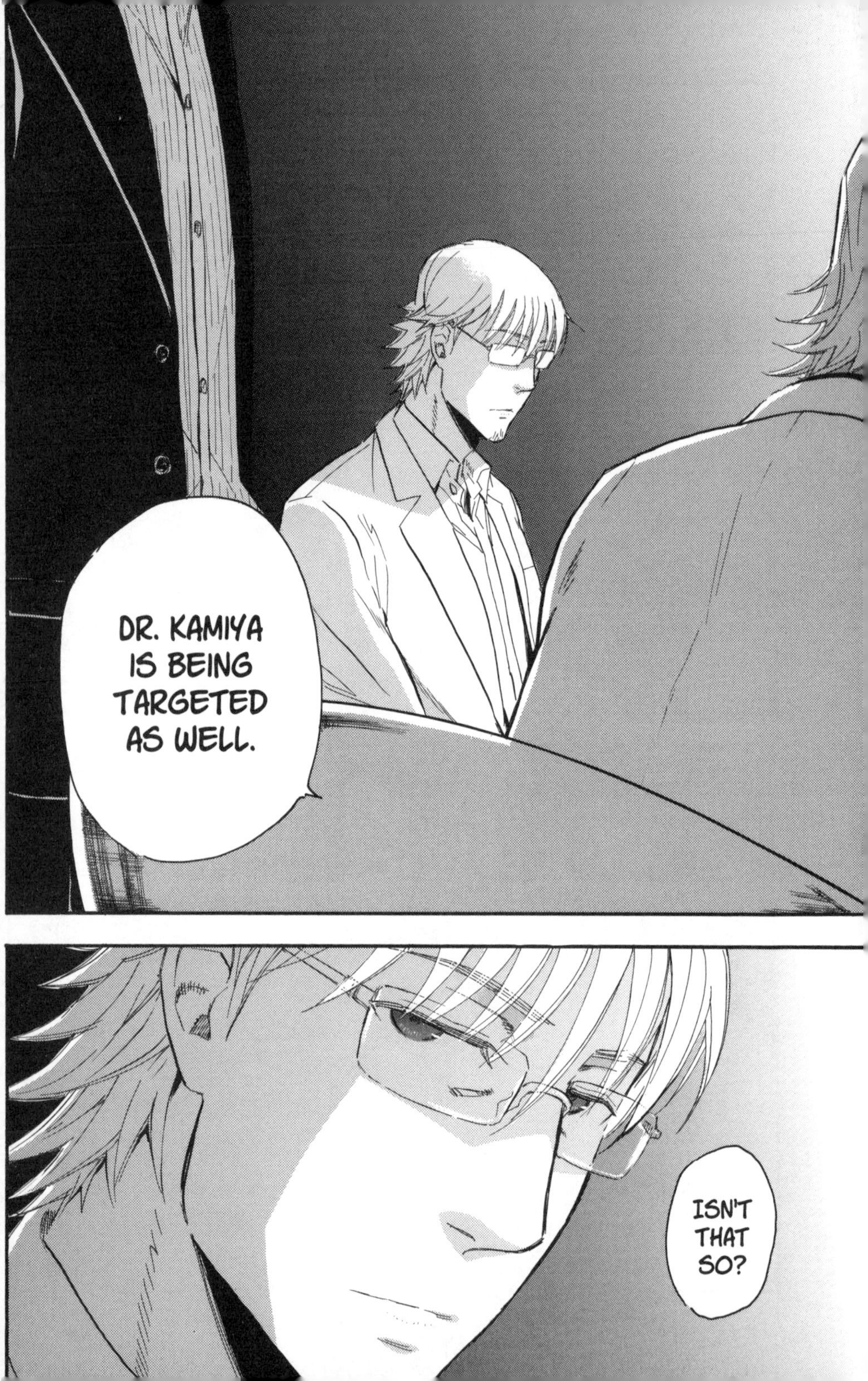
DR. KAMIYA IS BEING TARGETED AS WELL.
ISN'T THAT SO?

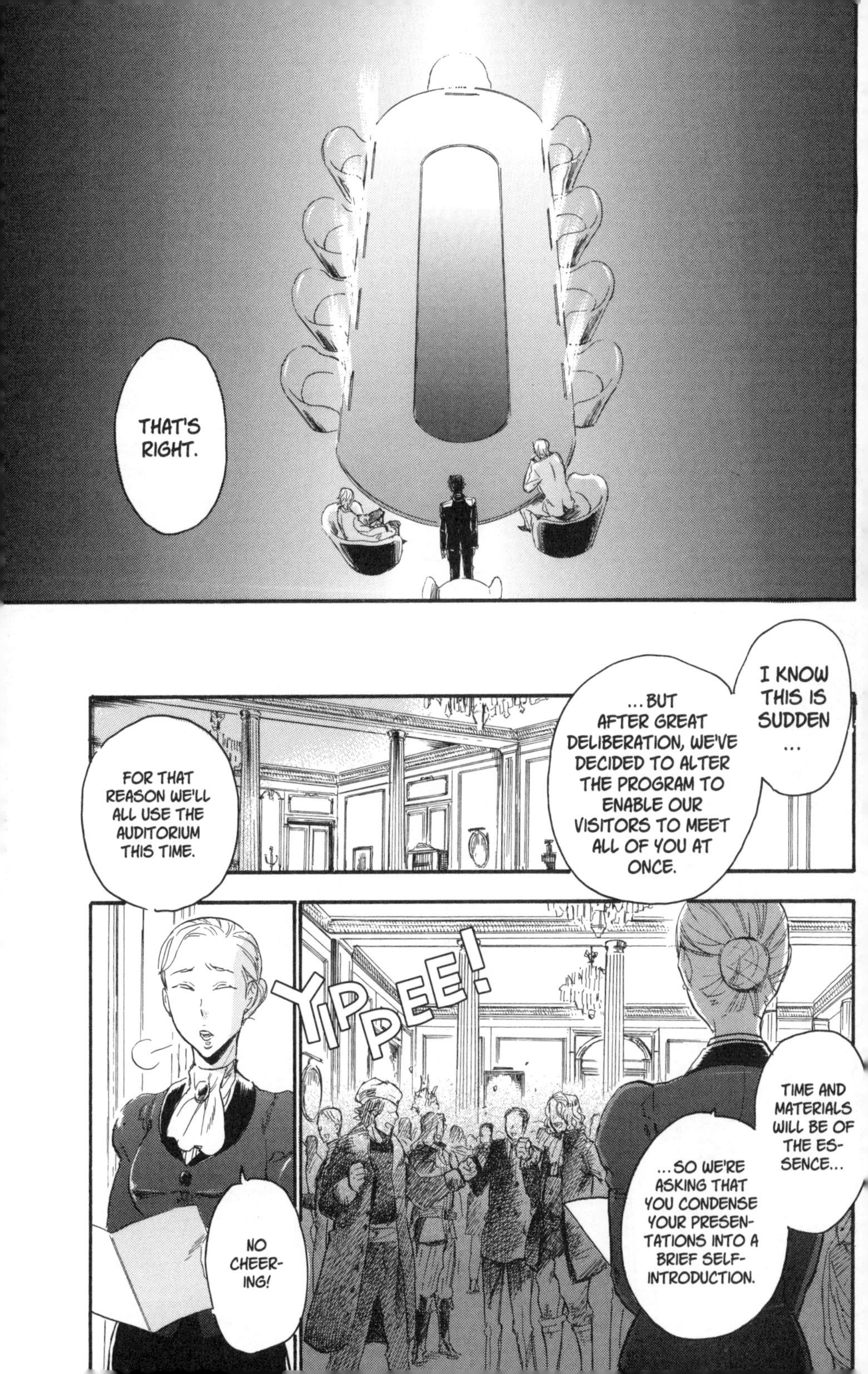
THAT'S RIGHT.
I KNOW THIS IS SUDDEN ...
...BUT AFTER GREAT DELIBERATION, WE'VE DECIDED TO ALTER THE PROGRAM TO ENABLE OUR VISITORS TO MEET ALL OF YOU AT ONCE.
FOR THAT REASON WE'LL ALL USE THE AUDITORIUM THIS TIME.
TIME AND MATERIALS WILL BE OF THE ES-SENCE...
...SO WE'RE ASKING THAT YOU CONDENSE YOUR PRESEN-TATIONS INTO A BRIEF SELF-INTRODUCTION.
YIPPEE!
NO CHEER-ING!

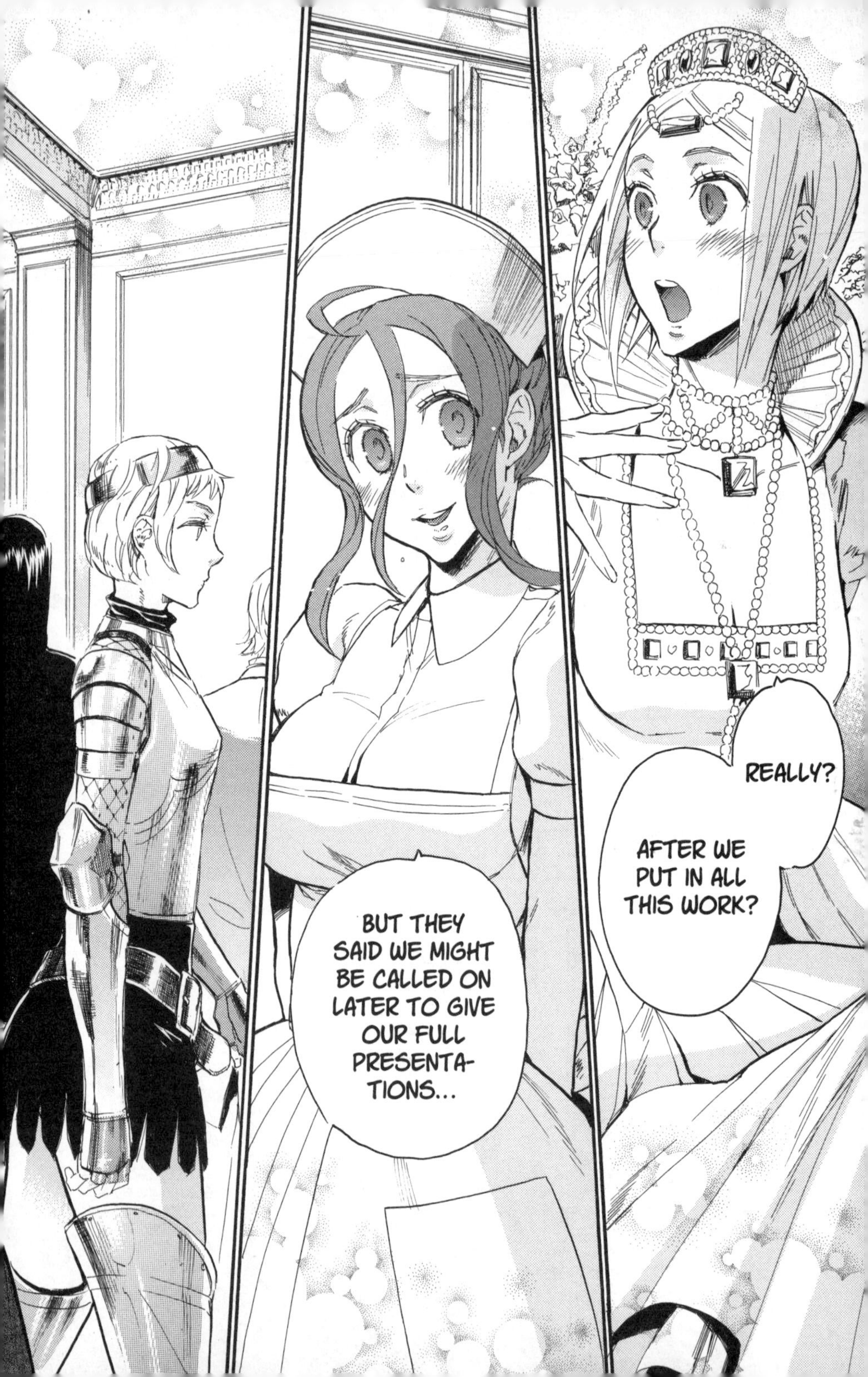
REALLY?
AFTER WE PUT IN ALL THIS WORK?
BUT THEY SAID WE MIGHT BE CALLED ON LATER TO GIVE OUR FULL PRESENTA-TIONS...

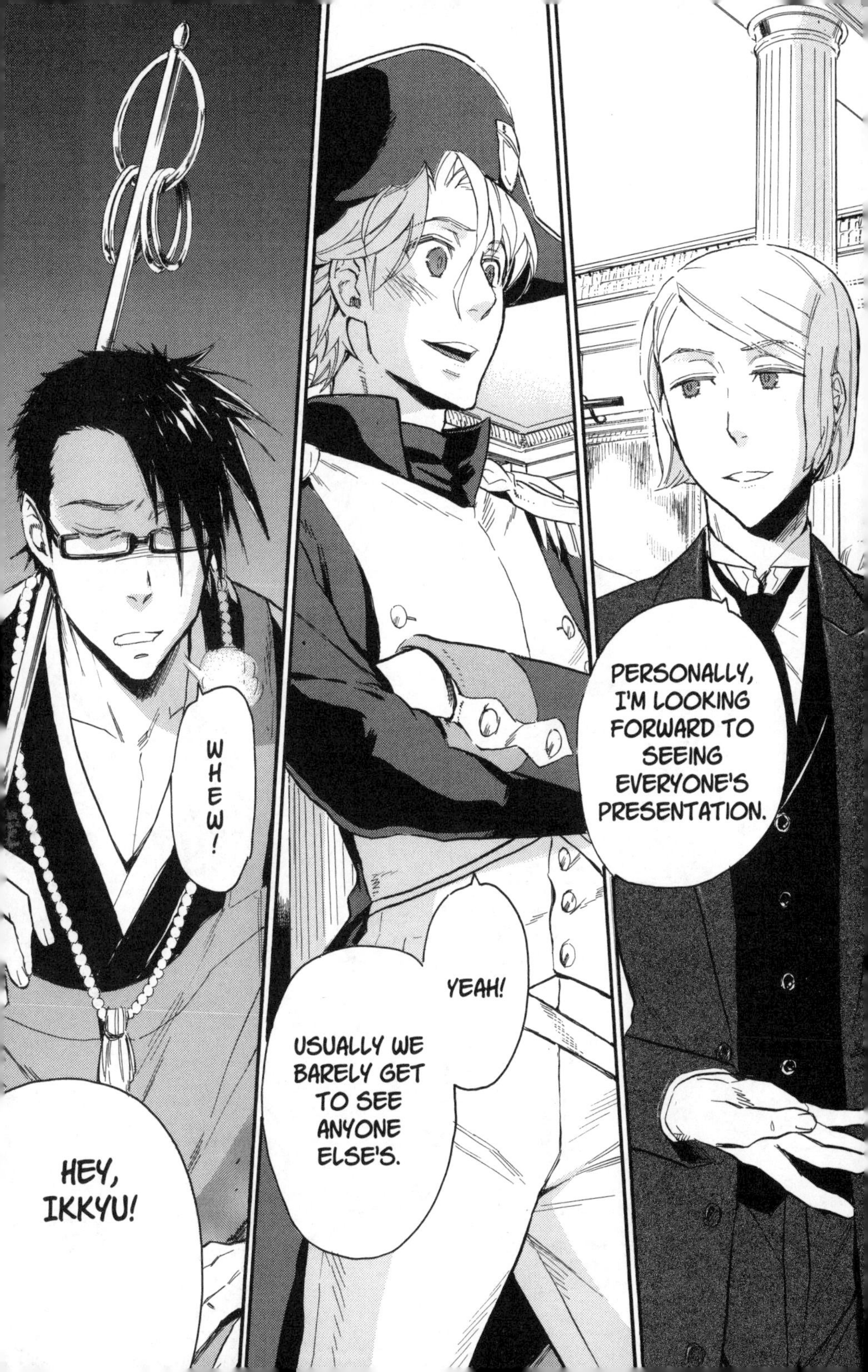
PERSONALLY, I'M LOOKING FORWARD TO SEEING EVERYONE'S PRESENTATION.
YEAH!
USUALLY WE BARELY GET TO SEE ANYONE ELSE'S.
WHEW!
HEY, IKKYU!

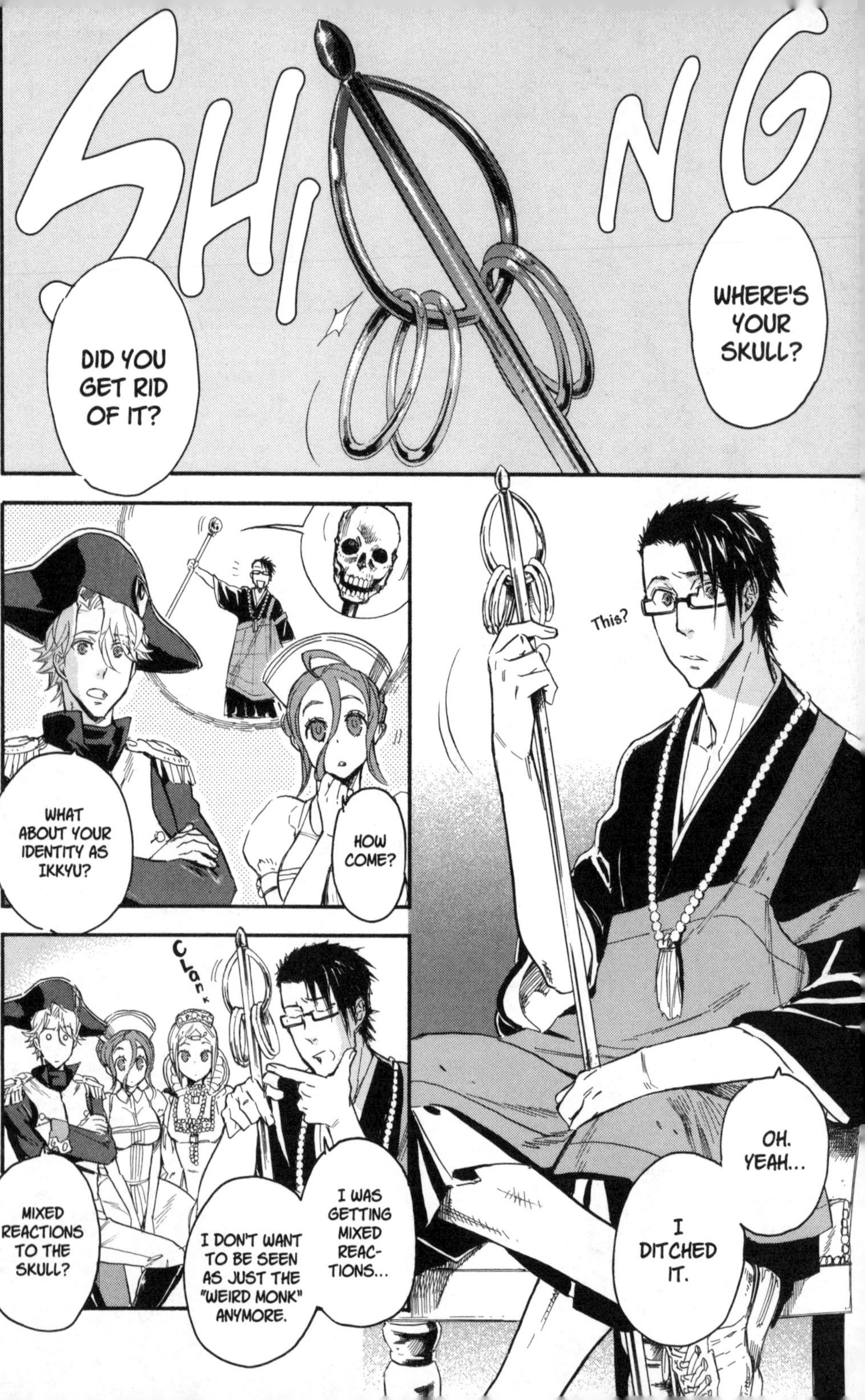
SHING
WHERE'S YOUR SKULL?
DID YOU GET RID OF IT?
This?
OH. YEAH...
I DITCHED IT.
HOW COME?
WHAT ABOUT YOUR IDENTITY AS IKKYU?
Clank
I WAS GETTING MIXED REAC-TIONS...
I DON'T WANT TO BE SEEN AS JUST THE "WEIRD MONK" ANYMORE.
MIXED REACTIONS TO THE SKULL?

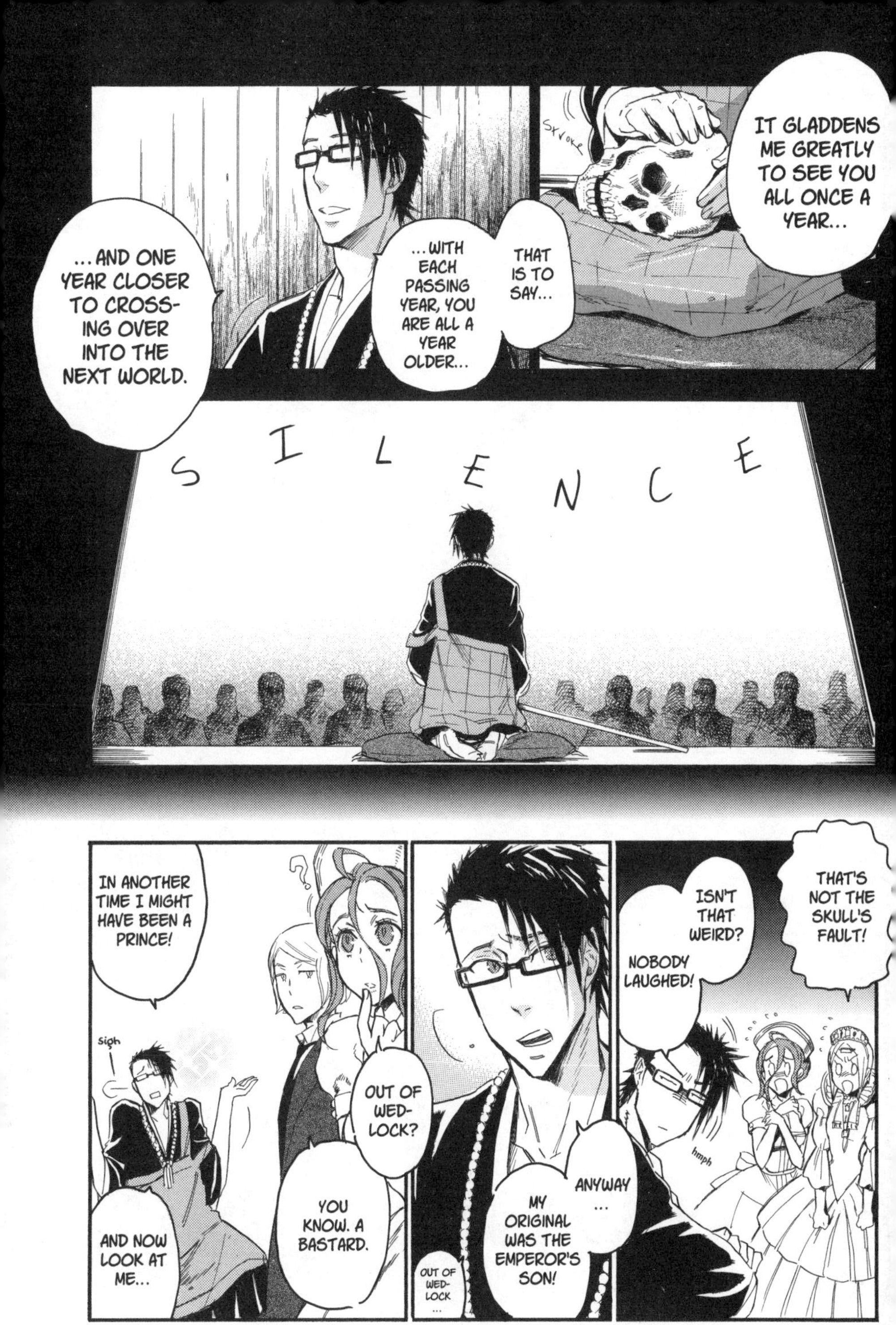
IT GLADDENS ME GREATLY TO SEE YOU ALL ONCE A YEAR...
THAT IS TO SAY...
...WITH EACH PASSING YEAR, YOU ARE ALL A YEAR OLDER...
...AND ONE YEAR CLOSER TO CROSS-ING OVER INTO THE NEXT WORLD.
SILENCE
THAT'S NOT THE SKULL'S FAULT!
ISN'T THAT WEIRD?
NOBODY LAUGHED!
hmph
ANYWAY...
MY ORIGINAL WAS THE EMPEROR'S SON!
OUT OF WED-LOCK...
OUT OF WED-LOCK?
YOU KNOW. A BASTARD.
IN ANOTHER TIME I MIGHT HAVE BEEN A PRINCE!
Sigh
AND NOW LOOK AT ME...

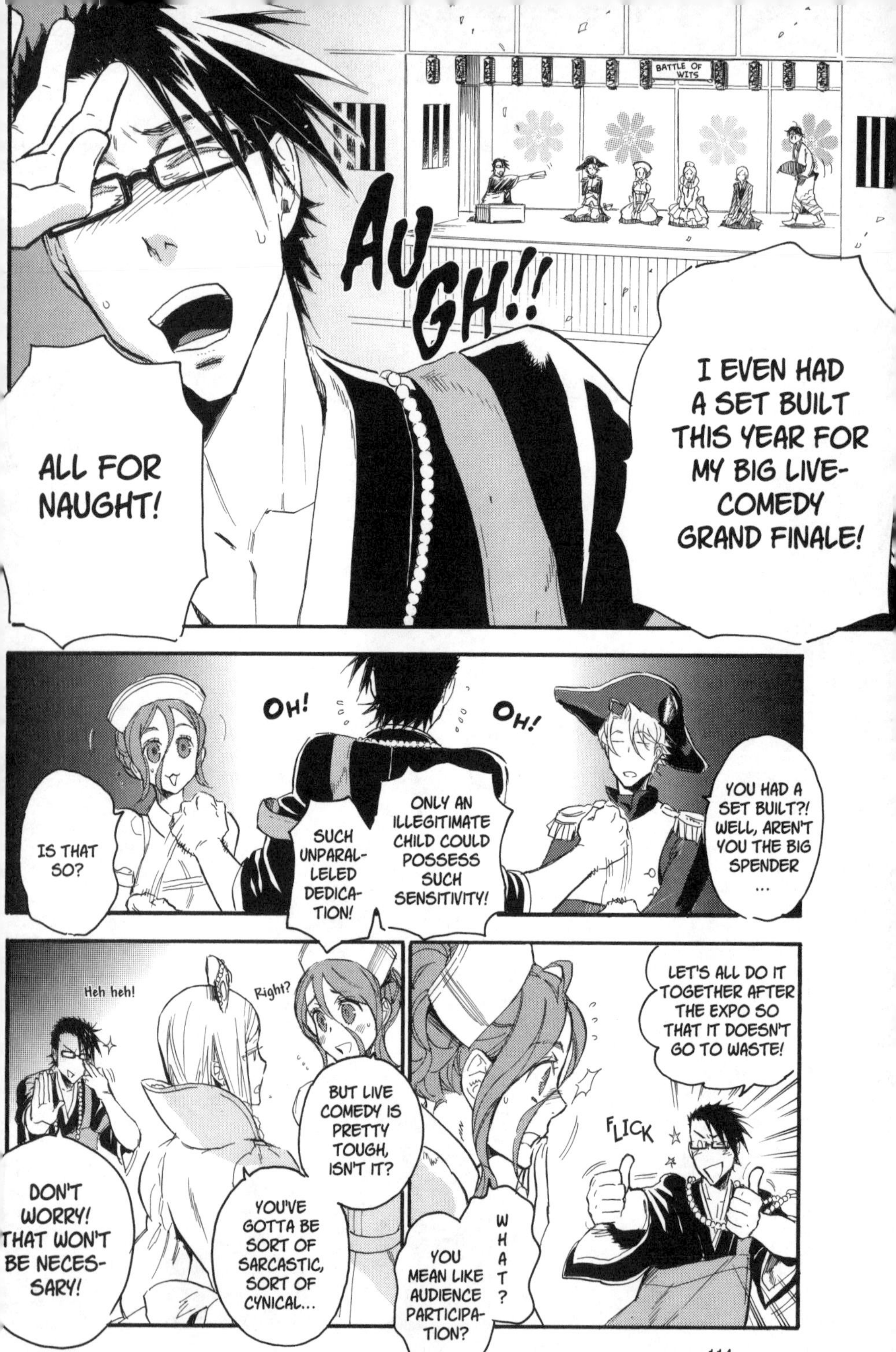
BATTLE OF WITS
I EVEN HAD A SET BUILT THIS YEAR FOR MY BIG LIVE-COMEDY GRAND FINALE!
AUGH!!
ALL FOR NAUGHT!
OH!
YOU HAD A SET BUILT?! WELL, AREN'T YOU THE BIG SPENDER ...
ONLY AN ILLEGITIMATE CHILD COULD POSSESS SUCH SENSITIVITY!
OH!
SUCH UNPARALLELED DEDICATION!
IS THAT SO?
LET'S ALL DO IT TOGETHER AFTER THE EXPO SO THAT IT DOESN'T GO TO WASTE!
FLICK
WHAT?
Right?
BUT LIVE COMEDY IS PRETTY TOUGH, ISN'T IT?
YOU'VE GOTTA BE SORT OF SARCASTIC, SORT OF CYNICAL...
YOU MEAN LIKE AUDIENCE PARTICIPATION?
Heh heh!
DON'T WORRY! THAT WON'T BE NECESSARY!

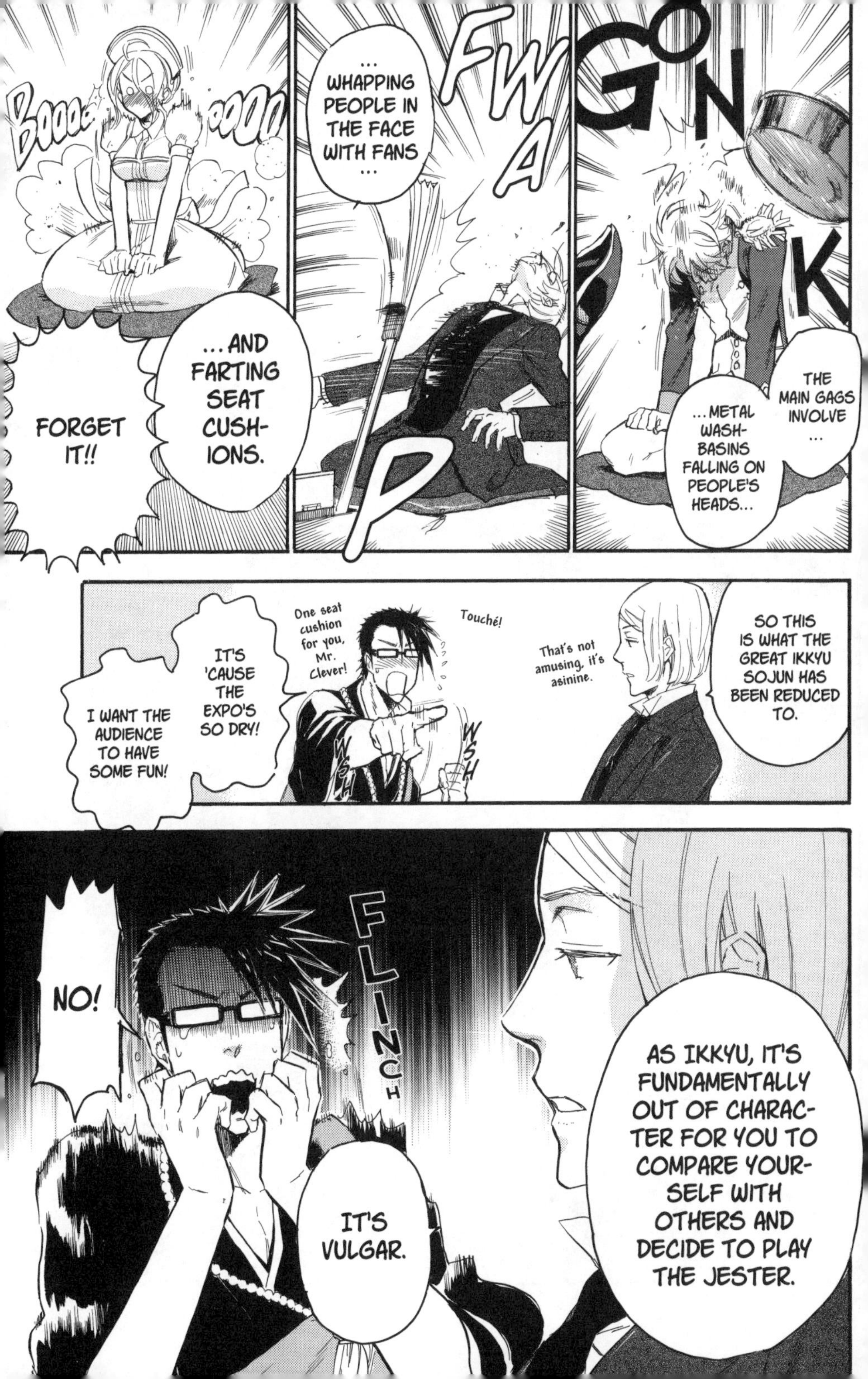
GONK
THE MAIN GAGS INVOLVE ...
...METAL WASH-BASINS FALLING ON PEOPLE'S HEADS...
FWAP
... WHAPPING PEOPLE IN THE FACE WITH FANS ...
...AND FARTING SEAT CUSH-IONS.
FORGET IT!!
SO THIS IS WHAT THE GREAT IKKYU SOJUN HAS BEEN REDUCED TO.
That's not amusing, it's asinine.
Touché!
One seat cushion for you, Mr. Clever!
WSH
WSH
IT'S 'CAUSE THE EXPO'S SO DRY!
I WANT THE AUDIENCE TO HAVE SOME FUN!
AS IKKYU, IT'S FUNDAMENTALLY OUT OF CHARAC-TER FOR YOU TO COMPARE YOUR-SELF WITH OTHERS AND DECIDE TO PLAY THE JESTER.
IT'S VULGAR.
FLINCH
NO!

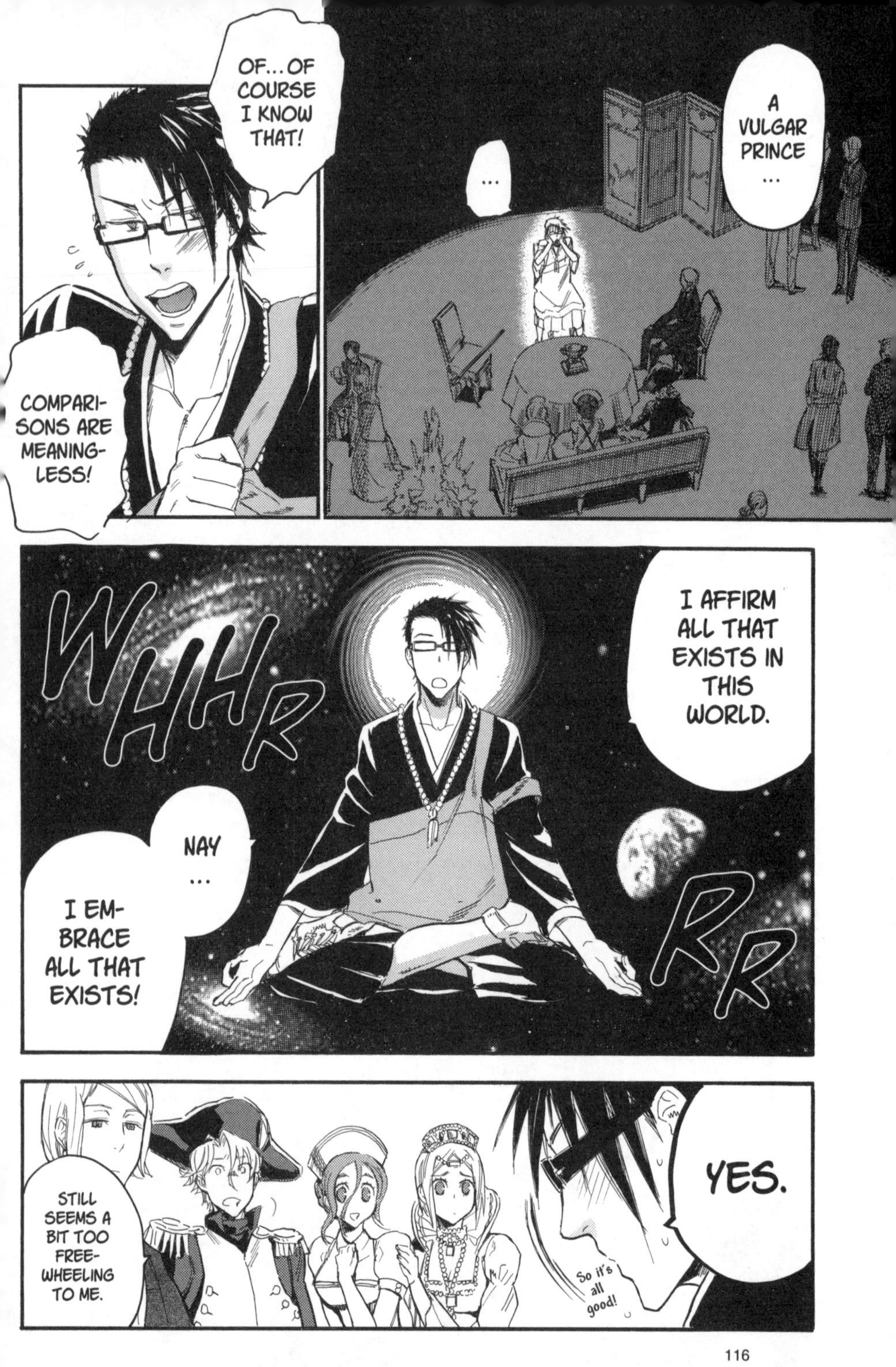
A VULGAR PRINCE ...
...
OF... OF COURSE I KNOW THAT!
COMPARISONS ARE MEANINGLESS!
I AFFIRM ALL THAT EXISTS IN THIS WORLD.
WHHR
RR
NAY ...
I EMBRACE ALL THAT EXISTS!
YES.
So it's all good!
STILL SEEMS A BIT TOO FREE-WHEELING TO ME.

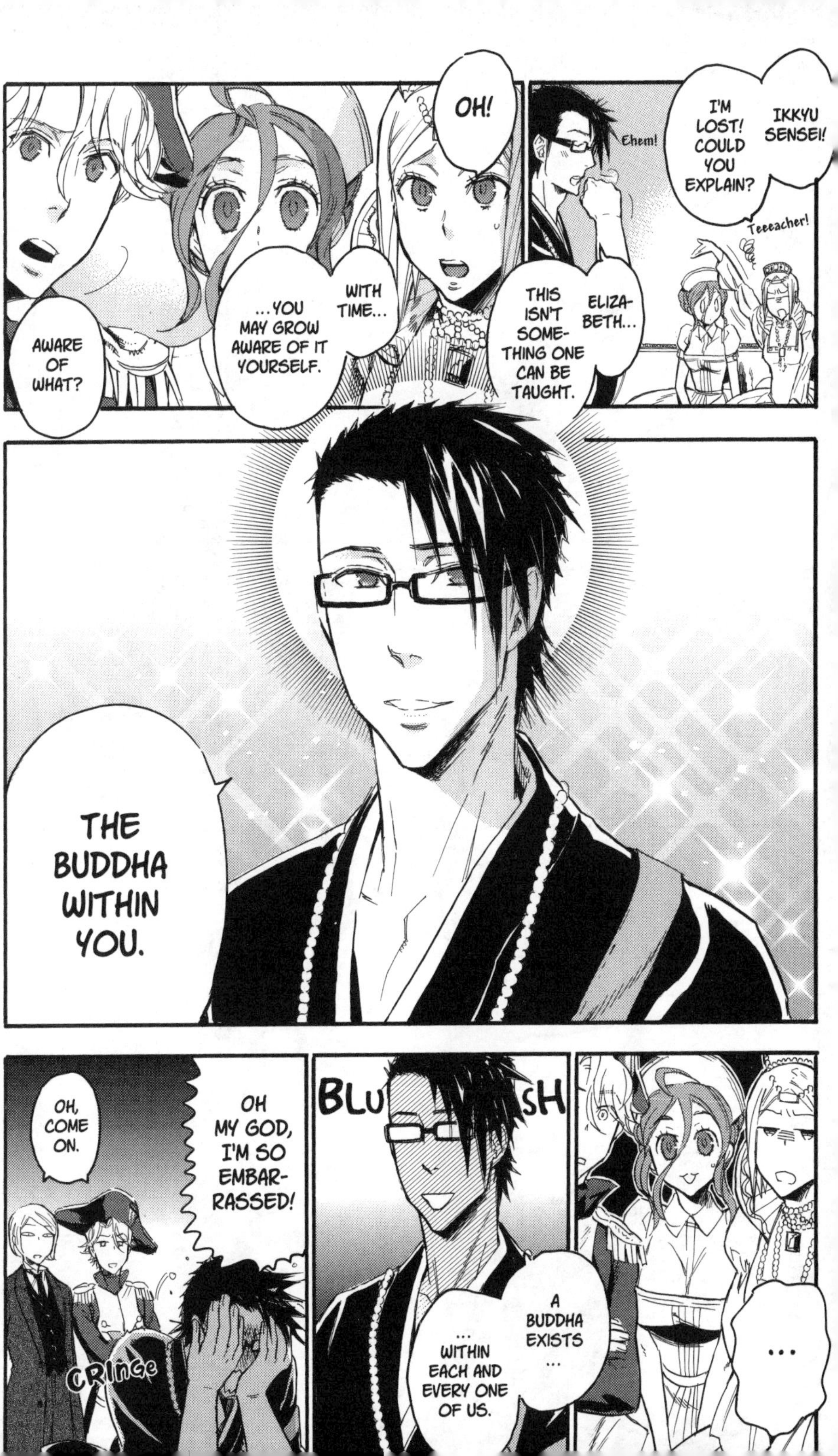
IKKYU SENSEI!
I'M LOST! COULD YOU EXPLAIN?
Ehem!
Teeeacher!
ELIZABETH...
THIS ISN'T SOMETHING ONE CAN BE TAUGHT.
OH!
WITH TIME...
...YOU MAY GROW AWARE OF IT YOURSELF.
AWARE OF WHAT?
THE BUDDHA WITHIN YOU.
...
BLU
SH
A BUDDHA EXISTS ...
... WITHIN EACH AND EVERY ONE OF US.
OH MY GOD, I'M SO EMBARRASSED!
OH, COME ON.
CRINGE

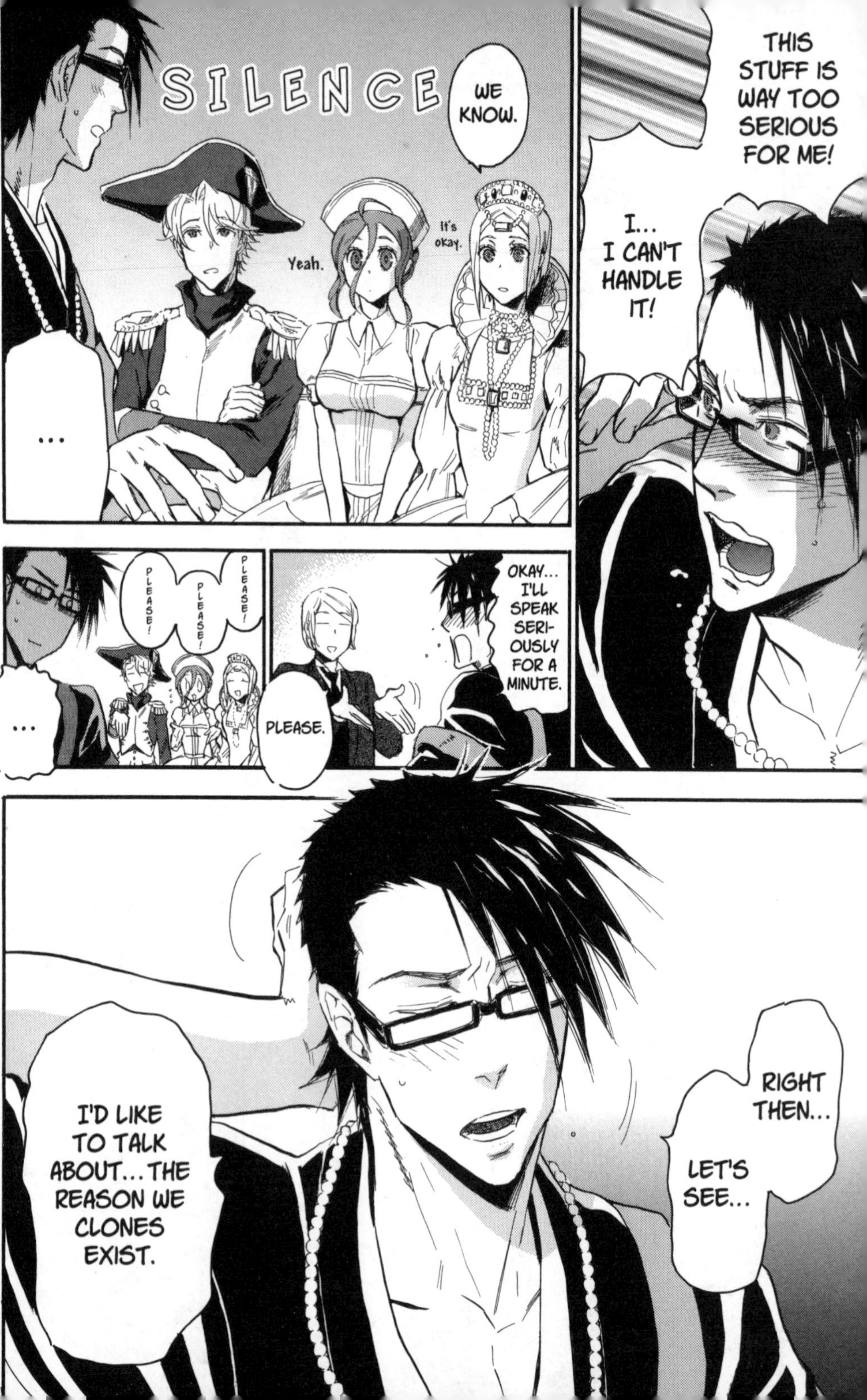
THIS STUFF IS WAY TOO SERIOUS FOR ME!
I... I CAN'T HANDLE IT!
WE KNOW.
SILENCE
It's okay.
Yeah.
...
OKAY... I'LL SPEAK SERI-OUSLY FOR A MINUTE.
PLEASE.
PLEASE!
PLEASE!
PLEASE!
...
RIGHT THEN...
LET'S SEE...
I'D LIKE TO TALK ABOUT... THE REASON WE CLONES EXIST.

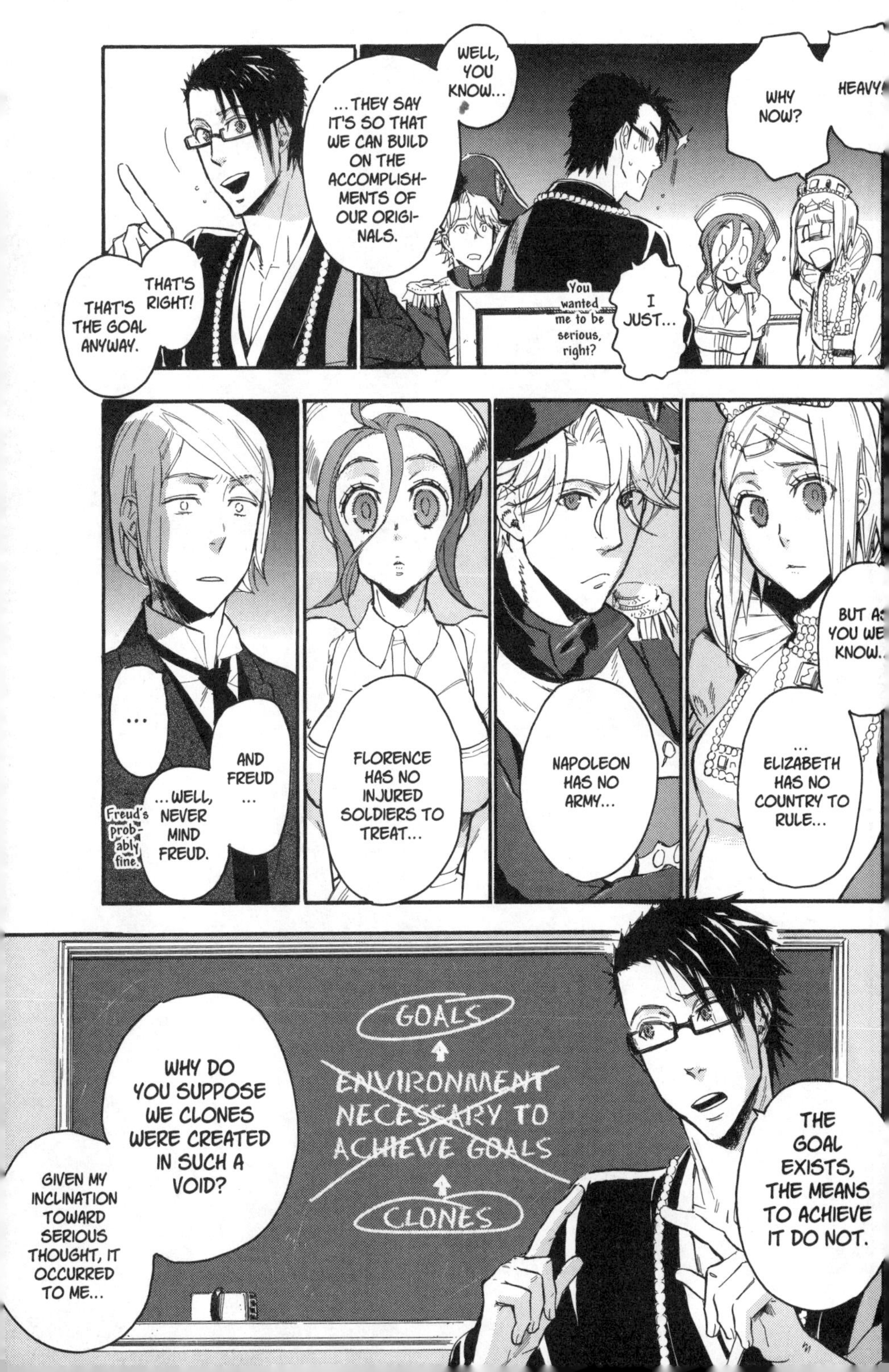

HEAVY!
WHY NOW?
WELL, YOU KNOW...
...THEY SAY IT'S SO THAT WE CAN BUILD ON THE ACCOMPLISHMENTS OF OUR ORIGINALS.
I JUST...
You wanted me to be serious, right?
THAT'S RIGHT!
THAT'S THE GOAL ANYWAY.
BUT AS YOU WE KNOW...
...ELIZABETH HAS NO COUNTRY TO RULE...
NAPOLEON HAS NO ARMY...
FLORENCE HAS NO INJURED SOLDIERS TO TREAT...
...
AND FREUD...
...WELL, NEVER MIND FREUD.
Freud's probably fine.
THE GOAL EXISTS, THE MEANS TO ACHIEVE IT DO NOT.
GOALS
ENVIRONMENT NECESSARY TO ACHIEVE GOALS
CLONES
WHY DO YOU SUPPOSE WE CLONES WERE CREATED IN SUCH A VOID?
GIVEN MY INCLINATION TOWARD SERIOUS THOUGHT, IT OCCURRED TO ME...

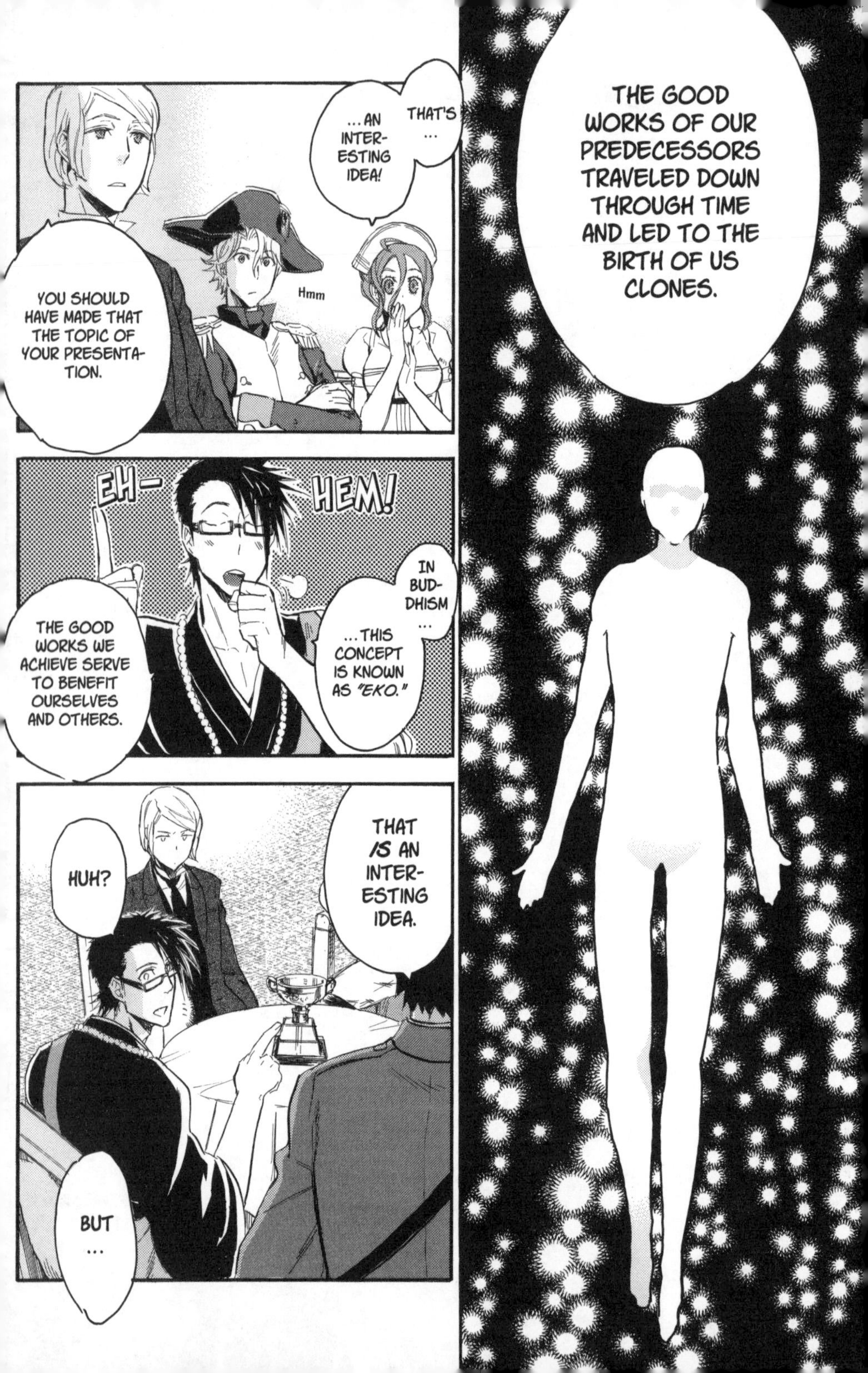
THE GOOD WORKS OF OUR PREDECESSORS TRAVELED DOWN THROUGH TIME AND LED TO THE BIRTH OF US CLONES.
THAT'S ...
...AN INTER-ESTING IDEA!
Hmm
YOU SHOULD HAVE MADE THAT THE TOPIC OF YOUR PRESENTA-TION.
EH-HEM!
IN BUD-DHISM ...
...THIS CONCEPT IS KNOWN AS "EKO."
THE GOOD WORKS WE ACHIEVE SERVE TO BENEFIT OURSELVES AND OTHERS.
THAT *IS* AN INTER-ESTING IDEA.
HUH?
BUT ...

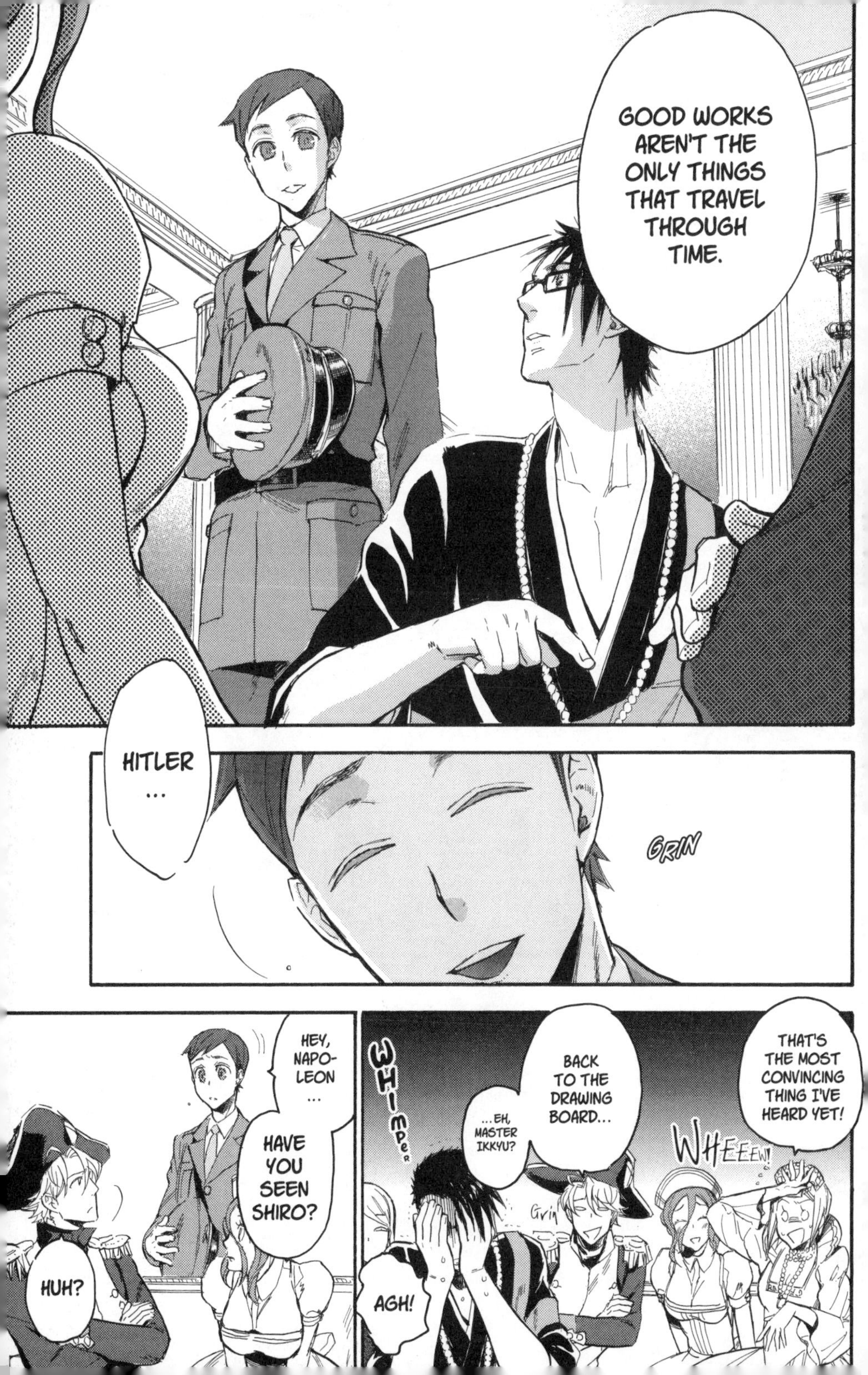
GOOD WORKS AREN'T THE ONLY THINGS THAT TRAVEL THROUGH TIME.
HITLER ...
GRIN
THAT'S THE MOST CONVINCING THING I'VE HEARD YET!
WHEEEW!
BACK TO THE DRAWING BOARD...
...EH, MASTER IKKYU?
Grin
WHIMPER
AGH!
HEY, NAPOLEON ...
HAVE YOU SEEN SHIRO?
HUH?

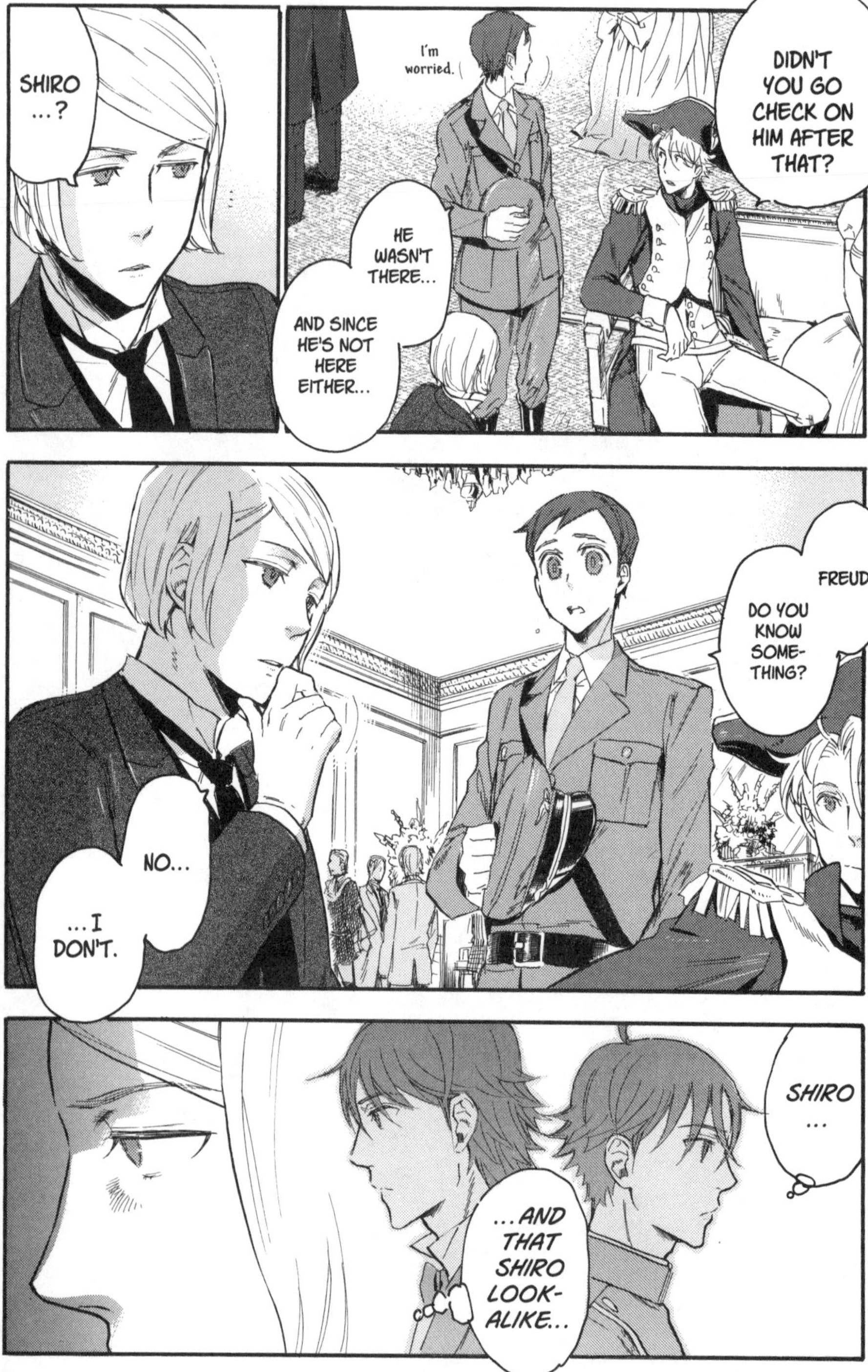
DIDN'T YOU GO CHECK ON HIM AFTER THAT?
I'm worried.
HE WASN'T THERE...
AND SINCE HE'S NOT HERE EITHER...
SHIRO ...?
FREUD?
DO YOU KNOW SOME-THING?
NO...
...I DON'T.
SHIRO ...
...AND THAT SHIRO LOOK-ALIKE...

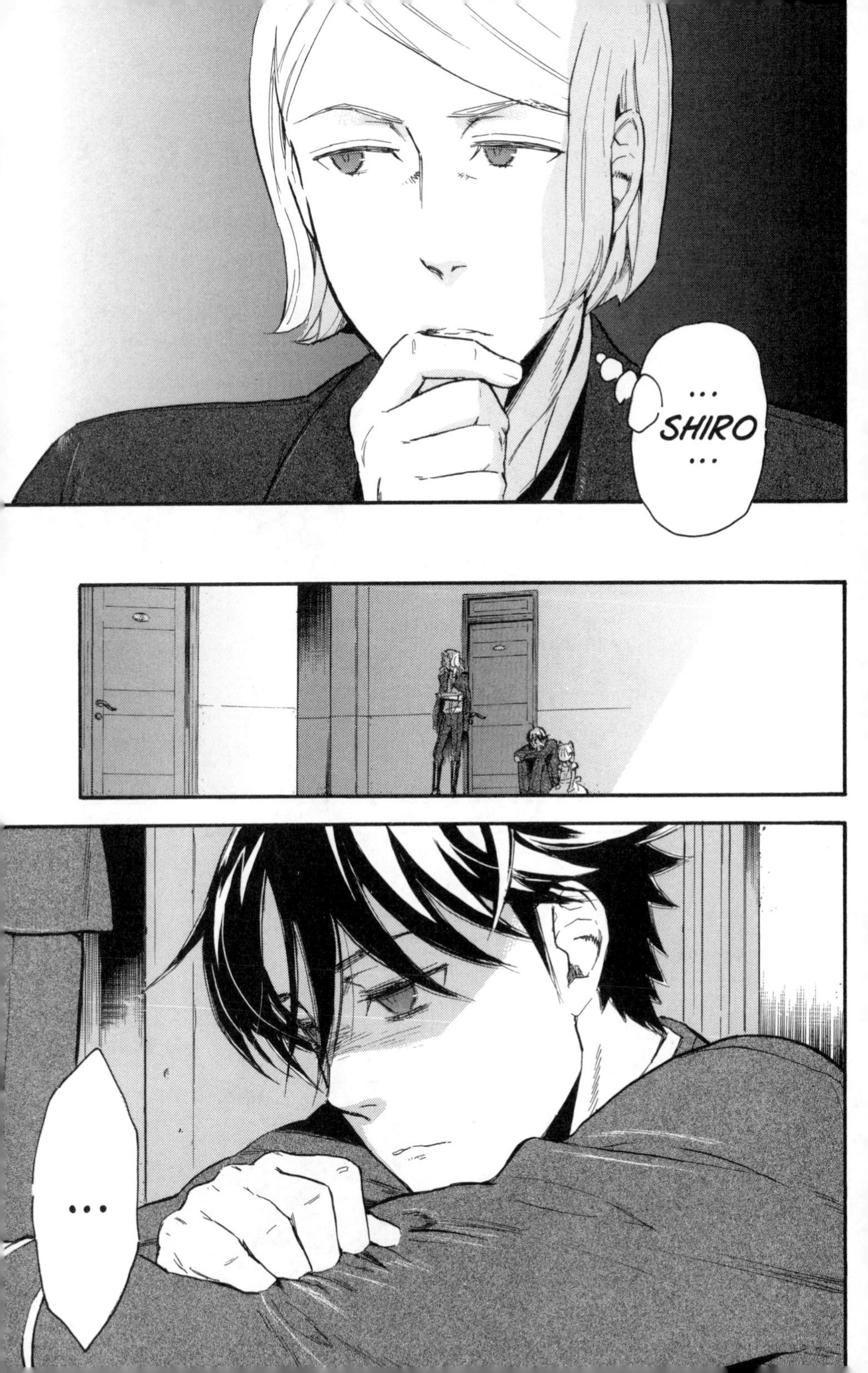
... SHIRO ...
...

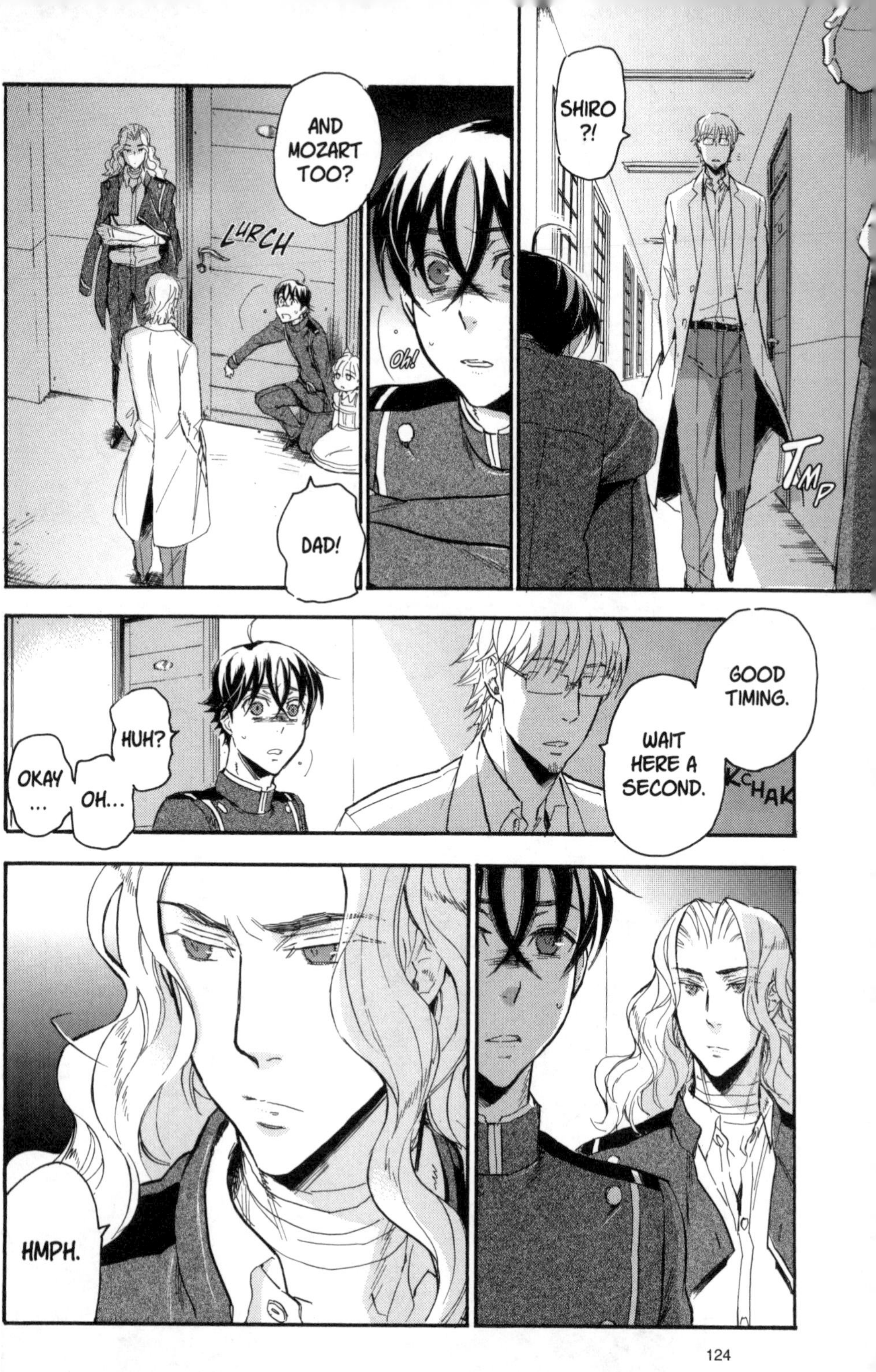
SHIRO ?!
TMP
AND MOZART TOO?
Oh!
LURCH
DAD!
GOOD TIMING.
WAIT HERE A SECOND.
KCHAK
HUH?
OH...
OKAY ...
HMPH.

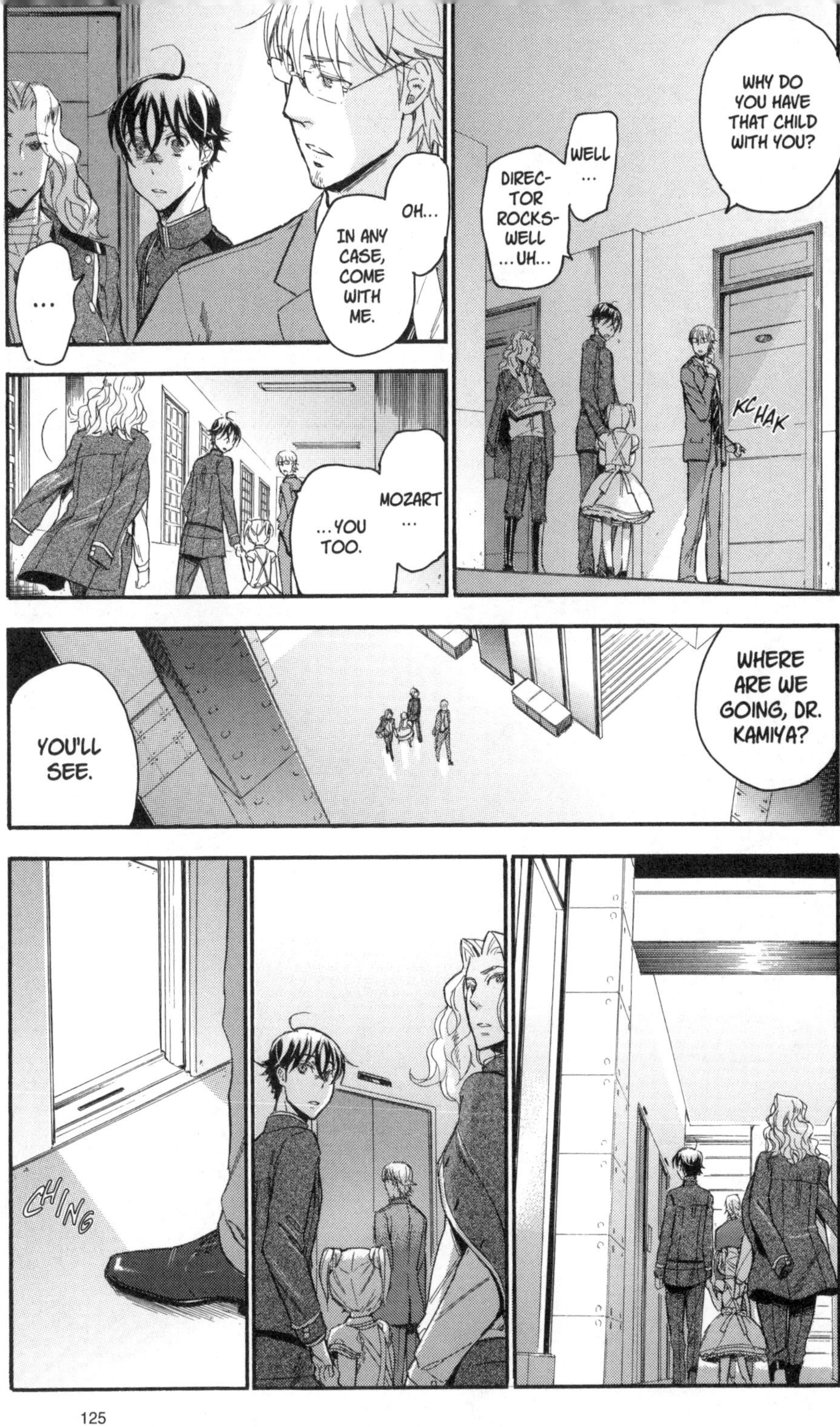
WHY DO YOU HAVE THAT CHILD WITH YOU?
WELL...
DIRECTOR ROCKSWELL... UH...
KCHAK
OH... IN ANY CASE, COME WITH ME.
...
MOZART...
...YOU TOO.
WHERE ARE WE GOING, DR. KAMIYA?
YOU'LL SEE.
CHING

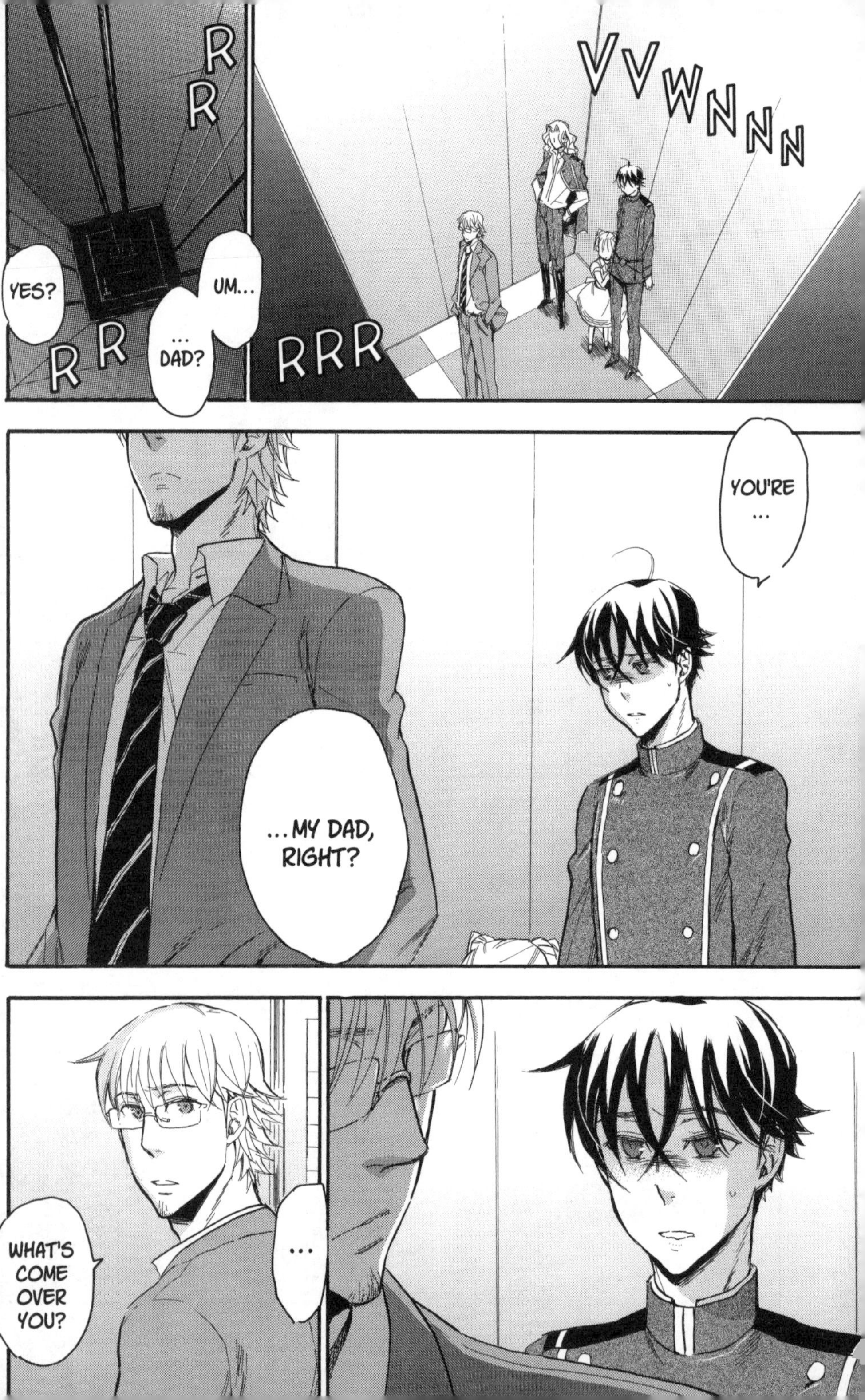
VVWNNNN
RRR
RR
UM...
...DAD?
YES?
RR
YOU'RE...
...MY DAD, RIGHT?
...
WHAT'S COME OVER YOU?

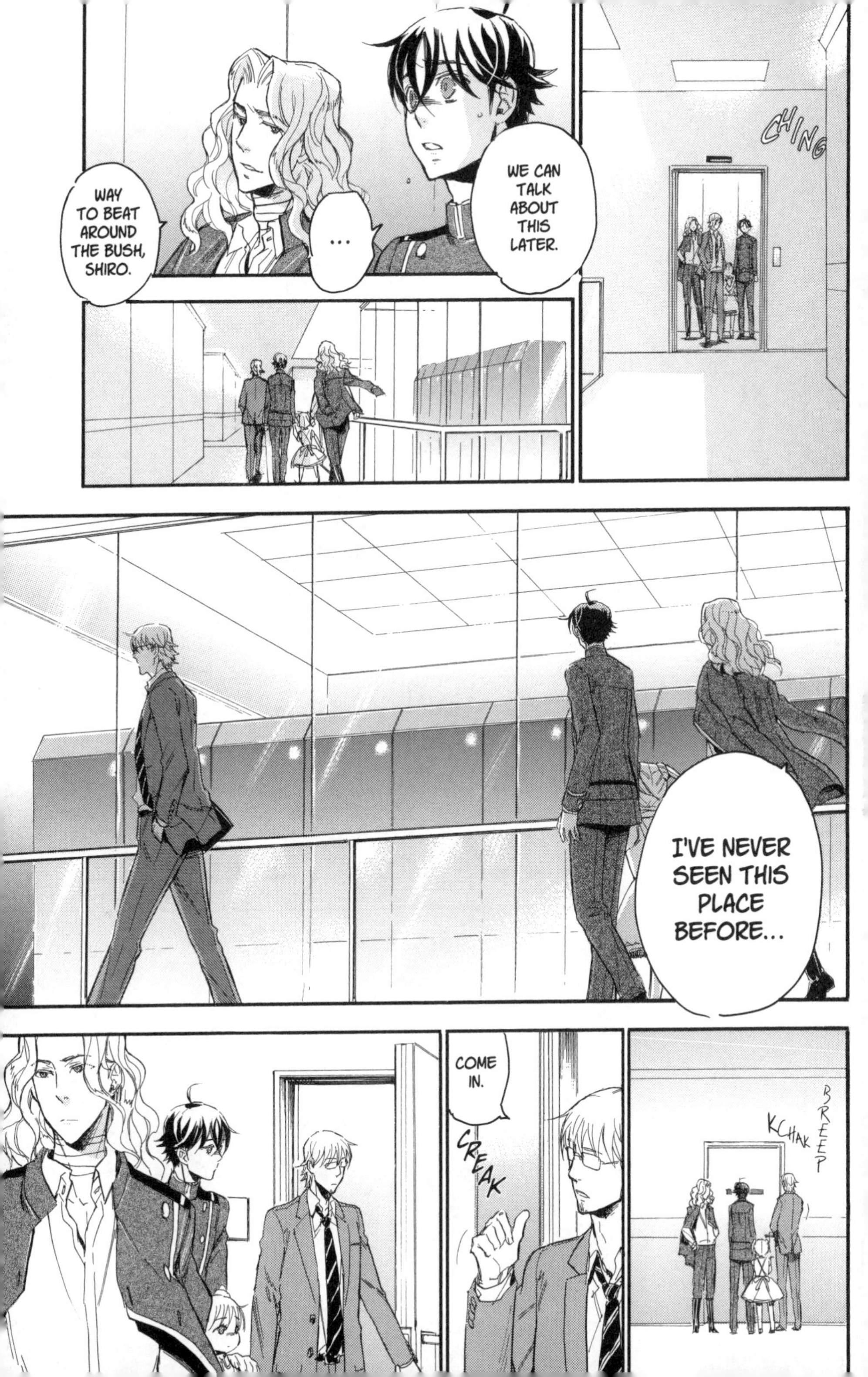
CHING
WE CAN TALK ABOUT THIS LATER.
...
WAY TO BEAT AROUND THE BUSH, SHIRO.
I'VE NEVER SEEN THIS PLACE BEFORE...
BREEEP
KCHAK
COME IN.
CREAK

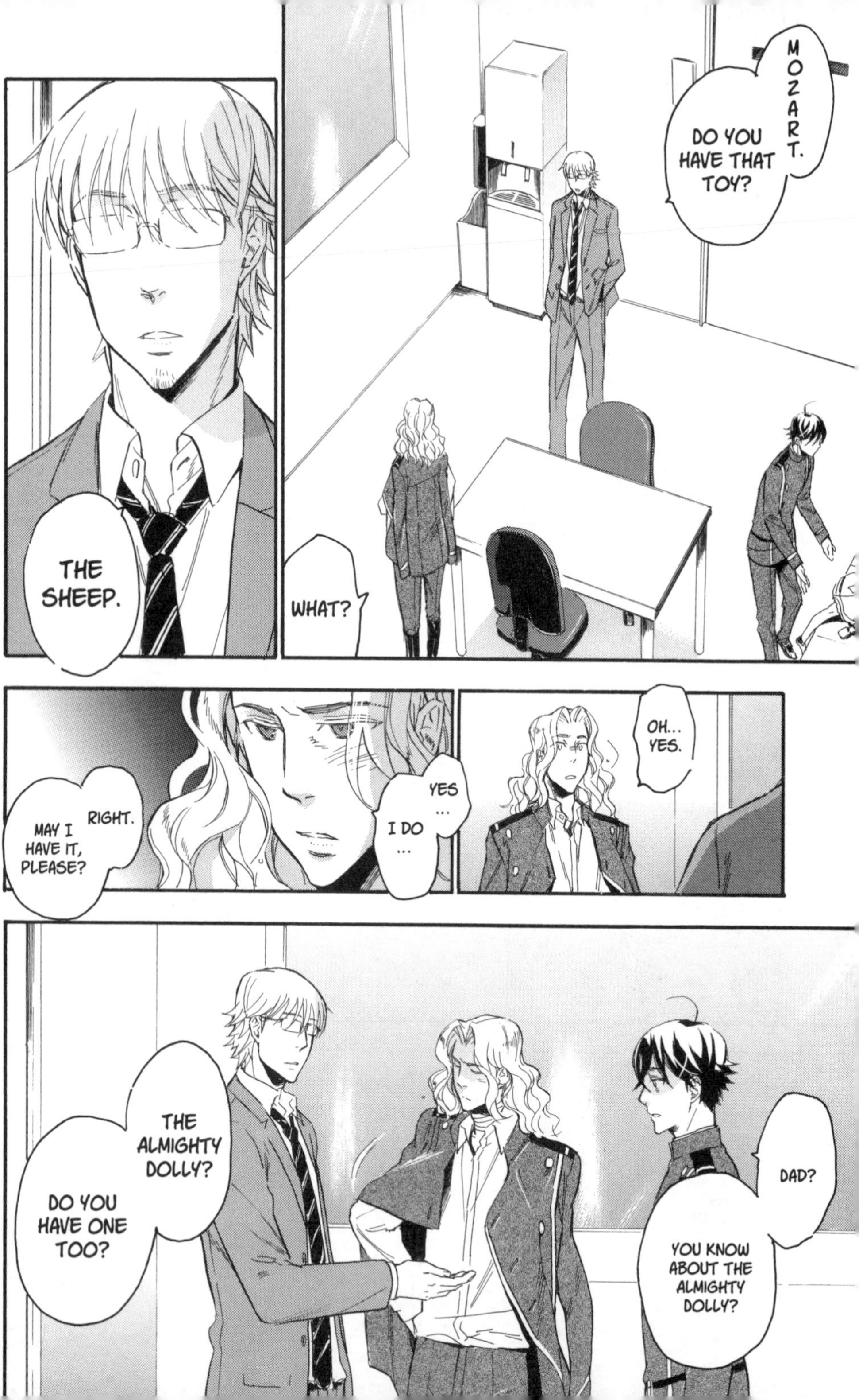
MOZART.
DO YOU HAVE THAT TOY?
WHAT?
THE SHEEP.
OH... YES.
YES... I DO...
RIGHT.
MAY I HAVE IT, PLEASE?
DAD?
YOU KNOW ABOUT THE ALMIGHTY DOLLY?
THE ALMIGHTY DOLLY?
DO YOU HAVE ONE TOO?

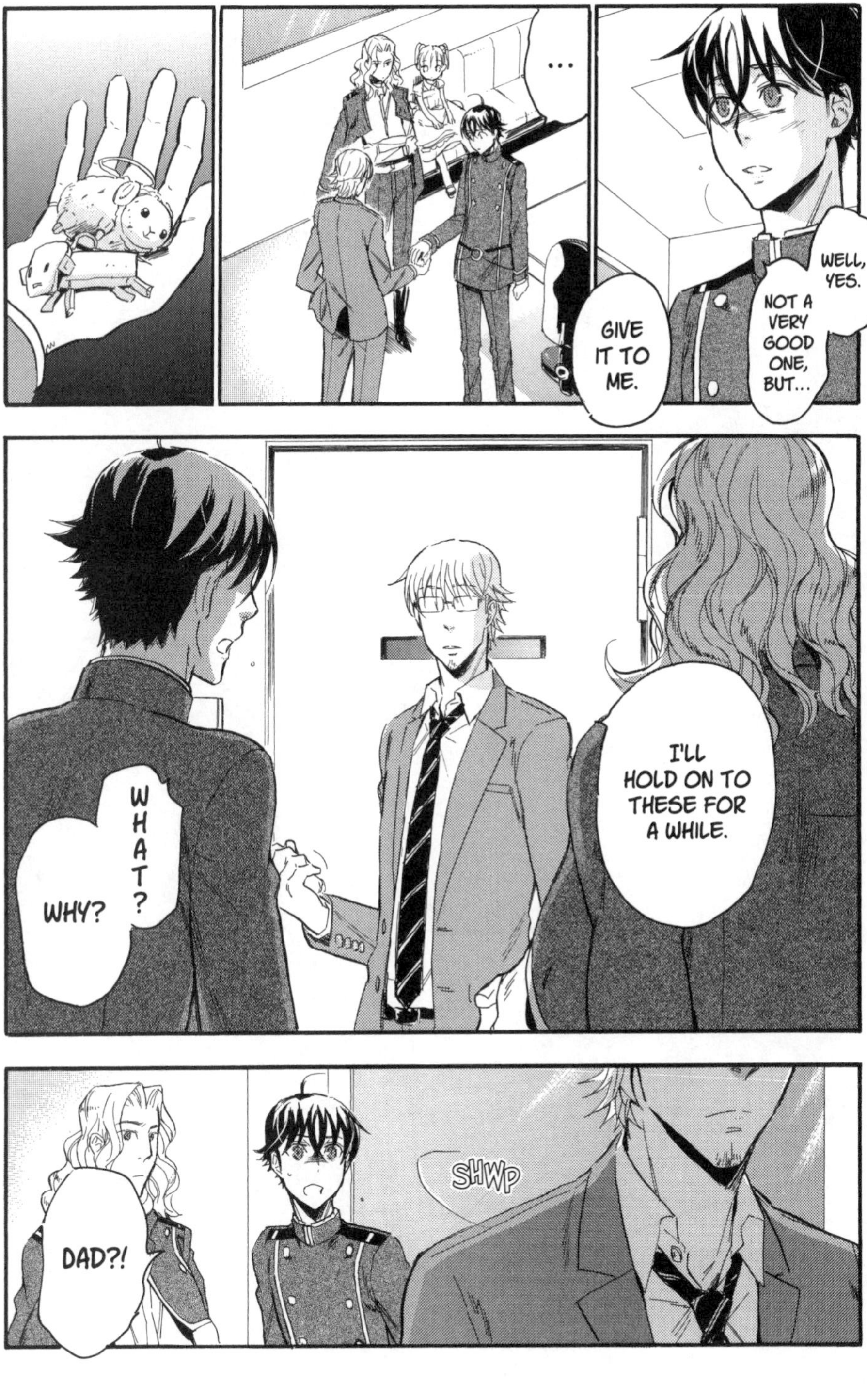
WELL, YES.
NOT A VERY GOOD ONE, BUT...
GIVE IT TO ME.
...
I'LL HOLD ON TO THESE FOR A WHILE.
WHAT?
WHY?
SHWP
DAD?!

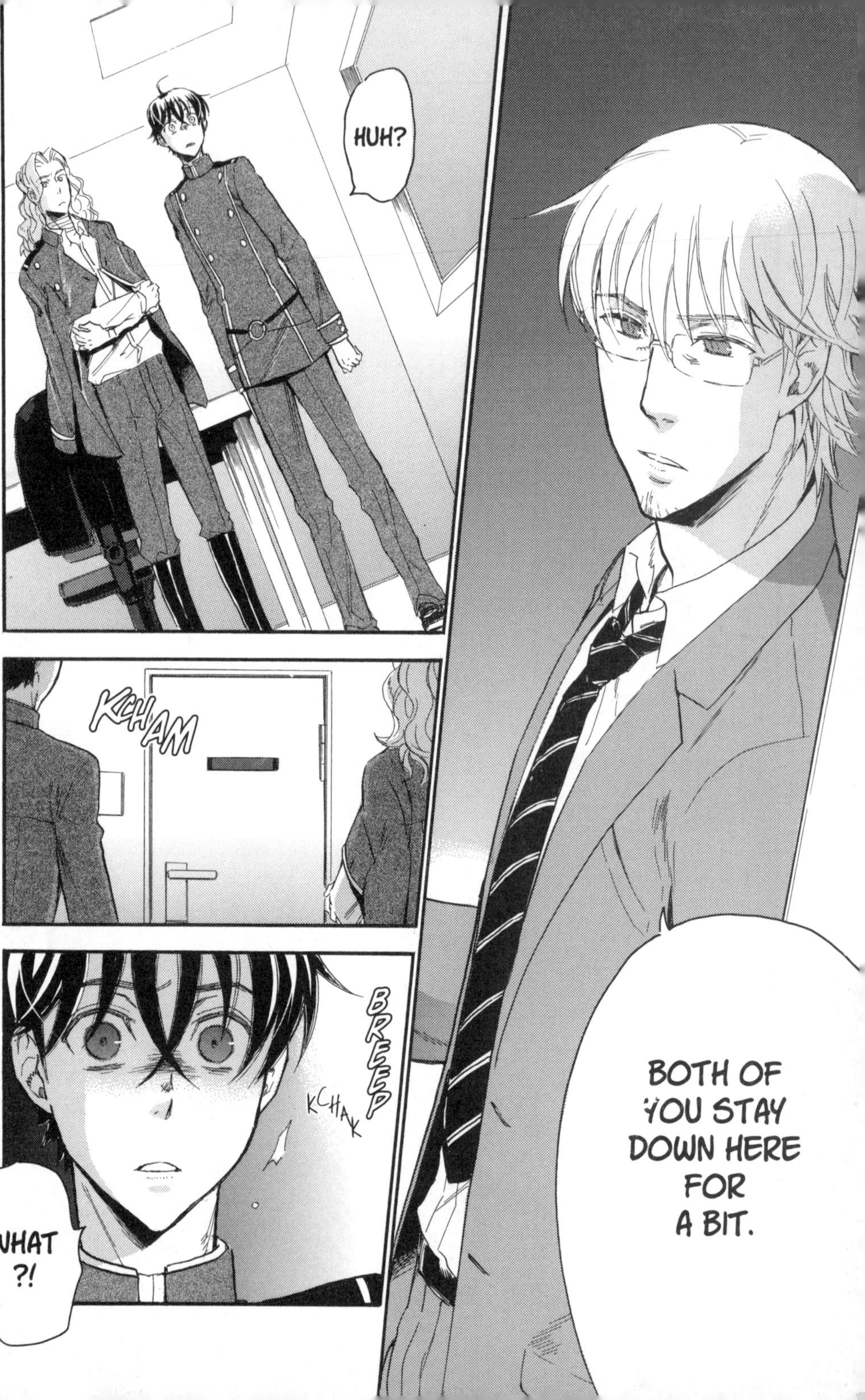
BOTH OF YOU STAY DOWN HERE FOR A BIT.
HUH?
KCHAM
BREEP
KCHAK
WHAT?!

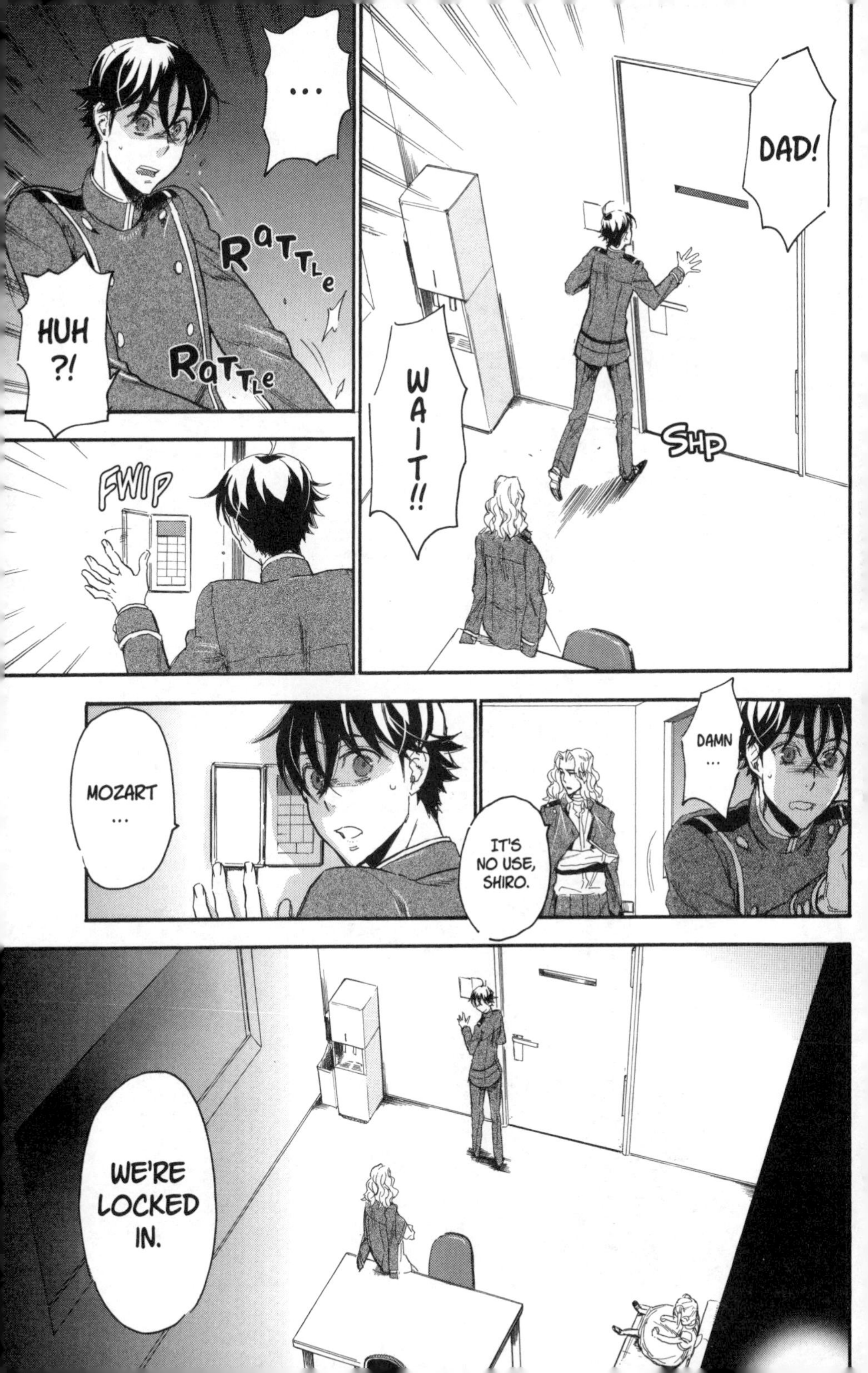
DAD!
WAIT!!
SHP
...
RATTLE
RATTLE
HUH?!
FWIP
DAMN...
IT'S NO USE, SHIRO.
MOZART...
WE'RE LOCKED IN.

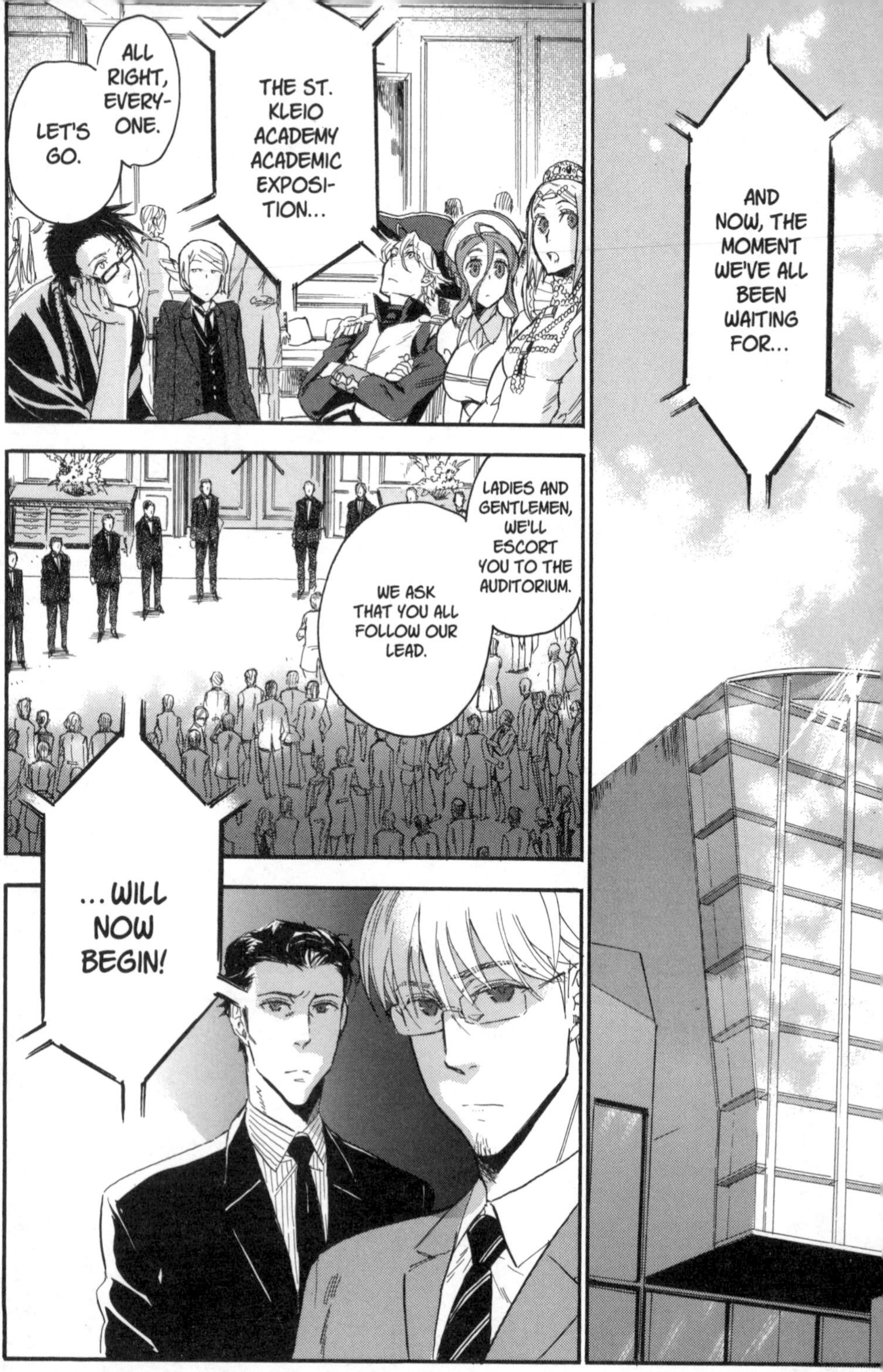
AND NOW, THE MOMENT WE'VE ALL BEEN WAITING FOR...
THE ST. KLEIO ACADEMY ACADEMIC EXPOSITION...
ALL RIGHT, EVERYONE.
LET'S GO.
LADIES AND GENTLEMEN, WE'LL ESCORT YOU TO THE AUDITORIUM.
WE ASK THAT YOU ALL FOLLOW OUR LEAD.
...WILL NOW BEGIN!

# Chapter seventeen

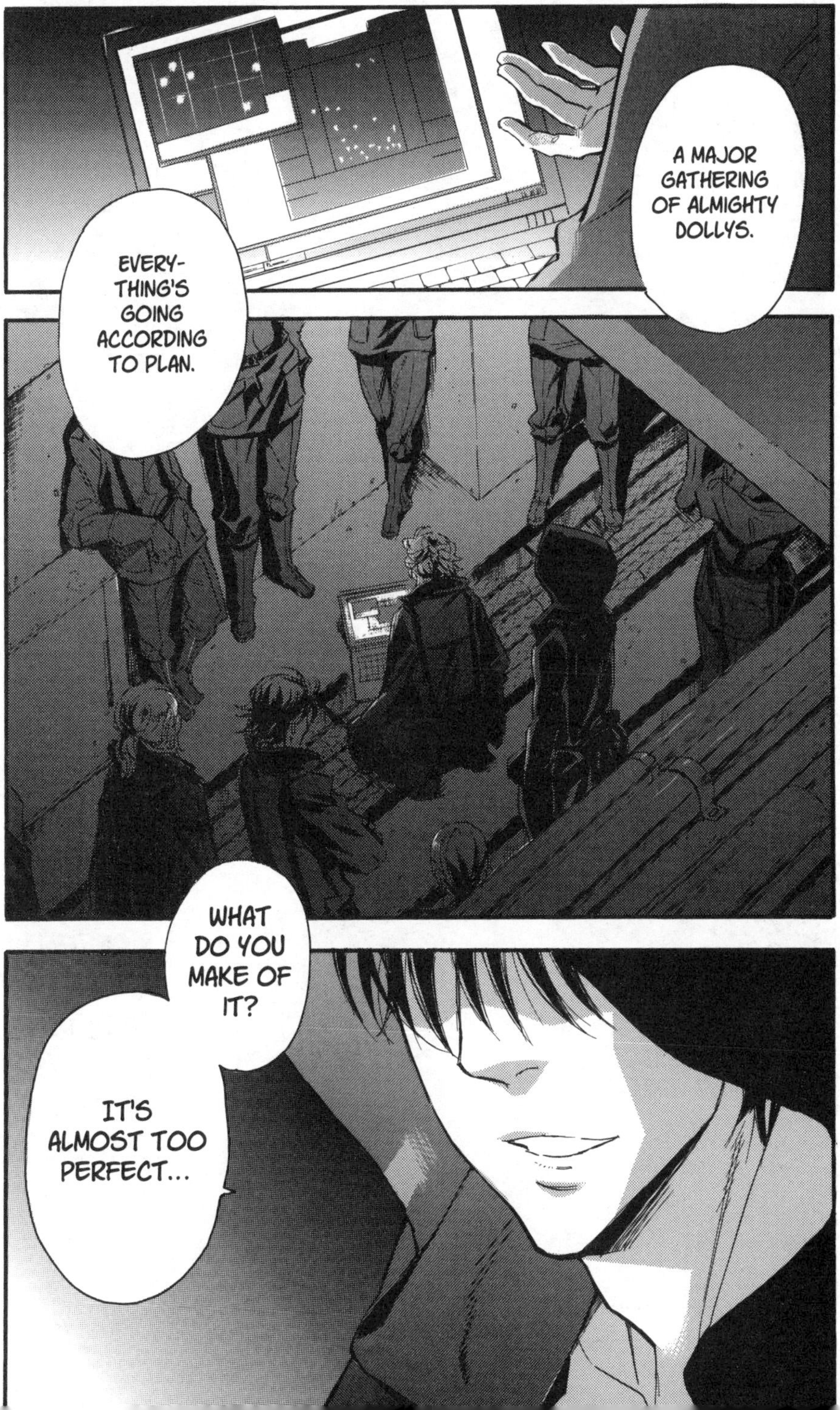
A MAJOR GATHERING OF ALMIGHTY DOLLYS.
EVERY-THING'S GOING ACCORDING TO PLAN.
WHAT DO YOU MAKE OF IT?
IT'S ALMOST TOO PERFECT...

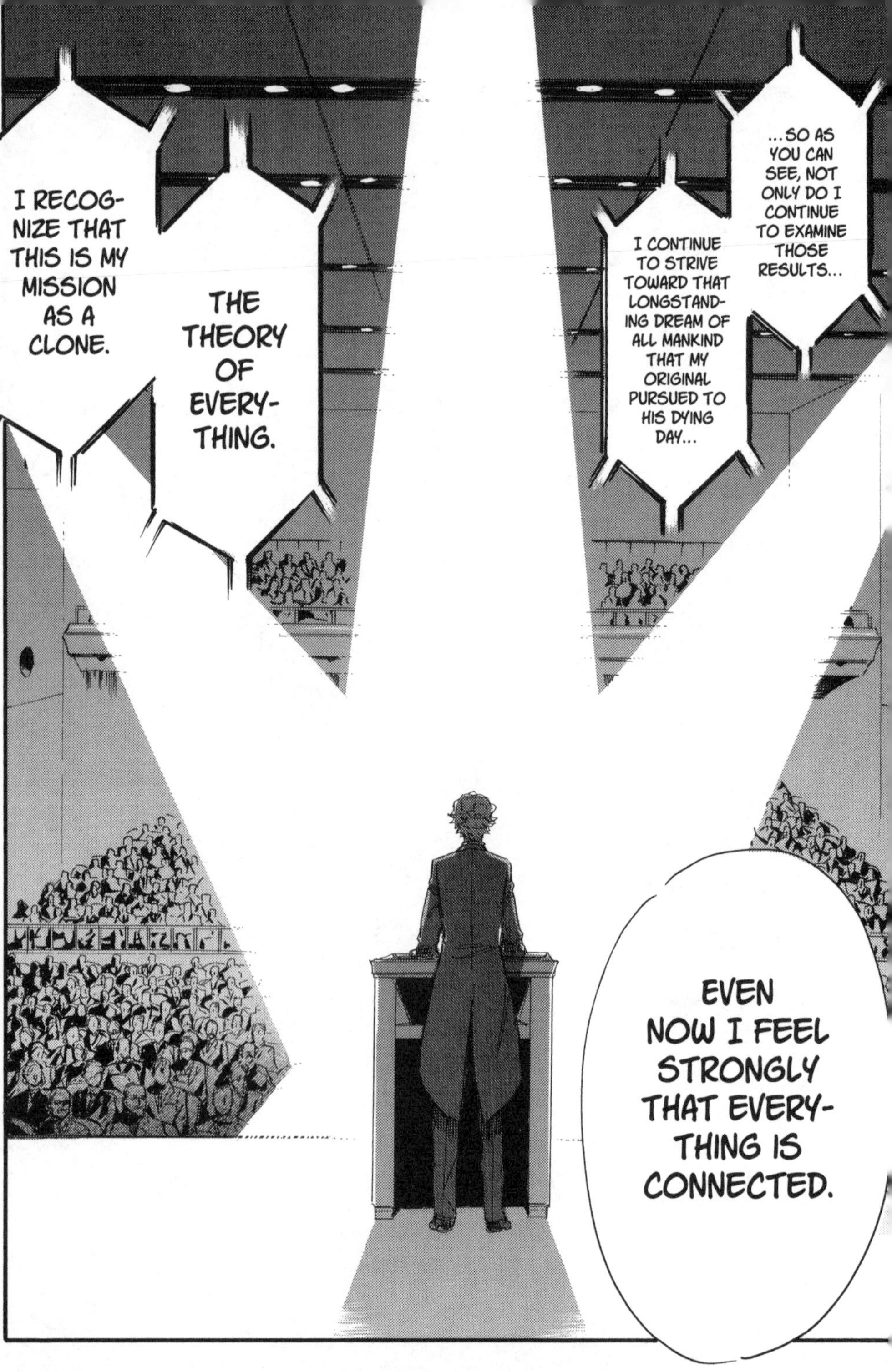
...SO AS YOU CAN SEE, NOT ONLY DO I CONTINUE TO EXAMINE THOSE RESULTS...
I CONTINUE TO STRIVE TOWARD THAT LONGSTANDING DREAM OF ALL MANKIND THAT MY ORIGINAL PURSUED TO HIS DYING DAY...
THE THEORY OF EVERYTHING.
I RECOGNIZE THAT THIS IS MY MISSION AS A CLONE.
EVEN NOW I FEEL STRONGLY THAT EVERYTHING IS CONNECTED.

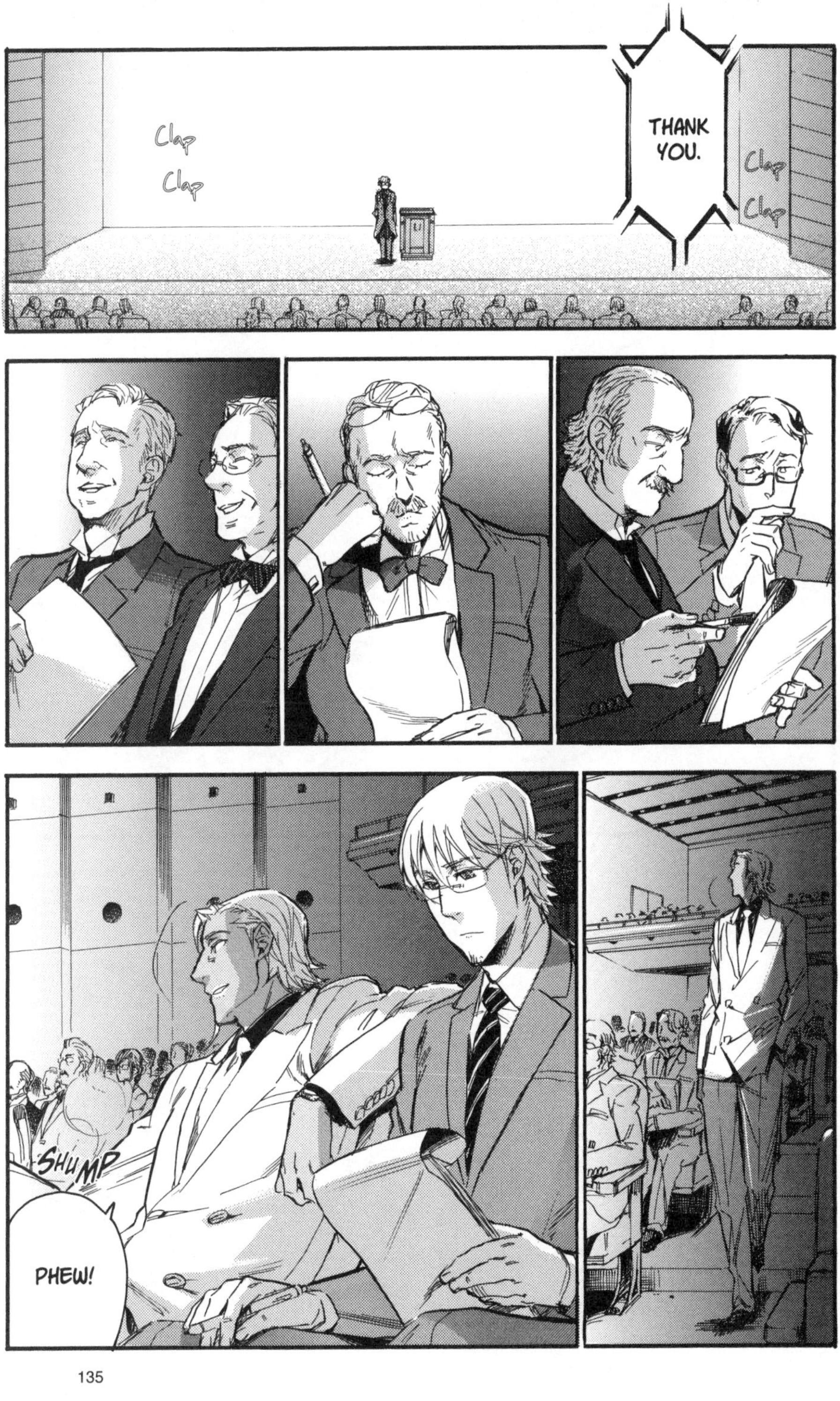
THANK YOU.
Clap
Clap
Clap
Clap
SHUMP
PHEW!

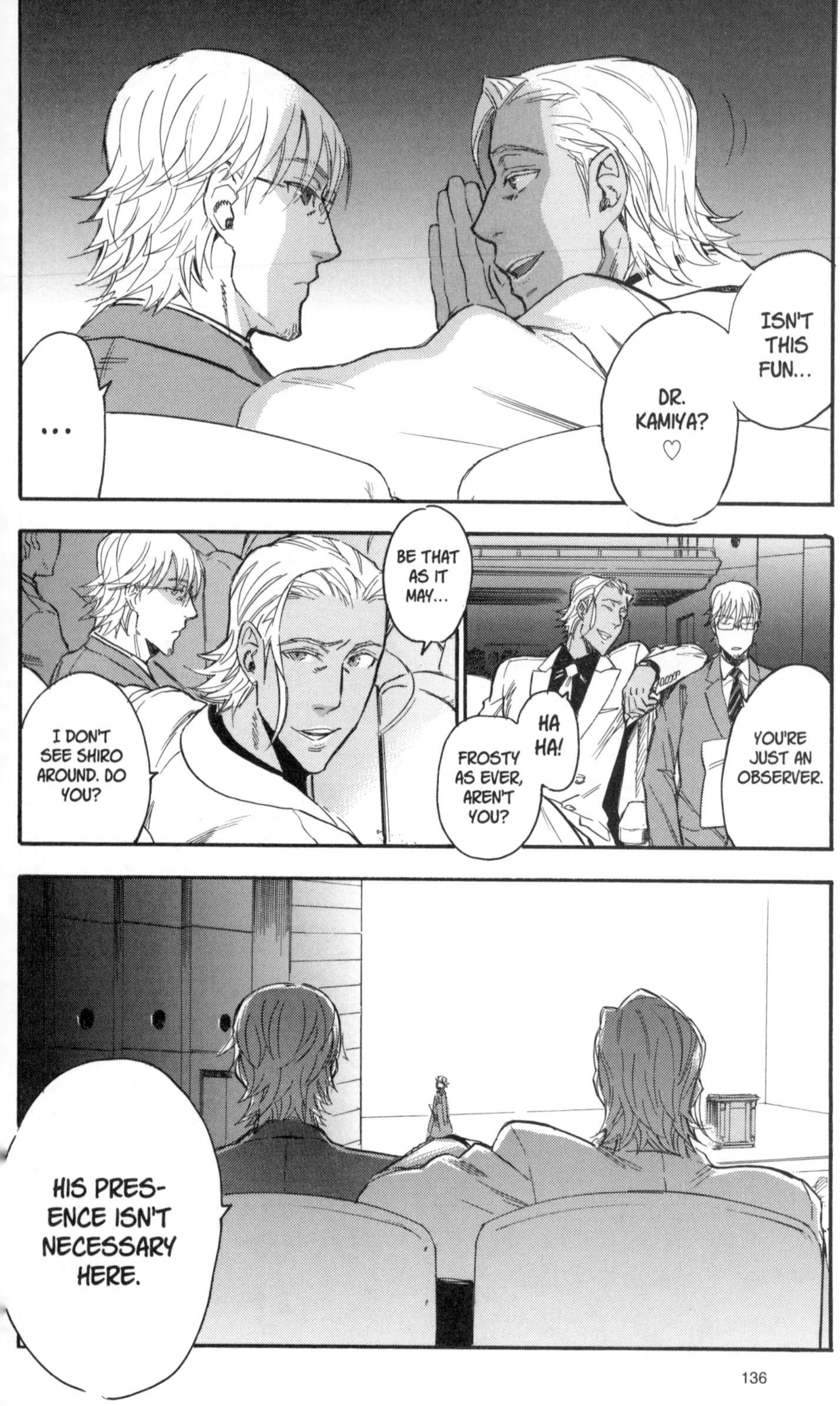
ISN'T THIS FUN...
DR. KAMIYA? ♡
...
YOU'RE JUST AN OBSERVER.
HA HA!
FROSTY AS EVER, AREN'T YOU?
BE THAT AS IT MAY...
I DON'T SEE SHIRO AROUND. DO YOU?
HIS PRES-ENCE ISN'T NECESSARY HERE.

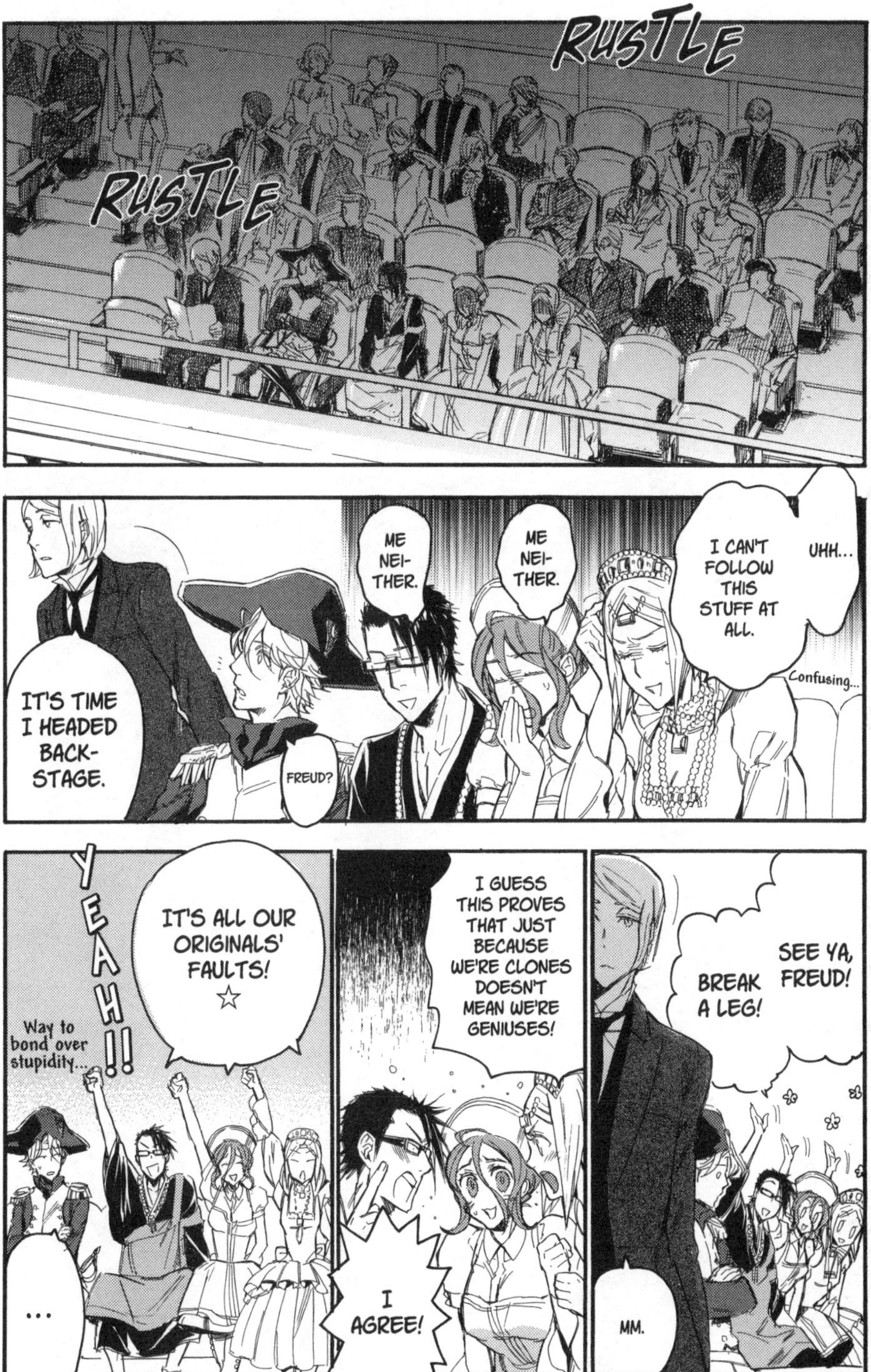
RUSTLE
RUSTLE
UHH...
I CAN'T FOLLOW THIS STUFF AT ALL.
Confusing...
ME NEI-THER.
ME NEI-THER.
IT'S TIME I HEADED BACK-STAGE.
FREUD?
SEE YA, FREUD!
BREAK A LEG!
MM.
I GUESS THIS PROVES THAT JUST BECAUSE WE'RE CLONES DOESN'T MEAN WE'RE GENIUSES!
I AGREE!
YEAH!!
IT'S ALL OUR ORIGINALS' FAULTS! ☆
Way to bond over stupidity...
...

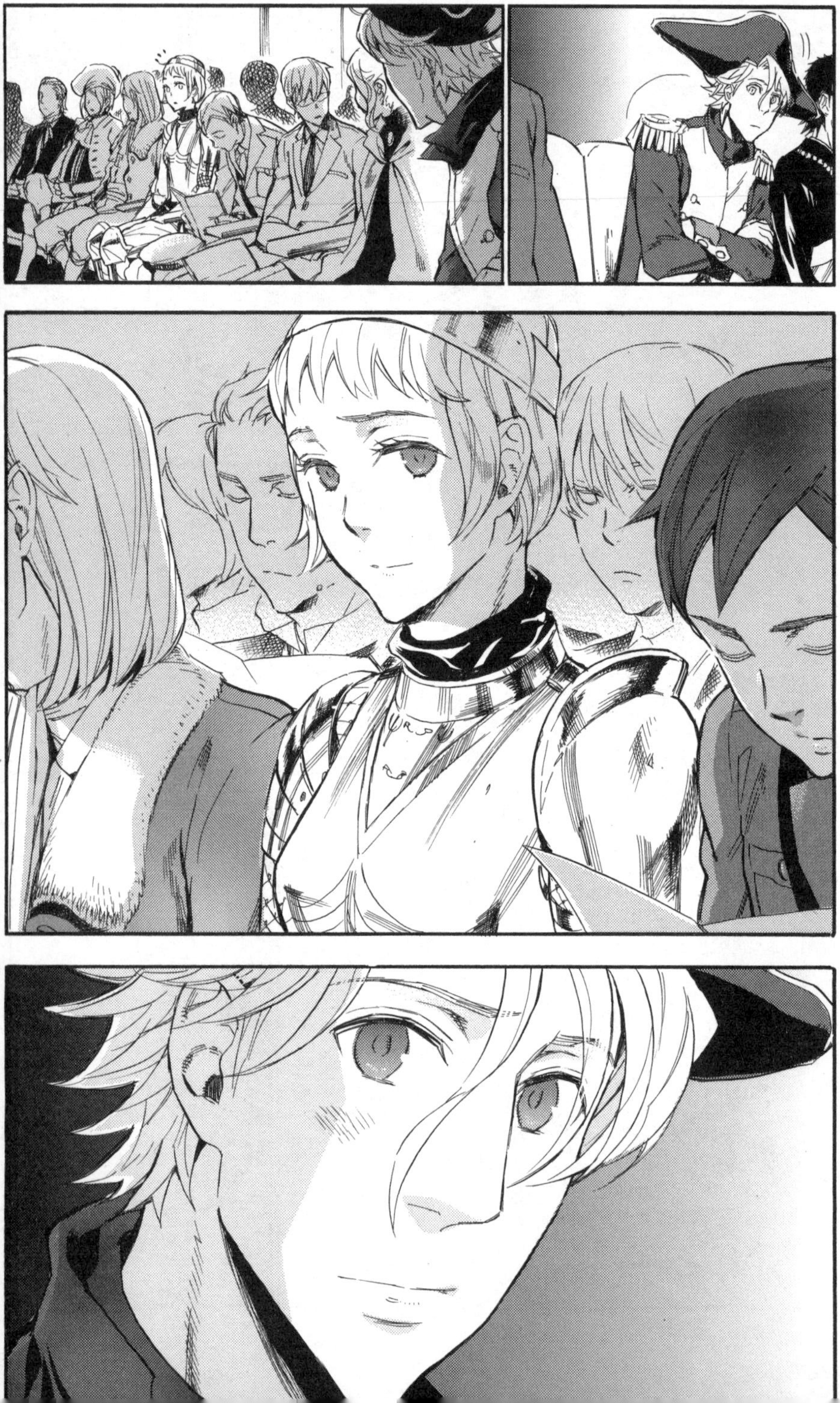

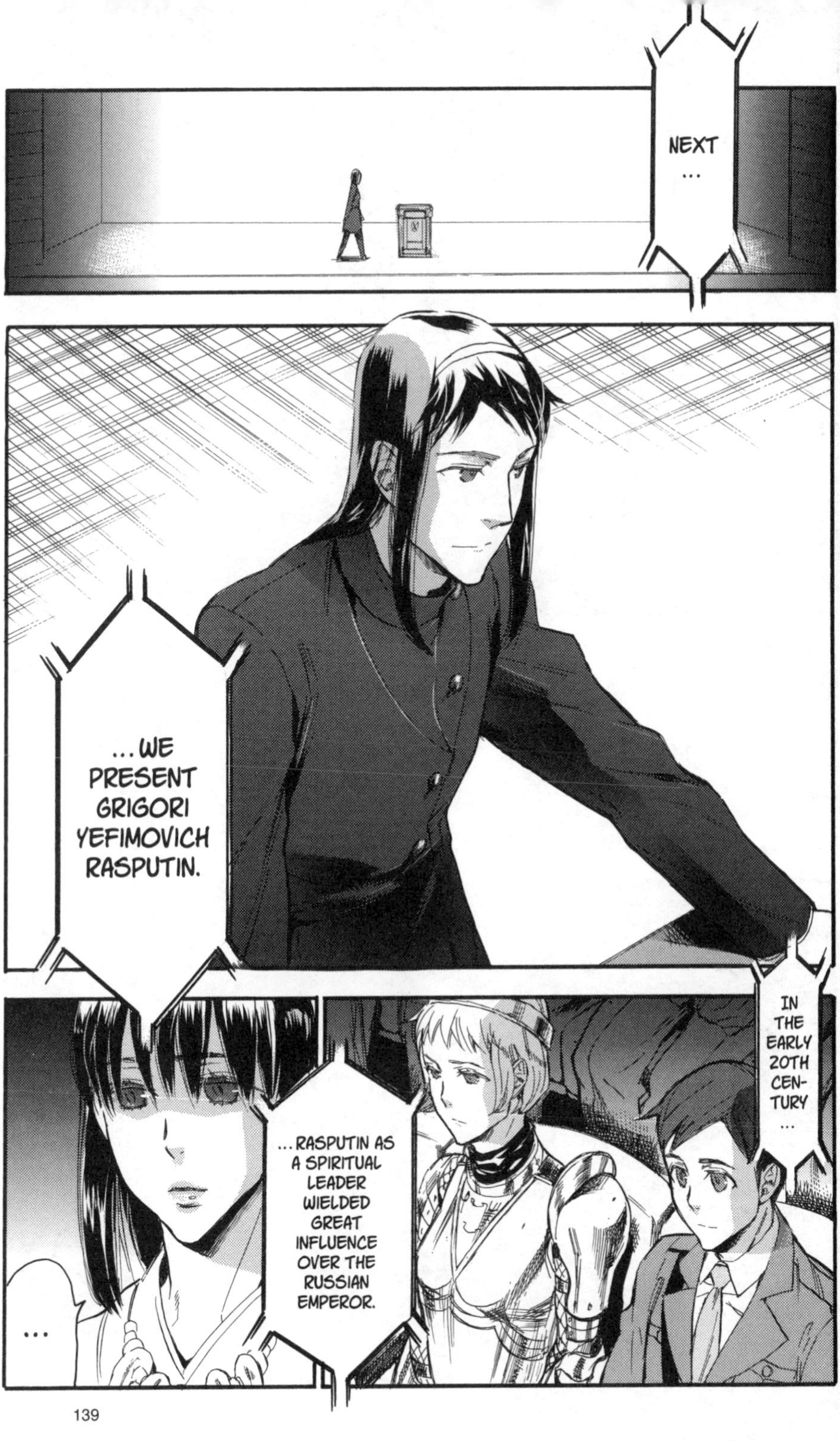
NEXT ...
...WE PRESENT GRIGORI YEFIMOVICH RASPUTIN.
IN THE EARLY 20TH CEN-TURY ...
...RASPUTIN AS A SPIRITUAL LEADER WIELDED GREAT INFLUENCE OVER THE RUSSIAN EMPEROR.
...

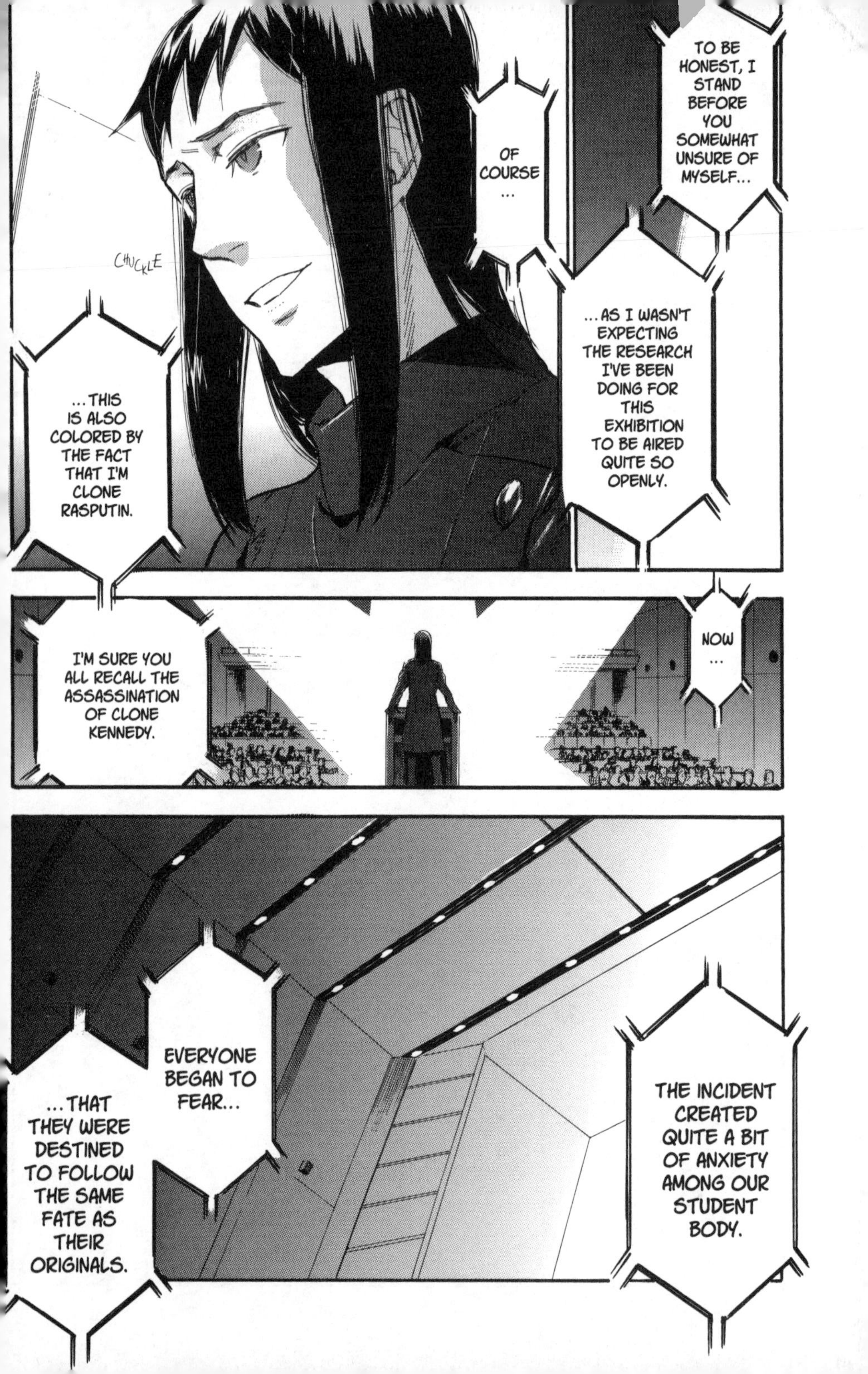
TO BE HONEST, I STAND BEFORE YOU SOMEWHAT UNSURE OF MYSELF...
...AS I WASN'T EXPECTING THE RESEARCH I'VE BEEN DOING FOR THIS EXHIBITION TO BE AIRED QUITE SO OPENLY.
OF COURSE...
CHUCKLE
...THIS IS ALSO COLORED BY THE FACT THAT I'M CLONE RASPUTIN.
NOW...
I'M SURE YOU ALL RECALL THE ASSASSINATION OF CLONE KENNEDY.
THE INCIDENT CREATED QUITE A BIT OF ANXIETY AMONG OUR STUDENT BODY.
EVERYONE BEGAN TO FEAR...
...THAT THEY WERE DESTINED TO FOLLOW THE SAME FATE AS THEIR ORIGINALS.

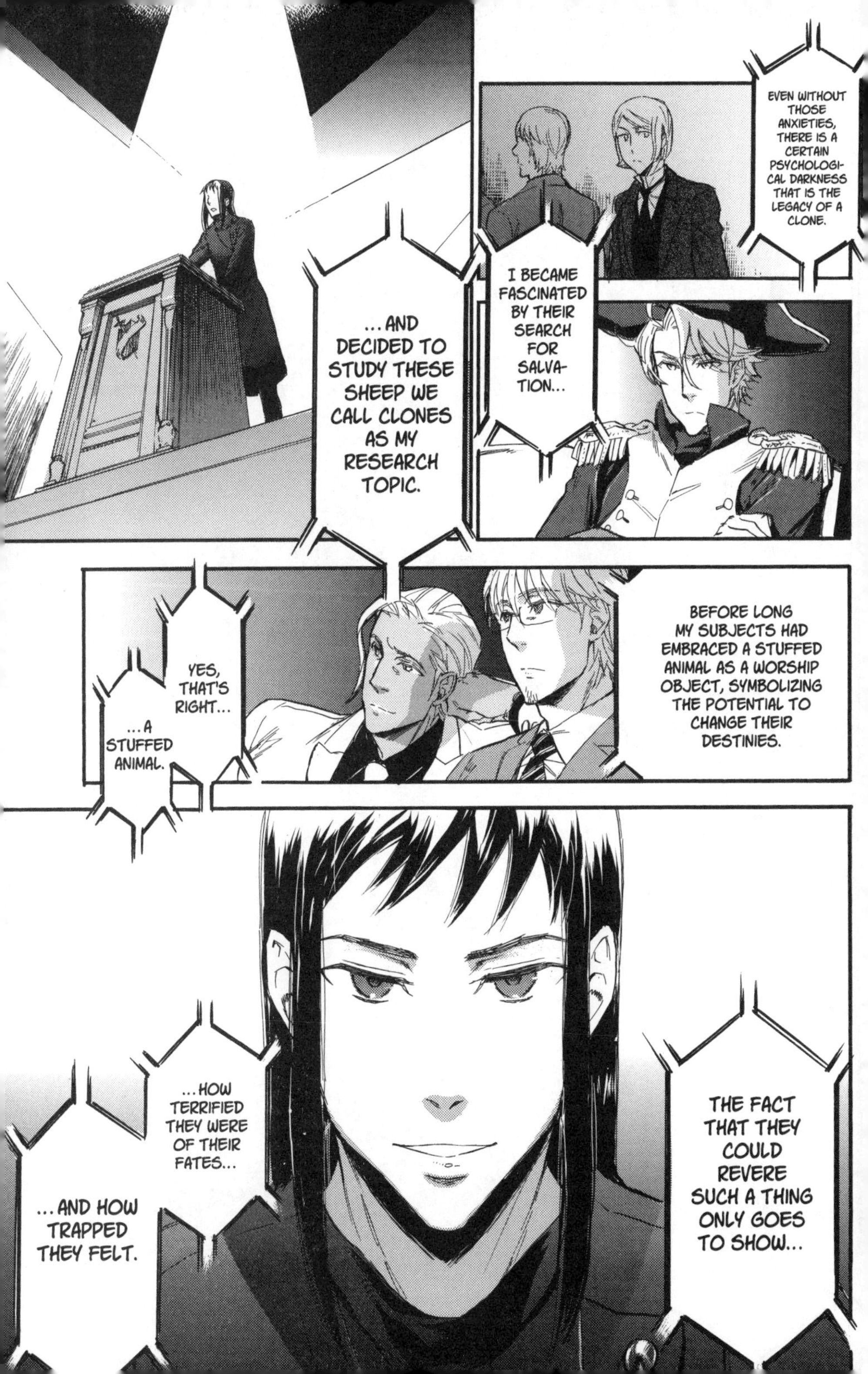
EVEN WITHOUT THOSE ANXIETIES, THERE IS A CERTAIN PSYCHOLOGICAL DARKNESS THAT IS THE LEGACY OF A CLONE.
I BECAME FASCINATED BY THEIR SEARCH FOR SALVATION...
...AND DECIDED TO STUDY THESE SHEEP WE CALL CLONES AS MY RESEARCH TOPIC.
BEFORE LONG MY SUBJECTS HAD EMBRACED A STUFFED ANIMAL AS A WORSHIP OBJECT, SYMBOLIZING THE POTENTIAL TO CHANGE THEIR DESTINIES.
YES, THAT'S RIGHT...
...A STUFFED ANIMAL.
THE FACT THAT THEY COULD REVERE SUCH A THING ONLY GOES TO SHOW...
...HOW TERRIFIED THEY WERE OF THEIR FATES...
...AND HOW TRAPPED THEY FELT.

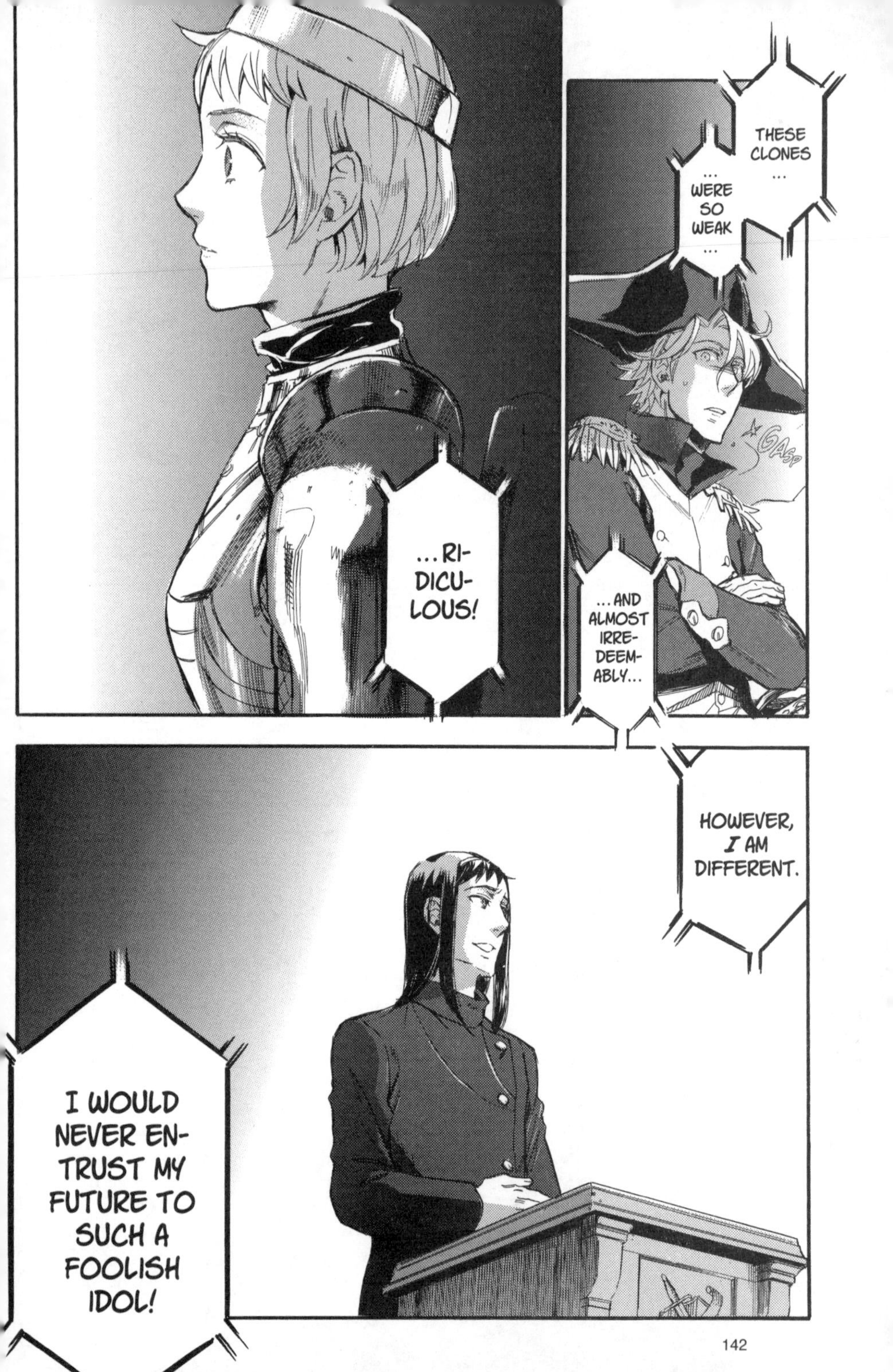
THESE CLONES ...
... WERE SO WEAK ...
GASP
...AND ALMOST IRRE-DEEM-ABLY...
...RI-DICU-LOUS!
HOWEVER, *I* AM DIFFERENT.
I WOULD NEVER EN-TRUST MY FUTURE TO SUCH A FOOLISH IDOL!

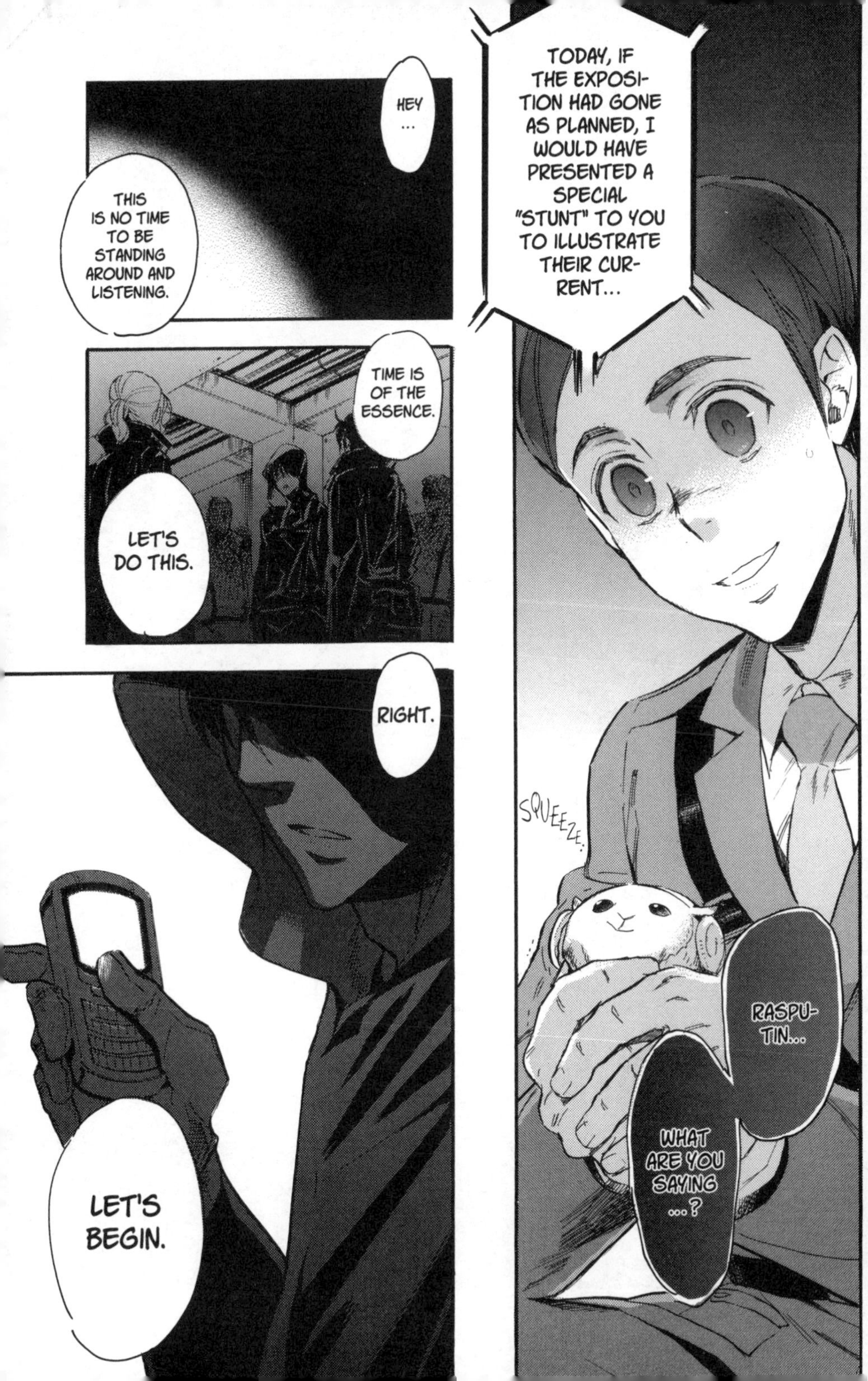
TODAY, IF THE EXPOSITION HAD GONE AS PLANNED, I WOULD HAVE PRESENTED A SPECIAL "STUNT" TO YOU TO ILLUSTRATE THEIR CURRENT...
SQUEEZE
RASPUTIN...
WHAT ARE YOU SAYING ...?
HEY ...
THIS IS NO TIME TO BE STANDING AROUND AND LISTENING.
TIME IS OF THE ESSENCE.
LET'S DO THIS.
RIGHT.
LET'S BEGIN.

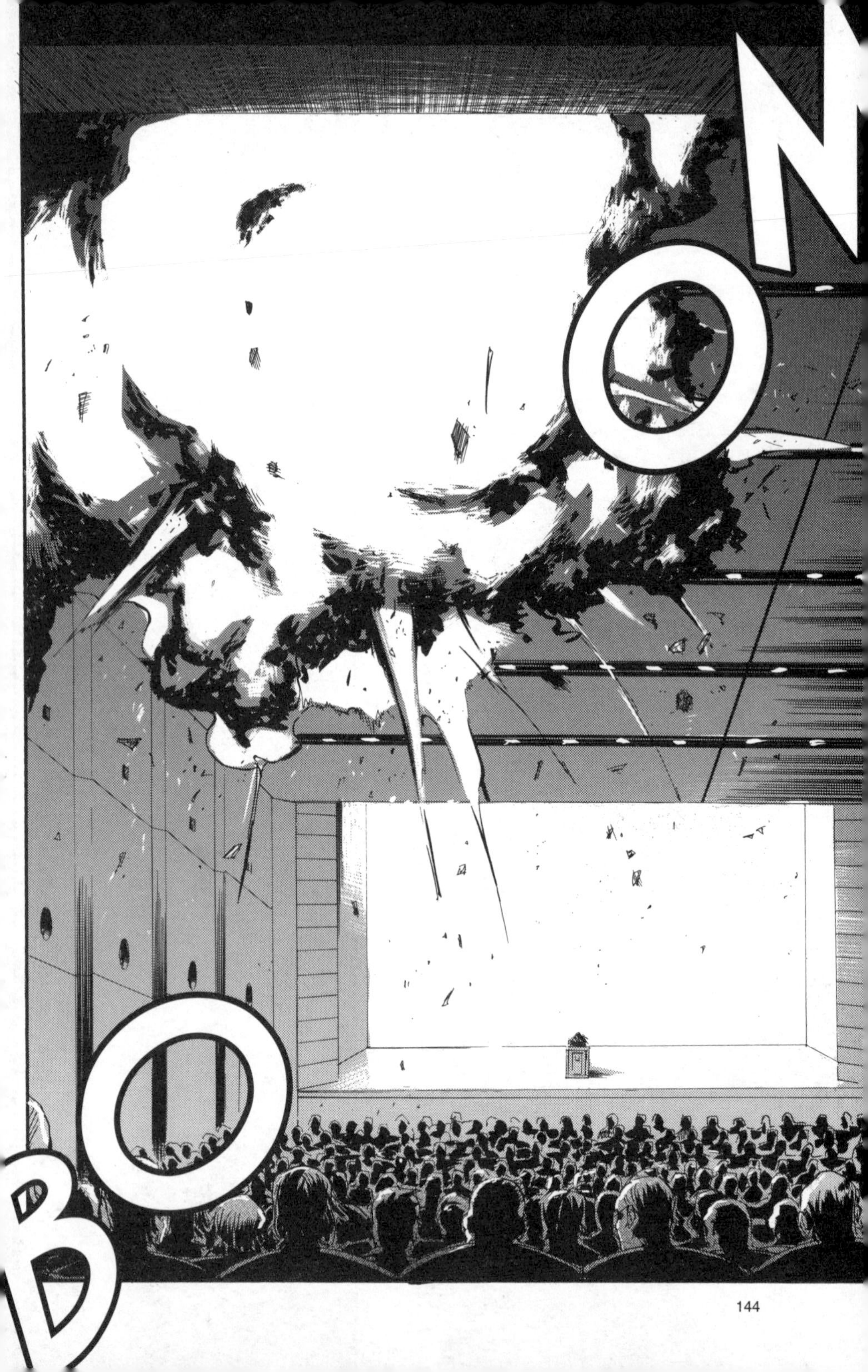
BOON

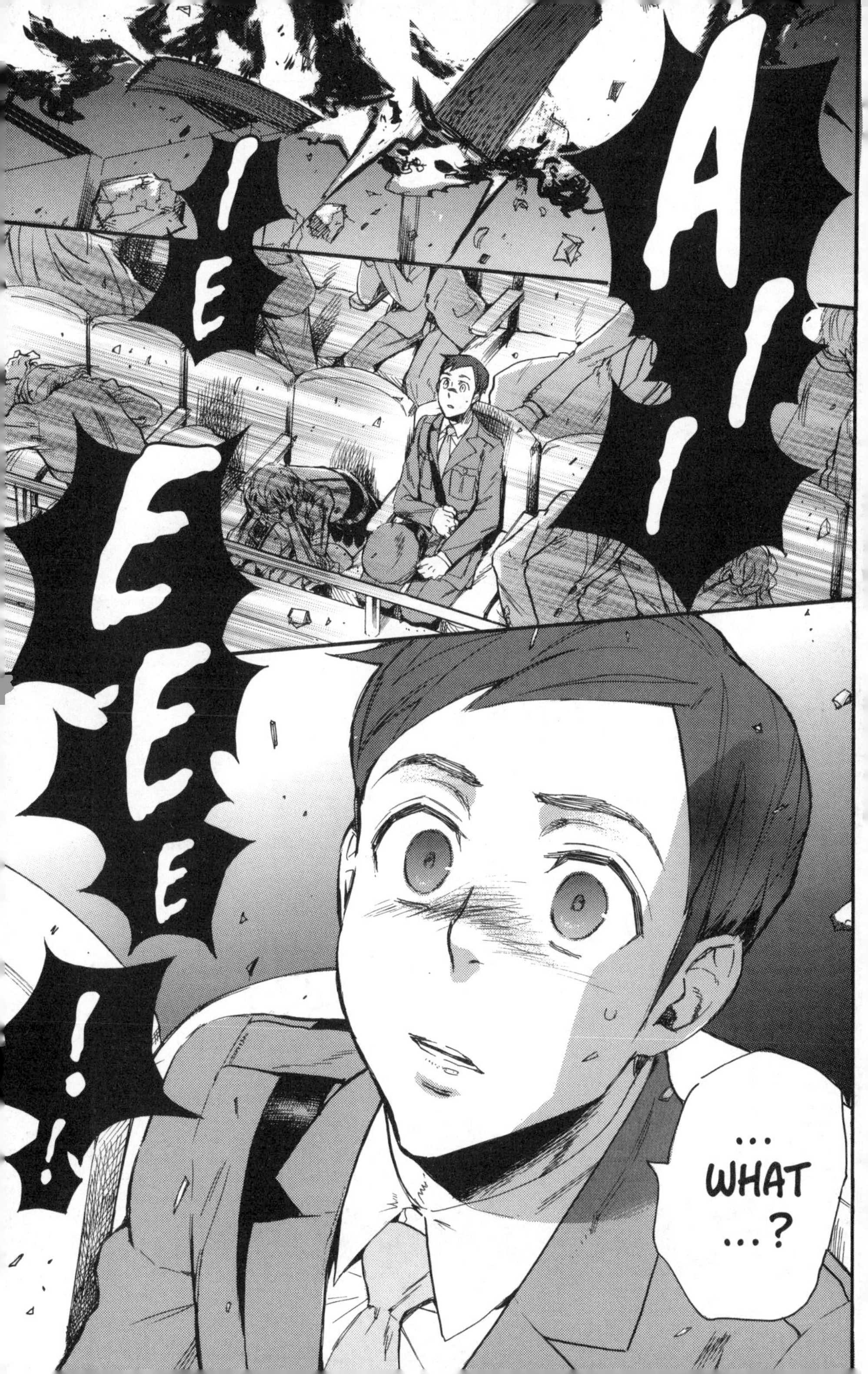
AIII
IEEEEE!!
...WHAT...?

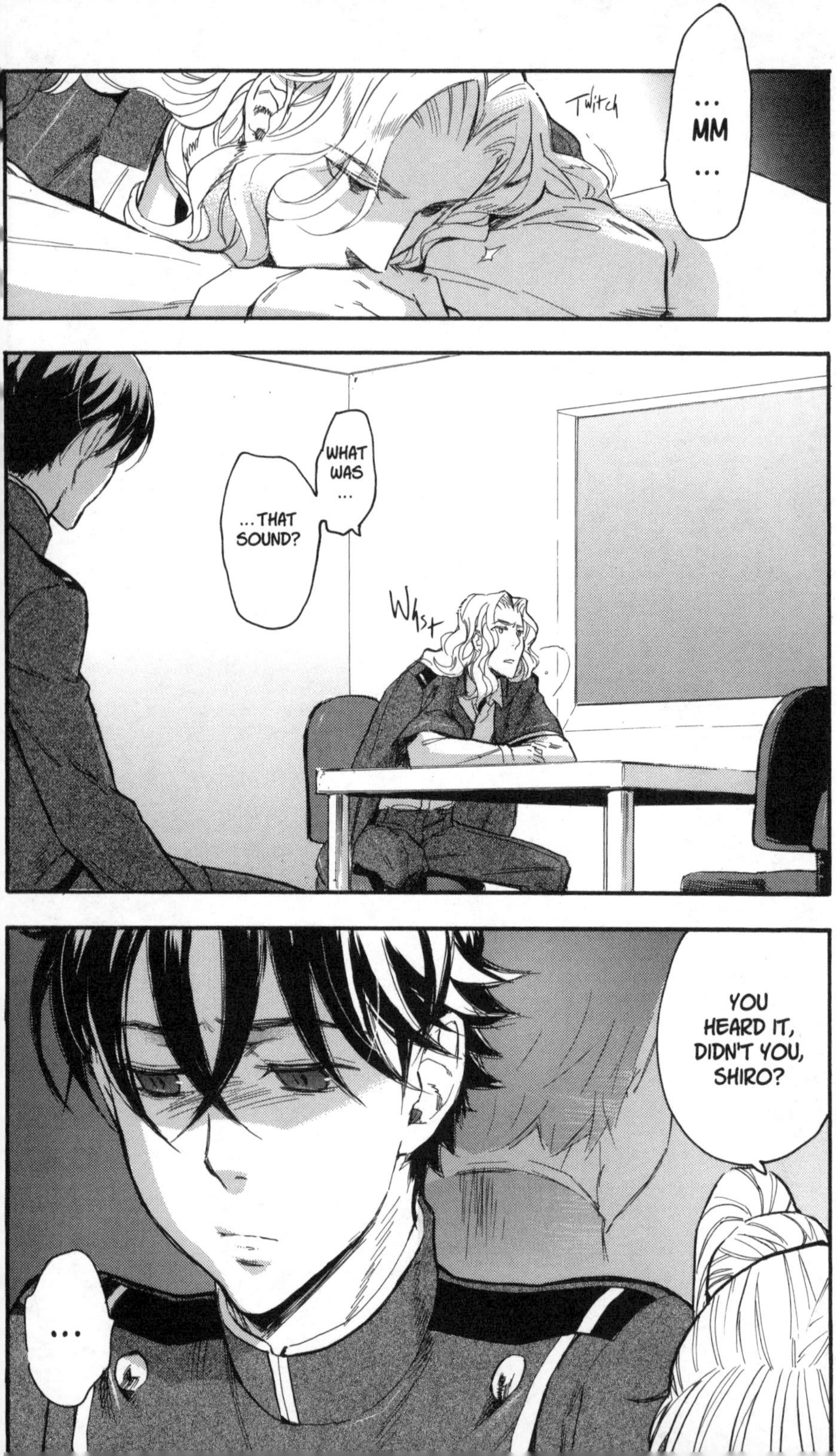
... MM ...
Twitch
WHAT WAS ...
...THAT SOUND?
Whst
YOU HEARD IT, DIDN'T YOU, SHIRO?
...

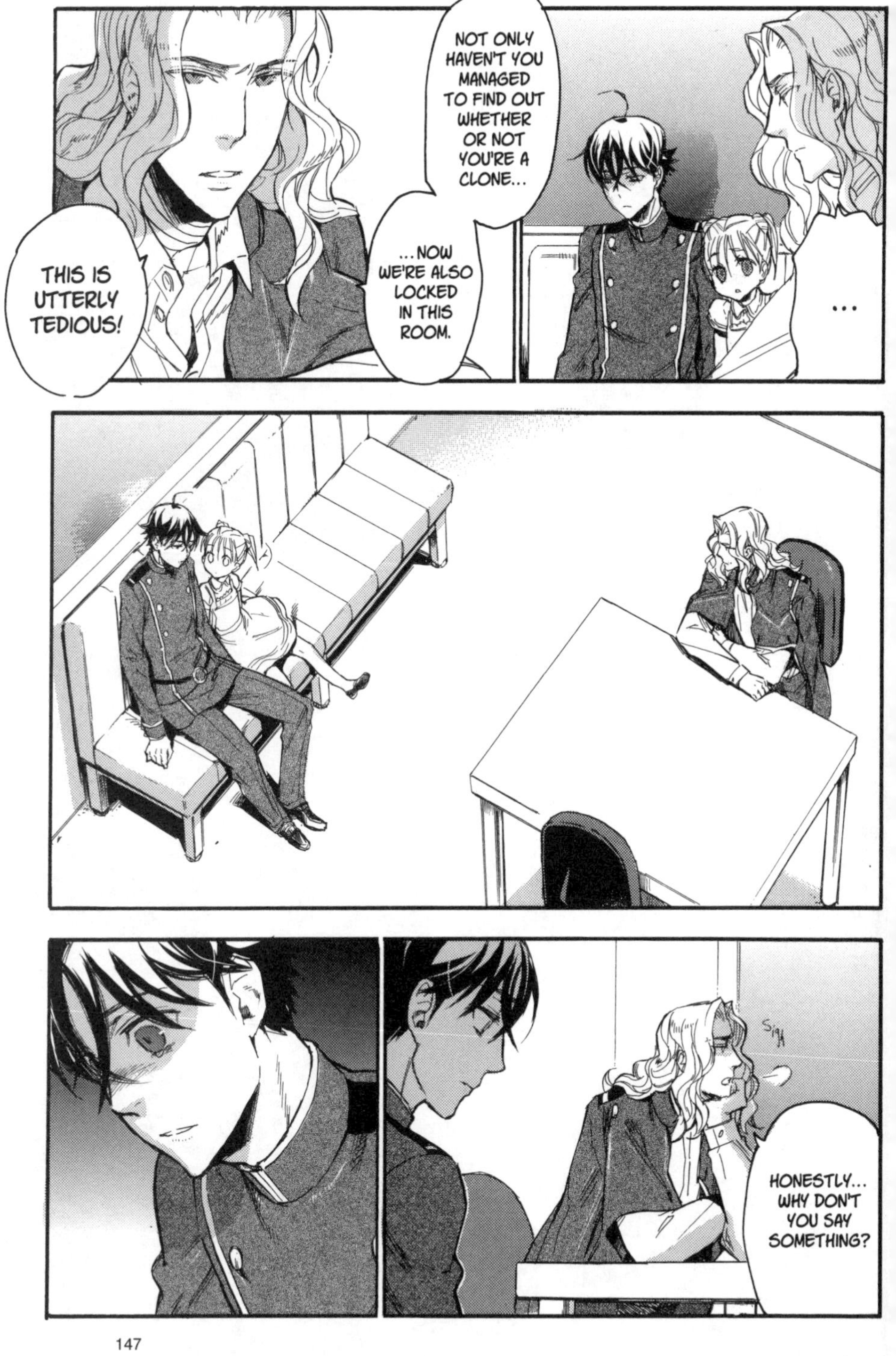
...
NOT ONLY HAVEN'T YOU MANAGED TO FIND OUT WHETHER OR NOT YOU'RE A CLONE...
...NOW WE'RE ALSO LOCKED IN THIS ROOM.
THIS IS UTTERLY TEDIOUS!
Sigh
HONESTLY... WHY DON'T YOU SAY SOMETHING?

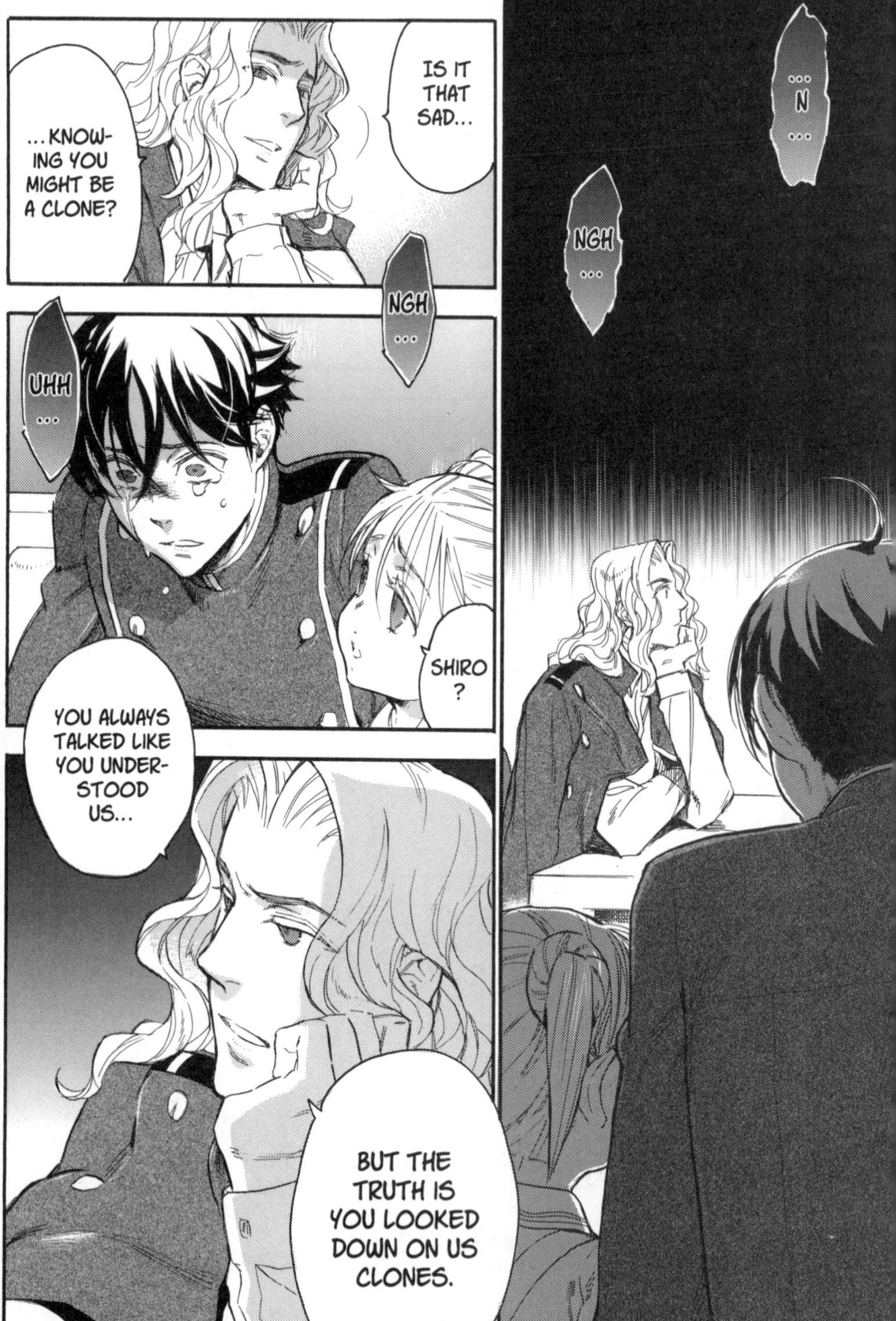
...N...
NGH...
IS IT THAT SAD...
...KNOWING YOU MIGHT BE A CLONE?
NGH...
SHIRO?
UHH...
YOU ALWAYS TALKED LIKE YOU UNDERSTOOD US...
BUT THE TRUTH IS YOU LOOKED DOWN ON US CLONES.

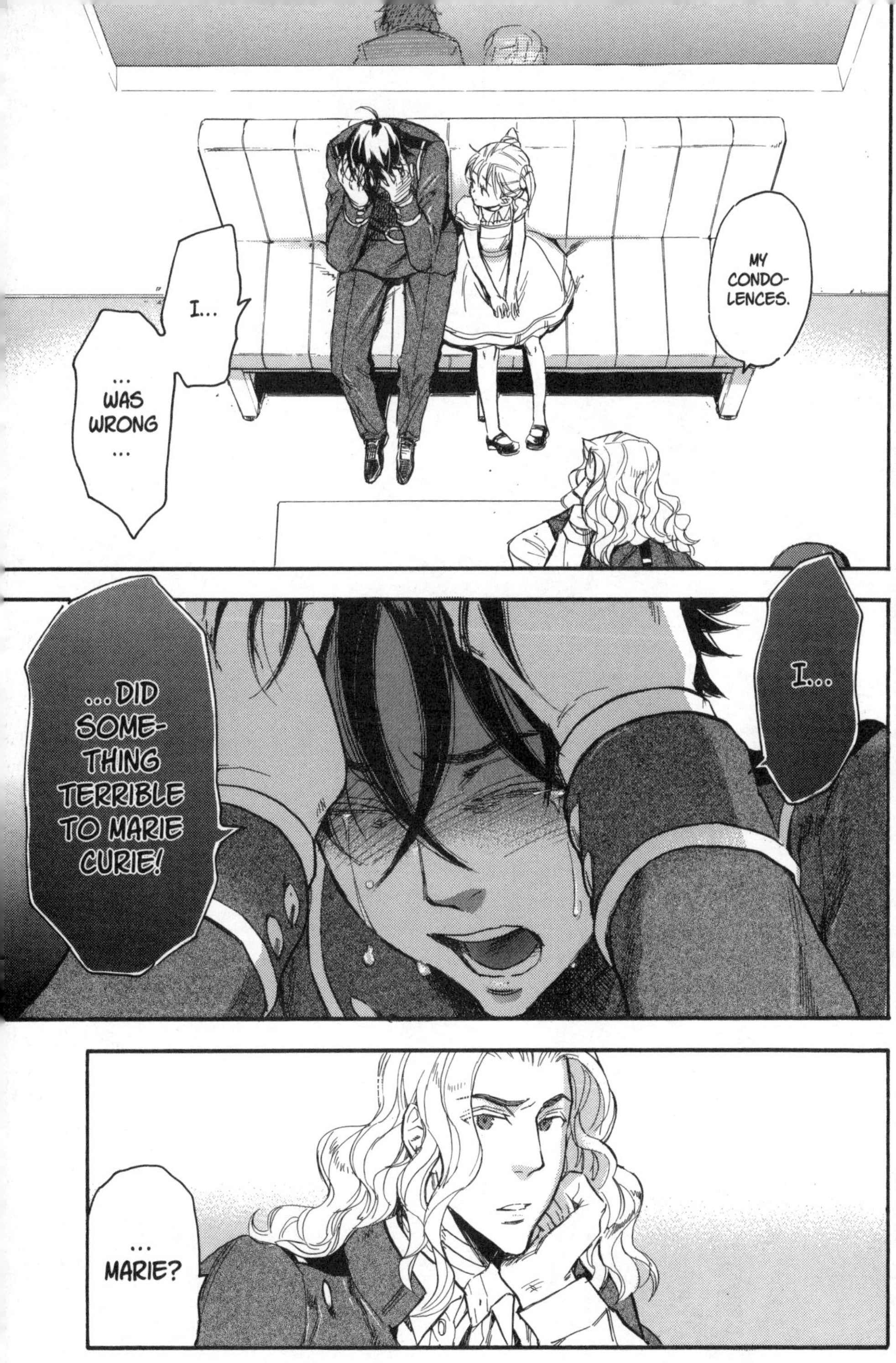
MY CONDO- LENCES.
I...
...WAS WRONG...
I...
...DID SOME- THING TERRIBLE TO MARIE CURIE!
...MARIE?

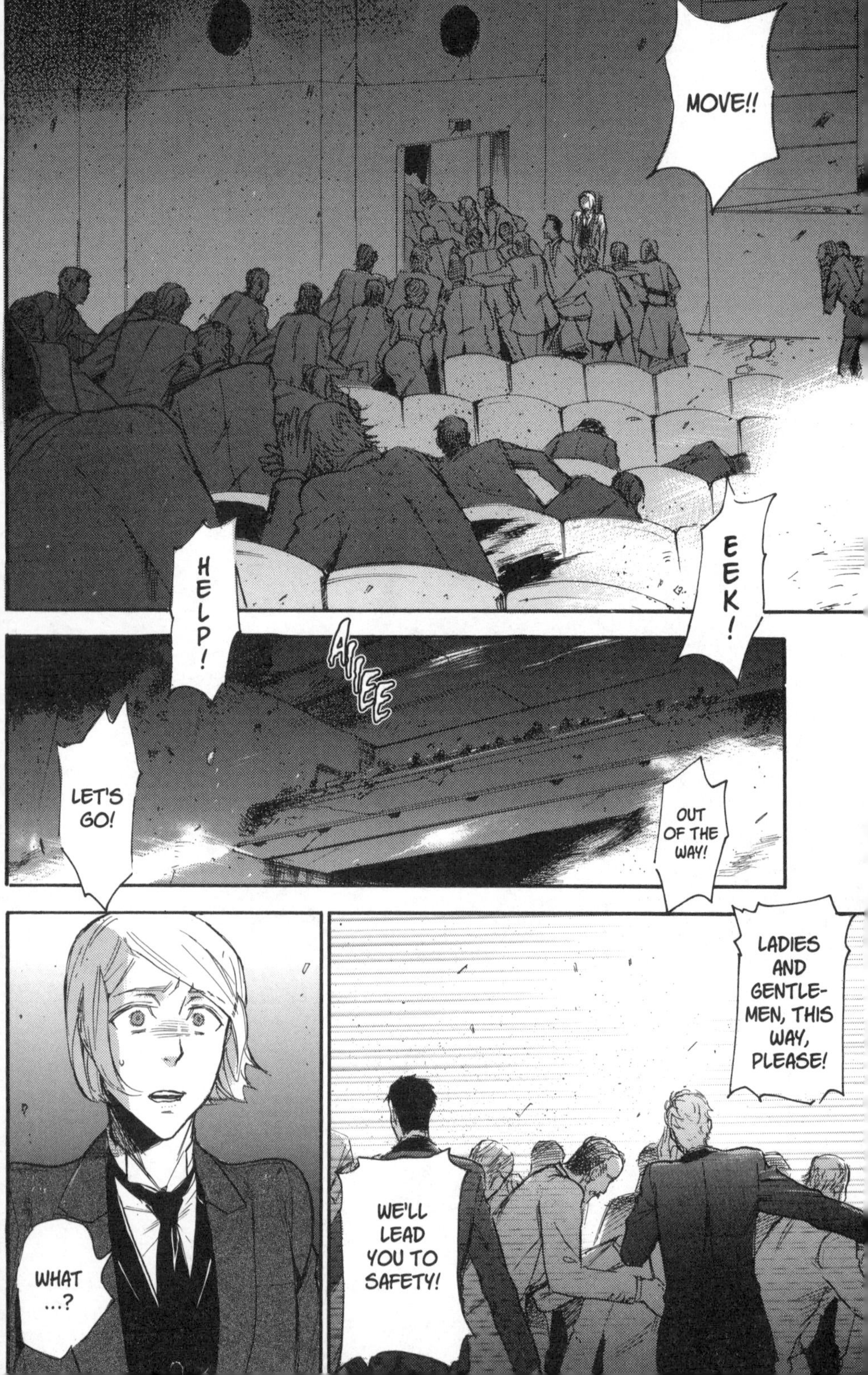
MOVE!!
EEK!
HELP!
AIIEE
OUT OF THE WAY!
LET'S GO!
LADIES AND GENTLE-MEN, THIS WAY, PLEASE!
WE'LL LEAD YOU TO SAFETY!
WHAT ...?

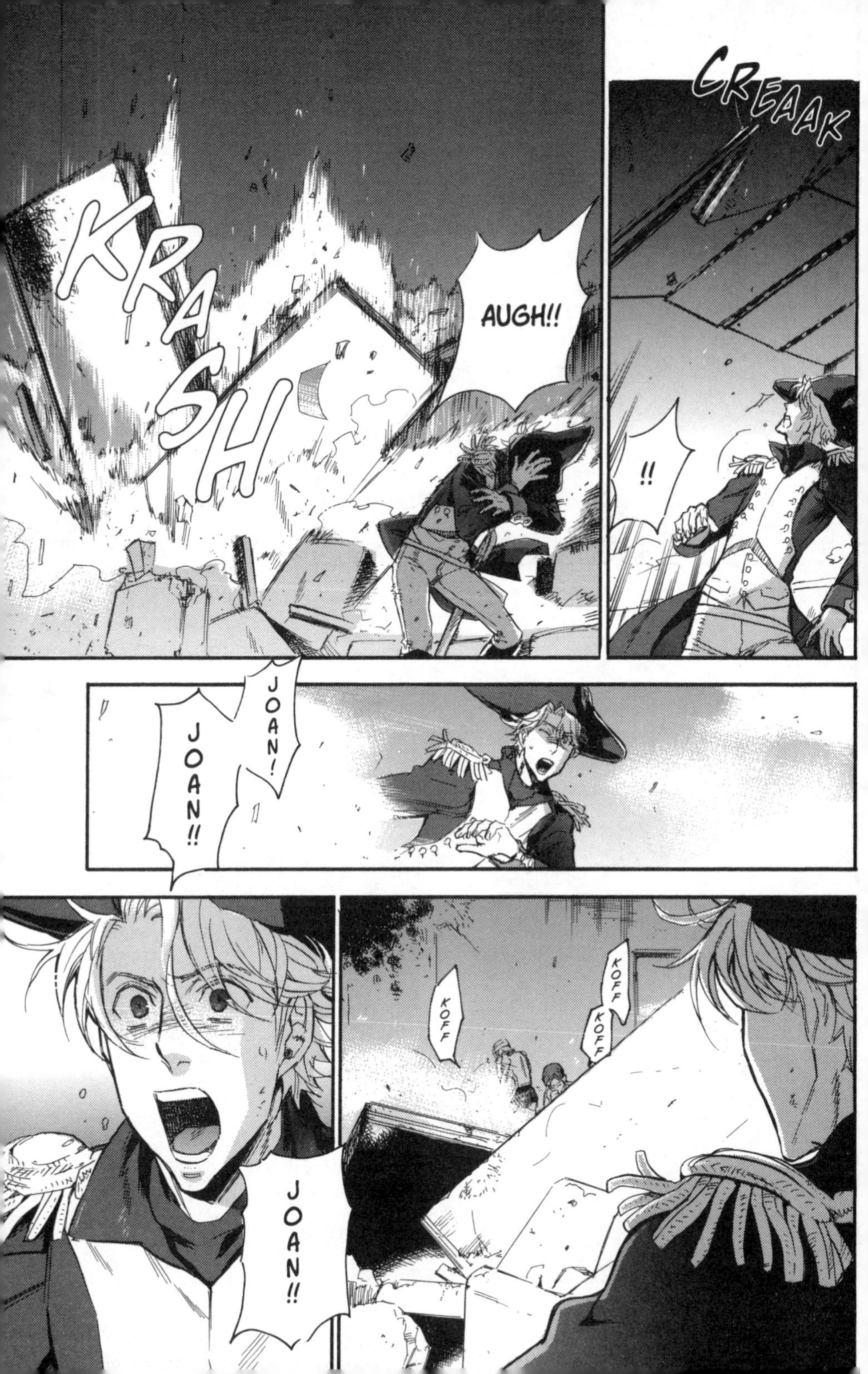
CREAAK
!!
KRASH
AUGH!!
JOAN!
JOAN!!
KOFF KOFF
KOFF
JOAN!!

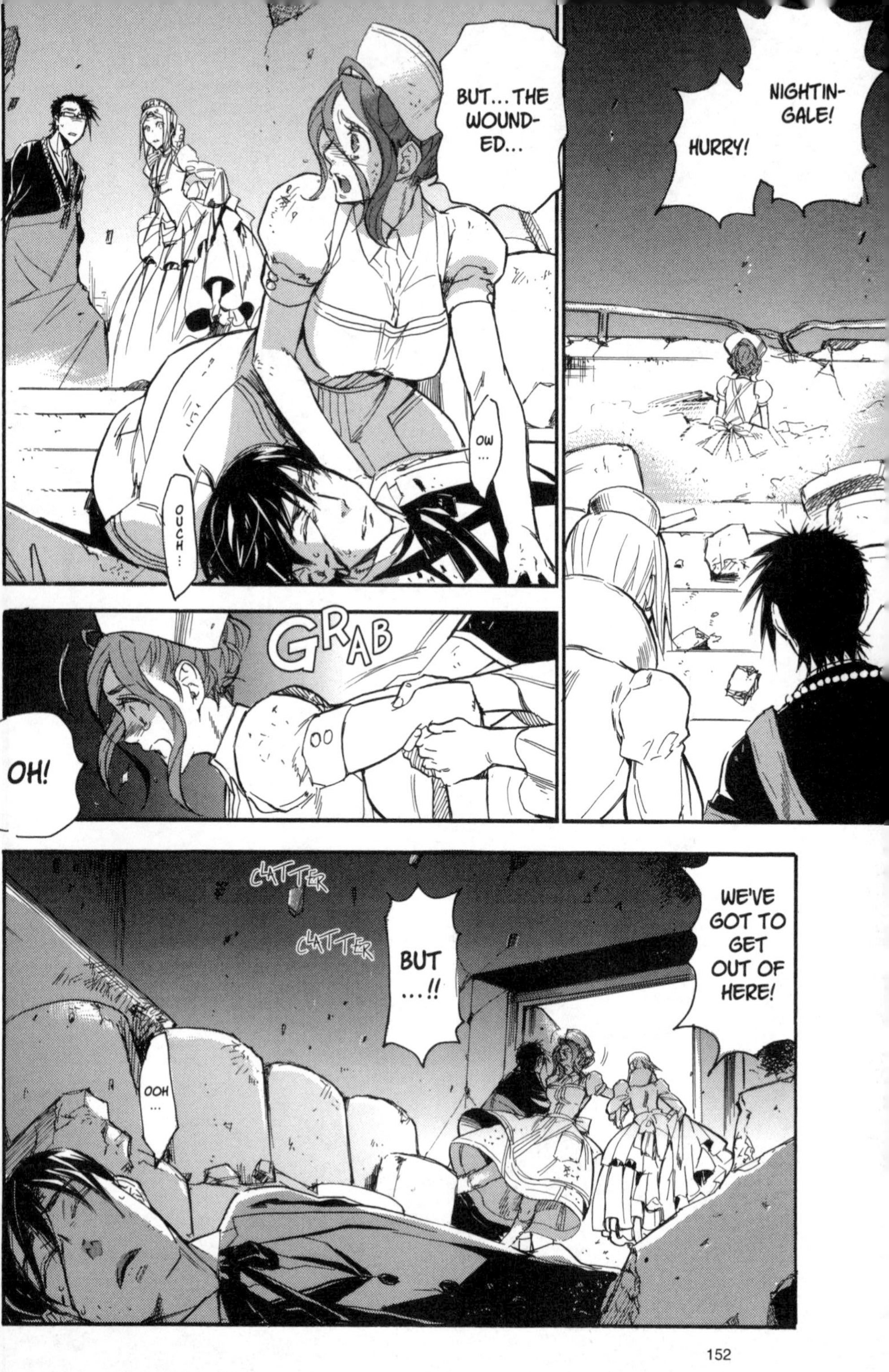
NIGHTIN-GALE!
HURRY!
BUT... THE WOUND-ED...
OW...
OUCH...
GRAB
OH!
WE'VE GOT TO GET OUT OF HERE!
BUT...!!
CLATTER
CLATTER
OOH...

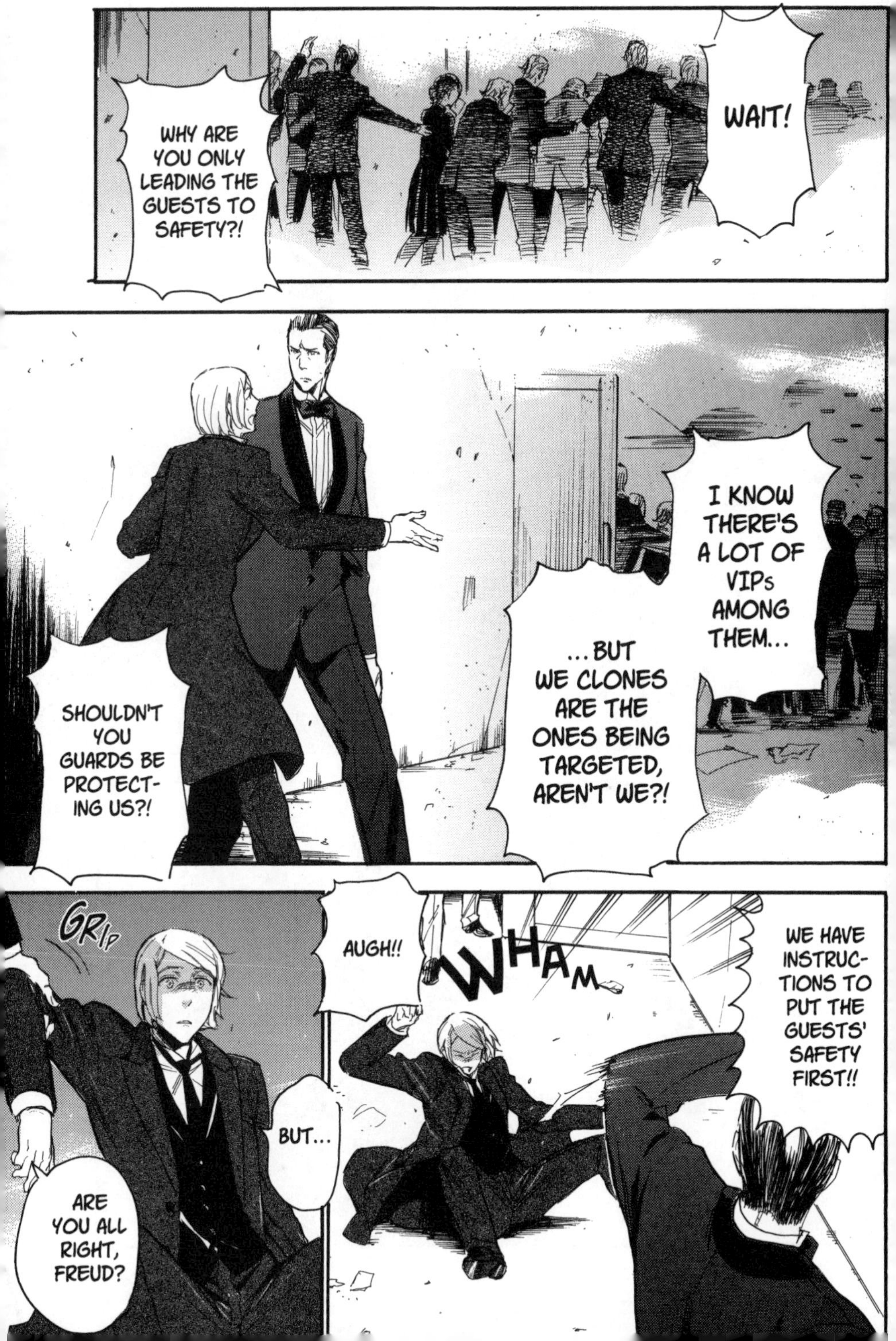
WAIT!
WHY ARE YOU ONLY LEADING THE GUESTS TO SAFETY?!
I KNOW THERE'S A LOT OF VIPs AMONG THEM...
...BUT WE CLONES ARE THE ONES BEING TARGETED, AREN'T WE?!
SHOULDN'T YOU GUARDS BE PROTECTING US?!
WE HAVE INSTRUCTIONS TO PUT THE GUESTS' SAFETY FIRST!!
WHAM
AUGH!!
BUT...
GRIP
ARE YOU ALL RIGHT, FREUD?

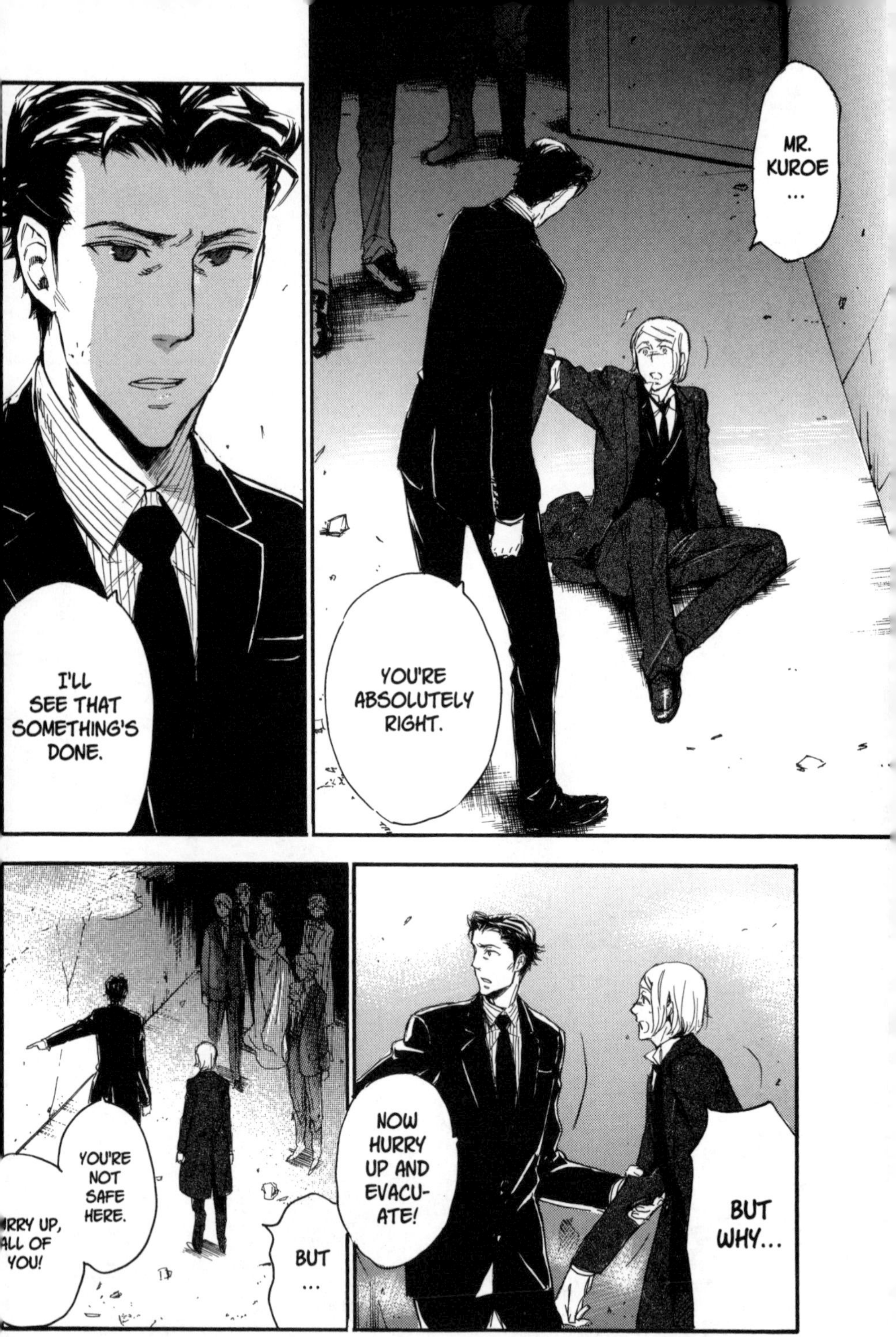

MR. KUROE ...
YOU'RE ABSOLUTELY RIGHT.
I'LL SEE THAT SOMETHING'S DONE.
BUT WHY...
NOW HURRY UP AND EVACU-ATE!
YOU'RE NOT SAFE HERE.
RRY UP, LL OF YOU!
BUT ...

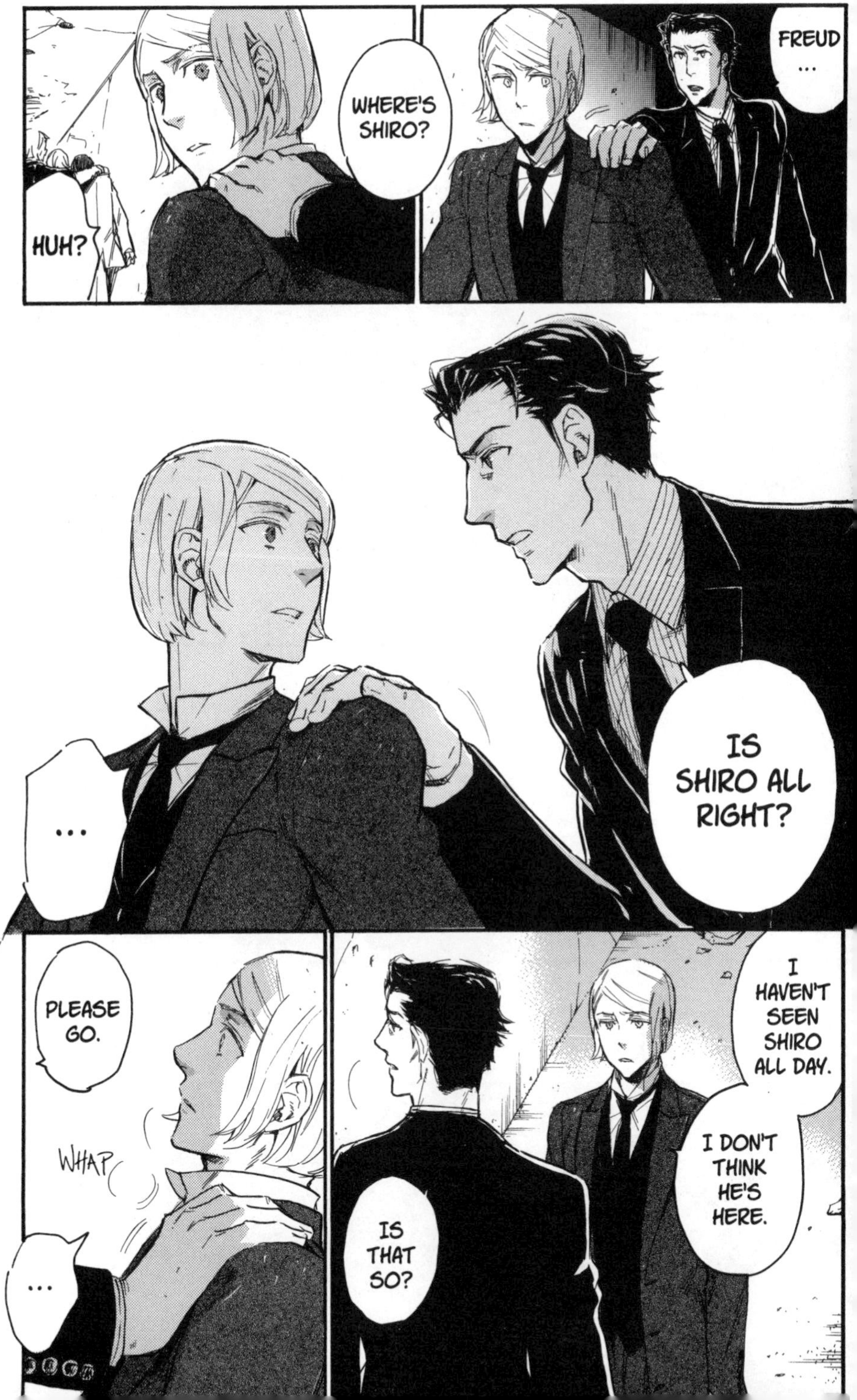
FREUD ...
WHERE'S SHIRO?
HUH?
IS SHIRO ALL RIGHT?
...
I HAVEN'T SEEN SHIRO ALL DAY.
I DON'T THINK HE'S HERE.
IS THAT SO?
PLEASE GO.
WHAP
...

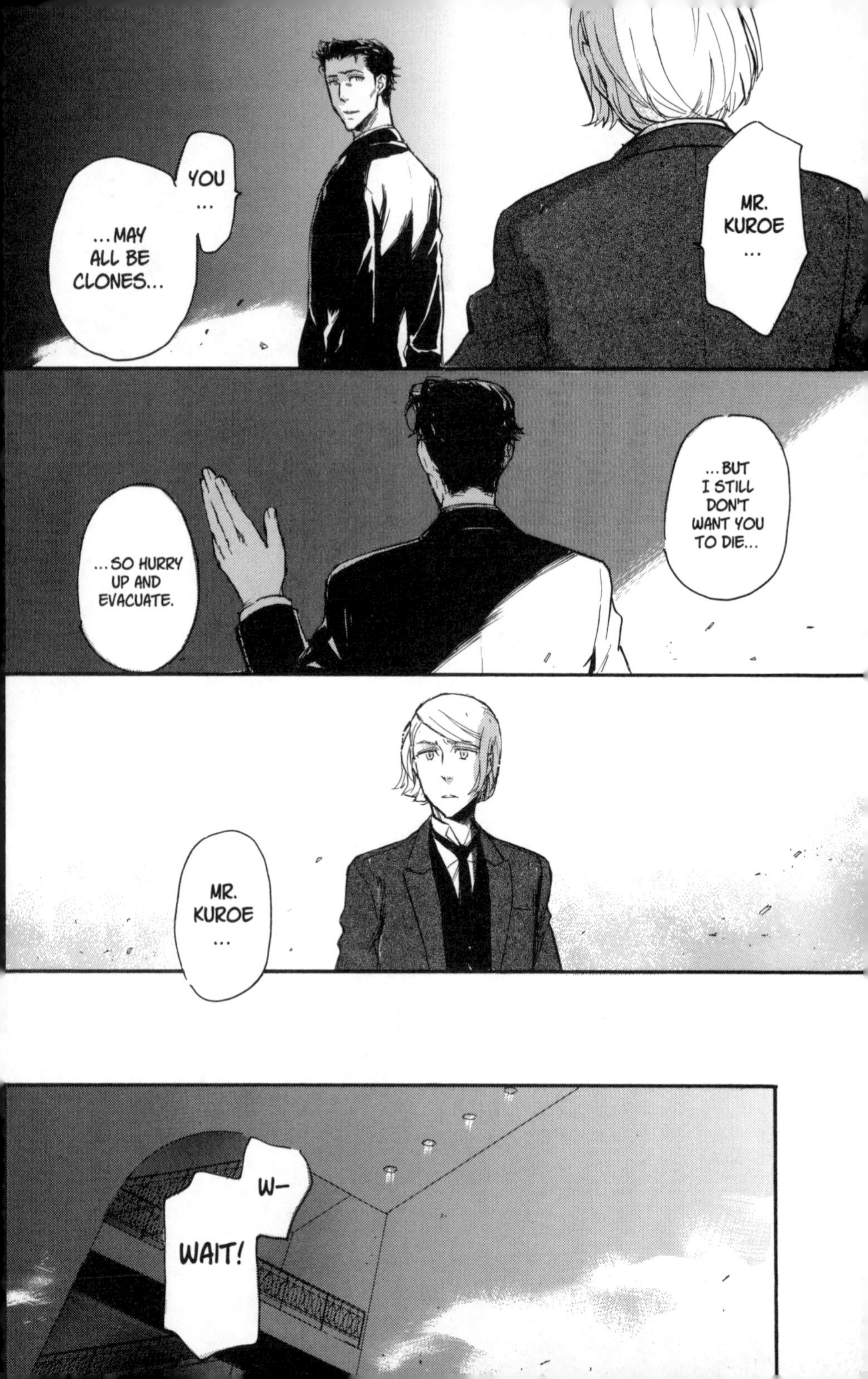
MR. KUROE ...
YOU ... ...MAY ALL BE CLONES...
...BUT I STILL DON'T WANT YOU TO DIE...
...SO HURRY UP AND EVACUATE.
MR. KUROE ...
W— WAIT!

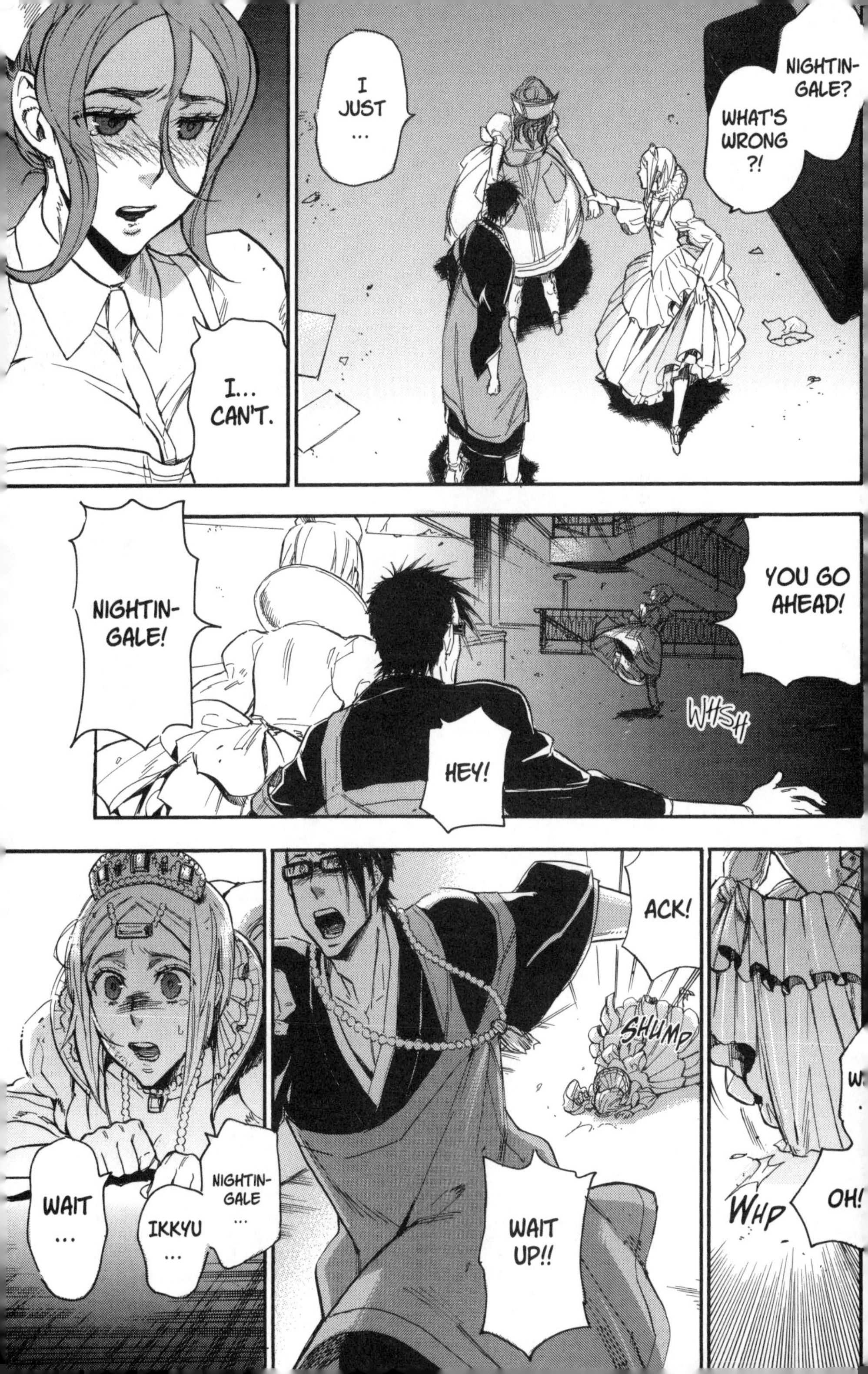
NIGHTIN-GALE? WHAT'S WRONG ?!
I JUST ...
I... CAN'T.
YOU GO AHEAD!
WHSH
NIGHTIN-GALE!
HEY!
OH!
WHP
ACK!
SHUMP
WAIT UP!!
NIGHTIN-GALE ...
IKKYU ...
WAIT ...

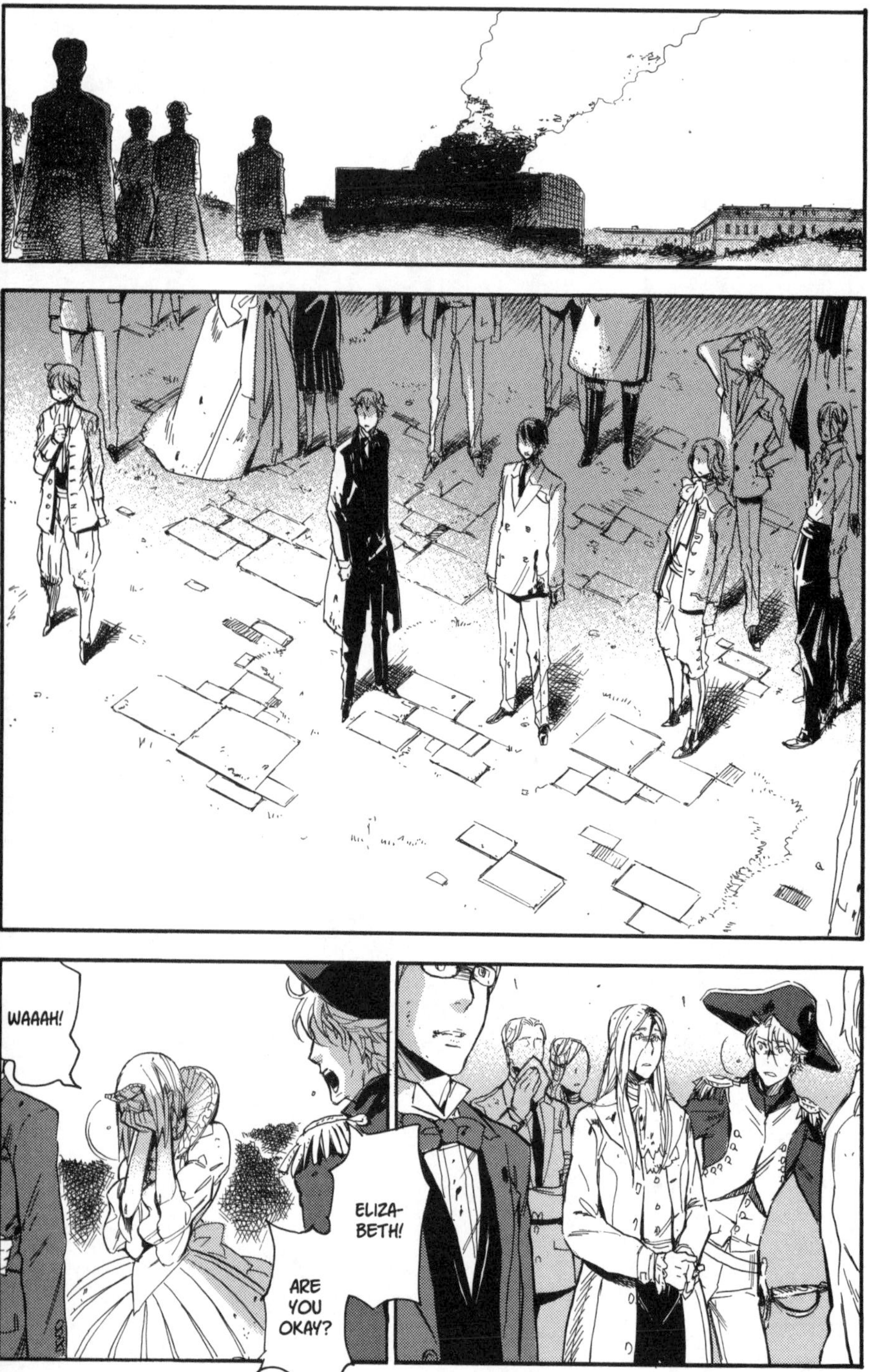
WAAAH!
ELIZA-BETH!
ARE YOU OKAY?

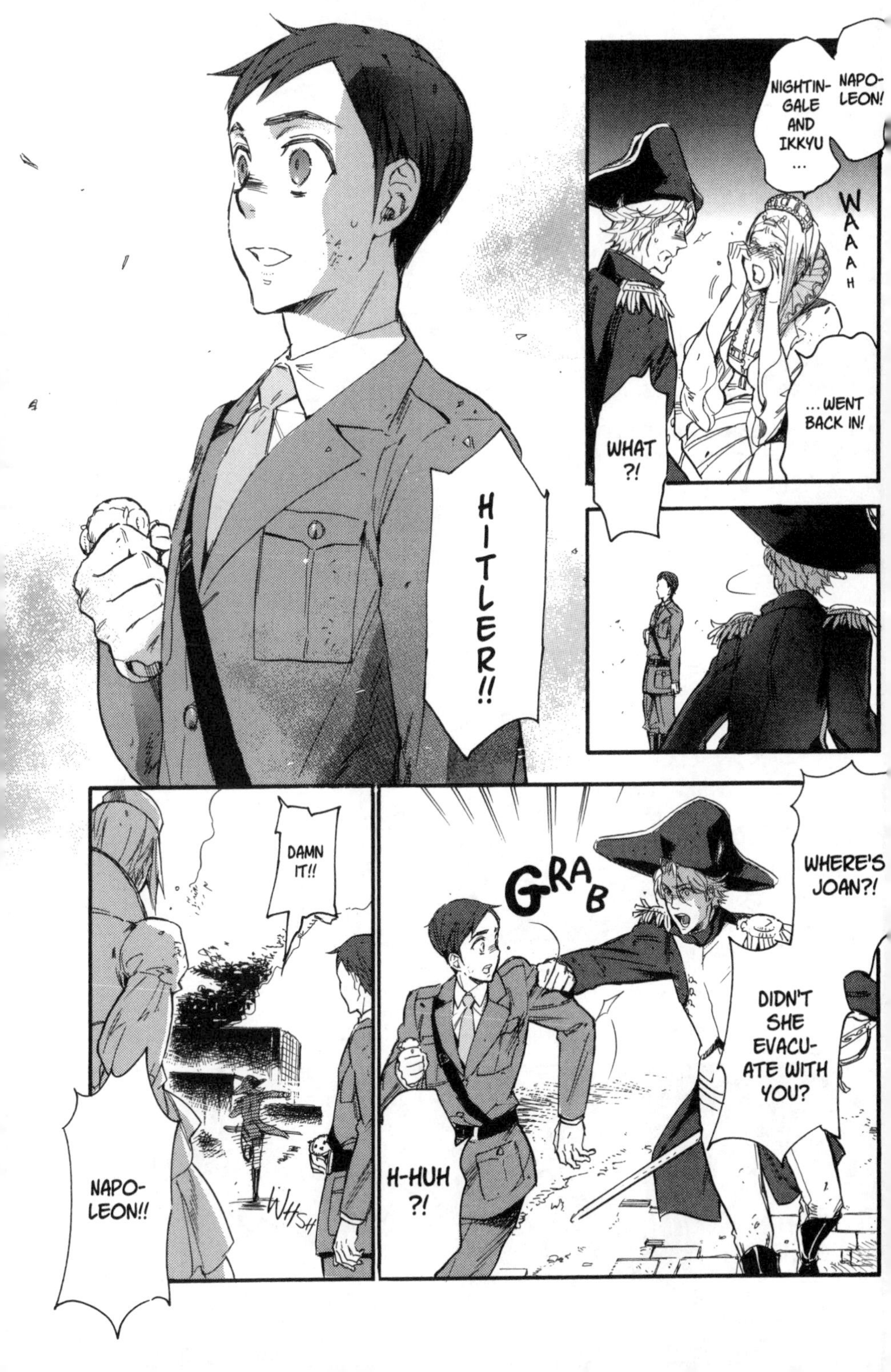
NAPOLEON!
NIGHTINGALE AND IKKYU...
WAAAAH
...WENT BACK IN!
WHAT?!
HITLER!!
WHERE'S JOAN?!
GRAB
DIDN'T SHE EVACUATE WITH YOU?
H-HUH?!
DAMN IT!!
WHSH
NAPOLEON!!

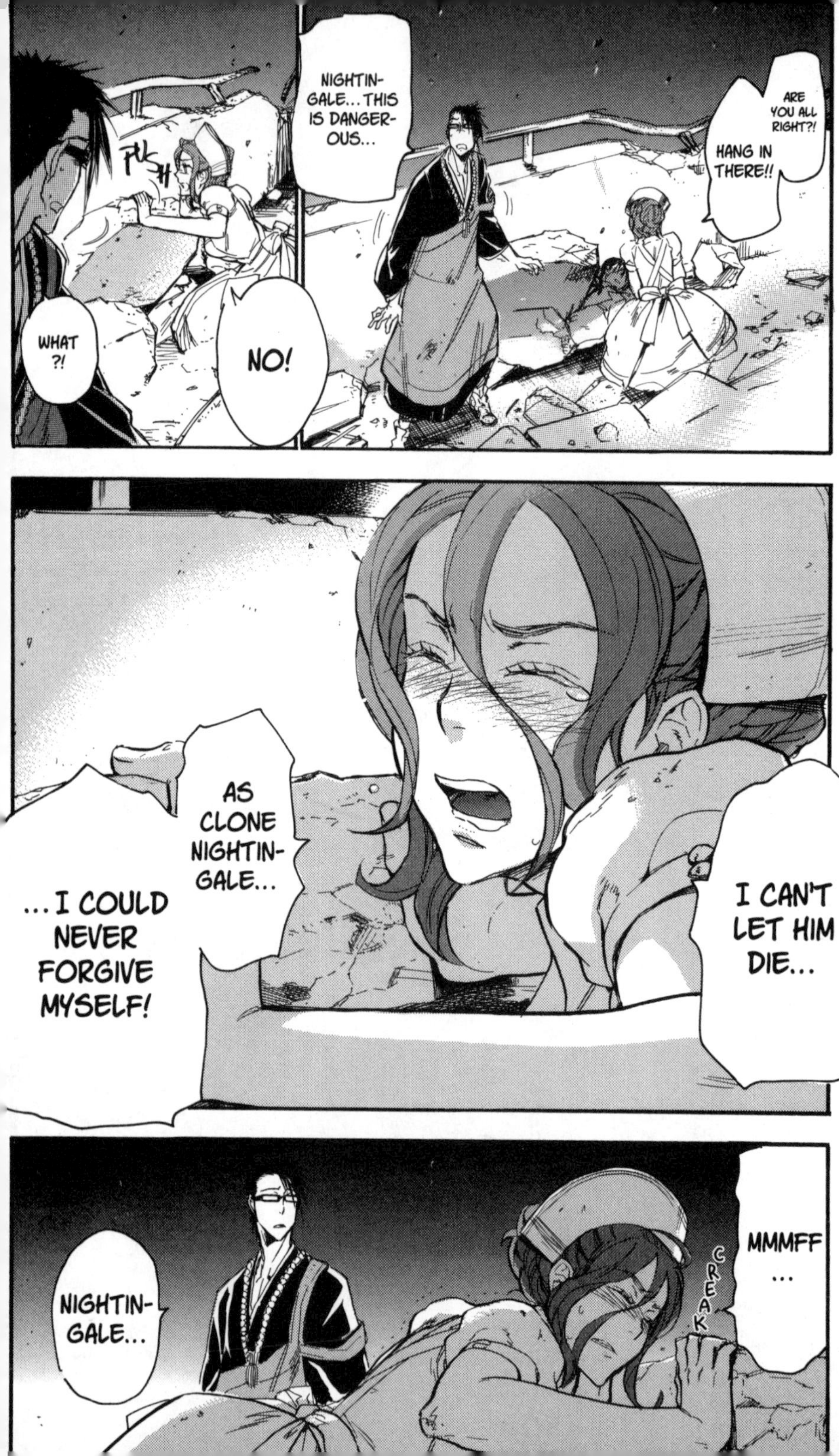
ARE YOU ALL RIGHT?!
HANG IN THERE!!
NIGHTIN-GALE... THIS IS DANGER-OUS...
NO!
WHAT?!
I CAN'T LET HIM DIE...
AS CLONE NIGHTIN-GALE...
...I COULD NEVER FORGIVE MYSELF!
MMMFF...
CREAK
NIGHTIN-GALE...

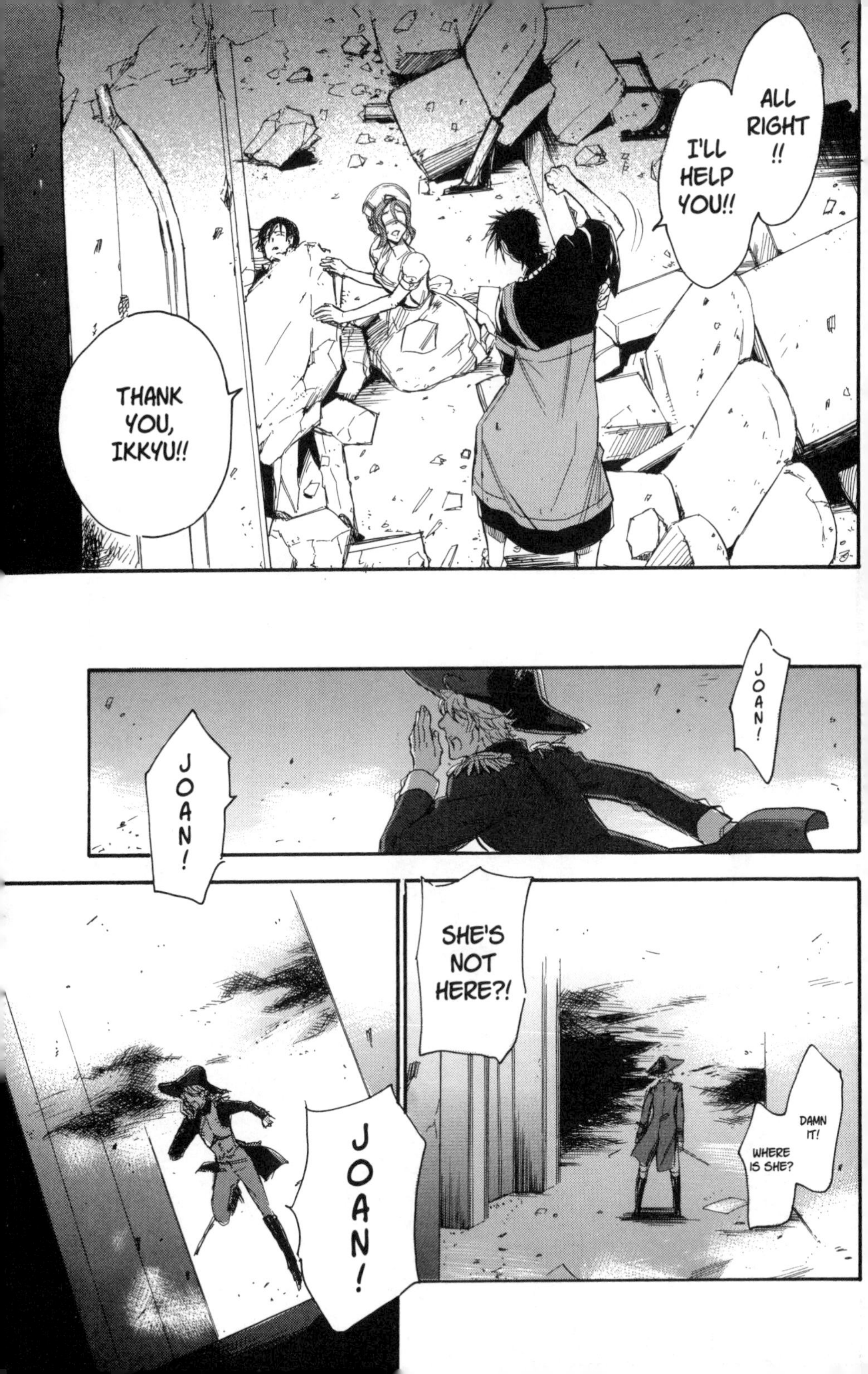
ALL RIGHT!!
I'LL HELP YOU!!
THANK YOU, IKKYU!!
JOAN!
JOAN!
SHE'S NOT HERE?!
DAMN IT!
WHERE IS SHE?
JOAN!

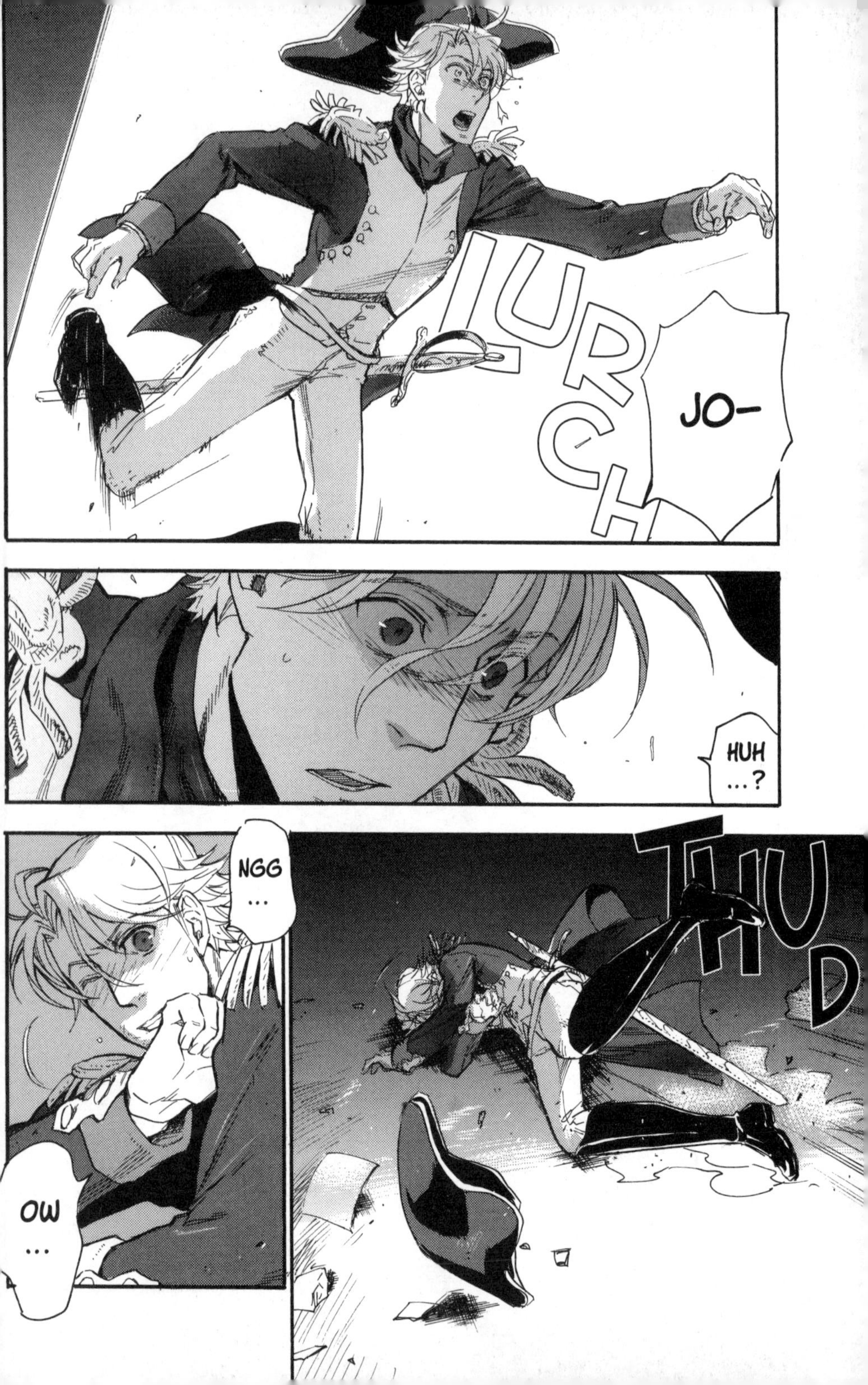
LURCH
JO-
HUH ...?
THUD
NGG ...
OW ...

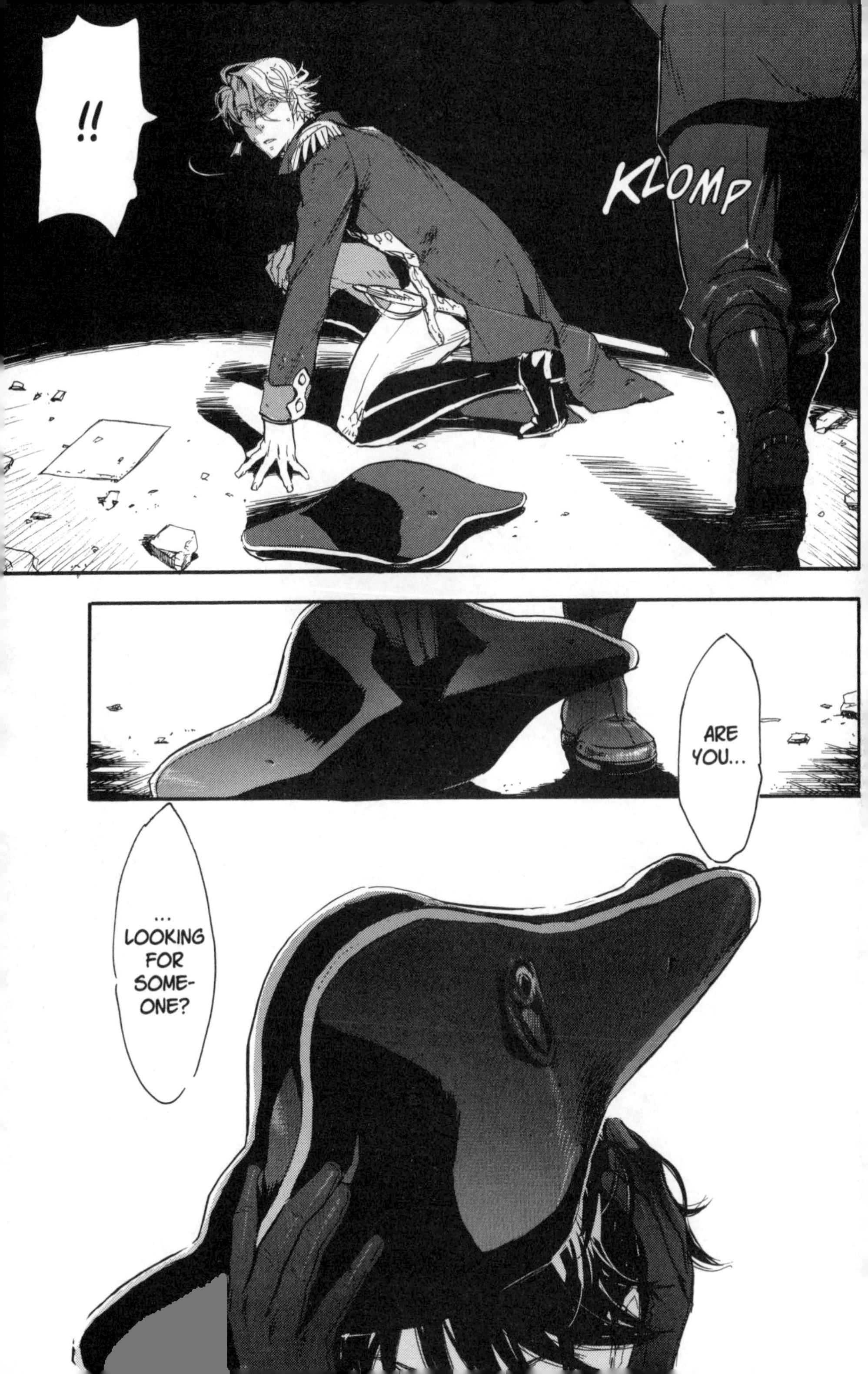
KLOMP
!!
ARE YOU...
...LOOKING FOR SOME-ONE?

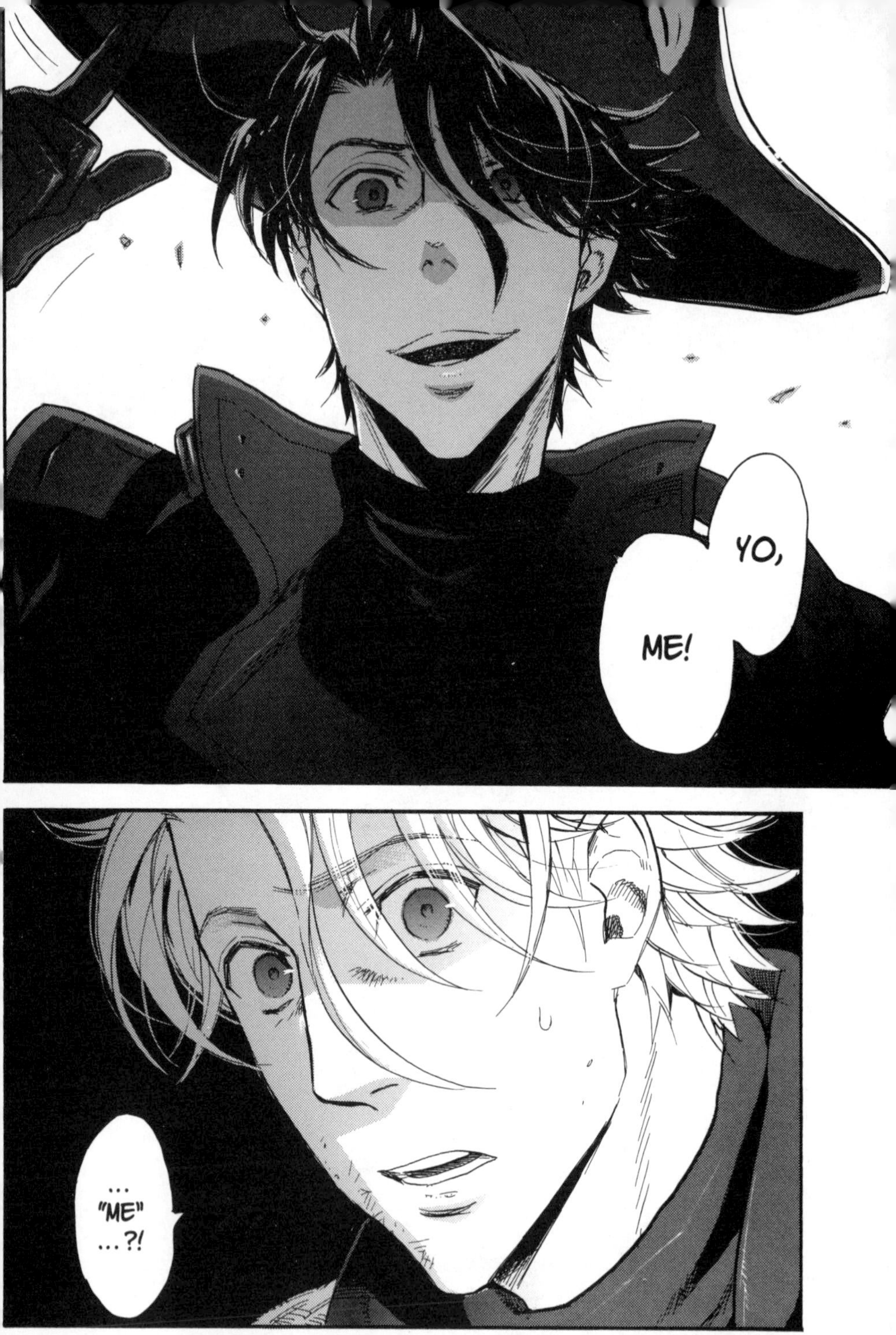
YO, ME!
..."ME"...?!

# Chapter eighteen

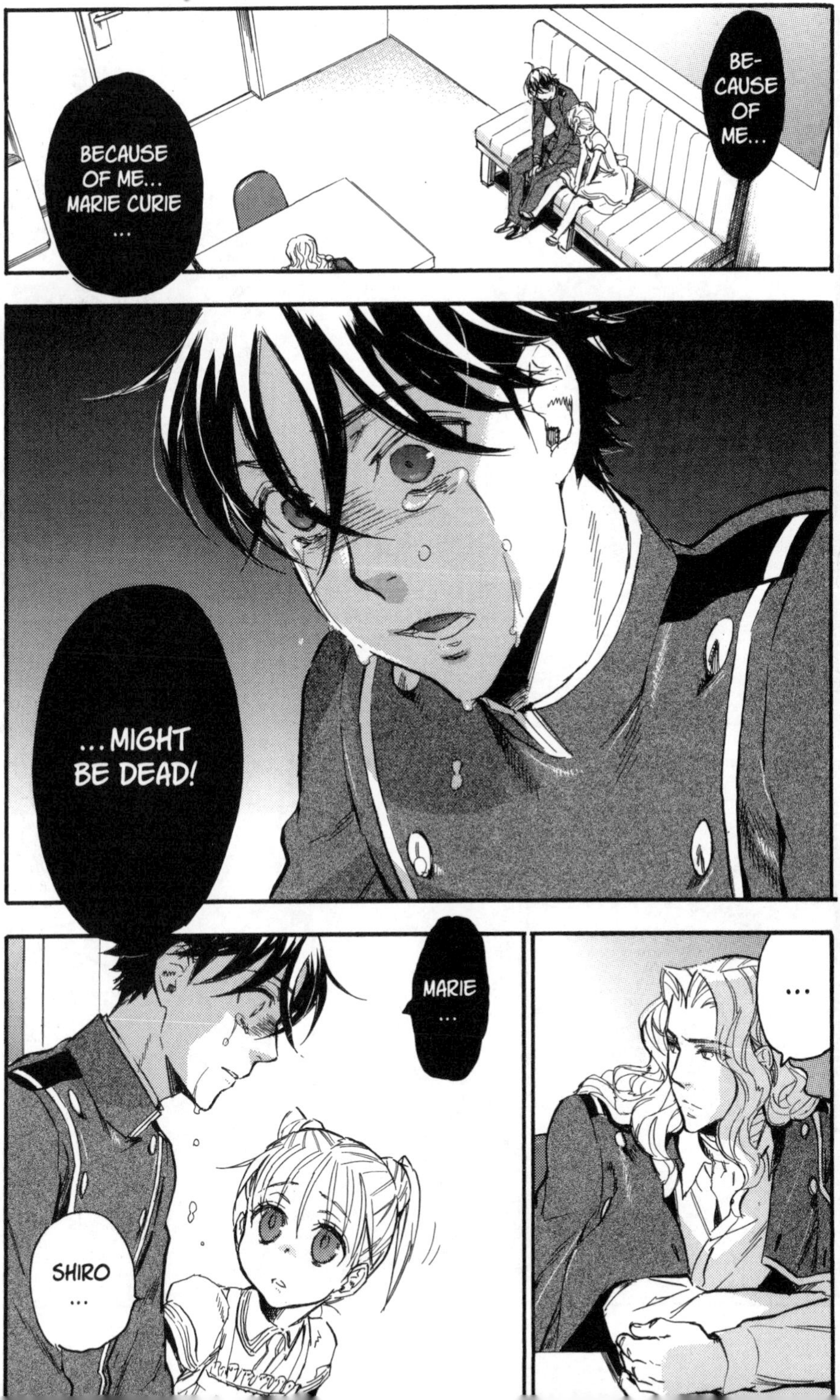
BE-CAUSE OF ME...
BECAUSE OF ME... MARIE CURIE ...
...MIGHT BE DEAD!
...
MARIE ...
SHIRO ...

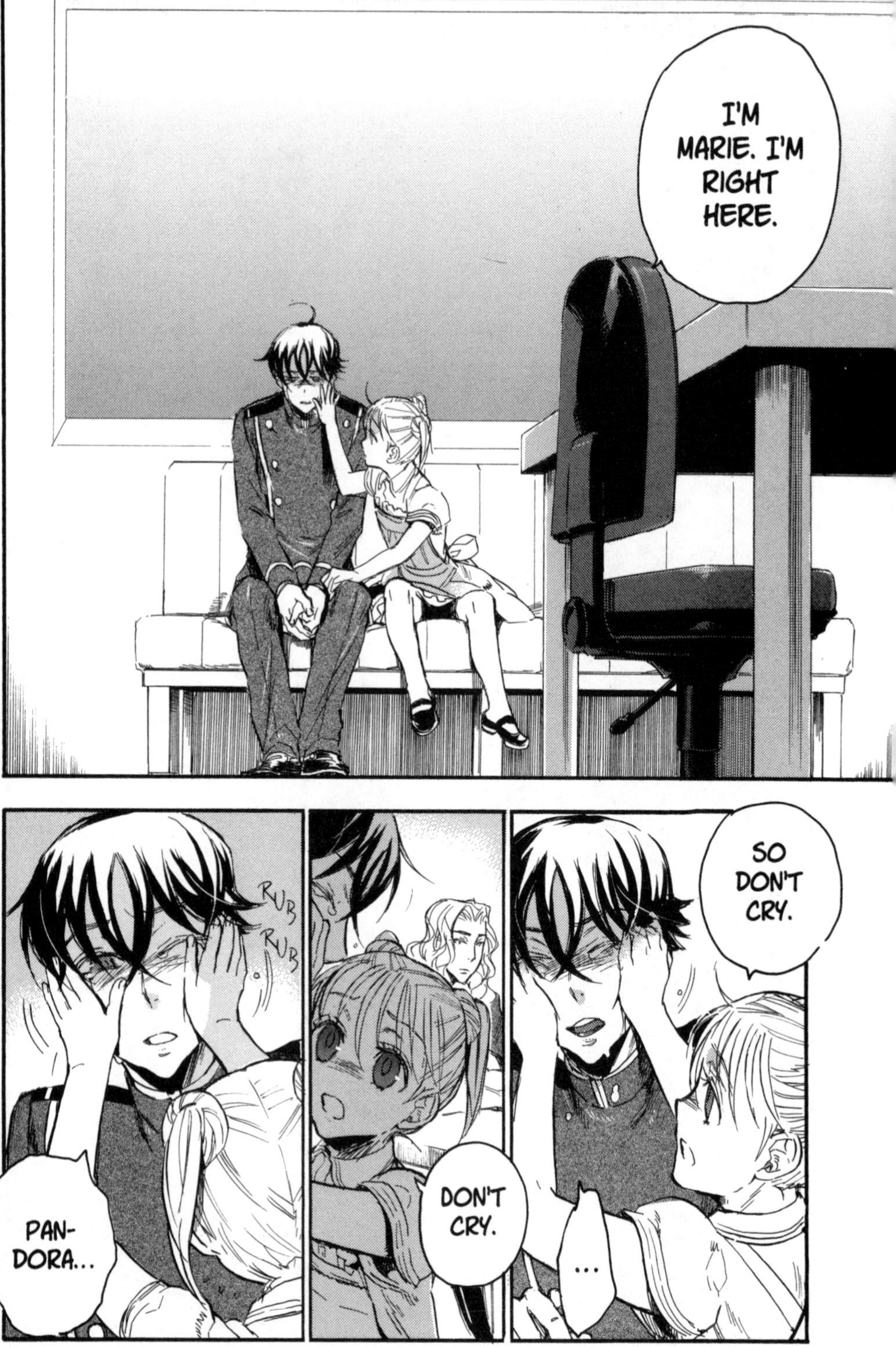
I'M MARIE. I'M RIGHT HERE.
SO DON'T CRY.
...
DON'T CRY.
RUB RUB
PAN-DORA...

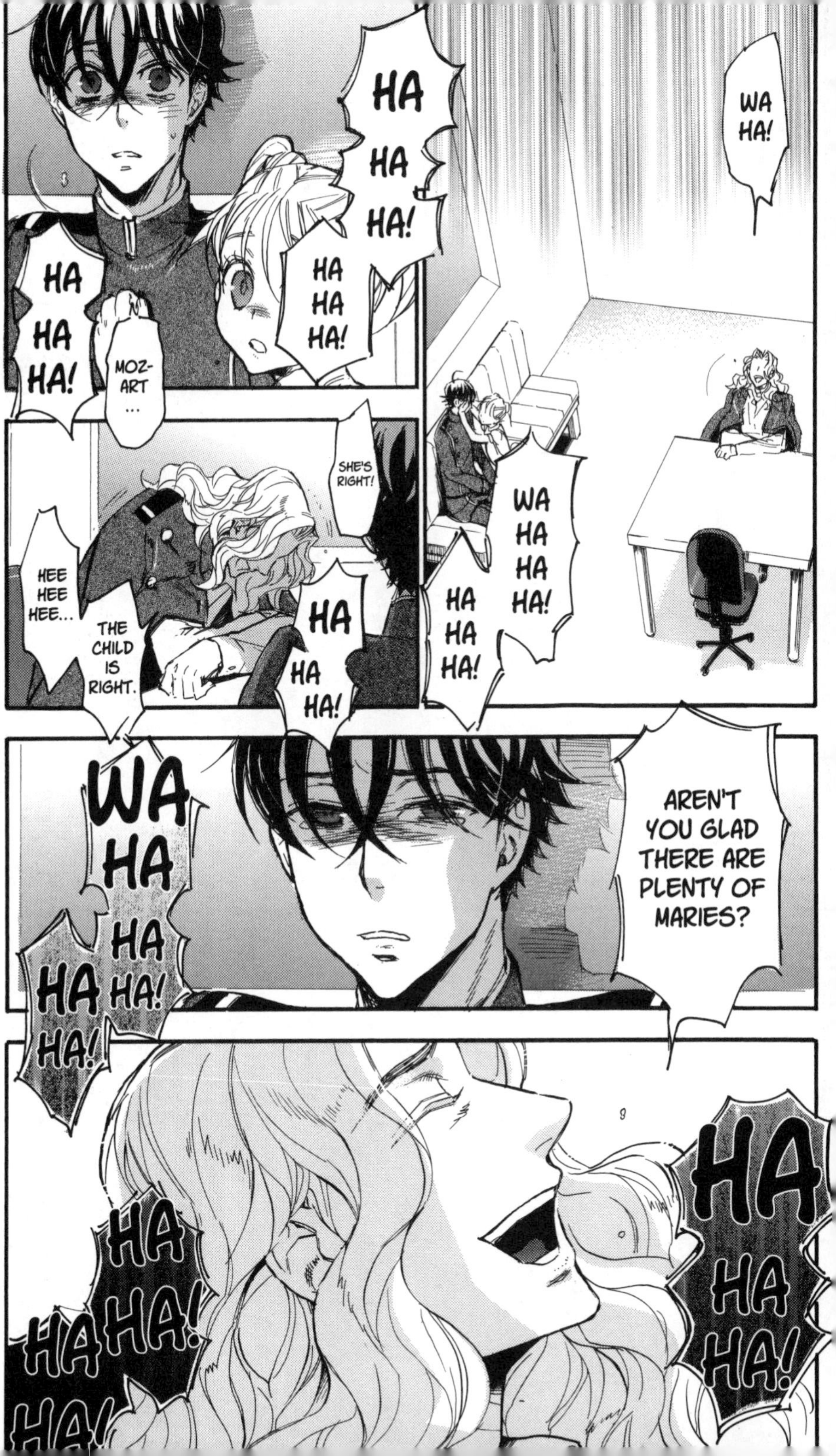
WA HA!
WA HA HA HA!
HA HA HA!
HA HA HA!
HA HA HA!
HA HA HA!
MOZ-ART...
SHE'S RIGHT!
HA HA HA!
HEE HEE HEE...
THE CHILD IS RIGHT.
AREN'T YOU GLAD THERE ARE PLENTY OF MARIES?
WA HA HA HA!
HA HA HA!
HA HA HA HA!
HA HA HA!
HA HA HA!

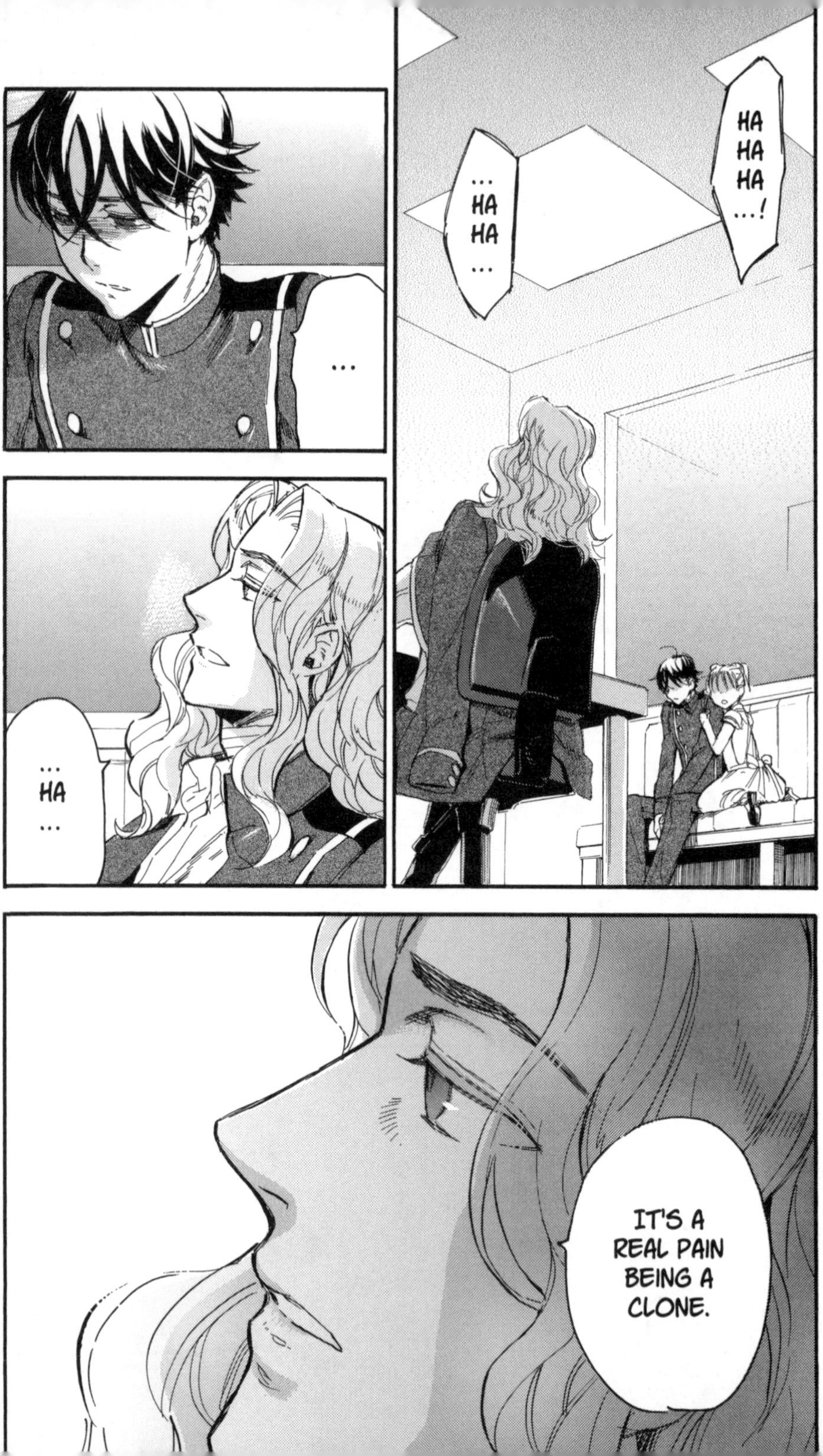
HA HA HA ...!
... HA HA ...
...
... HA ...
IT'S A REAL PAIN BEING A CLONE.

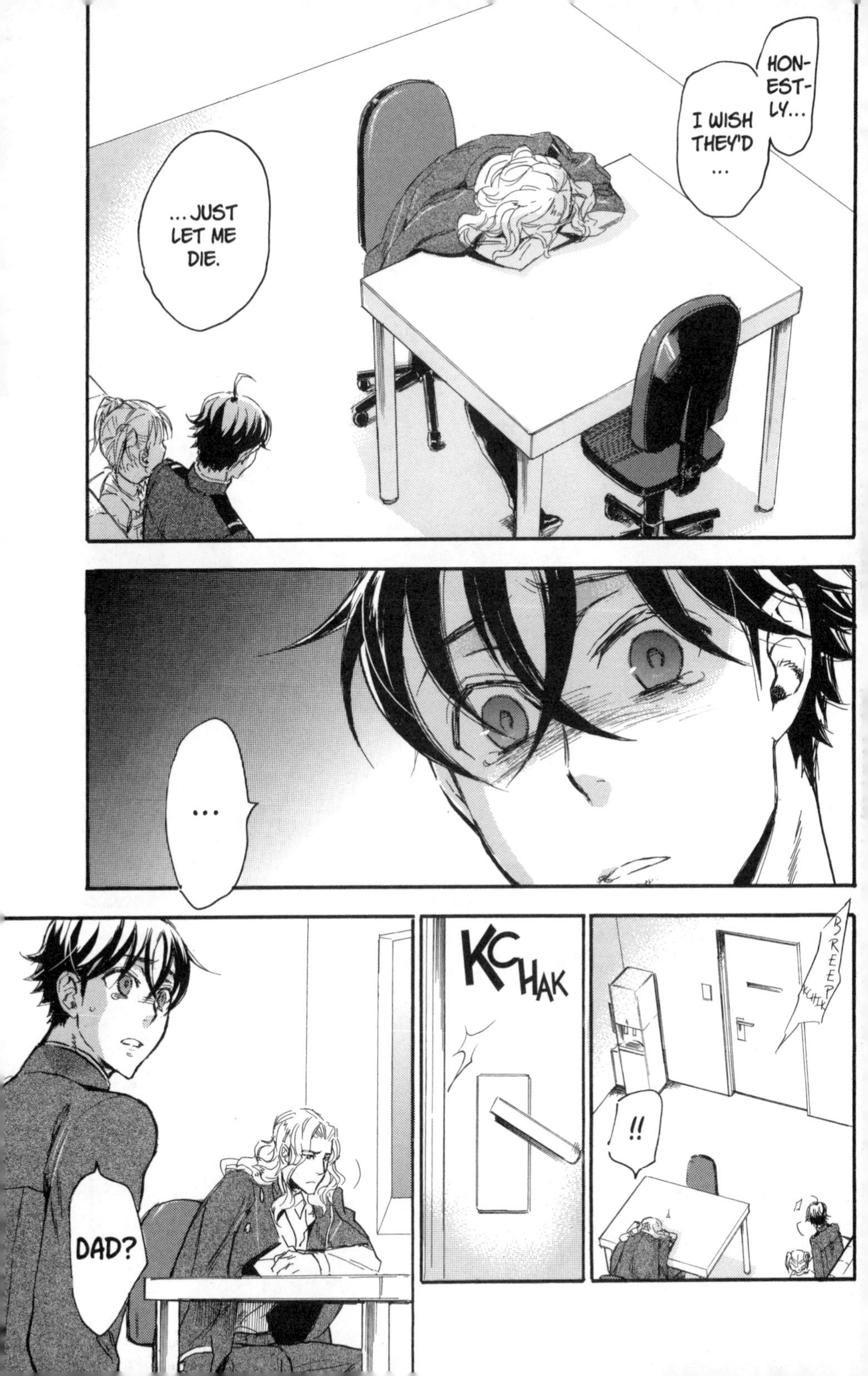
HON-EST-LY...
I WISH THEY'D ...
...JUST LET ME DIE.
...
BREEP
KCHIK
!!
KCHAK
DAD?

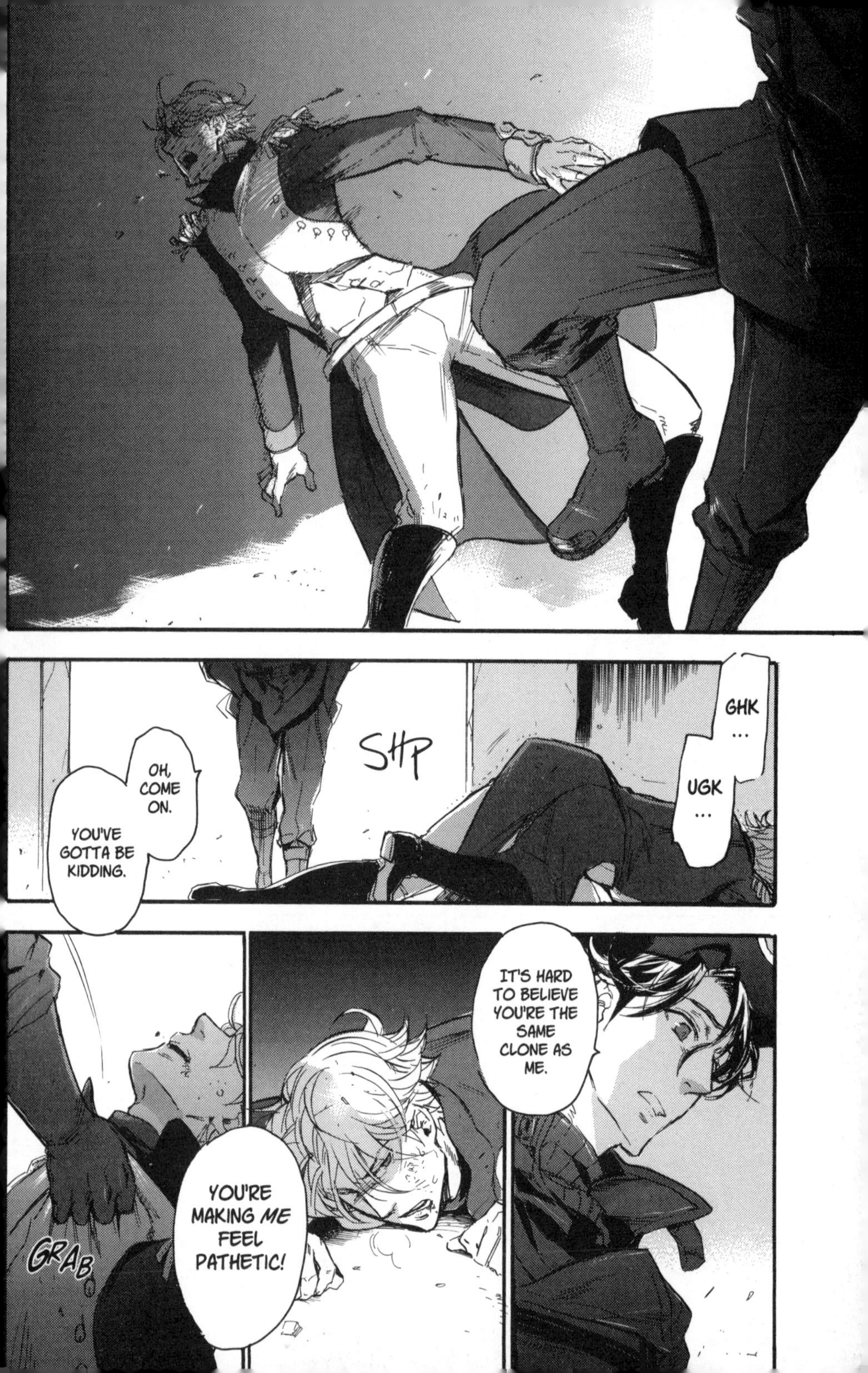
GHK …
UGK …
SHP
OH, COME ON.
YOU'VE GOTTA BE KIDDING.
IT'S HARD TO BELIEVE YOU'RE THE SAME CLONE AS ME.
YOU'RE MAKING *ME* FEEL PATHETIC!
GRAB

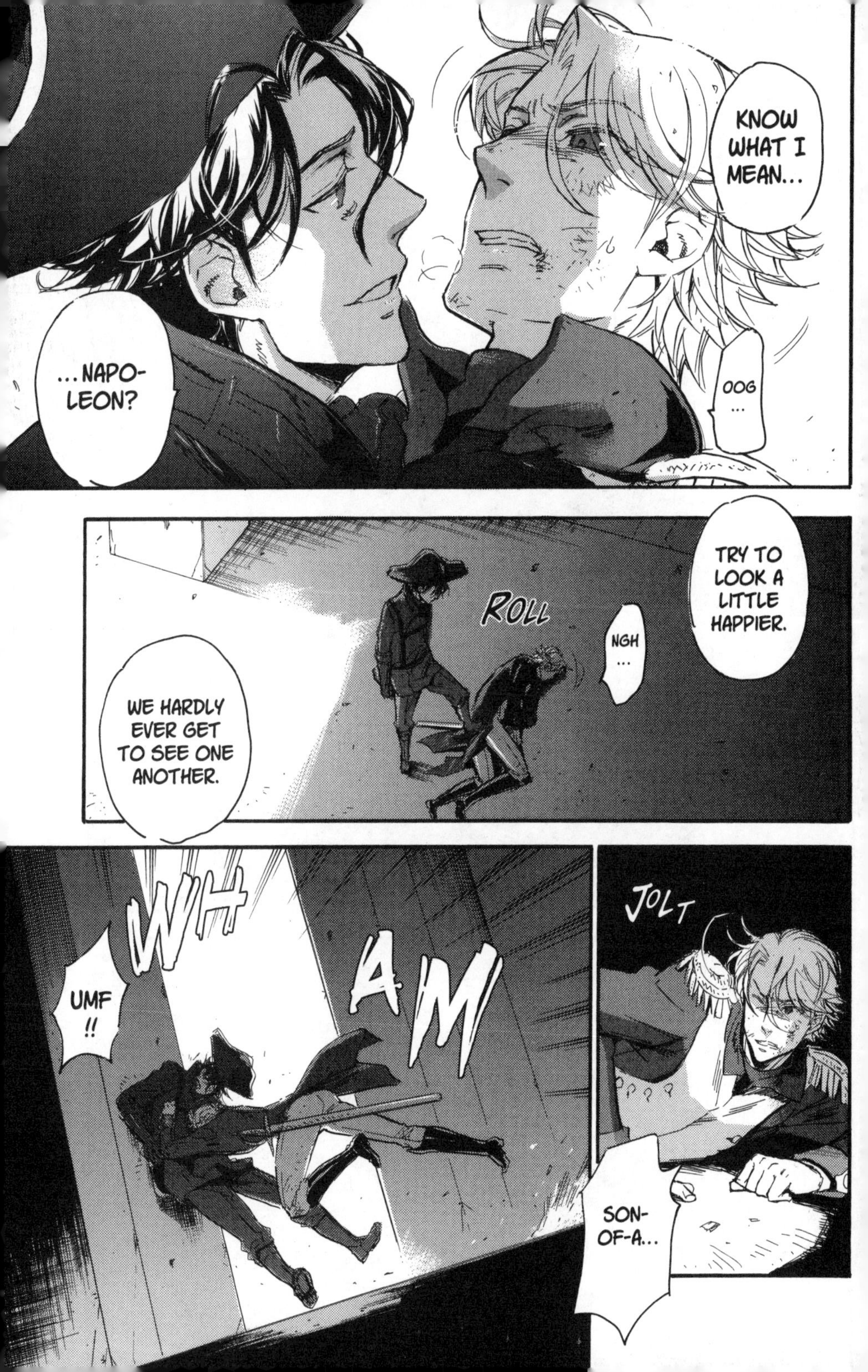
KNOW WHAT I MEAN...
OOG ...
...NAPO-LEON?
TRY TO LOOK A LITTLE HAPPIER.
NGH ...
ROLL
WE HARDLY EVER GET TO SEE ONE ANOTHER.
JOLT
SON-OF-A...
WHAM
UMF !!

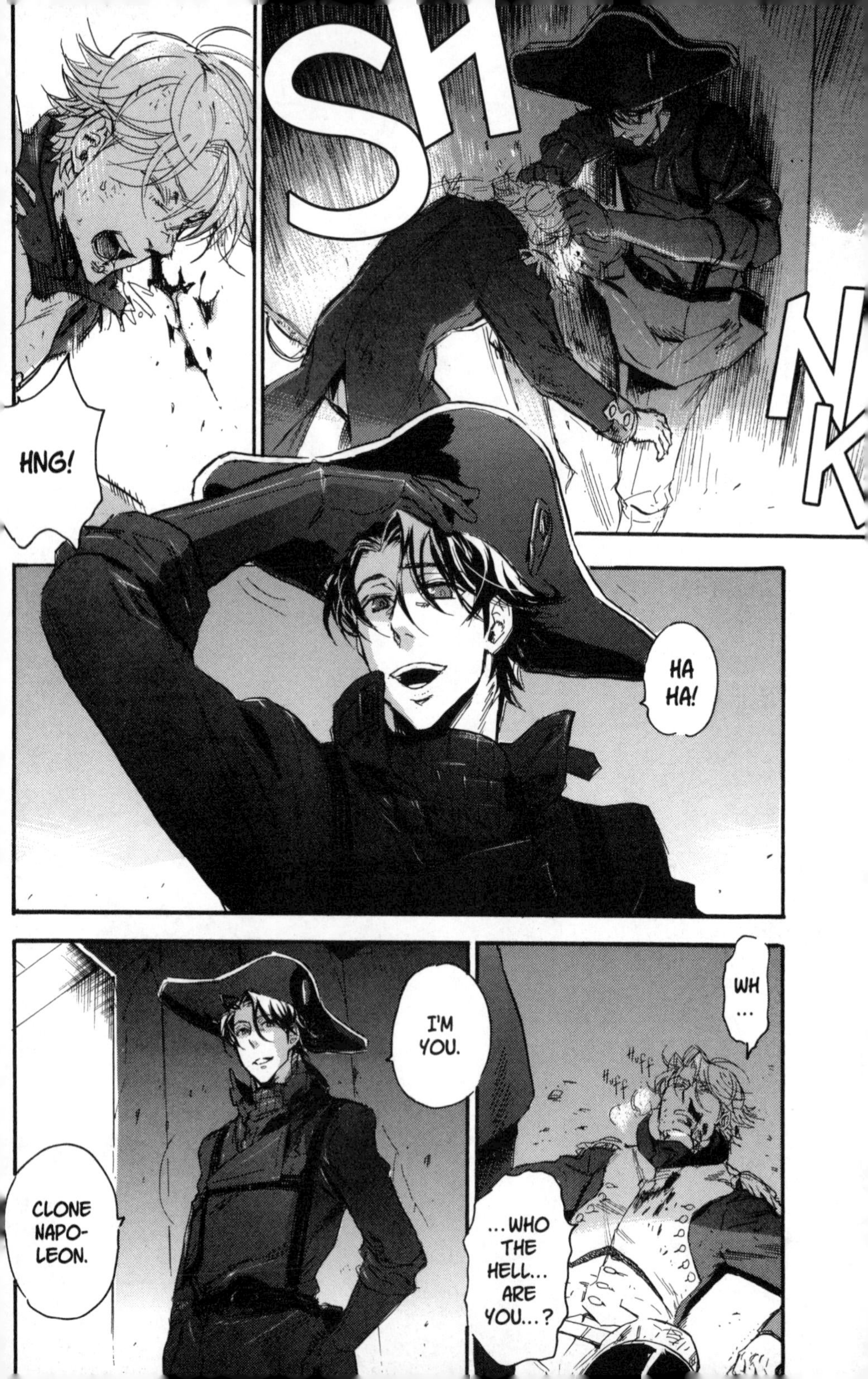
SHNK
HNG!
HA HA!
WH...
...WHO THE HELL... ARE YOU...?
I'M YOU.
CLONE NAPOLEON.

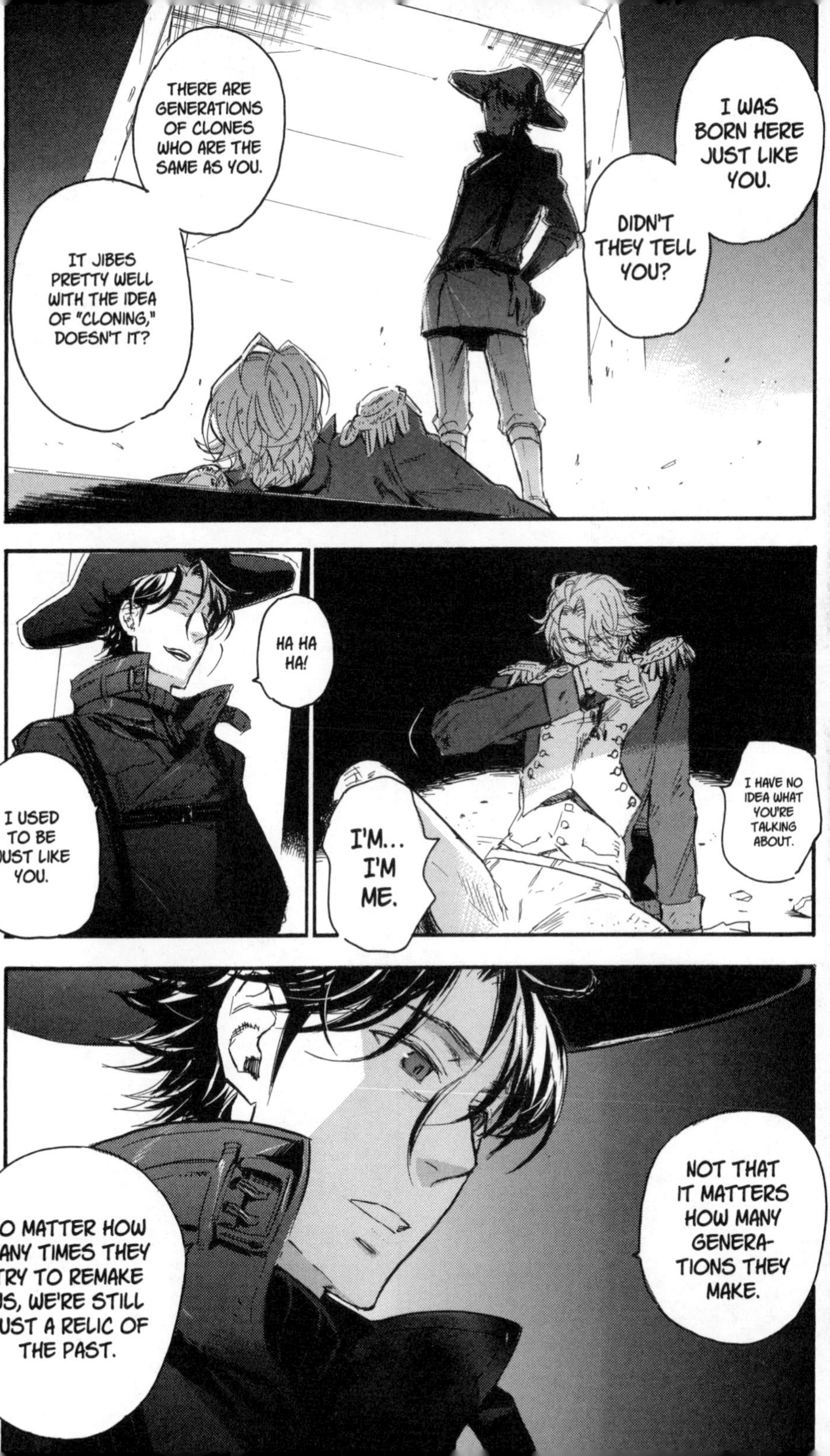
I WAS BORN HERE JUST LIKE YOU.
DIDN'T THEY TELL YOU?
THERE ARE GENERATIONS OF CLONES WHO ARE THE SAME AS YOU.
IT JIBES PRETTY WELL WITH THE IDEA OF "CLONING," DOESN'T IT?
I HAVE NO IDEA WHAT YOU'RE TALKING ABOUT.
I'M... I'M ME.
HA HA HA!
I USED TO BE JUST LIKE YOU.
NOT THAT IT MATTERS HOW MANY GENERATIONS THEY MAKE.
NO MATTER HOW MANY TIMES THEY TRY TO REMAKE US, WE'RE STILL JUST A RELIC OF THE PAST.

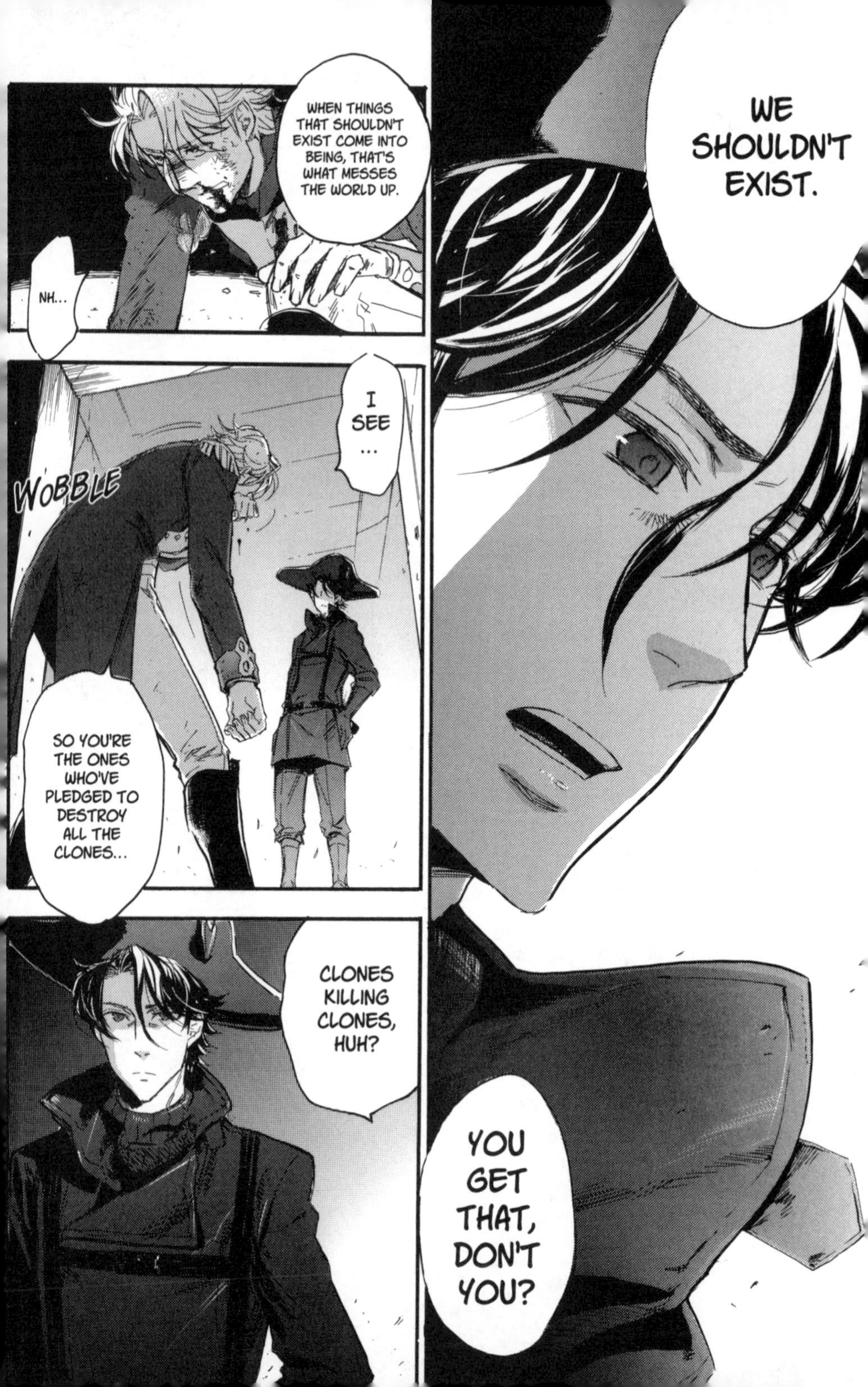
WHEN THINGS THAT SHOULDN'T EXIST COME INTO BEING, THAT'S WHAT MESSES THE WORLD UP.
NH...
I SEE...
WOBBLE
SO YOU'RE THE ONES WHO'VE PLEDGED TO DESTROY ALL THE CLONES...
CLONES KILLING CLONES, HUH?
WE SHOULDN'T EXIST.
YOU GET THAT, DON'T YOU?

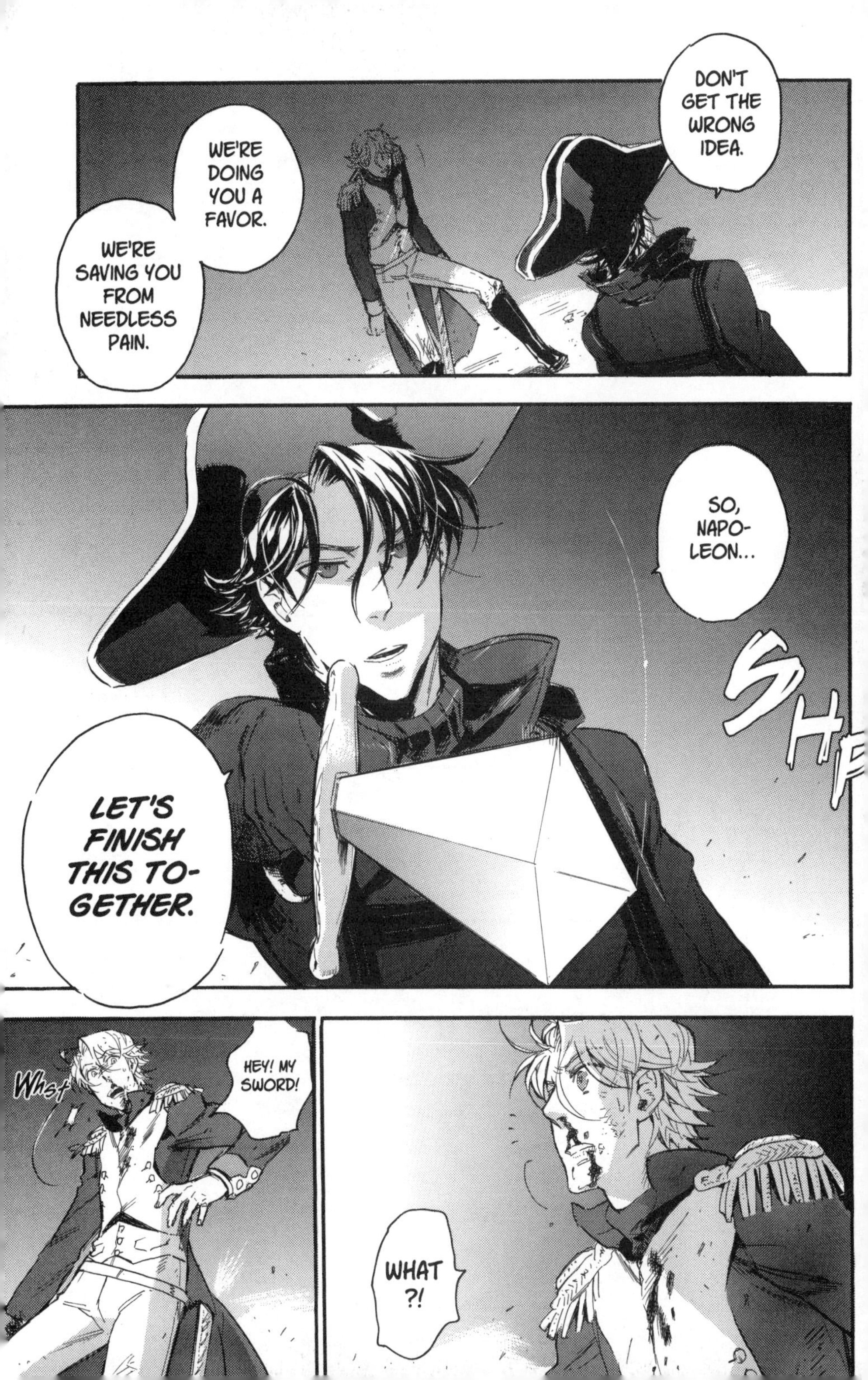
DON'T GET THE WRONG IDEA.
WE'RE DOING YOU A FAVOR.
WE'RE SAVING YOU FROM NEEDLESS PAIN.
SO, NAPOLEON...
SH
LET'S FINISH THIS TOGETHER.
WHAT?!
HEY! MY SWORD!
Whsf

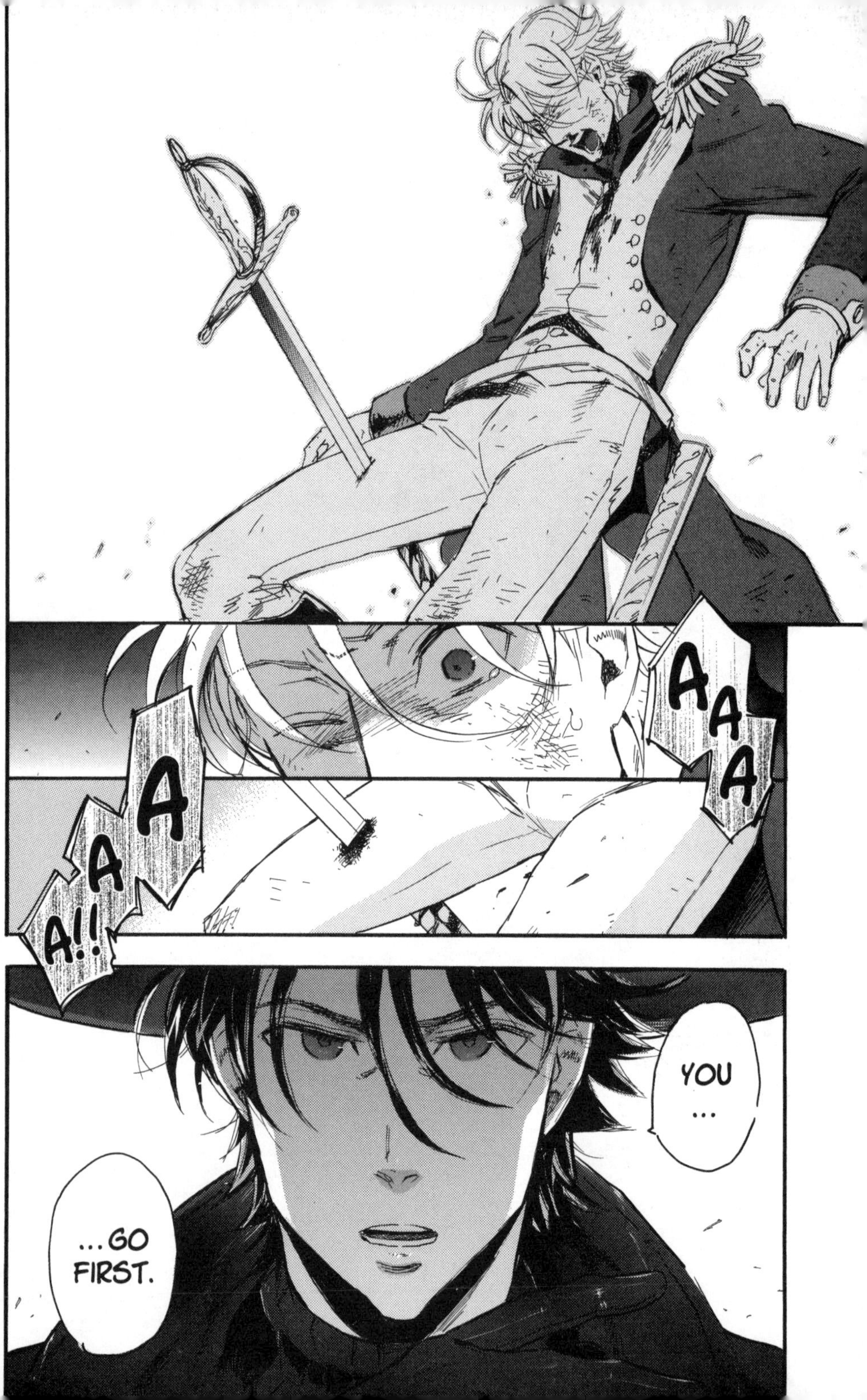
AAA
AAAA!!
YOU ...
...GO FIRST.

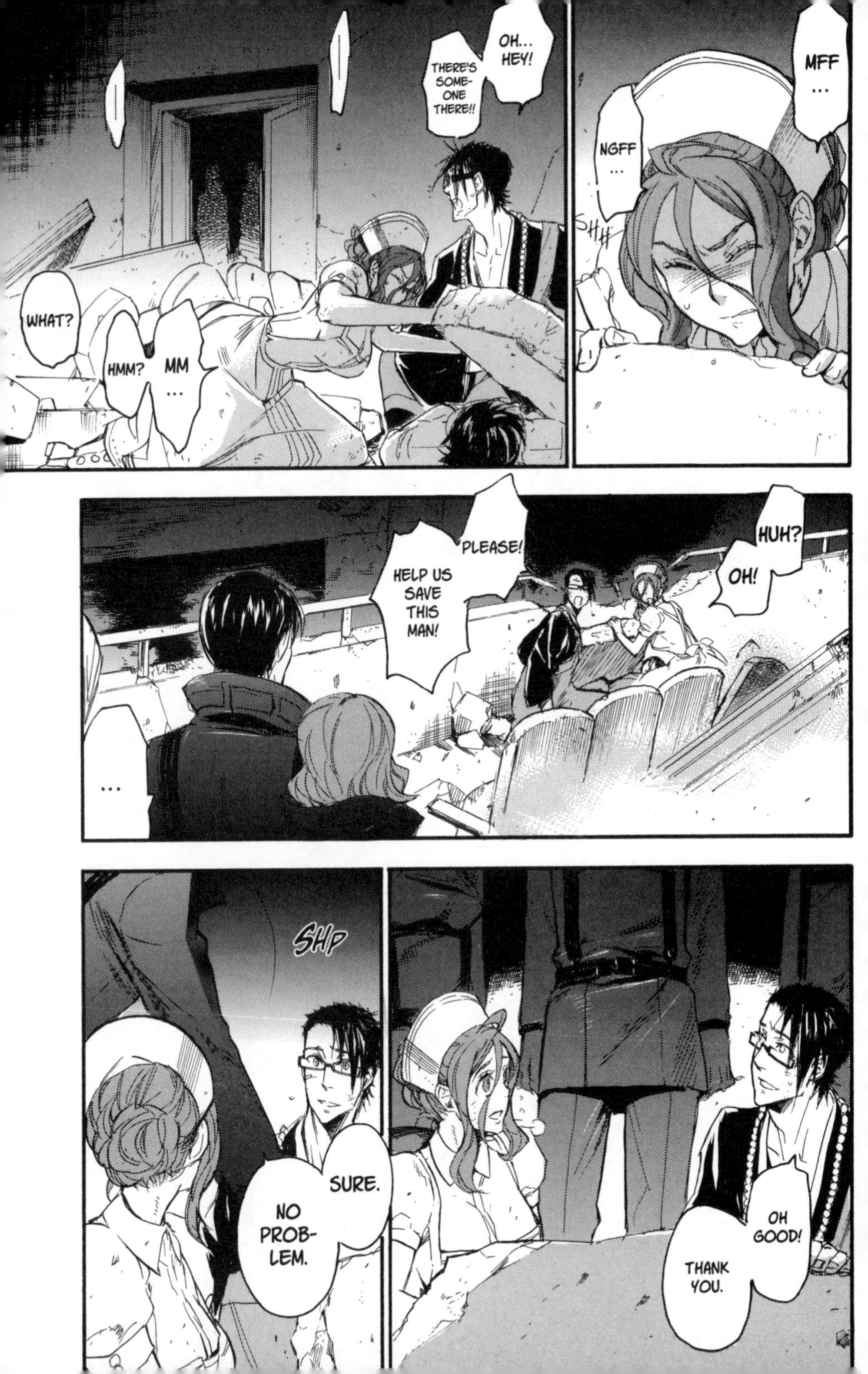

MFF ...
NGFF ...
SHH
OH... HEY!
THERE'S SOME-ONE THERE!!
!
!
MM ...
HMM?
WHAT?
HUH?
OH!
PLEASE!
HELP US SAVE THIS MAN!
...
OH GOOD!
THANK YOU.
SHP
SURE.
NO PROB-LEM.

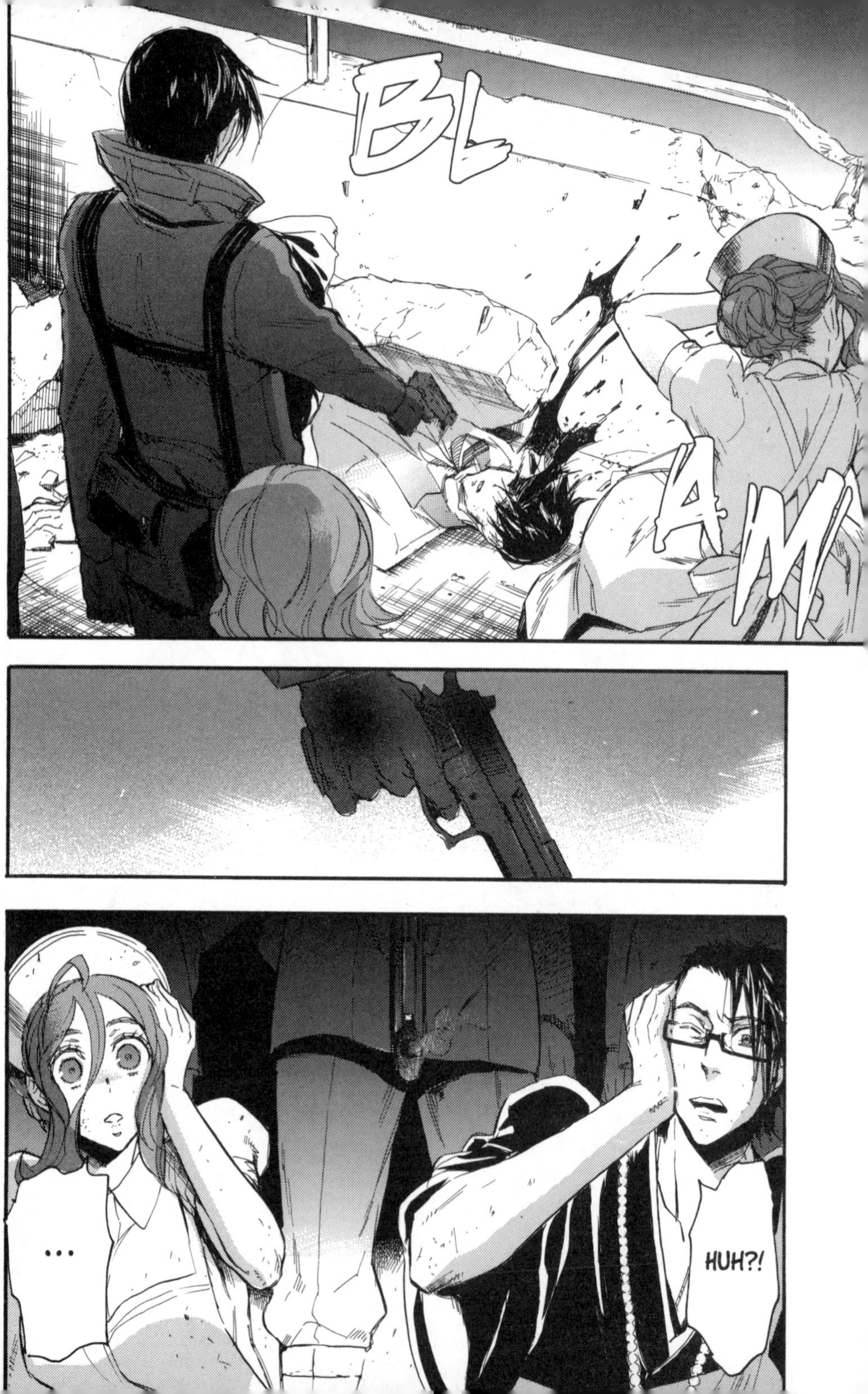
BLAM
HUH?!
...

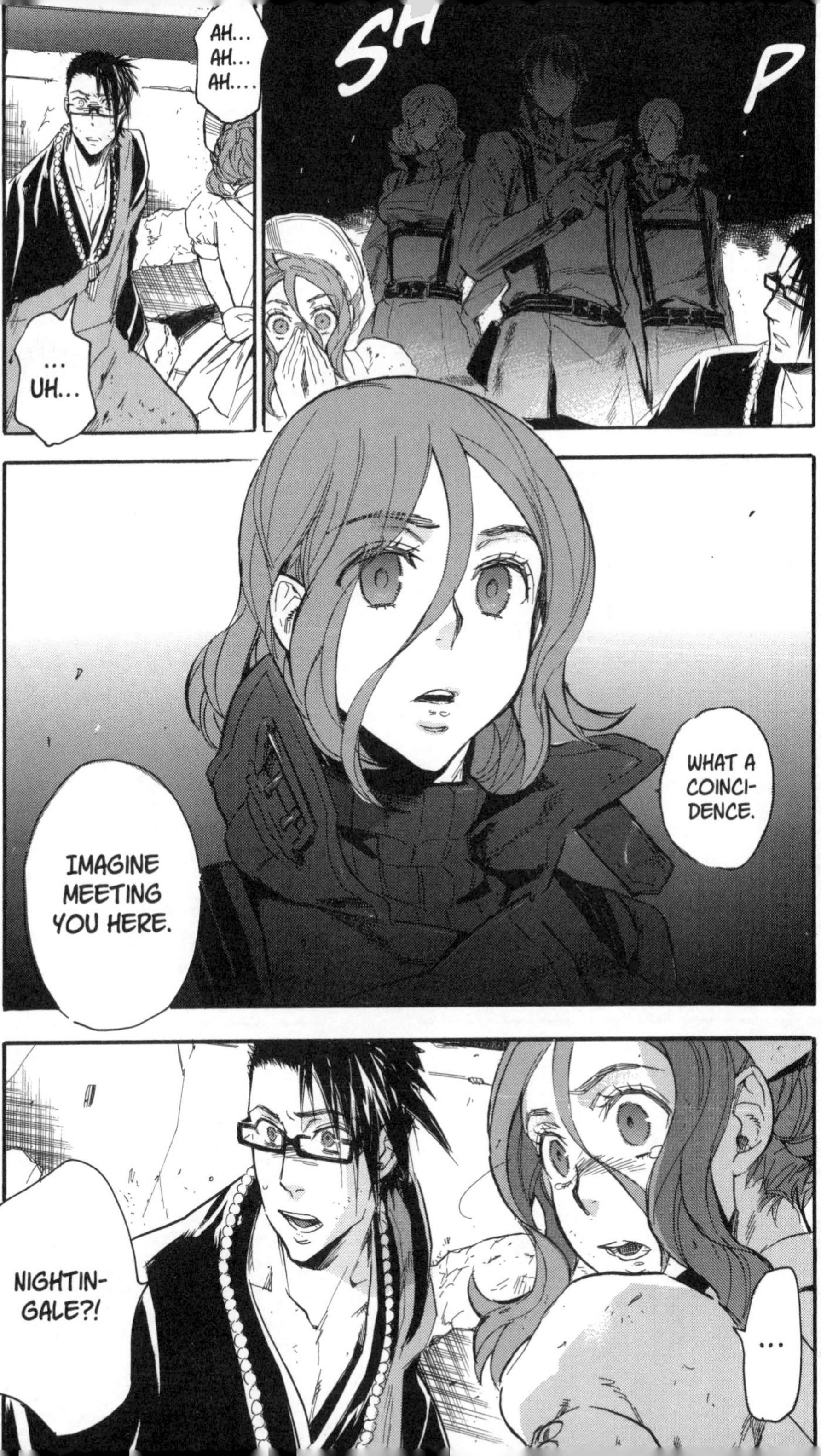
SH
P
AH... AH... AH....
... UH...
WHAT A COINCI-DENCE.
IMAGINE MEETING YOU HERE.
NIGHTIN-GALE?!
...

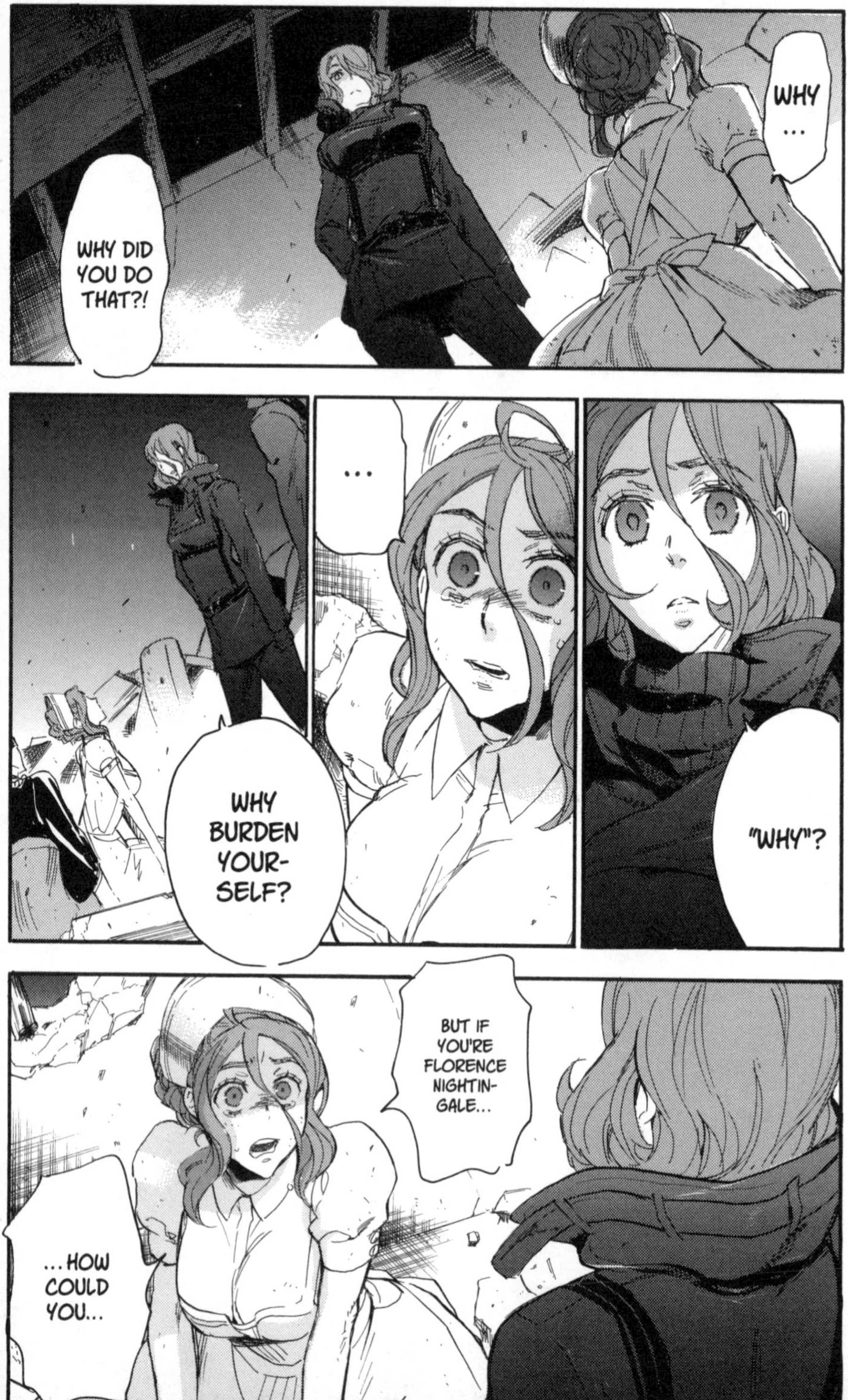
WHY ...
WHY DID YOU DO THAT?!
"WHY"?
...
WHY BURDEN YOUR-SELF?
BUT IF YOU'RE FLORENCE NIGHTIN-GALE...
...HOW COULD YOU...

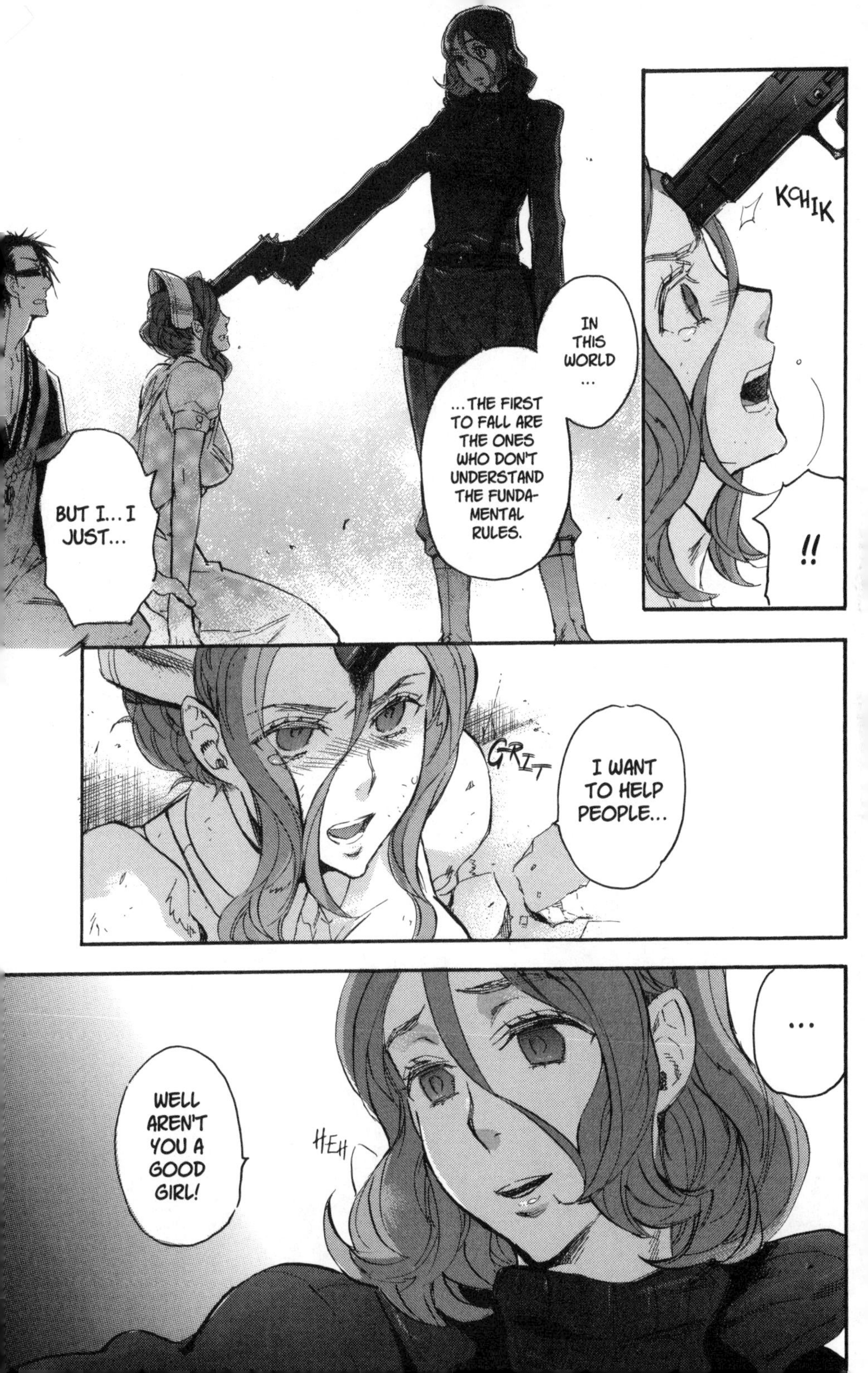
KCHIK
!!
IN THIS WORLD...
...THE FIRST TO FALL ARE THE ONES WHO DON'T UNDERSTAND THE FUNDA-MENTAL RULES.
BUT I... I JUST...
GRIT
I WANT TO HELP PEOPLE...
...
HEH
WELL AREN'T YOU A GOOD GIRL!

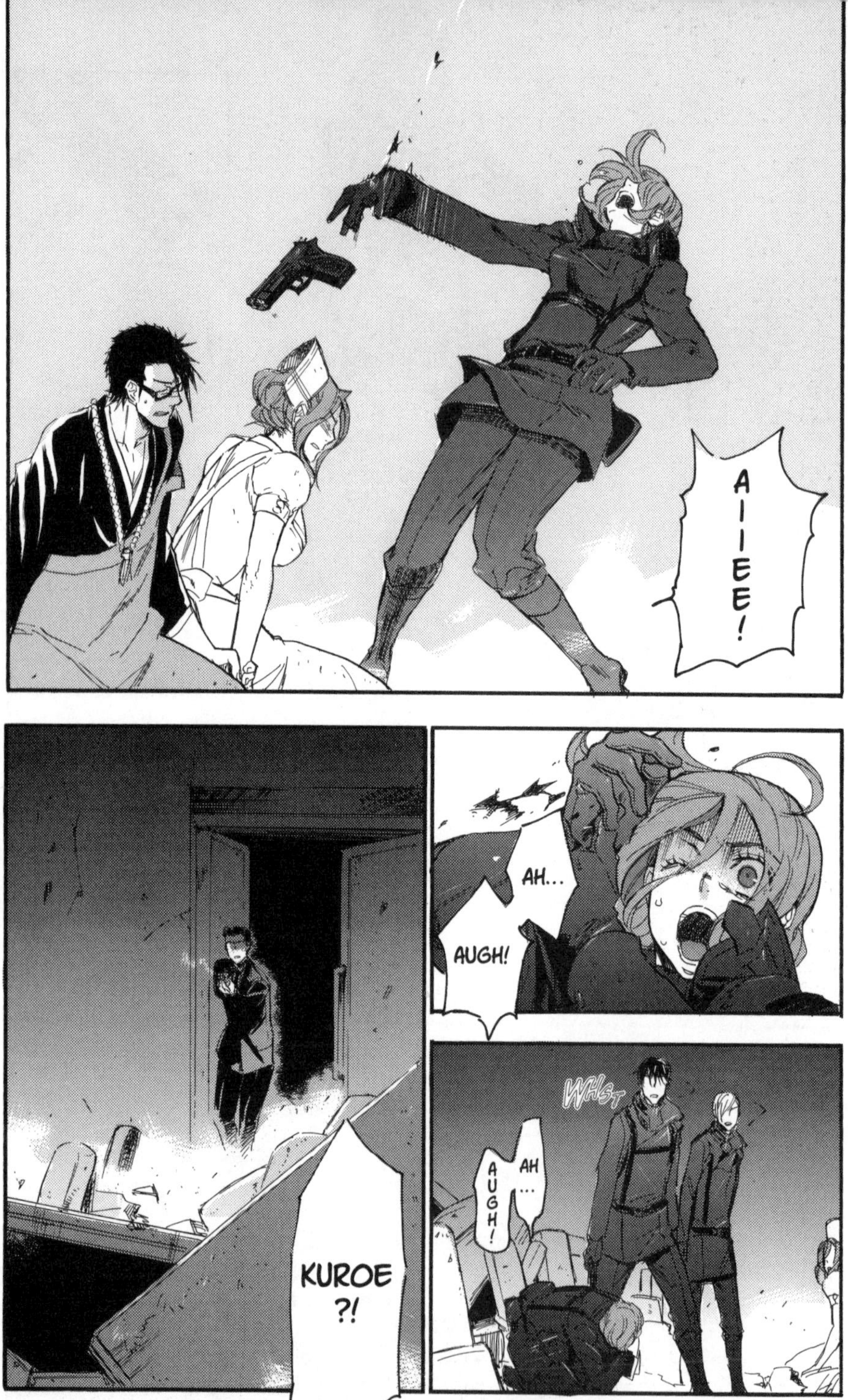
AIIEEE!
AH...
AUGH!
WHST
AH...
AUGH!
KUROE ?!

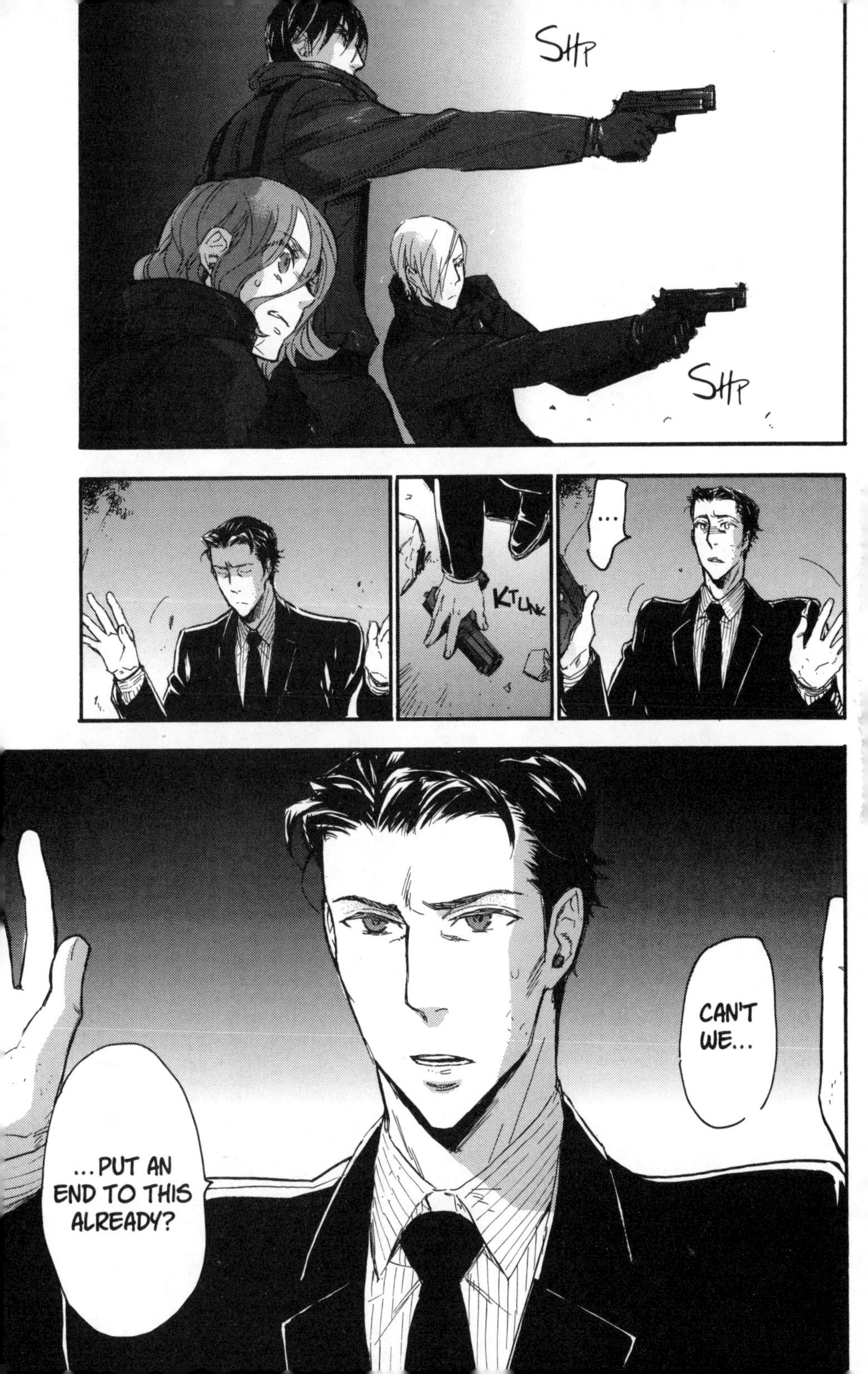
SHP
SHP
...
KTUNK
CAN'T WE...
...PUT AN END TO THIS ALREADY?

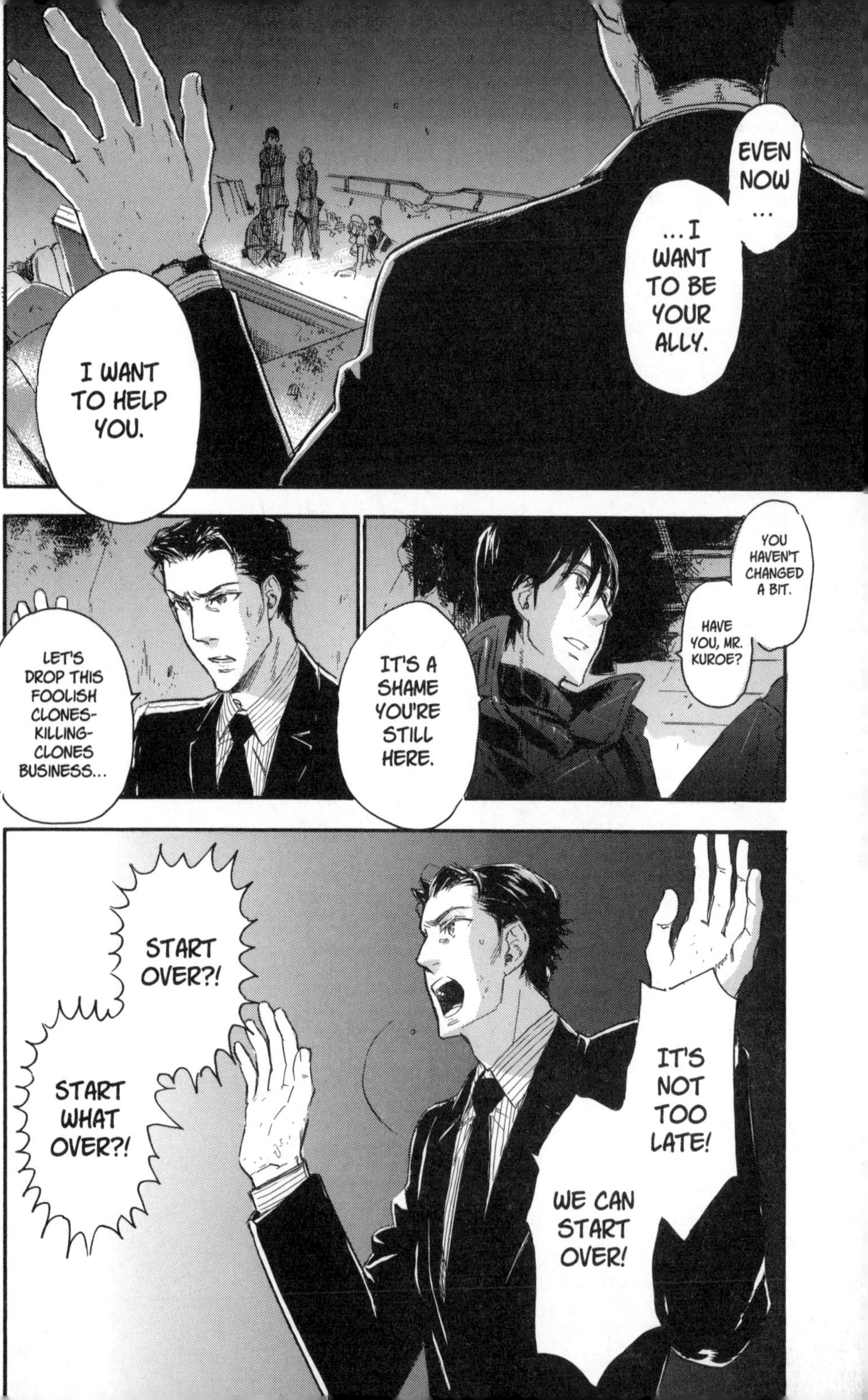
EVEN NOW...
...I WANT TO BE YOUR ALLY.
I WANT TO HELP YOU.
YOU HAVEN'T CHANGED A BIT.
HAVE YOU, MR. KUROE?
IT'S A SHAME YOU'RE STILL HERE.
LET'S DROP THIS FOOLISH CLONES-KILLING-CLONES BUSINESS...
IT'S NOT TOO LATE!
WE CAN START OVER!
START OVER?!
START WHAT OVER?!

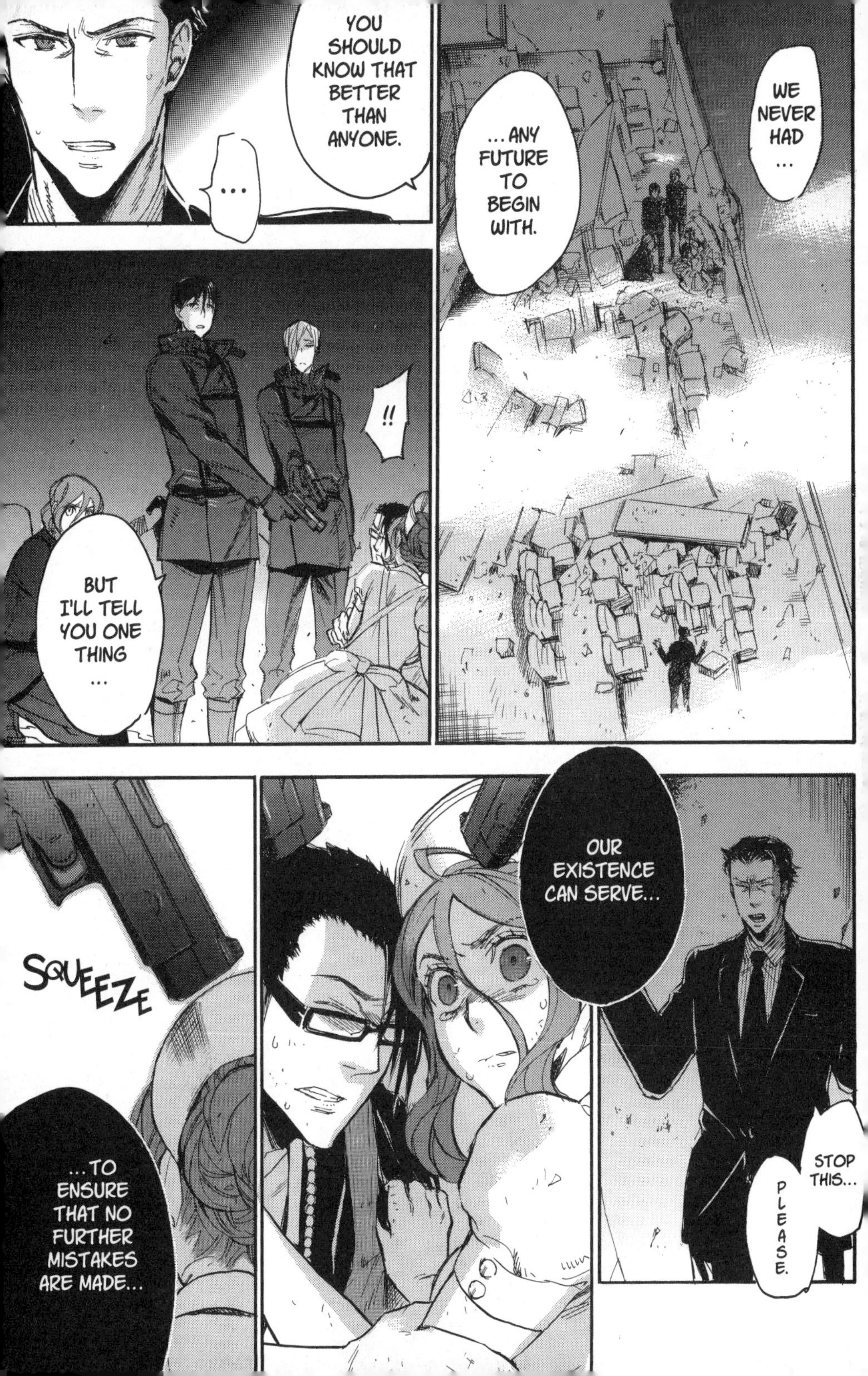
WE NEVER HAD...
...ANY FUTURE TO BEGIN WITH.
YOU SHOULD KNOW THAT BETTER THAN ANYONE.
...
!!
BUT I'LL TELL YOU ONE THING...
STOP THIS...
PLEASE.
OUR EXISTENCE CAN SERVE...
SQUEEZE
...TO ENSURE THAT NO FURTHER MISTAKES ARE MADE...

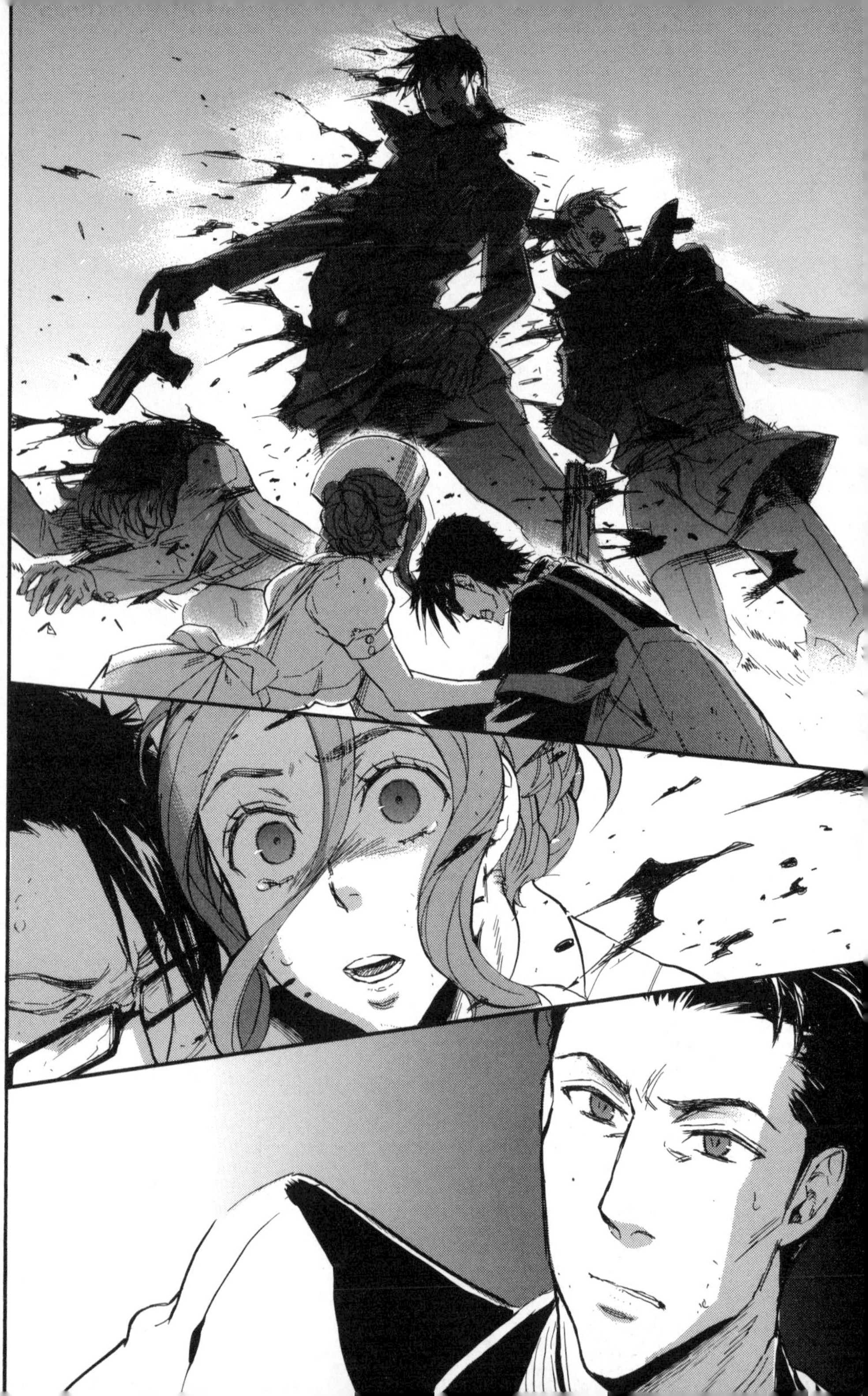

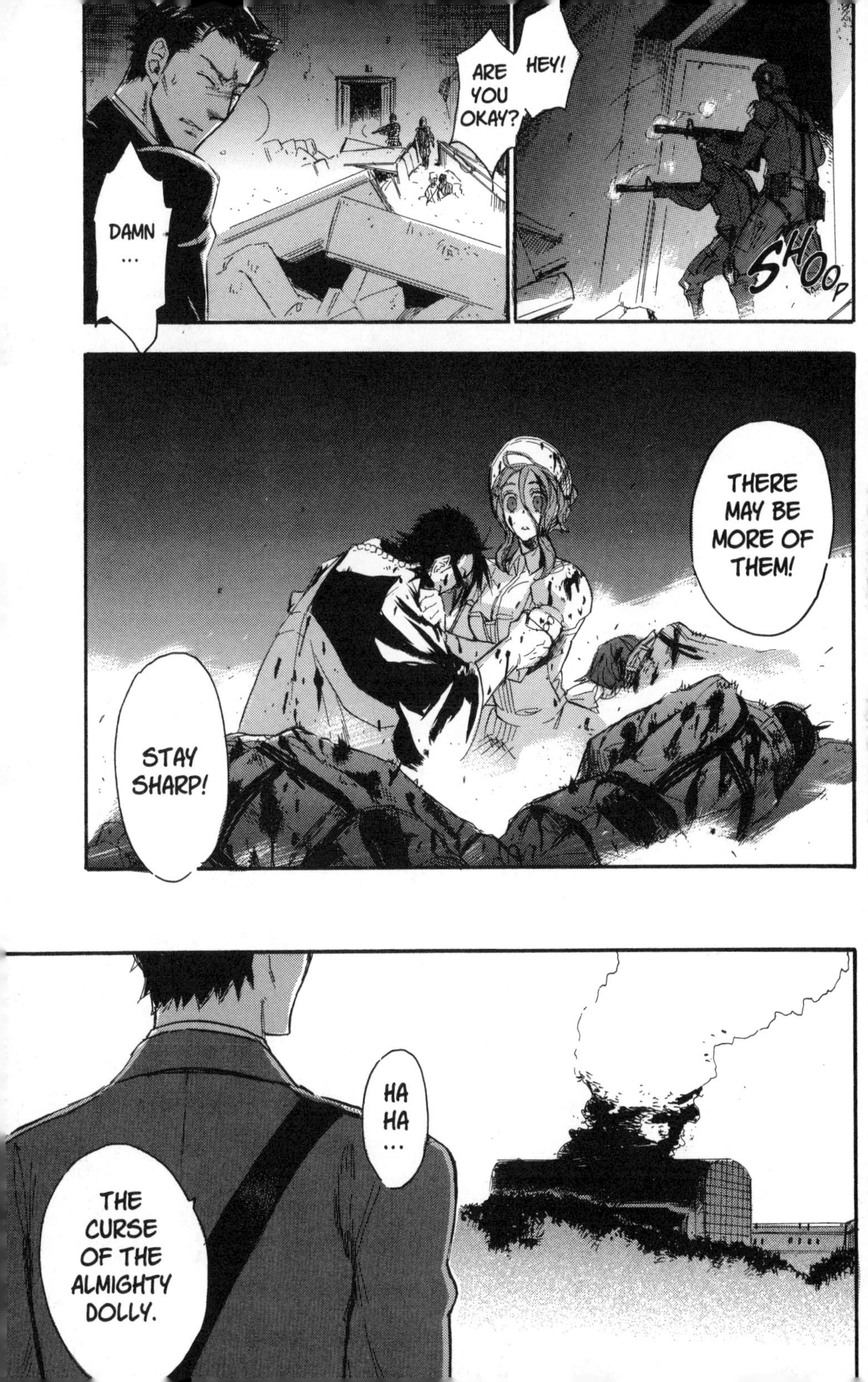
HEY! ARE YOU OKAY?
SHOOP
DAMN...
THERE MAY BE MORE OF THEM!
STAY SHARP!
HA HA...
THE CURSE OF THE ALMIGHTY DOLLY.

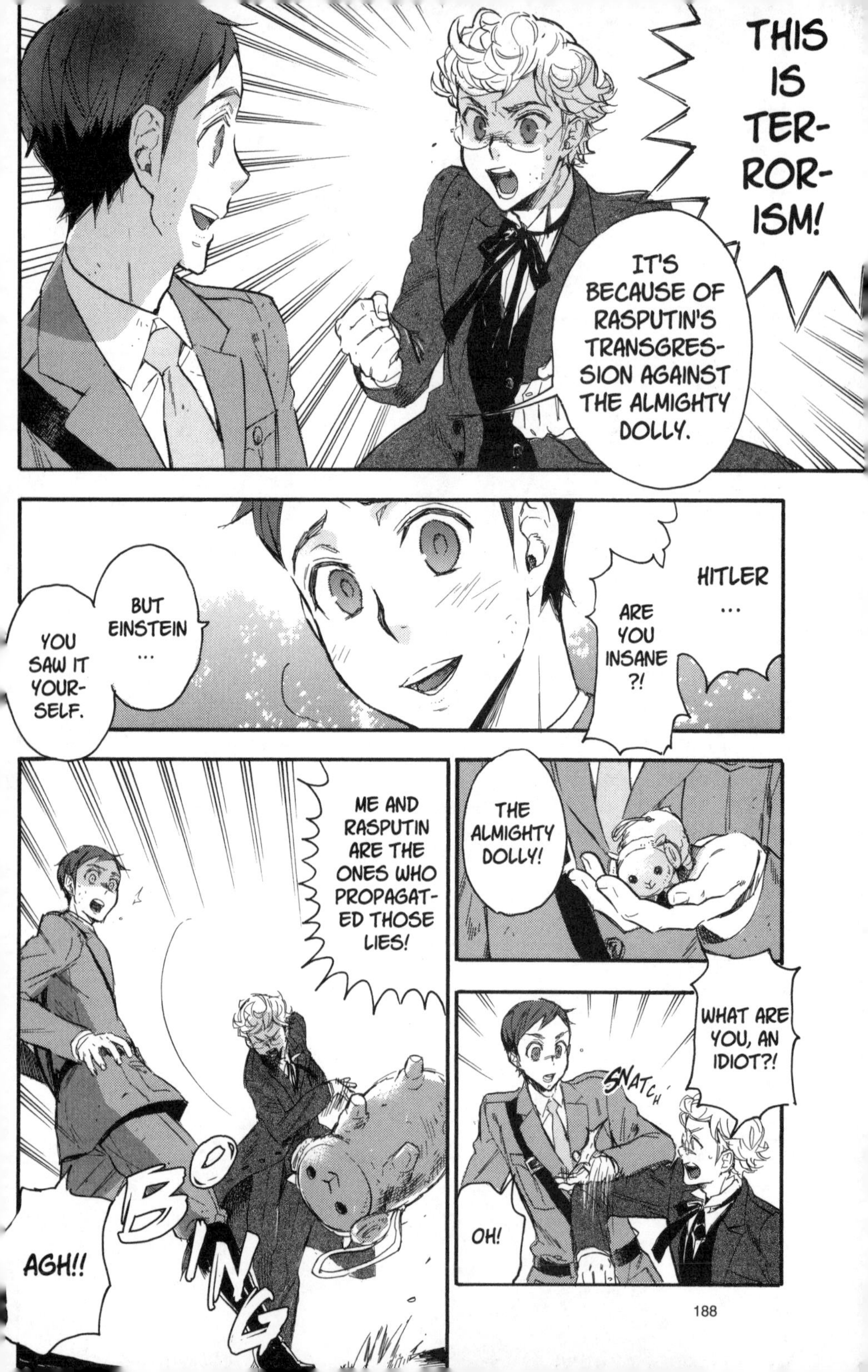
THIS IS TER-ROR-ISM!
IT'S BECAUSE OF RASPUTIN'S TRANSGRES-SION AGAINST THE ALMIGHTY DOLLY.
HITLER ...
ARE YOU INSANE?!
BUT EINSTEIN ...
YOU SAW IT YOUR-SELF.
THE ALMIGHTY DOLLY!
WHAT ARE YOU, AN IDIOT?!
SNATCH
OH!
ME AND RASPUTIN ARE THE ONES WHO PROPAGAT-ED THOSE LIES!
BOING
AGH!!

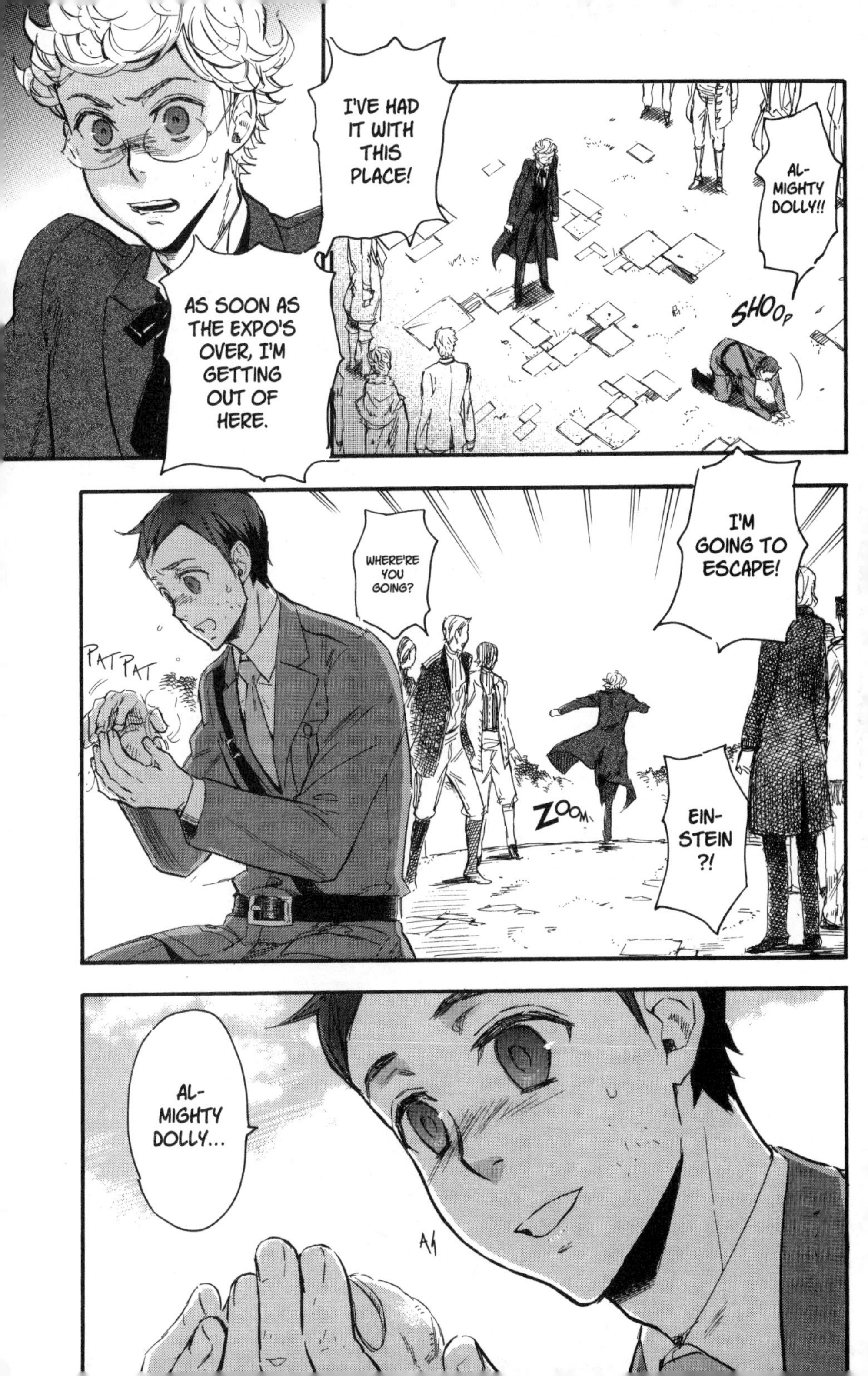
AL-MIGHTY DOLLY!!
SHOOP
I'VE HAD IT WITH THIS PLACE!
AS SOON AS THE EXPO'S OVER, I'M GETTING OUT OF HERE.
I'M GOING TO ESCAPE!
WHERE'RE YOU GOING?
EIN-STEIN?!
ZOOM
PAT PAT
AL-MIGHTY DOLLY...

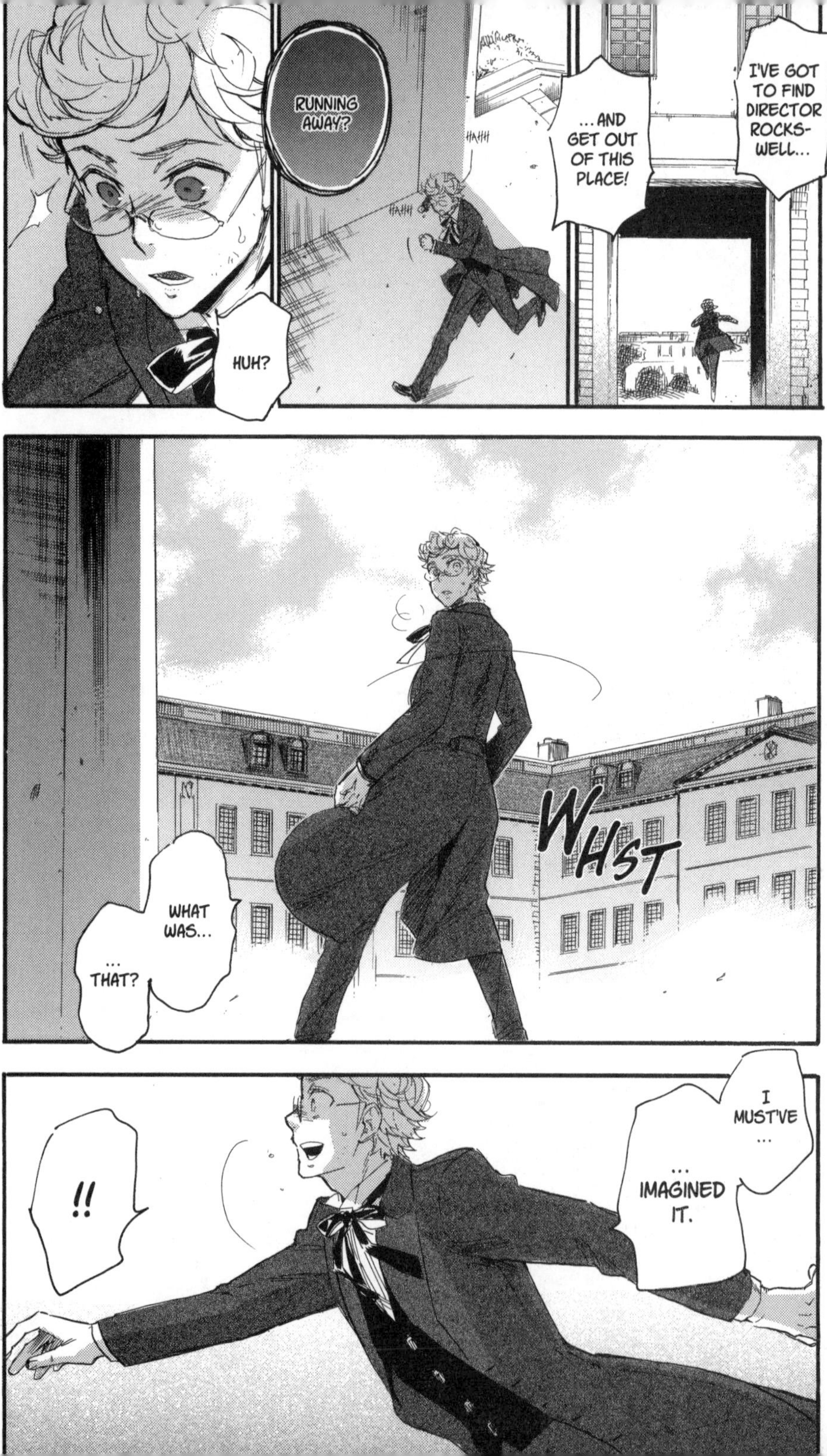
I'VE GOT TO FIND DIRECTOR ROCKS-WELL...
...AND GET OUT OF THIS PLACE!
RUNNING AWAY?
HUH?
WHST
WHAT WAS...
...THAT?
I MUST'VE...
...IMAGINED IT.
!!

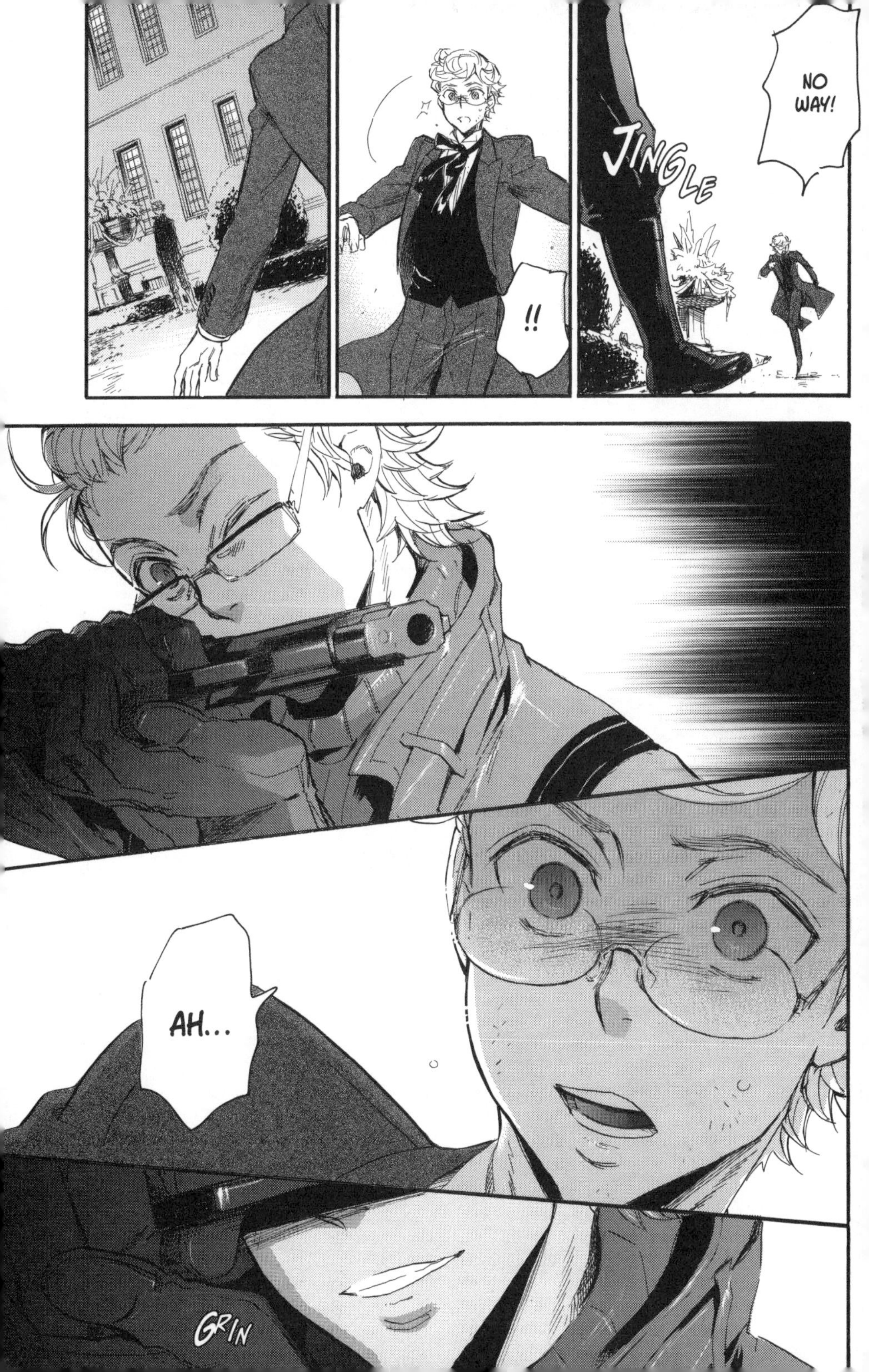
NO WAY!
JINGLE
!!
AH...
GRIN

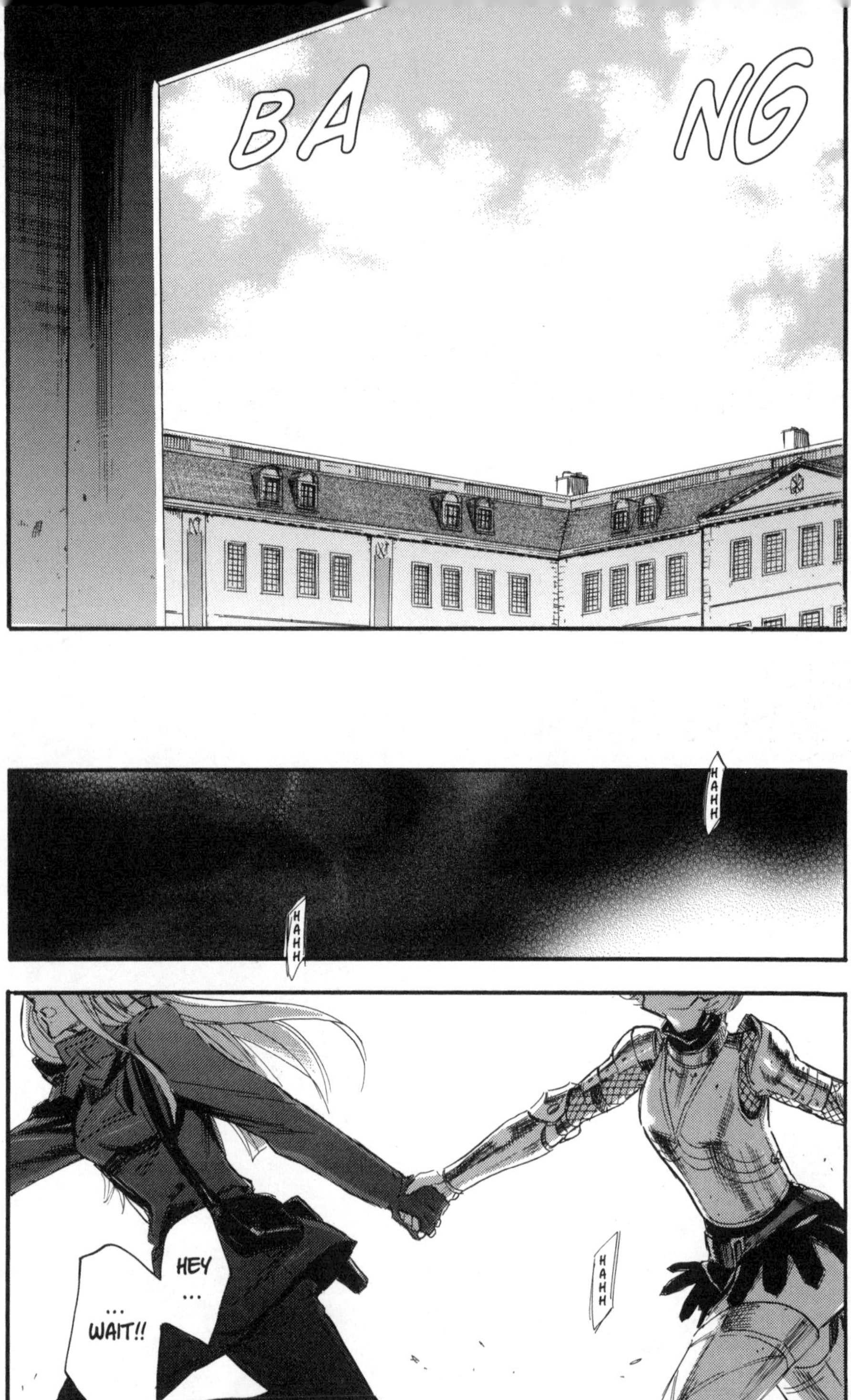
BANG
HAHH
HAHH
HAHH
HEY...
...WAIT!!

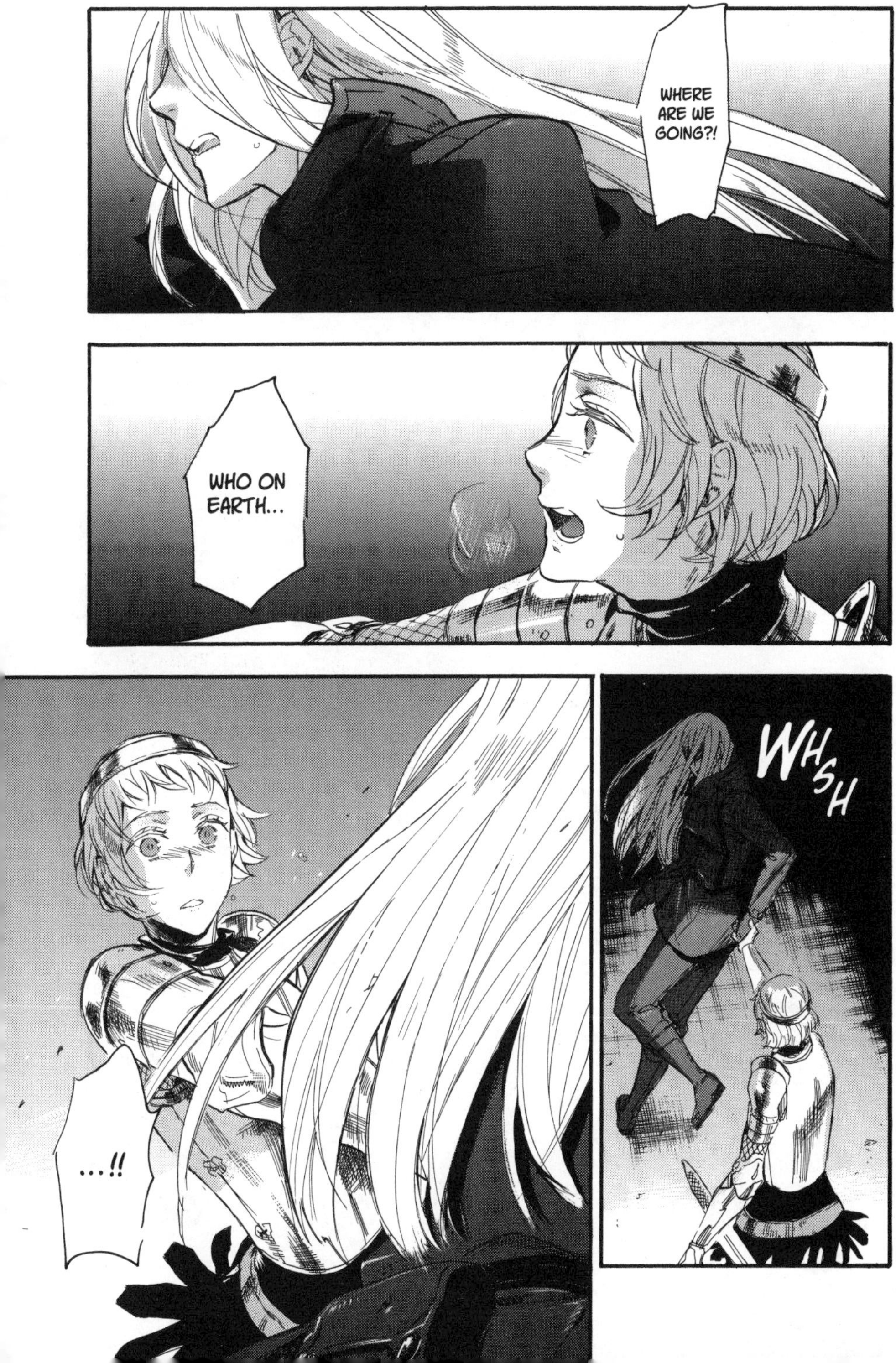
WHERE ARE WE GOING?!
WHO ON EARTH...
WHSH
...!!

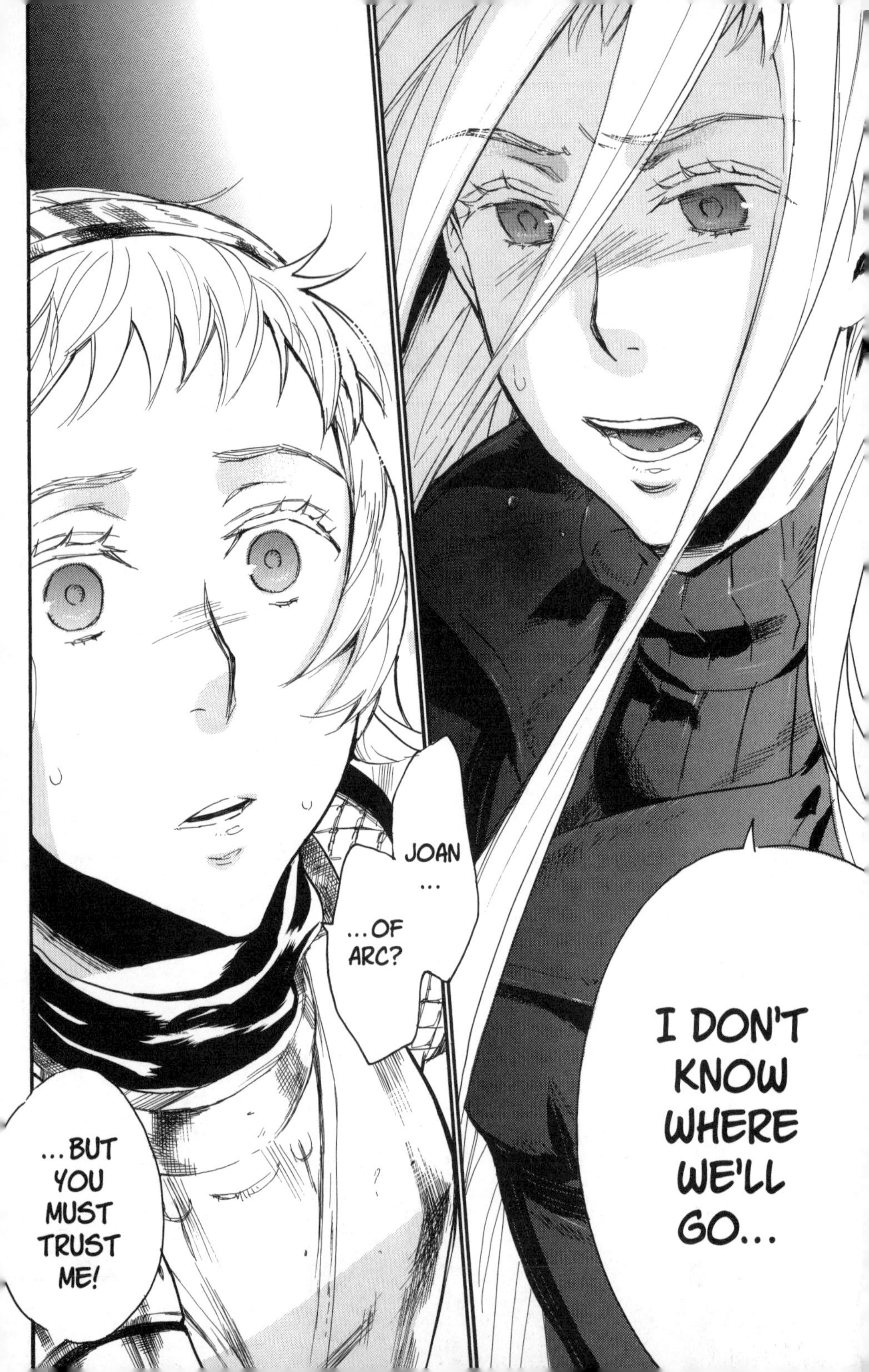
I DON'T KNOW WHERE WE'LL GO...
JOAN ...
...OF ARC?
...BUT YOU MUST TRUST ME!

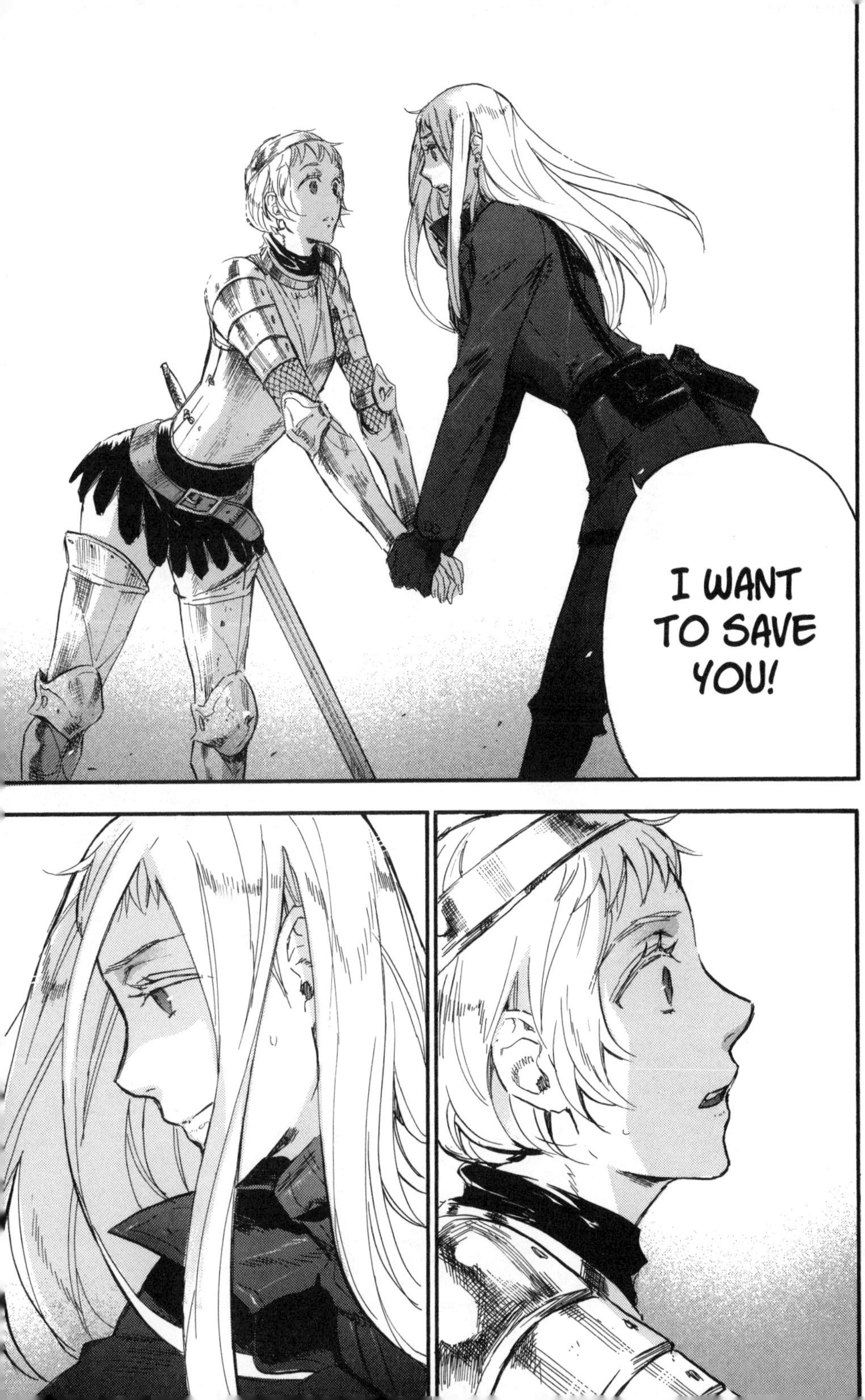
I WANT TO SAVE YOU!

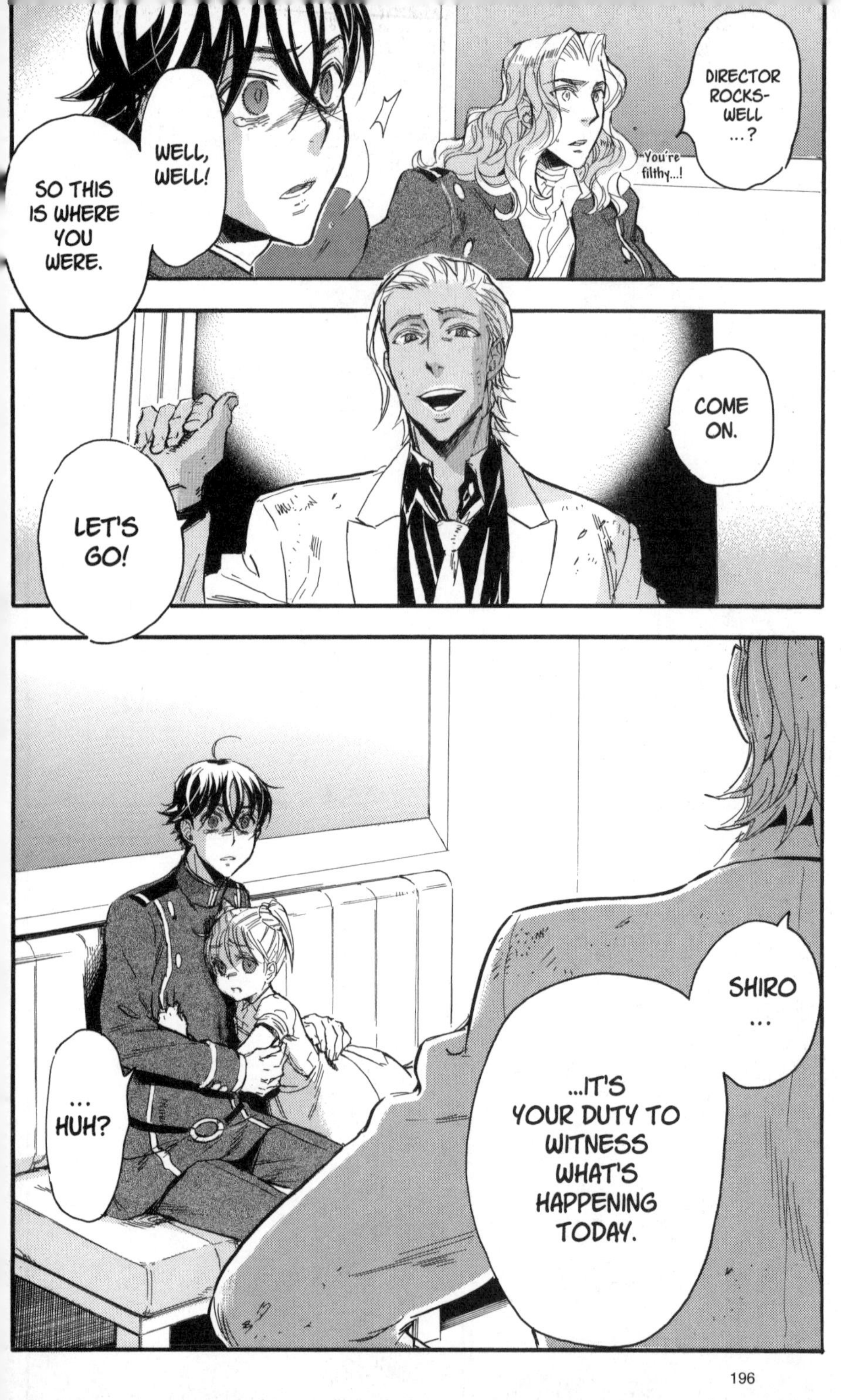
DIRECTOR ROCKS-WELL ...?
You're filthy...!
WELL, WELL!
SO THIS IS WHERE YOU WERE.
COME ON.
LET'S GO!
SHIRO ...
...IT'S YOUR DUTY TO WITNESS WHAT'S HAPPENING TODAY.
... HUH?

afterschool charisma

VOLUME THREE

end

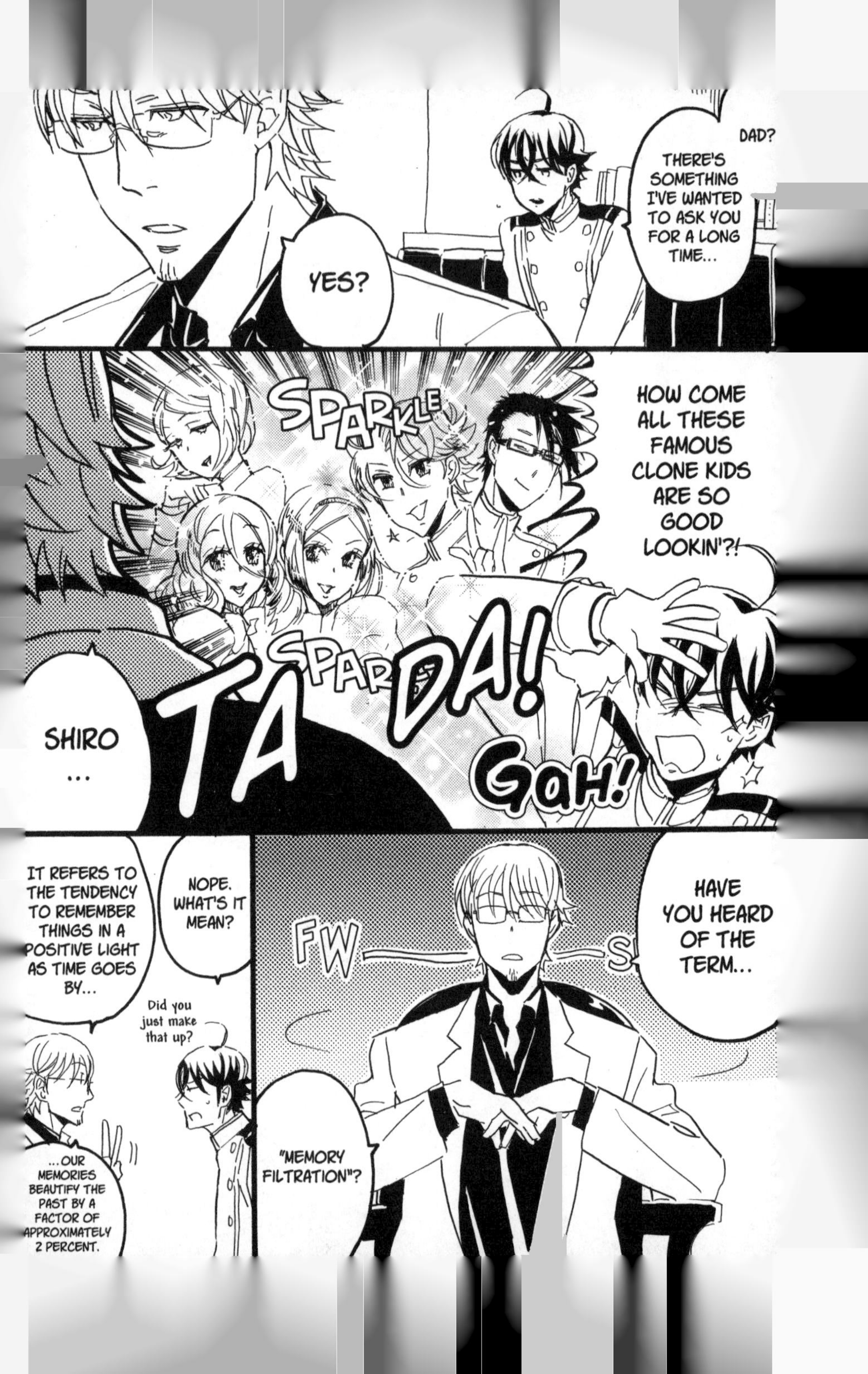
DAD?
THERE'S SOMETHING I'VE WANTED TO ASK YOU FOR A LONG TIME...
YES?
HOW COME ALL THESE FAMOUS CLONE KIDS ARE SO GOOD LOOKIN'?!
SPARKLE
TA DA!
SPARKLE
GAH!
SHIRO...
HAVE YOU HEARD OF THE TERM...
FW——S
"MEMORY FILTRATION"?
NOPE. WHAT'S IT MEAN?
IT REFERS TO THE TENDENCY TO REMEMBER THINGS IN A POSITIVE LIGHT AS TIME GOES BY...
Did you just make that up?
...OUR MEMORIES BEAUTIFY THE PAST BY A FACTOR OF APPROXIMATELY 2 PERCENT.

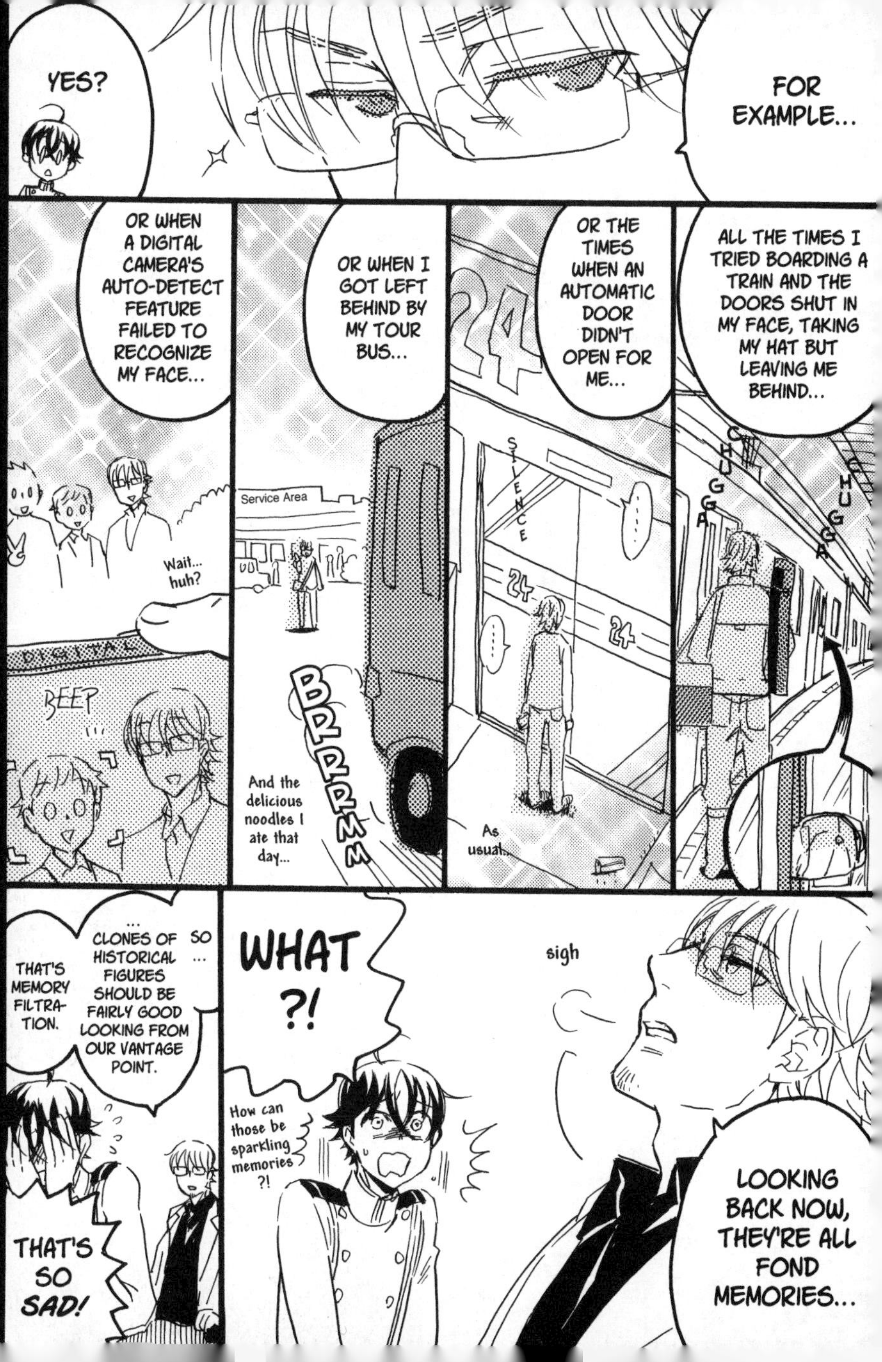
FOR EXAMPLE...
YES?
ALL THE TIMES I TRIED BOARDING A TRAIN AND THE DOORS SHUT IN MY FACE, TAKING MY HAT BUT LEAVING ME BEHIND...
CHUGGA
CHUGGA
OR THE TIMES WHEN AN AUTOMATIC DOOR DIDN'T OPEN FOR ME...
SILENCE
...
...
As usual...
OR WHEN I GOT LEFT BEHIND BY MY TOUR BUS...
Service Area
BRRRRMM
And the delicious noodles I ate that day...
OR WHEN A DIGITAL CAMERA'S AUTO-DETECT FEATURE FAILED TO RECOGNIZE MY FACE...
Wait... huh?
DIGITAL
BEEP
sigh
LOOKING BACK NOW, THEY'RE ALL FOND MEMORIES...
WHAT?!
How can those be sparkling memories?!
SO...
...CLONES OF HISTORICAL FIGURES SHOULD BE FAIRLY GOOD LOOKING FROM OUR VANTAGE POINT.
THAT'S MEMORY FILTRATION.
THAT'S SO SAD!

# AFTERSCHOOL CHARISMA
## VOLUME 3
### VIZ SIGNATURE EDITION

### STORY & ART BY KUMIKO SUEKANE

© 2009 Kumiko SUEKANE/Shogakukan
All rights reserved.
Original Japanese edition "HOUKAGO NO CARISMA"
published by SHOGAKUKAN Inc.

Original Japanese cover design by Mitsuru KOBAYASHI (GENI A LÒIDE)

TRANSLATION ─○─ CAMELLIA NIEH
TOUCH UP ART & LETTERING ─○─ ERIKA TERRIQUEZ
DESIGN ─○─ FAWN LAU
EDITOR ─○─ MEGAN BATES

Printed in Canada

Published by VIZ Media, LLC
P.O. Box 77010
San Francisco, CA 94107

10 9 8 7 6 5 4 3 2 1
First printing, June 2011

**PARENTAL ADVISORY**
AFTERSCHOOL CHARISMA is rated T+
for Older Teen and is recommended for
ages 16 and up.
ratings.viz.com

**VIZ SIGNATURE**
WWW.SIGIKKI.COM